Instructional Technology and Media for Learning

12th Edition

Sharon E. Smaldino
Northern Illinois University

Deborah L. Lowther
University of Memphis

Clif Mims
University of Memphis

D1567938

 Pearson

330 Hudson Street, NY NY 10013

Editorial Director: Kevin Davis
Portfolio Manager: Drew Bennett
Managing Content Producer: Megan Moffo
Senior Content Editor: Max Effenson Chuck
Content Producer: Yagnesh Jani
Portfolio Management Assistant: Maria Feliberty
Digital Development Editor: Carolyn Schweitzer
Senior Digital Producer: Allison Longley
Executive Product Marketing Manager: Christopher Barry
Executive Field Marketing Manager: Krista Clark
Procurement Specialist: Deidra Smith
Cover Design: Studio Montage
Cover Art: Shutterstock
Editorial Production and Composition Services: SPi Global
Full-Service Project Manager: Heather Winter, SPi Global
Printer/Binder: LSC Communications
Cover Printer: Phoenix Color
Text Font: Palatino LT Pro 9.5/13

Acknowledgments of third party content appear on the approriate page within the text

Library of Congress Cataloging-in-Publication Data

Names: Smaldino, Sharon E., author. | Lowther, Deborah L., author. | Mims,
    Clif, 1971- author. | Russell, James D., author.
Title: Instructional technology and media for learning / Sharon E.
    Smaldino, Northern Illinois University, Deborah L. Lowther, University of Memphis,
    Clif Mims, University of Memphis, James D. Russell, Purdue University.
Description: Twelfth Edition. | Boston : Pearson Education, Inc., [2018] |
    Includes bibliographical references and index.
Identifiers: LCCN 2017015584| ISBN 9780134287485 | ISBN 0134287487
Subjects: LCSH: Educational technology. | Audio-visual education.
Classification: LCC LB1028.3 .H45 2018 | DDC 371.33—dc23
LC record available at https://lccn.loc.gov/2017015584

1 17

ISBN 10: 0-13-428748-7
ISBN 13: 978-0-13-428748-5

Brief Contents

1   Exploring Student Learning   1

2   Designing Instruction and Assessing Learning   21

3   Integrating Technology and Media into Instruction: The ASSURE Model   39

4   Designing Digital Learning Environments   65

5   Engaging Learners with Digital Devices   95

6   Connecting Learners Using Web 2.0   118

7   Teaching at a Distance   139

8   Enhancing Learning with Multimedia   168

9   Preparing for Tomorrow's Challenges   209

Appendix Lesson Scenarios   231

Glossary   232

References   237

Name Index   241

Subject Index   243

Credits   250

Contents

About the Authors ix
Preface xi

1 Exploring Student Learning 1

Framework for Academic and Career Learning: Technology and Media in Today's Schools 2
    Instructional Technology 2
Technology for All Learners: Using Technology Tools to Differentiate Instruction 4
    Instructional Materials 6
    Roles of Technology and Media in Learning 7
The Digital Teacher 7
    Digital Instruction 8
    Technology Standards for Teachers 9
Video Example 1.1: How Do You Choose the Right Web Tools? 10
    National/State Curriculum Standards 10
The Digital Learner 11
    Digital Tools 11
    Digital Communication with Others 12
Video Example 1.2: Wiki Discussion 12
    Technology Guidelines for Students 13
    Technology for Inclusion 13
    Response to Intervention 13
    Universal Design 14
Framework for Academic and Career Learning Literacies 14
    Student Outcomes 14
    Support Systems 14
Effective Learning Environments 15
    The Learning Continuum: Traditional to Digital 15
    The Changing Role of Media Centers 16
Copyright Concerns: Copyright Law 16
    Educators and Copyright Law 17
    Fair Use 17
    Seeking Permission to Use Copyrighted Materials 17
    Term of Protection 18
    Changing the Material's Format 18
Summary 19
Professional Development 19
Suggested Resources 20

2 Designing Instruction and Assessing Learning 21

Learning Theories 22
    Behaviorist Perspective 22
    Cognitivist Perspective 22

    Constructivist Perspective 23
Video Example 2.1: Constructivism 23
    Social-Psychological Perspective 24
Principles of Effective Instruction for Learners 24
    Information and Instruction 25
    Bloom's Digital Taxonomy and The "Four Cs" 26
Taking a Look at Technology Integration: The New Tech Network 28
    Multiple Intelligences 28
    Meeting Learner Needs 29
Principles of Effective Technology Use 29
Video Example 2.2: Media Literacy Skills 30
Principles of Effective Media Use 31
Video Example 2.3: Using Online Resources 31
Principles of Effective Learning Assessment 32
    Authentic Assessment 32
    Portfolio Assessment 34
Technology Resources: Rubrics 36
    Traditional Assessment 37
Summary 37
Professional Development 38
Suggested Resources 38

3 Integrating Technology and Media into Instruction: The ASSURE Model 39

ASSURE Classroom Case Study 40
The ASSURE Model 40
ASSURE A Model to Help Assure Learning 41
Analyze Learners 41
    General Characteristics 41
    Specific Entry Competencies 42
    Learning Differences and Needs 42
ASSURE Classroom Case Study: Analyze Learners 43
Video Example 3.1: Analyze Learners 43
State Standards and Objectives 44
    Importance of Standards and Objectives 44
    The ABCDs of Well-Stated Learning Objectives 45
    ABCD Objectives Checklist 46
    Learning Objectives and Individual Differences 47
ASSURE Classroom Case Study: State Standards and Objectives 48
Select Strategies and Resources 48
    Select Strategies 48
    Select Resources 49
    Selecting, Modifying, or Designing Materials 49

ASSURE Classroom Case Study: Select Strategies and Resources 51

Video Example 3.2: Select Strategies and Resources 51

Utilize Resources 52
   Preview Resources 52
   Prepare Resources 52
   Prepare the Environment 52
   Prepare the Learners 52

ASSURE Classroom Case Study: Utilize Resources 53

Video Example 3.3: Utilize Resources 53
   Provide the Learning Experience 54

Require Learner Participation 54
   Practice 54

ASSURE Classroom Case Study: Require Learner Participation 56

Video Example 3.4: Require Learner Participation 56
   Feedback 56

Evaluate and Revise 57
   Evaluate Impact on Student Learning 57
   Evaluate and Revise Strategies and Resources 57
   Revision of Strategies and Resources 58

ASSURE Classroom Case Study: Evaluate and Revise 60

Video Example 3.5: Evaluate and Revise 60
Summary 61
ASSURE Lesson Plan Template: Analyze Learners 62
Professional Development 62
Suggested Resources 63

4   Designing Digital Learning Environments 65

ASSURE Classroom Case Study 65

Types of Learning Strategies 66
   Presentations 66
   Demonstrations 67
   Drill-and-Practice 68

Technology for All Learners: English Language Learners 68
   Tutorials 69
   Discussions 69
   Problem-Based Learning 70

Video Example 4.1: Problem-Based Learning 71
   Cooperative Learning 71
   Gaming 72
   Simulations 73
   Discovery 74

Integration of Technology and Media into Learning Strategies 75
   Presentations: Integration of Technology and Media 75
   Demonstrations: Integration of Technology and Media 76

   Drill and Practice: Integration of Technology and Media 76
   Tutorials: Integration of Technology and Media 76
   Discussions: Integration of Technology and Media 77
   Problem-Based Learning: Integration of Technology and Media 77

Video Example 4.2: Integrating WebQuests 78
   Cooperative Learning: Integration of Technology and Media 78
   Gaming: Integration of Technology and Media 78

Taking a Look at Technology Integration: Cooperative Learning 79
   Simulations: Integration of Technology and Media 79

Selection Rubric Games and Simulations 80
   Discovery: Integration of Technology and Media 82

When to Use Learning Strategies 82

Learning Contexts in Today's Classrooms 83
   Face-to-Face Instruction 83

Video Example 4.3: Face-to-Face Learning Context 85
   Distance Learning 85
   Blended Instruction 86
   Structured Independent Study 87
   Nonstructured Informal Study 87

Integrating Free and Inexpensive Materials 87
   Advantages of Free and Inexpensive Materials 88
   Limitations of Free and Inexpensive Materials 88
   Integration of Free and Inexpensive Materials 88
   Sources for Free and Inexpensive Materials 89
   Obtaining Free and Inexpensive Materials 90
   Evaluating Free and Inexpensive Materials 90

Innovations in Teaching: Interactive Multitouch Desks 90
Summary 91
ASSURE Lesson Plan 91
Professional Development 93
Suggested Resources 94

5   Engaging Learners with Digital Devices 95

ASSURE Classroom Case Study 96

Using Digital Devices in the Classroom 96

Video Example 5.1: Planning Digital Lessons 97
   Desktop to Mobile Continuum 97
   Strategies and Approaches 98

Copyright Concerns: Software 98
   Types of Digital Resources 99

Video Example 5.2: Preparing Students to Create Digital Presentations 101

Advantages of Using Digital Devices 102

Limitations of Using Digital Devices 103

Integrating Technology for Learning   103
**Taking a Look at Technology Integration: Testing
the Waters**   104
When to Use Technology   104
Application Selection   105
Technology for All Learners: Software and Apps   105
Selection Rubric   Software   106
Hardware   108
The Digital Classroom   110
  Single-Device Classroom   110
  Multi-Device Classroom   111
Video Example 5.3: Multiple Device Classroom   113
**Innovations in Teaching: Digital Fabricator: A Printer
for Real Objects**   113
Summary   114
ASSURE Lesson Plan   115
Professional Development   117
Suggested Resources   117

6 Connecting Learners
       Using Web 2.0   118
ASSURE Classroom Case Study   118
Web 2.0 Functions   119
  Collaborative Contributions   119
  Social Networking   119
  Mashups   120
Integrating Web 2.0 Resources into Instruction   120
**Video Example 6.1: Students Learning to
Use Web 2.0**   120
  Blogs   121
  Wikis   121
Video Example 6.2: Integrating Web 2.0   122
  Productivity Apps   123
**Taking a Look at Technology Integration:
Productivity App**   124
  Social Bookmarking   124
  Multimedia Sharing   125
When to Use Web 2.0   125
  Social Networks   127
  Mashups   128
  Selecting Web 2.0 Resources   129
Selection Rubric   Web 2.0 Resources   130
Advantages of Using Web 2.0 for Instruction   132
Technology for All Learners: Web 2.0 Tools   132
Limitations of Using Web 2.0 for Instruction   133
Video Example 6.3: Issues of Web 2.0 Use   133
**Innovations on the Horizon: Semantic-Aware
Applications**   134
Summary   134

ASSURE Lesson Plan   135
Professional Development   137
Suggested Resources   138

7 Teaching at a Distance   139
ASSURE Classroom Case Study   139
Designing Learning at a Distance   140
Video Example 7.1: Blackboard Design   141
  Student Access to Resource Materials   142
Copyright Concerns: Distance Learning   142
Teaching at a Distance   143
  Strategies and Approaches   143
  Types of Technology Resources   144
Video Example 7.2: Online Academic Discussion   145
Video Example 7.3: Video Discussion   146
Video Example 7.4: Video Class   148
  Critical Issues   148
Advantages of Distance Learning   150
Limitations of Distance Learning   151
Copyright Concerns: Online Learning   152
Integrating Distance Resources into Learning   152
  Virtual Public Schools   153
  Connecting with Text   153
  Integrating WebQuests   153
**Taking a Look at Technology Integration:
Key Pals**   154
**Taking a Look at Technology Integration:
Extending Knowledge through WebQuests**   155
  Connecting with Computer Conferencing   155
  Connecting with Parents   155
  Connecting with Other Teachers   155
  Connecting with Communities   156
  Course Connections   156
**Taking a Look at Technology Integration: GLOBE:
Networking Students, Teachers, and Scientists**   156
**Technology for All Learners: Distance Learning
Resources**   157
Video Example 7.5: Blackboard Benefit   157
Network Resources   158
  Types of Networks   158
  The World Wide Web   159
  Evaluating Online Resources   160
Technology Resources: Search Engines for Kids   160
Selection Rubric   Online Resources   161
Innovations in Teaching: Mobile Learning   163
Summary   163
ASSURE Lesson Plan   164
Professional Development   165
Suggested Resources   166

8 Enhancing Learning with Multimedia   168

ASSURE Classroom Case Study   168

Incorporating Multimedia Literacies into Teaching   169

Enhancing Learning with Audio   170
Advantages of Audio   170
Limitations of Audio   171
When to Integrate Audio into Instruction   171

When to Use Audio   172
How to Integrate Audio into Instruction   172

Technology for All Learners: Audio   173
Selection of Audio Resources   174
Types of Digital Audio   174

Selection Rubric   Audio Resources   175
Producing Audio   177

Copyright Concerns: Audio—Music   177

Video Example 8.1: Audio in Learning   178

Enhancing Learning with Video   178
Advantages of Video   179
Limitations of Video   179
Integration of Video   180

Technology for All Learners: Adapting Video   181

When to Use Video   181
Types of Educational Videos   181

Taking a Look at Technology Integration: Video   182
Selection of Video Resources   182

Selection Rubric   Video Resources   183
Producing Video   185

Copyright Concerns: Video   186

Video Example 8.2: Video in Learning   186

Enhancing Learning with Text   187
Advantages of Text   187
Limitations of Text   187
Integration of Text   188
Types of Text Resources   188

Technology for All Learners: Text   189
Selection of Text Resources   189
Producing Text   189

Selection Rubric   Text Resources   190

Video Example 8.3: Text in Learning   192

Enhancing Learning with Visuals   192
Advantages of Visuals   192
Limitations of Visuals   193
Integration of Visuals   193

Selection of Visual Materials   194
Types of Visuals   194

Selection Rubric   Visual Resources   195

Technology for All Learners: Visuals   197
Producing Visuals   199
Capturing Digital Visuals   202

Copyright Concerns: Visuals   202

Video Example 8.4: Visuals in Learning   203

Innovations in Teaching: The Maker Movement   203
Summary   204

ASSURE Lesson Plan   204
Professional Development   206
Suggested Resources   207

9 Preparing for Tomorrow's Challenges   209

The ASSURE Model for Tomorrow's Learning   210

Video Example 9.1: Digital Conversion   210

Tomorrow's Thinking and Learning   211
Tomorrow's Models   211
Tomorrow's Learning Environments   213

Tomorrow's Teachers   218

Video Example 9.2: Capturing Learning with ePortfolios   218
Exemplify Digital Age Thinking   218
Ubiquitously Integrate Emerging Technologies   219
Support Global Collaboration   219

Future Ready Professional Learning   220
Professional Engagement   220

Video Example 9.3: Professional Development and Online Communities   221
Professional Organizations   221
Professional Journals   223

Funding Technology for Tomorrow   224
Types of Grants   225
Writing a Grant Proposal   226
Summary   228
Professional Development   228
Suggested Resources   229

Appendix Lesson Scenarios   231

Glossary   232

References   237

Name Index   241

Subject Index   243

Credits   250

About the Authors

Sharon E. Smaldino

Sharon served for many years as a speech therapist and special educator in school districts from Florida to Minnesota. She spent many years working with PK-12 aged deaf and hearing-impaired students in public schools and in residential programs. For several years she worked with hearing impaired students who were placed in a residential program for social and emotional issues. During the time she was working with those students Sharon began a doctoral program at Southern Illinois University-Carbondale with a focus on instructional design and technology integration. Sharon brought her personal computer into her classroom to help her deaf students explore new technology-integrated learning experiences. Following completion of her degree, Sharon started her career as a teacher educator where she focused on working with teacher candidates, faculty, and PK-12 teachers to integrate technology into the learning process. Presenting at state, national, and international conferences, Sharon has become an important voice on applications of technology in the classroom and in distance education. In addition to her teaching, Sharon has written articles for state and national journals, chapters, and books on her primary research interest—effective technology integration in learning. She has worked on the development and implementation of grants that are designed to support teachers to integrate technology into their teaching. Sharon has received several awards for her teaching and professional activities. She has served as a journal editor and has held leadership positions in several state and national professional associations.

Deborah L. Lowther

Deborah has been an educator for over 30 years. For the first seven years of her career she taught middle school science and was highly engaged with providing professional development to teachers within and beyond her district. Because of her desire to work with teachers, she received her PhD in educational technology in 1994 and accepted a faculty position at the University of Memphis in 1995. At the University of Memphis, Deborah served as Department Chair for Instruction and Curriculum Leadership (ICL). The ICL department offers eight initial teacher licensure programs as well as several MS and EdD options. Prior to accepting the chair positon, Deborah served as the senior technology researcher for the Center for Research in Educational Policy, through which she researched PK-12 technology integration issues. She has personally conducted observations in PK-12 classrooms and interviewed students, teachers, and principals in numerous schools across the country. She has used the knowledge and experiences gained through engagement in applied research to develop the iNtegrating Technology for inquiry (NTeQ) Model with Dr. Gary Morrison. This model has been the foundational approach for several high-profile state-level technology initiatives. With regard to scholarship, Deborah has coauthored several books, chapters, and refereed journal articles; presented at numerous national and international conferences; and provided professional development to educational institutions across the nation.

Clif Mims

Clif is a teacher, researcher, author, speaker, and educational consultant specializing in the effective integration of technology with teaching and learning. His teaching career began more than 20 years ago as an elementary and middle school teacher. He also coached basketball and math teams to numerous championships. While earning his doctorate in instructional technology at the University of Georgia, Clif began focusing on teacher education and professional development. He is a professor of instructional design and technology at the University of Memphis and is the founding executive direction of the Martin Institute for Teaching Excellence. Clif is both a Project Zero Faculty Fellow and a Future of Learning Fellow at Harvard University. He and his wife have three children.

Preface

About This Book

Instructional Technology and Media for Learning, Twelfth Edition, shows how a complete range of technology and media formats can be integrated into classroom instruction using the ASSURE model for lesson planning. Written from the viewpoint of the teacher, the text shows specifically and realistically how technology and media fit into the daily life of the classroom. This book is intended for educators at all levels who place a high value on learning. Its purpose is to help educators incorporate technology and media into their repertoire—to use them as teaching tools and to guide students in using them as learning tools. We draw examples from elementary and secondary education because we know that instructors in these PK–12 settings have found previous editions of this book useful in their work.

New to This Edition

This edition is necessitated by the amazing pace of innovation in all aspects of technology, particularly in those related to computers and mobile technologies, as well as the Internet. The text has been updated to reflect the accelerating trend toward technology advances and changes in educational use of technology resources. We have combined two former chapters, audio and video, to reflect the multimedia concepts relevant today. The twelfth edition also addresses the interaction among the roles of teachers, technology coordinators, and school media specialists, all complementary and interdependent teams within the school.

- The explanation of the ASSURE model has been revised to be more clear, practical, and focused on PK–12 teaching and learning. Several chapters include ASSURE Classroom Case Study features that show how teachers can effectively integrate technology and media into instruction to augment their students' learning experiences.

- The chapters have been revised with updated information about designing instruction for learning that focuses on current learning standards and learning environments. Every effort has been made to identify the most current technology to support learning, providing an overview of how to use the technologies with students of all ages. We've included end-of-chapter professional development activities that guide the user through teacher performance assessment using technology standards as part of the process.

- We have updated several of the *Taking a Look at Technology Integration* features with examples of how actual classroom teachers use technology to support student learning. The examples place emphasis on integrating the learning standards and learner-centered instructional strategies.

- We have focused on enhancing the use of technology to meet the learning needs of all students in a classroom. With the increase in student diversity, classroom teachers are expected to meet the learning needs of all students. We have expanded the *Technology for All Learners* feature to help consider options that will be useful to facilitate learning experiences for all students in the classroom.

- We have added self-check items throughout each chapter to give the reader opportunities to recall the material just read and make connections to learning experiences. The reader can respond to questions that help them check for understanding. These replace the former end-of-chapter demonstration of professional knowledge exercises that were in previous editions.

Key Content Updates by Chapter

Specific chapter-by-chapter updates and additions include the following:

- **Chapter 1:** The first chapter reflects an extended discussion of academic and career learning experiences with updates on media and technology integration in classrooms. It includes an overview of effective learning environments. Key components of copyright issues are presented. Video segments offer ideas from the classroom. An updated description of the use of media and technology in instruction is present. An overview of assessment options is provided. Questions and discussion options are embedded throughout the chapter to provide learners with opportunities to explore the topics.

- **Chapter 2:** The chapter provides an updated overview of learning theories and principles of effective instruction. Video examples provide examples of ways that the technology offers support for learning and the embedded questions provide ways for learners to explore their thinking.

- **Chapter 3:** The foundational components of the ASSURE model have been updated and further supported with targeted, short video examples of actual classroom practice. The video examples demonstrate each step of the model and offer higher-level questions to deepen the learning experience.

- **Chapter 4:** Expanded discussion of digital learning environments explores a variety of learning strategies and contexts from a teacher's perspective. New examples, tips, and ideas reflect current classroom use of technology and media.

- **Chapter 5:** This chapter has been updated to align with digital devices used in today's classrooms to enhance learning. Video examples are revised to better demonstrate use of technology in classrooms. We embed new and thought-provoking questions and interactive application exercises throughout to keep readers engaged and increase learning.

- **Chapter 6:** This chapter has been revised to demonstrate the expanded role of Web 2.0 and social media in today's schools. New terminology aligns with current apps and digital devices used to support learning. The video examples provide insight into the ideas explored within the chapter. The embedded questions provide ways to engage the learners as they read the chapter.

- **Chapter 7:** An updated description of planning and implementing instruction at a distance is presented. An overview of resources to enhance learning opportunities in distance settings is included. Video of classroom use of distance learning provides examples within the chapter and, along with the embedded questions and discussion points, serves to guide the reader towards understanding the topics.

- **Chapter 8 (formerly chapters 8 and 9):** Chapters are combined, with integrated material covering four types of multimedia used to enhance learning: audio, video, text, and visuals. Integration examples are updated to illustrate ways new technologies and media are used in the classroom. Selection Rubrics for each type of media are embedded for quick access.

- **Chapter 9 (formerly chapter 10):** The Preparing for Tomorrow's Challenges chapter is fully updated with new Learning Outcomes, exciting video examples, and cutting-edge practices emerging on the horizon. Among the new topics are: coding as literacy, transdisciplinary learning, artificial intelligence, and augmented reality. The chapter also provides a new discussion of future ready professional development.

Pearson REVEL™

REVEL™ is Pearson's newest way of delivering our respected content. Fully digital and highly engaging, REVEL offers an immersive learning experience designed for the way today's students read, think, and learn. Enlivening course content with media interactives and assessments, REVEL empowers educators to increase engagement with the course to better connect with students.

REVEL™ Offers:

Dynamic content matched to the way today's students read, think, and learn, including:

- **Integrated Videos and Interactive Media** Integrated within the narrative, videos empower students to engage with concepts and take an active role in learning. REVEL's unique presentation of media as an intrinsic part of course content brings the hallmark features of Pearson's bestselling titles to life.
  - **Video examples within ASSURE Case Study boxes** offer students the opportunity to see key technologies at work, putting the ASSURE model into practice in different classrooms throughout the text.
  - **Application Exercises** are interactive activities that allow students to test their understanding of skills and concepts throughout each chapter, using formative and summative assessment tools. These include fill-in-the-blank, drag-and-drop tables, and journal exercises.
  - **Interactive Check Your Understanding items** are multiple choice assessment questions that test students' knowledge of the content they have just read at the end of each major section. Feedback for the correct answer is provided.
  - **Interactive Shared Writing activities** allow students to answer questions and share their responses with others.
- **Interactive Glossary** The material links bolded key terms in the text to glossary definitions, enabling students to read and comprehend with clarity without skipping concepts they do not understand.

Our Approach

We share a number of convictions that underlie this edition. First, we believe in an *eclectic* approach to instruction. Advocates cite an abundance of theories and philosophies in support of different approaches to instruction—behaviorist, cognitivist, constructivist, and social-psychological. We view these theoretical positions as differing *perspectives*— different vantage points—from which to examine the complex world of teaching and learning. We value each of them and feel that each is reflected in the guidance we offer.

Second, we have a balanced posture regarding the role of technology in instruction. Because of this perspective, we consider each technology in light of its advantages, limitations, and range of applications. No technology can be described solely as being either "good" or "bad," so we strive to give a balanced treatment to a range of technologies and media resources.

Third, we believe that technology can best be integrated into instruction when viewed from a learner's perspective. Therefore, throughout the book we attempt to approach technology and media solutions in terms of a teacher's day-to-day challenges and to avoid technical jargon as much as possible. Our examples deal with everyday teaching issues in a range of content areas.

The ASSURE Model for Technology Integration

To ensure our approach is applied effectively, we created the ASSURE Model for planning that included considerations for technology integration. This model presents a procedure that helps teachers consider appropriate technology that aligns with content standards while meeting the learning needs of all of their students. We have further refined this model in this current edition.

Focus on Professional Development

To help readers develop their ongoing professional knowledge and skills with regard to effectively using technology and media for learning, we have expanded the **Professional Development** feature.

In the first section, **Demonstrate Professional Skills,** readers integrate their learning through activities that are aligned with the ISTE Standards for Educators. The final section, **Building Your Professional Portfolio,** includes three parts: **Creating My Lesson, Reflecting on My Lesson,** and **Enhancing My Lesson.** These are also linked to the ISTE Standards for Educators.

- **Creating My Lesson** asks readers to select their own topics and settings for developing lessons that integrate the technology and media discussed in the chapter. Chapter-specific ideas help readers make decisions to create their own lesson plan using appropriate instructional strategies, technology, and media.

- **Reflecting on My Lesson** prompts readers to reflect on their lesson design, the process used to develop it, and different types of students who could benefit from it. Readers are also asked to reflect on what they learned about the process of matching audience, content, strategies, technology, media, and materials.

- **Enhancing My Lesson** asks the reader to describe other strategies, technologies, media, and materials that could enhance the lesson. The reader addresses how the lesson could be enhanced to meet the diverse needs of learners, including students who already possess the knowledge and skills targeted in the lesson plan.

Additional Features

ASSURE Classroom Case Study

Chapter opening "ASSURE Classroom Case Studies" (in Chapters 3 through 9) each presents a video clip of a specific classroom that will be revisited periodically throughout the chapter in the "ASSURE Case Study Reflections." These are brief notes and reflection questions that extend the opening case study by addressing the questions that a teacher may face when considering technology integration in the context of specific chapter content. At the end of the chapter, the "ASSURE Lesson Plan" provides a fuller version of the instructional or classroom situation outlined at the beginning of the chapter and offers a possible solution.

Taking a Look at Technology Integration

Cooperative Learning

Connie Courbat, a third-grade teacher, was aware of the various ability levels of her students and wanted them all to have a positive experience studying the westward movement of the 1800s. The lesson objectives were focused on helping students gain a better understanding of the impact of historical events on lifestyle choices. She introduced the topic by forming cooperative groups that used the Oregon Trail app on the one computer in her classroom to experience the adventures of a pioneer traveling the Oregon Trail. The app presented students with various scenarios as they worked their way through the trail, for example, equipment failure—losing a wagon wheel; managing supply shortages, and how to treat illnesses. She grouped the students to ensure that all ability levels were represented within each group, thus allowing all students to benefit from the experience. Ms. Courbat was careful to establish roles for each member of the group, such as team leader, recorder, and materials manager. She moved among the groups as they worked together, helping them to address questions and ensuring that they were accomplishing the tasks. Each group gave a presentation of their travels westward, explaining their successes and failures in achieving the goal of reaching Oregon.

The Stock Market Game, offered by the Simfa Foundation, is very effective in helping your students gain financial skills. This online, multiuser game requires that your students invest their online $100,000 portfolio, tracking their investments and working toward the goal of developing the highest performing portfolio among those who are participating. They work in teams, assuming leadership roles and building skills in cooperation and collaboration as they learn about investing. The game also provides your students with opportunities to practice their language arts and math skills as they work through their investment strategies.

Simulations: Integration of Technology and Media

Interpersonal skills and science experiments are popular subjects for simulations. In some simulations, learners manipulate mathematical models to determine the effect of changing certain variables, such as controlling the speed of a skier by changing the degree of incline.

Role-playing is another form of simulation to build communication and social skills needed in today's careers. As an example, the award winning simulation, Extreme Event, provides group-member roles in a simulated disaster situation that needs to be resolved through community efforts and information to help members as they move along in the process. The simulation is designed for students aged 14+ and focuses on building critical thinking skills associated with disaster resilience, while learning to prioritize resources and build coalitions to improve civic literacy.

You can simulate an event that occurred locally or a major event that occurred a century ago, like the sinking of the *Titanic*. One teacher engages her students in understanding the impact of the decisions made that eventful night by assigning roles of actual passengers to her students to reenact. While they are participating in "onboard" activities, such as playing card games, dancing, eating a meal, or taking a stroll along the deck of the boat, she guides their scurry to deal with the accident. Before the experience is over, she identifies who must leave the area because they have drowned. Her students better understand the devastating event as many of their classmates are escorted to a back section of the room. She shares implications of how an event such as this affects family members and what can be done to prevent such catastrophes.

When deciding which games or simulations will support your instructional goals, use the guidelines in the Selection Rubric: Games and Simulations to assist with the selection. For example, with the rubric you can assess the quality with which the game or simulation aligns with the lesson objective, provides accurate and current information, provides practice for relevant skills, and has the potential to hold the interest of your students.

Taking a Look at Technology Integration

These miniature case studies of technology and media applications demonstrate how teachers are using technology in a variety of settings. Like the ASSURE Classroom Case Study, they show technology and media use *in* context.

---

devices such as tablets and smart phones. Students will be expected to be able to use all the devices as appropriate for their learning experiences. As a teacher, you will decide which of the devices that you have in your classroom will be most effective in providing your students with quality learning experiences.

Strategies and Approaches

Educating today's students has shifted from providing information to opening doors for them to explore topics and create meaningful learning experiences for themselves. Technology has been incorporated as a central feature of this process. The implication is that educators are moving away from the idea of school as a place to *get knowledge* to the view that school is a place to *learn how to learn*. The challenge for you as a teacher is to provide opportunities for all students to use technology in meaningful ways to accomplish learning tasks. This may mean selecting specific software for individual students—for example, to practice math skills or to search online databases. This may mean changing your entire approach to a lesson. Student projects, such as working on an ecology report, are not new within the school curriculum, but the approach certainly can be.

You should be a model user of technology for your students. Students will quickly notice if the teacher makes illegal copies of programs and apps and doesn't follow copyright guidelines. Remember, actions speak louder than words. Check with your technology coordinator, library media specialist, or principal for the specific guidelines and licensing agreements that you should follow. See Copyright Concerns.

Students can interact directly with various technologies as part of their instructional activities in a variety of ways, from working with material presented by the computer or mobile device in a controlled sequence, such as a drill-and-practice program, to a student-initiated creative activity, such as a digitally published book of student poems. Learners may take tests on the computer or a mobile device or input information into personal e-portfolios. Students can use the e-portfolio to demonstrate specific learning or to create a catalog of their work over time to record their educational progress. The technology can help both the teacher and students in maintaining information about their learning and in guiding instruction. That is, the digital device can organize and store easily retrievable

Copyright Concerns

Software

Congress amended the Copyright Act to clear up questions of fair use of copyrighted programs. The changes defined the term *computer program* for copyright purposes and set forth rules on permissible and nonpermissible use of copyrighted computer software. According to the amended law, you are permitted to do the following with a single copy of a program:

- Make one backup or archival copy of the program.
- Use a "locksmith" program to bypass the copy-prevention code on the original to make the archival copy.
- Install one copy of the program onto a computer hard drive.
- Adapt a computer program from one language to another if the program is not available in the desired language.
- Add features to a copyrighted program to make better use of the program.
- Adapt a copyrighted program to meet local needs.

Without the copyright owner's permission, you are prohibited from doing the following:

- Making multiple copies of a copyrighted program.
- Making additional copies from an archival or backup copy.
- Making copies of copyrighted programs to be sold, leased, loaned, transmitted, or given away.
- Selling a locally produced adaptation of a copyrighted program.
- Making multiple copies of an adaptation of a copyrighted program even for use within a school or school district.
- Putting a single copy of a program onto a network without permission or a special site license.
- Duplicating the printed copyrighted software documentation unless allowed by the copyrighted software company.

Copyright Concerns

This feature provides an integrated discussion of copyright issues linked to specific chapter content.

The URL incorporates the name of the host computer (server), the directory on the server, and the title of the webpage (actual file). Within and among webpages relies on hypertext links that, when selected, move users to another location on the same page, another website on the same host computer, or to a different computer on the Web.

To use the Web for online learning, webpages have to be designed and written, and a host computer must be available to house them. Universities and large companies are usually directly connected to the Internet and run the necessary web-hosting (server) software. A popular resource in online distance education, the **Learning Management System (LMS)**, is software designed to make it easier for the teacher to design and deliver instruction and to use the resources that are part of the system, such as the discussion board, test options, and grade book. When using an LMS program such as Blackboard or Moodle, the teacher can concentrate on the instruction and not have to be concerned with computer programming issues.

Evaluating Online Resources

There are so many resources available for students and learners on the Web that it can be difficult to determine which are the best to support learning. You can start with those provided in Technology Resources: Search Engines for Kids.

See the **Selection Rubric: Online Resources** provided to guide you in identifying online resources that will benefit your professional development or support your students' learning. You can even ask students to use the rubric to evaluate sites they find while exploring new resources for their learning experiences.

Technology Resources

Search Engines for Kids

KidRex.org

This is a colorful, fun, and safe search site for kids that is designed by kids. KidRex searches the Internet for kid topic sites and employs the Google SafeSearch technology.

GoGooligans.com

This is an advanced academic and educational search engine for kids and teens. The search engine site offers additional resources for children with disabilities. For older teens, there is an advanced search engine, GoogleScholastic.com. Both search engines use Google SafeSearch technology to ensure that children are guided to sites that are appropriate for them.

FactMonster.com

FactMonster offers text, video, and other resources on many topics. A reference desk with access to a dictionary, atlas, and encyclopedia is included. A Homework Center is available with ideas about how to develop homework habits and skills and how to use the available resources. It is available for grade levels K–12 and includes topics covering math, language arts, social studies, and science.

Askkids.com

This is a student version of Ask.com that uses age-appropriate content, filtering, and search terms to help kids narrow their searches by asking questions.

Kidsclick.org

Librarians created this site to help students conduct searches. Main topic menus and helpful links make it a kid-friendly search engine.

Technology Resources

Because many schools have tight budgets, this feature offers a list of practical and valuable resources that are free or inexpensive. They also inform the reader how to obtain the resources. These are listed at the ends of chapters along with helpful web links.

Selection Rubrics

These rubrics are related to each of the technology and media formats, making it easy to preview materials systematically and to preserve the information for later reference. Textbook users have permission to print these rubrics for personal use.

---

80 Chapter 4

SELECTION RUBRIC Games and Simulations

Complete and save the following interactive evaluation to reference when selecting Games or Simulations to integrate into lessons.

Search Terms
_____
_____
_____

Title _____

Format

Source/Location _____ _____ Game

© Date _____ Cost _____ Length _____ Minutes _____ _____ Simulation

Subject Area _____ Grade Level _____

Instructional Strategies _____

Brief Description

Standards/Outcomes/Objectives

Prerequisites (e.g., prior knowledge, reading ability, vocabulary level, etc.)

Strengths

Limitations

Special Features

Name _____ Date _____

(Continued)

- *Limited view.* Every student may not have an equal view of the demonstration, thus possibly missing some aspect of the experience. A technological solution involves using a document camera to project the demonstration.
- *Nonflexible pacing.* Not all students may be able to follow the demonstration's pace of presentation. Recording the procedure on video will allow students to review the demonstration as needed.

Drill-and-Practice

In **drill-and-practice**, learners complete practice exercises to refresh or increase fluency in content knowledge and skills, most commonly in mathematics, language arts, and second languages. Use of this strategy assumes that your learners have received some instruction on the concept, principle, or procedure they are practicing. To be effective, the drill-and-practice exercises should include feedback to reinforce correct responses and to remediate errors learners might make along the way. As seen in the Technology for All Learners: English Language Learners, digital drill-and-practice works well for students who are learning English.

ADVANTAGES OF DRILL-AND-PRACTICE. Drill-and-practice is a commonly used learning strategy due to advantages such as:

- *Corrective feedback.* Students receive feedback on their responses.
- *Information chunking.* Information is presented in small chunks, allowing students to review the material in small bits.
- *Built-in practice.* Practice is built into the small chunks of information, giving immediate opportunities to try out the new knowledge in some positive way.

LIMITATIONS OF DRILL-AND-PRACTICE. Along with advantages, there are also some limitations associated with the use of drill-and-practice, which include:

- *Repetitive.* Not all students respond well to the repetitive nature of drill-and-practice. It is important to limit the time spent or number of exercises to prevent monotony.

Technology for All Learners: English Language Learners

Nearly 10% of public school students are English language learners (ELLs) with approximately 75% of those speaking Spanish (NCES, 2017). Thus, teachers often need to help ELL students with learning English as well as content area knowledge and skills. Excellent digital resources are readily available to engage students in drill-and-practice activities to help students learn to speak, read, and write in English. Examples include:

- *Listen and repeat videos.* Free online videos, often on YouTube, provide vocabulary words in the student's home language and also in English, followed by the narrator pronouncing the word in English.
- *Alphabet Books.* Online books are organized by the English alphabet. For each letter, an English word that starts with the letter is provided (e.g., Flower) along with the same word in the student's home language (e.g., Flor for Spanish) and an image to help understanding (e.g., a daisy). Students can also create their own digital or paper alphabet books.
- *Matching Games.* Online matching games in which students must select the English word to match an image or a word in their home language. Free games are readily available for multiple topics, such as animals, family, shapes, fruit, transportation, etc.
- *Flashcards.* Digital flashcards are another option for teachers with ELL students. Free online ELL flashcards sometimes offer options for listening to the pronunciation of the word, using a timed setting for recognizing the name from three or four options, or using them in a traditional fashion for learning the new words.

Technology for All Learners

This feature describes technology and media that can be used to meet the learning needs of diverse learners, ranging from those with learning disabilities to gifted and talented students.

---

90 Chapter 4

There are a number of websites that serve as repositories for open source materials, or online products that are available for sharing. Among the websites are Curriki and Gooru, which are communities for sharing educational resources. Teachers, students, and families can use these sources for lessons, practice on specific topics, or to share resources they've designed themselves. Gooru uses a media-based format and actually includes the lesson's media, such as videos, as part of the lesson resources. Illustrative Mathematics is another website that provides games and activities to practice math concepts for grades 7 through 12. The Illustrative Mathematics author has years of experience teaching mathematics and offers many ideas for helping young people learn math concepts while enjoying the learning experiences.

Obtaining Free and Inexpensive Materials

Most classroom materials are available in a format that can easily be downloaded from the provider's website. For those resources that are not available online, you can submit your request via email, phone, fax, or mail. Some agencies may require the request to be submitted on school letterhead and signed by your principal, such as scheduling a police officer for a guest presentation. Any student requests should include your endorsement. When ordering hard copies of materials, ask for a preview copy before requesting multiple copies and, when appropriate, share the resources with other teachers. When obtaining online resources from sites with feedback options, respond with descriptions of how the materials were used along with student reactions. Be courteous, but be honest! Many suppliers attempt to improve free and inexpensive materials on the basis of user comments. When online feedback isn't possible, send a thank you note.

Evaluating Free and Inexpensive Materials

As with all types of materials, evaluate the educational value of free and inexpensive materials critically. Some are very "slick" (technically well presented) but not educationally sound. Use the appropriate selection rubric for the type of media (web resources, video, etc.) you are evaluating. All the selection rubrics in this book have the rating criterion "bias free." Use it judiciously when reviewing free and inexpensive materials.

Innovations in Teaching

Interactive Multitouch Desks

Classrooms of the future will no longer have desks and separate laptops. Interactive multitouch desks resemble the navigational interface used in science fiction movies, such as *Star Trek*. The screen serves as an individual workspace, an interactive whiteboard, and a collaboration tool for several students. Students use fingers or pens to interact with the desk and can define their own space with an icon or avatar. The desks are connected through a fully interactive classroom system, which is monitored with a teacher's console that can also be used to view student work on every screen or display example work.

☑ Check Your Understanding 4.4

Innovations in Teaching

This feature presents chapter-specific examples of innovative trends and technologies in teaching and learning.

When to Use

This feature gives specific tips on using technology and media with clarity, flair, and dramatic effect. It goes with the U of the ASSURE Model (Utilize Technology, Media, and Materials).

Support Materials for Instructors

The following resources are available for instructors to download on www.pearsonhighered.com/educators. Instructors enter the author or title of this book, select this particular edition of the book, and then click on the Resources tab to log in and download textbook supplements.

The Instructor's Guide (0134298284)

The Instructor's Guide provides chapter-by-chapter tools for use in class. Teaching strategies, in-class activities, student projects, key term definitions, and helpful resources will reinforce key concepts or applications and keep students engaged.

PowerPoint® Presentations (0134298276)

Designed as an instructional tool, the presentations can be used to elaborate on chapter material. They are available for both students and instructors and reinforce key concepts and ideas presented throughout the text.

TestGen (0134287479)

Test Gen is a powerful test generator available exclusively from Pearson Education. You install TestGen on your personal computer (Windows or Macintosh) and create your own tests for classroom testing and for other specialized delivery options, such as a local area network or the web. A test bank, which is also called a Test Item File (TIF), typically contains a large set of test items organized by chapter and ready for your use in creating a test based on the associated textbook material.

The tests can be downloaded in the following formats:

- TestGen Testbank file—PC
- TestGen Testbank file—MAC
- TestGen Testbank—Blackboard 9 TIF

- TestGen Testbank—Blackboard CE/Vista (WebCT) TIF
- Angel Test Bank (zip)
- D2L Test Bank (zip)
- Moodle Test Bank
- Sakai Test Bank (zip)

Authors' Services

The authors are eager to assist you in putting together an outstanding course. We offer the following services to instructors who have adopted this book:

- *Online dialog.* The authors are available to "meet" with your students if you are using an online course delivery learning management tool.
- *Telelectures and Videoconferences.* Contact any of the authors in advance to arrange a guest lecture in your class via telephone or video. Some instructors find this a good way to demonstrate the use of this technology for learning about distance learning options. The authors' e-mail addresses are listed in the Instructor's Guide.
- *Workshops.* The authors have conducted workshops across the country. This is a forum for exchange of ideas and networking among instructors of courses on technology and media. They are also available to provide a workshop in your area if you wish to arrange one.
- *Consulting.* The authors are available for consulting and conducting workshops at the local, state, and national level. They are regular presenters and workshop facilitators across the country and around the world.

If you are a student or an instructor using this text and wish to share your comments with us, please email them to Sharon Smaldino (smaldinos@comcast.net), Deborah Lowther (dlowther@memphis.edu), or Clif Mims (clifmims@memphis.edu).

Acknowledgments

Through each of the editions we have been fortunate to have guidance from the people who teach the courses for which this book is designed. In preparing this edition, again we surveyed a sample of adopters and other leaders in the field to elicit their advice about content and emphases. We also asked other well-respected colleagues in the field to critique the text. We thank all those who gave their time and expertise to help make this textbook what it is. In particular we want to acknowledge those talented individuals who reviewed the twelfth edition and suggested improvements: 1) Rob Branch, University of Georgia 2) Jennifer Richey, Texas Woman's University 3) Mary Smith, Texas A&M Texarkana 4) Matthew A. Williams, Ph.D., Kent State University

We offer an extended appreciation to these teachers for sharing their expertise and allowing us to record their technology integration lessons: Tiare Ahu, high school; Lindsay Kaiser and Jena Marshall, fifth grade; Kerry Bird, fourth grade; Vicki Davis, high school; Jimmy Chun, high school; and Scott James, fifth grade.

We would like to thank the editorial and production staff of Pearson Education, especially Drew Bennett, Max Chuck, Carolyn Schweitzer, and Yagnesh Jani, and members of the editorial and production team: Heather Winter, Raja K, Linda Duerte, Kay Brymer, Kevin Campbell, and Matthew Shaw. We have never had such intense and helpful support from any previous publication team.

We are grateful to our colleagues from our own universities—Northern Illinois University and the University of Memphis—for their many and valuable forms of support over the years.

And, we are especially grateful for the opportunity to have worked with Jim Russell, one of the original authors of this text's long-time contribution to the field. Jim is a professor emeritus of Educational Technology at Purdue University, where he was a faculty member for 38 years, having received numerous honors for his teaching. During those years, he also engaged in working with classroom teachers to improve their classroom practice and use of technology. Prior to joining the faculty at Purdue, Jim was a high school mathematics and science teacher. As authors, we have heart-felt gratitude for Jim's guidance, patience, and insights that helped us with this book and with our professional endeavors.

Finally, we thank our families for all they do to make this project possible. Their patience and support have been invaluable in helping us finish this project.

Sharon E. Smaldino

Deborah L. Lowther

Clif Mims

Features

ASSURE CASE STUDIES, REFLECTIONS, AND LESON PLANS

Chapter 3, pp. 40, 41, 43, 48, 51, 53, 56, 60, 62
Chapter 4, pp. 65, 91
Chapter 5, pp. 96, 115
Chapter 6, pp. 118, 135
Chapter 7, pp. 139, 164
Chapter 8, pp. 168, 204

COPYRIGHT CONCERNS

Software, p. 98
Distance Learning, p. 142
Online Learning, p. 152
Audio—Music, p. 177
Video, p. 186
Visuals, p. 202

INNOVATIONS IN TEACHING

Interactive Multitouch Desks, p. 90
Mobile Learning, p. 163
The Maker Movement, p. 203

SELECTION RUBRIC

Games and Simulations, p. 80
Software, p. 106
Web 2.0 Resources, p. 130
Online Resources, p. 161
Audio Resources, p. 176
Video Resources, p. 184
Text Resources, p. 191
Visual Resources, p. 196

TAKING A LOOK AT TECHNOLOGY INTEGRATION

The New Tech Network, p. 28
Cooperative Learning, p. 79
Testing the Waters, p. 104
Productivity App, p. 124
Key Pals, p. 154
Extending Knowledge through WebQuests, p. 155
GLOBE: Networking Students, Teachers, and Scientists, p. 156
Audio, p. 173
Video Resources, p. 183

TECHNOLOGY FOR ALL LEARNERS

Using Technology Tools to Differentiate Instruction, p. 4
English Language Learners, p. 68
Software and Apps, p. 105
Web 2.0 Tools, p. 132
Distance Learning Resources, p. 157
Audio, p. 173
Adapting Video, p. 181
Text Resources, p. 190
Visuals, p. 197

TECHNOLOGY RESOURCES

Rubrics, p. 36
Search Engines for Kids, p. 160

VIDEO EXAMPLE

How Do You Choose the Right Web Tools?, p. 10
Wiki Discussion, p. 12
Constructivism, p. 23
Media Literacy Skills, p. 30
Using Online Resources, p. 31
Analyze Learners, p. 43
Select Strategies and Resources, p. 51
Utilize Resources, p. 53
Require Learner Participation, p. 56
Evaluate and Revise, p. 60
Problem-Based Learning, p. 71
Integrating WebQuests, p. 78
Face-to-Face Learning Context, p. 85
Planning Digital Lessons, p. 97
Preparing Students to Create Digital Presentations, p. 101
Multiple Device Classroom, p. 113
Students Learning to Use Web 2.0, p. 120
Integrating Web 2.0, p. 122
Issues of Web 2.0 Use, p. 133
Blackboard Design, p. 141
Online Academic Discussion, p. 145
Video Discussion, p. 146
Video Class, p. 148
Blackboard Benefit, p. 157

Audio in Learning, p. 178
Video in Learning, p. 186
Text in Learning, p. 192
Visuals in Learning, p. 203
Digital Conversion, p. 210
Capturing Learning with ePortfolios, p. 218
Professional Development and Online Communities, p. 221

WHEN TO USE

Learning Strategies, p. 82
Technology, p. 104
Web 2.0, p. 125
Audio, p. 172
Video, p. 181

Chapter 1
Exploring Student Learning

 ## Learning Outcomes

This chapter addresses ISTE Standards for Teachers 2, 4, and 5.

1.1 Identify key components of the framework for academic and career learning and how technology and media are integrated into today's classrooms.

1.2 Explain the role of the digital teacher, the tools and resources available to fully integrate technology into teaching, and the guidelines and standards for teaching content knowledge and skills.

1.3 Describe the role of the digital learner.

1.4 Discuss the framework for academic and career learning literacies.

1.5 Describe effective environments.

1.6 Describe the key concerns regarding copyright law for educational uses.

 ## Goal

Learn about the uses of technology and media to ensure successful student learning.

Introduction

This book offers a systematic approach for selecting and using technology and media to facilitate student learning to enhance academic and career preparation. This approach is based on the ASSURE model, which helps teachers plan effective, integrated lessons by following a six-step process. Exploring both traditional technologies used in PK–12 classrooms today as well as innovative and cutting-edge approaches that may be commonplace in the future, we describe technology and media that teachers can use to promote learning both within and beyond the classroom. We describe how to select, use, and evaluate resources to ensure that learners emerge with the knowledge and skills needed for their successful future careers.

We begin by exploring the influence of technology and media within the learning process on the new roles of teachers to engage students in the classroom. No longer are teachers and textbooks the sources of all information. Instead, the teacher has become the facilitator of knowledge and skills acquisition. With a few keystrokes or taps, students can explore the world using boundless online resources and a wide array of digital media to obtain the information they seek. Students can discuss their findings in real-time conversations with experts and with other students representing a global array of cultures and experiences.

These exciting technology innovations provide unlimited ways to expand educational opportunities for our students, but they also present new challenges to teachers. As a teacher, how will you go beyond the textbook? How will you select the "right" technology and media when so many choices are available? And more importantly, how will you create learning experiences that effectively use these tools and resources to ensure that your students gain new knowledge and skills?

Framework for Academic and Career Learning: Technology and Media in Today's Schools

As we continue to move into the future, it is critical that the foundational components of PK–12 education keep pace with evolving societal needs to prepare students for citizenship and successful careers. As a teacher, you are challenged to help students achieve mastery of core subjects as well as gain contemporary knowledge and skills. Leaders from business and education, as well as other associations and institutions, are joining together to recommend new approaches and broader learning expectations for PK–12 students (ISTE, 2015; Partnership for 21st Century Learning, 2015). Foundational to knowledge and skills is the preparation of your students to meaningfully and purposefully use technology and media for creativity and innovation, communication, research, and problem solving. Themes based on global awareness, entrepreneurship, and lifelong learning skills, such as adaptability, leadership, and responsibility, are also recommended for inclusion within core subject area study. This text will serve as a guide to assist you in integrating contemporary knowledge and skills into your instructional planning and practices.

Instructional Technology

Currently, when most people hear the word *technology*, they think of products like computers, tablets, and mobile devices. In this text, we will be referring to **instructional technology**, which involves the integration of teacher and student use and knowledge of tools, resources, and techniques to improve learning.

To promote student learning, you need to create an appropriate learning environment. Throughout the book we will describe the decision-making processes that you can use and the factors you must balance in your decisions. You will need to know the characteristics of your learners. The expected outcomes (objectives) must be specified. You will need to select the appropriate strategies and materials. The best available technology and media must be used properly to promote optimal learning. You will need to get your learners involved through appropriate practice and feedback. Throughout the process, you will be assessing student learning and evaluating the instructional experience, as well as its components, so you can revise as necessary. We have put all of these steps together in the ASSURE model.

Although some educators view technology as a classroom cure-all, it is important to note that technology resources don't automatically make teachers more proficient. You will need to be versed in best practices for integrating technology into the curriculum. The ASSURE model provides a structure and easy-to-follow steps to guide teachers through the process of creating lessons that achieve the goals of effectively using technology and promoting learning. The model is applicable for all types of technology across all subject areas for different learners and learning conditions.

Developed as a planning aid to help ensure that technology and media are used to their maximum advantage, not just as interchangeable substitutes for printed or oral messages, the ASSURE model provides a systematic process for creating learning experiences. Indeed, one of the most important roles of technology and media is to serve as a catalyst for change in the whole instructional environment.

Current technology offers several benefits for teachers.

- One is the ability to digitally store and access large amounts of information, whether as text, audio, visuals, games, or videos, in computer files, on DVDs, or in a cloud storage space.

- Another unique advantage of current technology is its adaptability to meet the varying needs of your students. As seen in Technology for All Learners, you can differentiate instruction and access to learning experiences with a variety of technology tools.

- A third advantage of technology is that your students are no longer limited to the confines of the classroom. Through the school media center and computer networks such as the Internet, the world becomes each student's classroom.

STATUS OF THE TECHNOLOGY GAP.   As you plan different technology integration activities, it is important to stay current on technology issues, such as the "digital divide," which may influence your instructional choices. The digital divide—or technology gap—in PK–12 schools continues to narrow. Students of all economic levels have greater access to high-speed Internet-connected computers at school. Of note is that there are efforts to bridge the gap for students who may not have home computers (Barnett, 2013).

On the other hand, the technology gap varies when examining Internet usage by adults. Even though in 2014 approximately 80% of American households had access to the Internet at home, disparities in Internet use still exist based on ethnic groups and location (Rainie & Cohn, 2014). For example, the use was lower in more rural areas. A similar pattern was seen for use of smart phones (Lenart, 2015). Interestingly, the report revealed that smart phone use was higher among all teen groups, with text messaging being the highest use of the cell phone among all smart phone users. So, when you are thinking about using the Internet to communicate with your students' families, remember that not all of them will have access to your webpages or emails. Also, remember that your students may have better access to the Internet using their smart phones than using a computer. Another consideration for middle and high school teachers is to use text messaging to communicate with your students, as it is regularly used by this age group.

SIX MEDIA FORMATS.   Media, the plural of medium, are means of communication. Derived from the Latin medium ("between"), the term refers to anything that carries information between a source and a receiver. The purpose of media is to facilitate communication and learning.

Technology for All Learners
Using Technology Tools to Differentiate Instruction

As a result of educational policy advances, the characteristics of students in the general classroom are placing increased emphasis on meeting many different learning needs. Technology plays an important role in the education of students with exceptionalities. Adapted and specially designed technology and media can contribute enormously to effective instruction for all students and can help them achieve at their highest potential regardless of innate abilities.

Children with disabilities in particular need special instructional interventions. Children with mental disabilities have a greater opportunity to learn when presented with highly structured learning situations. Structure compensates for ill-structured prior knowledge that decreases students' abilities to incorporate messages into atypical mental constructs. The students benefit from having much more of the message placed within a familiar context.

Children with physical disabilities also benefit from the use of technology to enhance their learning experiences. Students with hearing or visual impairments require different kinds of learning materials. More emphasis should be placed on audio for students with visual impairments and on visuals for those with hearing problems. Adjusting instruction for all exceptional groups requires heavy reliance on technology and media, as well as the appropriate selection of these materials to fit specific purposes. Many teachers have found that these assistive strategies for students with disabilities have the added benefit of helping all students.

Assistive technologies can be classified as low tech, medium tech, or high tech. Low-tech devices do not use electricity or batteries. For example, a magnifying glass to enlarge printed material for a visually impaired student would be a low-tech assistive technology. The medium-tech category includes electrical devices. A mini book light to increase illumination would be representative of medium-tech equipment. High-tech assistance involves the use of a computer. The text to speech option is an example of high-tech assistive technology.

Students with language or cultural differences need to have opportunities to experience learning in appropriate ways. Students whose primary language is different than that used for instruction need to have materials and devices that allow them to have access to learning in their primary language. Translation software can help prepare materials for these students and allows them to continue to participate in classroom activities. Students who have diverse cultural backgrounds may need alternative images as part of their instructional materials. Teachers can easily access a variety of culturally sensitive images on the Web. By ensuring that the images are culturally sensitive, teachers augment the learning experience of all students in the classroom.

Diverse learners also include gifted and talented students who, for example, could use digital sources, DVDs, or archived text to explore topics beyond or in addition to regular classroom assignments. They can also use the Internet to search for current information or to engage in a live chat with the author of a book the class is reading or a state senator who will vote on an environmental issue being studied. They can be asked to analyze the information they locate and to synthesize a presentation for the class, perhaps using Prezi, or they can post their findings on a class webpage.

For more information, see the Technology for All Learners features throughout this book.

A braille display is an example of an assistive technology.

Media are discussed in more detail in later chapters, but as an overview, let's look at the six basic categories of media used in learning (Figure 1.1): text, audio, visuals, video, manipulatives (objects), and people.

1. Text, the most commonly used medium, is composed of alphanumeric characters that may be displayed in any format—whiteboard, computer screen, book, poster, and so on.

2. Audio, another medium commonly used in learning, includes anything you can hear—a person's voice, music, mechanical sounds (running car engine), noise, and so on. It may be live or recorded.

3. Visuals are also regularly used to promote learning and include diagrams on a computer screen, drawings on a whiteboard, photographs, graphics in a book, cartoons, and so on.

Figure 1.1 Six Basic Categories of Media

4. Video is a visual as well as audio medium that shows motion and can be stored on DVDs or flash drives, streamed from the Internet, be in the form of computer animation, and so on.

5. Although often not considered media, real objects and models are three-dimensional manipulatives that can be touched and handled by students. Growing in popularity are digital manipulatives, which represent three-dimensional objects and can be manipulated digitally.

6. The sixth and final category of media is people. In fact, people are critical to learning. Students learn from teachers, other students, and adults.

There are many types of media in each category, which we will refer to as **media formats**—the physical forms in which messages are incorporated and displayed. Media formats include, for example, whiteboards and books (text and visuals), PowerPoint or Prezi slides (text and visuals), CDs or podcasts (voice and music), DVDs (video and audio), and computer multimedia (audio, text, and video). Each has different strengths and limitations in terms of the types of messages that can be recorded and displayed. Choosing a media format can be a complex task, considering the vast array of media and technology available, the variety of learners, and the many objectives to be pursued (Table 1.1).

When selecting media formats, the instructional situation or setting (e.g., large group, small group, self-instruction), learner variables (e.g., reader, nonreader, auditory preference), and the nature of the objective (e.g., cognitive, affective, motor skill, interpersonal) must be considered, as well as the presentational capabilities of each of the media formats (e.g., still visuals, video, printed words, spoken words).

Application Exercise 1.1

Instructional Materials

Once you determine the media format, such as a DVD or web-based content, you must decide which of the appropriate media you will use. The specific medium becomes the instructional material.

Instructional materials are the specific items used within a lesson that influence student learning. For example, a middle school lesson may focus on adding polynomials with a computer software program that provides virtual manipulatives students use to create "concrete" examples of addition problems in order to reach solutions. The computer software offers feedback and opportunities to continue practicing. The

---

Table 1.1 Examples of Media Formats and Instructional Materials

Media	Media Formats	Instructional Materials Examples
Text	Printed book, computer software, e-book, webpages	A textbook StoryMaker software
Audio	CD, live presenter, podcast	State of the Union address on webcast
Visual	Drawing on interactive whiteboard Photo in a newspaper	Drawing of the musical scale Photo of local building
Video	DVD, IMAX documentary film, streamed video	*Lewis & Clark: Great Journey West* video
Manipulative	Real or virtual object	Algebra tiles
People	Teachers, subject-matter experts	The chief officer of NASA

specific math problems and feedback generated by this software are the instructional materials. Another example is this text that you are currently reading, which consists of the written information (text), visuals, interactive activities, and learning exercises found at the end of the chapter.

The design and use of instructional materials are critical, because it is the interaction of the students with those materials that generates and reinforces actual learning. If the materials are weak, improperly structured, or poorly sequenced, only limited learning will occur. On the other hand, powerful, well-designed instructional materials are experienced in such a way that they can be readily encoded, retained, recalled, and used in a variety of ways. Learners will remember these materials if they are created, integrated, and presented in a manner that allows them to have the needed impact.

Roles of Technology and Media in Learning

Jonathan Bergmann and Aaron Sams (2012) coined the phrase "the flipped classroom" to describe a model of instruction that mixes direct instruction with constructivist learning experiences. The idea merges technology-based instructional opportunities with teacher-guided learning. Students are able to gather information through video, online exploration, and audio formats outside the instructional setting that they then use in the classroom to extend their understanding of content with the teacher's guidance.

Technology and media play an important role in these types of learning experiences, either when you create them for your students to use or when your students explore new learning opportunities. Flipped classrooms provide you with the opportunity to bring technology more naturally into your classrooms and to explore more creative ways to engage students in learning (Hertz, 2012). The six step ASSURE model is an excellent foundation for planning and implementing innovative approaches, such as the flipped classroom.

 Check Your Understanding 1.1

The Digital Teacher

When instruction is teacher centered, technology and media are used to support the presentation of instruction. For example, you may use an electronic whiteboard to display variations of a bar graph as your students predict population growth over time. You may also use a pocket chart to show how the meaning of a sentence changes when word cards are rearranged. Projecting a live video feed from a zoo can facilitate a presentation on the feeding habits of birds. Certainly, properly designed instructional materials can enhance and promote learning. This book uses the ASSURE model to assist you in selecting and using instructional strategies, media, technology, and materials. However, the effectiveness of your choices depends on careful planning and selection of the appropriate resources.

Digital tools expand and enhance your capabilities to fulfill the numerous roles and responsibilities associated with being an educator. These tools better enable the "digital" teacher to plan for and provide interactive instruction while participating in a global community of practice with fellow educators. The following examples show the potential available in a well-equipped digital environment.

Digital Instruction

A "digital" teacher's instruction includes presentations that are media rich and interactive. Live digital videoconferences bring historians, novelists, and content experts into your classroom. Notes and concept maps from brainstorming sessions are captured on electronic whiteboards and instantaneously emailed to your students. Instructional presentations seamlessly integrate streamed digital video and audio from Internet-based files that range from short clips demonstrating specific concepts to full-length documentaries. You instantaneously go to a specific section of a DVD and show a segment in slow or fast motion or as a still image to reinforce targeted outcomes for your students. PowerPoint or Prezi presentations integrate strategically selected animations, sounds, and hyperlinks with digitized information to enhance learning.

PERSONAL RESPONSE SYSTEMS. Digital teachers use handheld digital devices, such as **personal response systems** (PRSs), to collect and graphically display student answers to teacher questions. The PRS, commonly called a "clicker," is a wireless keypad similar to a TV remote that transmits student responses. Because each PRS is assigned to a designated student, the system can be used to take attendance. However, its main benefit is to allow you to know each of your student's responses in a variety of circumstances. Using a PRS during instruction enhances learner–instructor interactivity in whole-class settings (Moss & Crowley, 2011). Educational uses of the PRS include measuring student understanding of concepts, comparing student attitudes about different ideas, predicting "What if" situations, and facilitating drill and practice of basic skills. The PRS graphs student responses to provide teachers and students immediate feedback. Teachers can use this information to guide the pace and direction of a discussion and to make instructional decisions to meet student learning needs.

MOBILE ASSESSMENT TOOLS. Mobile digital devices, such as smart phones and tablets, enable teachers to record student assessment data directly into a mobile device that transfers the data to a computer for report generation. For example, mobile digital devices are used to collect information on student academic performance (Gee, 2012). Teachers can gather the data over time and produce charts and graphs that help to show how a student's learning has changed over the school year.

Elementary teachers are fast becoming large-scale users of mobile assessment tools to monitor and record the reading abilities of their students. Many use mCLASS:

Personal response systems provide teachers with immediate feedback from students.

Reading 3D by Amplify Education, software that provides the text of a book the student is reading and a series of tools to let the teacher easily track performance while the student reads the book. The software also offers digital versions of leading reading assessment instruments, such as Dynamic Indicators of Basic Early Literacy Skills (DIBELS).

The mobile devices not only save you time, but the software also provides automatic timing and scoring of your student results. You can continually individualize instruction because of the availability of immediate results. Assessment data are easily downloaded to a secure, password-protected website that offers a variety of reporting options, from whole class to individual student.

Mobile devices allow teachers to gather information directly from their students. A fourth grade teacher uses **Quick Response (QR) Codes** to gather information about her students as they enter her classroom every morning. She assigns her students homework that is a summary of what the students learned and how they are feeling about school, which are then transmitted to her each morning. She uses the QR code system the school district installed as a quick way to gather the information. She scans through the student reports and adjusts her teaching to reflect her students' needs. While the data she gathers is informal, Ms. Unger feels that it helps her to ensure quality learning experiences for all her students.

Special education teachers often use a mobile device equipped with the Pivot 2.0 app as a mobile assessment tool. The program can be customized to record designated activities in a student's Individual Education Plan (IEP). During an observation of your student's performance or behavior, you use the stylus to record the observed strategies from a list of possible choices. As a teacher, you also can add written comments and notes to that student's record. After the observation, you can transfer the information to your computer to generate reports and graphs of student progress.

COMMUNITY OF PRACTICE.   Digital teachers participate in community of practice (CoP) activities, in which groups of educators with common goals from across the nation and around the world share ideas and resources. These Internet-based interactions allow teachers to collaborate and exchange ideas and materials. The CoP can include educators who are teaching the same subject area and grade level or educators with similar interests and needs, such as technology integration, classroom management, or working with gifted and talented students.

Teachers interested in integrating technology into their instruction can utilize the resources and networks of experts, mentors, and new colleagues supported by a variety of web communities. An example is TeacherFocus, a virtual community that offers you the opportunity to work collaboratively with teachers across the country and to learn about advances in best practice. TeacherFocus offers you topics of interest, event calendars, and focused discussions related to content and grade levels.

As members of the Virtual Math Teams (VMT) project at the Math Forum, math teachers can learn to enhance student use of technology in solving nonroutine, authentic problems requiring pre-algebra, algebra, or geometry knowledge and skills. Through the VMT, middle and high school teachers can work with peers in special Internet chat sessions with shared whiteboard software, which will then be used by their students.

The effective use of technology and media demands that teachers be better organized in advance, first thinking through their objectives, then altering the everyday classroom routine as needed, and finally evaluating to determine the impact of instruction on mental abilities, feelings, values, interpersonal skills, and motor skills. The increased access to digital resources will change not only how you function as a teacher, but also student roles, as we discuss next.

Technology Standards for Teachers

The ISTE Standards for Teachers provide five basic guidelines for becoming what we call a *digital teacher* (ISTE, 2012b). As seen in Table 1.2, these types of guidelines describe classroom practices, lesson development, and professional expectations.

Table 1.2 Technology Guidelines for Teachers

Technology Guideline	Description
Guide student learning and promote student creativity	Understanding learning skills and aligning knowledge of content, teachers incorporate technology to guide students in their learning and their ability to be innovative and creative.
Develop learning experiences that incorporate digital resources	Using digital resources, teachers can develop and implement lessons, as well as use the resources to assess learning growth.
Serve as a model for using technology	Teachers incorporate technology as part of their daily professional activities for planning and implementing learning with a focus on innovation and global understanding.
Guide student understanding of responsibilities for citizenship and social topics	Teachers provide students with learning experiences that guide their understanding of roles and responsibilities within society.
Expand knowledge and understanding through participation in professional development and leadership opportunities	Teachers participate in multiple opportunities to explore new models of learning and instruction, effective integration of technology, and leadership opportunities.

Source: Smaldino, Russell, Lowther, Mims, Instructional Technology and Media for Learning, 12e., © 2019, Pearson Education, Inc., New York, NY.

Each chapter of this text includes a Professional Development section to help emphasize the importance of the technology standards and to build your knowledge and skills through Demonstrating Professional Skills and Building My Professional Portfolio activities that are directly associated with the ISTE standards.

Technology guidelines serve to help you move forward in your understanding of providing effective learning settings and using technology to facilitate learning experiences for all your students. Most states and individual school districts have adopted a format for teachers to include technology into the classroom. Be certain to check on your own school's policies and check out professional development opportunities to expand your knowledge and skills with technology integration.

Video Example 1.1: How Do You Choose the Right Web Tools?

Watch this video and listen to Chris Gammon talk about the challenge of finding the "latest and greatest technology" for the classroom. How does he find that professional development and forming a learning community helps address this challenge?

National/State Curriculum Standards

All teachers are expected to consider learning outcomes for their students based on curriculum standards. These outcomes are often part of a larger-scale assessment practice that assures that all students have similar content knowledge and skills. Each teacher will want to be familiar with the appropriate grade and content standards for students when planning and implementing learning experiences for students. Adjustments in instructional strategies and materials will need to be made to ensure that all your students will have opportunities to be successful in their learning experiences.

The Common Core State Standards (CCSS) were developed over several years with an emphasis on higher-level learning (Calkins, Ehrenworth, & Lehman, 2012; CCSS, 2012). Students are expected to engage in reading and writing as an integral component of their learning within all content areas. The idea is that students can learn to read complex texts and then communicate their understanding of what they have read, whether the text is literature, mathematics, social science, or science. Also valued in the CCSS is the concept that learning is a process; thus, the standards are written so that each grade level's standards reflect what has been learned and what is to follow. Embedded in CCSS is the respect for the teacher's knowledge and skills in working with individual students to facilitate learning. The standards provide teachers with the flexibility to design instruction to meet their students' learning needs and to foster success in all aspects of their learning.

Even though the CCSS have become the focus of much of the implementation of standards throughout the United States, there is still the need to reflect individual learning needs within curricular areas. There are many common core content areas that have standards yet to be fully developed and some standards that will remain the domain of individual states. The state standards that are used to provide specific guidance for learning, for example, technology, are prominent at national and state levels.

 Check Your Understanding 1.2

The Digital Learner

When instruction is student centered, the primary users of technology and media are the students themselves. Student-centered activities allow teachers to spend more of their time assessing and directing student learning, consulting with individual students, and teaching one on one and in small groups. How much time you can spend on such activities will depend on the extent of the instructional role assigned to technology and media. Indeed, under certain circumstances, the entire instructional task can be left to technology and media. In fact, media are often "packaged" for this purpose—objectives are listed, guidance in achieving objectives is given, materials are assembled, and self-evaluation guidelines are provided. This is not to say, of course, that instructional technology can or should replace you as the teacher, but rather that technology and media can help you become a creative manager of the learning experience instead of a mere dispenser of information.

Digital students learn in classrooms where the technology is a seamless component of learning that expands the educational environment beyond the classroom walls. Devices and digital connections extend the existing capabilities of learners in many directions.

Digital Tools

The digital student uses mobile wireless devices in a variety of ways in and out of the school setting by taking technology where it is needed. For example, your students on the reading rug might find Internet resources on wireless tablets; other students might bring personal mobile devices (smart phones), tablets. or smaller and lighter computers to the library to take notes from archived online community newspaper articles; or student pairs might use a digital camera to capture examples of symmetry found on the school campus. Perhaps elementary students with digital probes might record the pH of six soil types used to grow radish plants or a high school student with a reading access barrier listens to an MP3, or compressed audio file, of David McCullough's "The Wright Brothers," a homework reading assignment for the class using devices such as those you find on the web site, *Assistive Media*. These types of wireless devices extend and embellish the learning experience beyond anything non-digital methods can produce.

Digital Communication with Others

Never before have your students been so connected with each other as they are in today's wireless digital environments. Smart phones, tablets, and laptops are used to send video, voice, text, and animated messages; to listen to lessons, music, news, and sports; and to watch the latest music videos and movies. Students communicate with their digital devices through voice commands, written notes, or by using a touch-screen or mini keyboard. Documents with digitally embedded comments and edits are instantaneously exchanged between students and their teachers, among students, and with experts. Student learning communities extend around the globe through web-based interactive communication tools and social media sites such as **blogs** (publicly accessible personal journals), **wikis** (web information that can be edited by any registered user), and **podcasts** (Internet-distributed audio and video files formatted for direct download to mobile devices). For example, your students can create a blog on global warming in which they regularly exchange commentary and related hyperlinks with students located around the world. Middle school students use wikis to interact with college students who respond to their writing activities, while a high school American literature class uploads podcasts of interviews with authors to the class website.

These tools are becoming increasingly popular, as seen in a 2015 Nielsen report that shows continued increase in the use of technology and in the time spent on social media sites (Nielsen Company, 2015). *Wikipedia* is similarly popular, with over 3 million entries

Video Example 1.2: Wiki Discussion

Watch this video to learn more about this constructivist approach to teaching and learning. How do wikis foster greater collaboration for students and teachers to all work together than do non-digital options?

available in over 200 languages in 2015. As with digital teachers, the digital students of today embrace and use technology to explore, inquire, and advance their personal learning, as well as contribute to the knowledge of others.

Technology Guidelines for Students

The ISTE Technology Standards for students provide six critical skills students need to achieve success in school and in future careers (ISTE, 2012a). Notice in Table 1.3 that guidelines for students align with the idea that knowledge and skills are important to academic and career success

It is important that as a teacher you are familiar with technology standards for your students and build your own technology skills to match what is expected of your students. Throughout the text we provide multiple examples of how the technology guidelines are integrated into ASSURE lesson plans.

Technology for Inclusion

In tomorrow's classrooms, teachers will be working with students who have a variety of learning needs. Many students will have English as their second language. Other students will have learning or physical challenges and will need assistance to be able to participate in classroom activities. Technology can provide the kinds of support these students need to be successful in their learning. Teachers will need to make choices and decisions about using technology to optimize learning for all the students in their classrooms. The ASSURE model can help you make technology decisions as you consider the learning needs of all your students. Throughout this textbook we have included a feature, Technology for All Learners, to share ideas with you about the types of resources available to help you with all your students.

For PK–12 students with disabilities, the National Instructional Materials Accessibility Standard (NIMAS) guides the production and electronic distribution of digital versions of textbooks and other instructional materials so they can be more easily converted to accessible formats, including Braille and text-to-speech.

Response to Intervention

There are many school resources available for students who have physical or learning challenges. With the addition of **Response to Intervention** (RtI), a program of assessment and appropriate instructional assistance in schools, challenged students are recognized earlier and their needs are more quickly met. Often these challenged students who are in the regular

Table 1.3 Technology Guidelines for Students

Technology Guideline	Description
Be creative and innovative when using technology as part of the learning experience	Students use technology in creative and innovative ways to demonstrate their learning outcomes.
Be effective in communication and use technology for collaboration	Students effectively use technology to communicate with peers and others and find ways to engage in collaborative opportunities as part of their learning experiences.
Use digital tools to collect, analyze, and apply information	Students use digital technology tools to collect and analyze information to share with others or to incorporate into their own learning experiences.
Use digital tools to demonstrate the ability to think critically, solve problems that lead to effective decisions	Students plan and incorporate technology to assist them as they engage in thinking critically and in solving problems, leading them to make data-informed decisions.
Demonstrate an understanding of being a global citizen	Students participate in multiple activities to demonstrate their understanding of their roles and responsibilities within a global society.
Competently use technology resources	Students use the technology resources available to them correctly and effectively to accomplish expected outcomes.

Source: Smaldino, Russell, Lowther, Mims, Instructional Technology and Media for Learning, 12e., © 2019, Pearson Education, Inc., New York, NY.

classroom setting are provided with technology resources that aid their ability to be successful in the classroom. As a teacher, you need to seek the assistance of school specialists to ensure that your students have access to the appropriate technology for their learning needs.

Universal Design

Additional guidelines include the concept of universal design for learning (UDL), which was created to expand learning opportunities for all individuals, especially those with disabilities (Center for Applied Special Technology [CAST], 2014). The UDL framework consists of three primary principles:

1. *Multiple means of representation,* to give diverse learners options for comprehension, language, mathematical expressions and symbols, and perception
2. *Multiple means of action and expression,* to provide learners options for executive functions, expression and communication, and physical action
3. *Multiple means of engagement,* to provide learners options for self-regulation, sustaining effort and persistence, and recruiting interest (CAST, 2014)

Application Exercise 1.2

 Check Your Understanding 1.3

Framework for Academic and Career Learning Literacies

Classroom experiences must provide multiple opportunities for gaining new knowledge and skills that are encompassed in a critical set of learning literacies. This text prepares you to embed key learning technologies that your students need to improve learning and achieve successful careers.

Student Outcomes

Teachers need an understanding of the ability of a student to comprehend or decode information and to use, transform, and create new information. As you follow the ASSURE model to develop your lesson plans, always include opportunities for students to build general literacy knowledge and skills.

You will also want to consider the standards for learning and recognize how to support your students' learning experiences so that they can be successful in demonstrating their knowledge and skills. By recognizing your students as individuals with unique learning needs, you will be able to help them achieve the targeted learning outcomes that indicate their knowledge, skill, and achievements.

Support Systems

As a classroom teacher you are not alone in helping your students achieve designated outcomes. There are many resources available to you, such as media specialists, technology coordinators, and area universities with courses and programs that can help you gain additional knowledge about technology. Many of these support systems are focused on ensuring student engagement and learning. Their intent is to help you make appropriate choices to meet your students' learning needs and to ensure you are able to use the resources successfully.

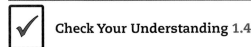

Effective Learning Environments

The trend for tomorrow's teachers is to shift from traditional teaching strategies and tools to using digital tools with instructional approaches that better meet the needs of students. However, the transition from traditional to digital classroom environments varies greatly from teacher to teacher and school to school. Prensky (2006) describes teachers in this variable process of technology adoption and adaptation as moving, whether slowly or quickly, through a four-phase process, which is still applicable for current teachers: (1) dabbling, (2) doing old things in old ways, (3) doing old things in new ways, and (4) doing new things in new ways (p. 43) (see Figure 1.2).

The process described by Prensky begins with Phase 1, "dabbling" with technology by randomly adding technology tools to a few learning situations. In Phase 2, technology is used to do old things in old ways, as when teachers display lecture notes in PowerPoint rather than using the white board and handouts. It is not until Phase 3, doing old things in new ways, that technology begins to show its promise, such as when a teacher uses a virtual 3-D model to demonstrate the structure of a compound rather than drawing it on a chalkboard, or students use word processing and clip art rather than notebook paper and hand-drawn images to create a short story. Finally, Phase 4, doing new things in new ways, fully utilizes the power of technology and media, but it requires providing our students with "future-oriented content [to] develop their skills in programming, knowledge filtering, using their connectivity . . . with cutting edge, powerful, miniaturized, customizable, one-to-one technology" (Prensky, 2006, p. 45).

The Learning Continuum: Traditional to Digital

Many of today's classrooms have achieved Prensky's Phase 4 by adopting and adapting their environments with digital tools that support and enhance "digital" teacher and student capabilities. For example, technology extends environments beyond the classroom walls by connecting students with other students, outside experts, and parents. Individual classroom websites provide access to homework calendars, assignment details, online resources, and often offer parents access to real-time reports of student progress.

Within these phases, three primary types of instruction are used: face-to-face instruction, **distance learning**, and **blended learning**. We have all experienced face-to-face instruction at school, at home, and during extracurricular activities. When done

Figure 1.2 Prensky's (2006) Technology Adoption and Adaptation Four-Phase Process

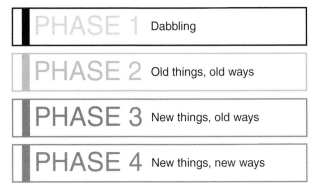

SOURCE: Pearson Education, Inc.

well, it is an excellent method of teaching that is prevalent in PK–12 schools. Distance learning occurs when the teacher and students are not in the same physical location during instruction. As of today, most states offer students opportunities to participate in middle or high school online virtual classes. Other schools are offering courses that combine face-to-face instruction with distance learning to create blended instruction, allowing students to see teacher demonstrations and work with other students during hands-on activities, such as labs, drama and musical arts performances, or building 3-D models. Many states have now added a graduation requirement that all high school graduates must have completed at least one blended or totally online course.

The Changing Role of Media Centers

Many school libraries have been merged into what are now called **library media centers,** which offer traditional library reading resources but now also include a variety of information technology assets. Most library media centers are equipped with multiple Internet-connected computers, often with subscriptions to PK–12 online resources such as libraries of digital books, reference materials, and educational software. The library media centers also provide you with a variety of classroom support materials ranging from lab kits to subject-specific software and videos. The role of the librarian and/or media specialist is continually expanding to require increasing expertise in accessing the array of digital resources, as well as understanding basic computer technology to assist your students using the equipment in the center.

 Check Your Understanding 1.5

Shared Writing Exercise 1.1

Copyright Concerns: Copyright Law

To protect the financial interests of the creators, producers, and distributors of original works of information and art, nations adopt copyright laws. **Copyright** refers to the legal rights to an original work. These laws set the conditions under which anyone may copy, in whole or part, original works transmittable in any medium. Without copyright laws, writers, artists, and media producers would not receive the compensation they deserve for their creations, the flow of creative work would be reduced to a trickle, and we would all be the losers.

Technology, especially the Internet, has made it much easier to copy from a variety of digital materials—text, visuals, audio, and video. All material on the Internet is copyrighted unless stated otherwise. In 1998, the Conference on Fair Use issued a report (Lehman, 1998) that, despite not being a legal document, provides a consensus view (until tested in a court of law) on use of copyrighted material.

You have a legal and ethical responsibility to serve as a role model for your students; therefore, use all materials in a professional and ethical manner. We also recommend teaching relevant aspects of copyright laws to your students, even very young students. If you are unsure what to do, ask for your school's copyright guidelines. Librarians and media/technology specialists at your school may be able to help you interpret the national guidelines. Ignorance of the law is no excuse!

Please note that the copyright information presented here is *not* legal advice. It is based on what the authors have read in the literature and online. For more information on copyright, refer to the Print Resources at the end of this chapter.

Educators and Copyright Law

What happens if an educator knowingly and deliberately violates copyright law? The Copyright Act of 1976 contains both criminal and civil sanctions. Possible fines for copyright infringement range from $750 to $30,000 per infringement. If it can be proven that the law was broken by willful intent, the fine may be raised to $150,000. Willful infringement for private or commercial gain carries a possible fine of $250,000 and up to 5 years in prison. Copyright violation is a serious crime.

Fair Use

Fair use provides an important copyright exception for teachers and students. Small portions of copyrighted works may be used in teaching when properly cited and noted that the materials are copyrighted and by whom. Although there are no absolute guidelines for determining what constitutes fair use in an education setting, the law sets forth four basic criteria for determining what is fair use:

- *Purpose and character of the use, including whether such use is for nonprofit educational purposes rather than of a commercial nature.* Using a copyrighted work for an educational objective is more likely to be considered fair use than using it for commercial gain or entertainment.

- *Nature of the copyrighted work.* If the work is for a general readership, such as a magazine or periodical not specifically designed for education, it would tend to support fair use in the classroom. Works of an entertainment nature, such as cartoons, movies, or music, are less likely to be considered fair use. If the work itself is educational in nature, a judgment of fair use may not be supported because of potential impact on sales.

- *Amount and substantiality of the portion used in relation to the copyrighted work as a whole.* Using a smaller amount of the total work is more likely to be considered fair use than using a larger amount.

- *Effect of the use on the potential market for or value of the copyrighted work.* Use that negatively affects potential sales of the original work weighs against fair use.

Until the courts decide otherwise, teachers and media professionals can use the fair use criteria to decide when to copy materials that would otherwise be protected. For example, if the school media center subscribes to a journal or magazine to which you refer students and you make digital slides of several graphics to help students understand an article, this would be fair use based on the following criteria:

- The nature of the work is general, and its audience (and market) is not predominantly the educational community.

- The character of use is nonprofit.

- The amount copied is minimal.

- There is no intent to replace the original, only to make it more useful to students in conjunction with the copyrighted words.

Seeking Permission to Use Copyrighted Materials

Aside from staying within the guidelines that limit but recognize our legal right to free use of copyrighted materials, what else can we do to ensure students have access to these materials? We can, obviously, seek permission from copyright owners and, if requested, pay a fee for their use. Certain requests will ordinarily be granted without payment of fee—transcripts for the blind, for example, or material to be tried out once in an experimental program. Permission is not needed for use of materials in the public domain—materials on which copyright protection has run out or materials produced by federal government employees in the course of their regular work.

In seeking permission to use copyrighted materials, it is generally best to contact the distributor or publisher of the material rather than its creator. Whether or not the creator is the holder of the copyright, the distributor or publisher generally handles permission requests and sets fees. If the address of the publisher is not given on the material, you can usually find it on the Internet.

When seeking permission:

- Be as specific as possible. For printed materials, give the page numbers and exact amount of print material you wish to copy. If possible, send along a photocopy of the material. Fully describe nonprint material. State how you intend to use the material, where you intend to use it, and the number of copies you wish to make.

- Remember that fees for reproduction of copyrighted materials are sometimes negotiable. If the fee is beyond your budget, do not hesitate to ask whether it can be lowered.

- If for any reason you decide not to use the requested material, make this fact known to the publisher or producer. Without this formal notice, it is likely to be assumed that you have in fact used it as requested and you may be charged a fee you do not actually owe.

- Keep copies of *all* your correspondence and records of *all* other contacts that you make relevant to seeking permission to use copyrighted instructional materials.

Another solution is to obtain "royalty free" collections of media. You can access collections of images and sounds that can be used in presentations or other products without payment of royalties using Internet resources. Many vendors now sell CDs that contain similar types of resources that you can share with your students for their productions. Be sure to read the fine print. What "royalty free" means varies from one collection to the next. In one case, there may be almost no restrictions on the use of the materials (such as materials found through Creative Commons); in another, you may not be allowed to use the materials in any kind of electronic product.

Term of Protection

The term, or duration, of copyright was changed by the Sonny Bono Copyright Term Extension Act of 1998. For an individual author, the copyright term continues for 70 years after his or her death. If a work is made for hire (i.e., by an employee or by someone commissioned to do the work), the term is 100 years from the year of creation or 75 years from the date of first publication or distribution, whichever comes first. Works copyrighted prior to January 1, 1978, are protected for 28 years and then may have their copyright renewed. The renewal protects them for a term of 75 years after their original copyright date.

Changing the Material's Format

Even though you (or your school) have the capability to convert analog materials to a digital format, it is usually a violation of copyright laws and guidelines. The originators of copyrighted material are granted the sole right to make derivatives of their original work. For example, it is illegal to purchase an analog VHS video and convert it to a digital format. Likewise, you cannot convert copyrighted printed materials into a digital format.

Copyright law protects the format in which ideas are expressed (Becker, 2003). Teachers cannot make audio recordings of library books or textbooks for student use. One exception in the law permits the audio recording of books for use by students who are legally blind.

 Check Your Understanding 1.6

Summary

In this chapter you read about the elements that will be important in your study of technology and media as they affect your students' learning.

- *Identify key components of the framework for academic and career learning and how technology and media are integrated into today's classrooms.* Information about the components associated with academic and career learning experiences were described. Ideas were presented on how technology and media are integrated into today's classrooms

- *Explain the role of the digital teacher, the tools and resources available to fully integrate technology into teaching, and the guidelines and standards for teaching content knowledge and skills.* Information about the role of a teacher in a digital learning setting was described. Ways to achieve effective learning based on using standards, as well as the variety of learning settings based on access to technology tools were

included. Guidelines were presented for how to plan the use of technology in your teaching.

- *Describe the role of the digital learner.* The digital learner was discussed as well as what a teacher needs to consider when using technology and media to help the learner gain knowledge and skills.

- *Discuss the framework for academic and career learning literacies.* A framework for academic and career literacies, important for your students' future success, were presented.

- *Describe effective learning environments.* What it means to develop an effective learning environment was discussed.

- *Describe key concerns regarding copyright law for educational uses.* Concepts related to educational copyright issues were discussed. Specific copyright concerns as they relate to specific technology and media will be presented in later chapters.

Professional Development

Demonstrating Professional Skills

1. Prepare a 10-minute presentation on your reaction to the framework for academic and career learning (ISTE Standards for Teachers 5.C).

2. Analyze an instructional situation (either real or hypothetical) and identify the learning standards being reinforced in the lesson (ISTE Standards for Teachers 2.C).

3. Prepare a concept map that depicts the benefits and concerns of the three types of instruction (face-to-face, distance, or blended) presented in this chapter (ISTE Standards for Teachers 5.C).

4. Create a one-page guide about copyrights that will assist you in following copyright laws for educational uses (ISTE Standards for Teachers 4.A).

Building Your Professional Portfolio

Reflecting on My Learning. Reflect on knowledge and digital skills for your future students as compared to the knowledge and digital skills required from

your own PK–12 educational experiences. What are the primary differences? What do you see as the greatest benefits and as your most difficult challenges in ensuring that your students build their own knowledge and digital skills to enhance their academic and career success (ISTE Standards for Teachers 2.B)?

Enhancing My Portfolio. Select a technology integration lesson from the Web. After citing the source of the lesson, analyze it according to topics discussed in this chapter. Specifically, take note of how or if the lesson addresses the following: (1) use of technology and media, (2) types of technology and media used, (3) types of learning standards identified, (4) type(s) of instruction, (5) teacher use of technology, (6) student use of technology, and (7) areas where copyright laws will need to be followed. Reflect on your lesson analysis and prepare a report, providing strengths, weaknesses, and recommendations for using technology and media to enhance student learning (ISTE Standards for Teachers 5.C).

Suggested Resources

Print Resources

Cennamo, K., Ross, J. & Ertmer, P. (2014). *Technology integration for meaningful classroom use: A standards-based approach*. Belmont, CA: Wadsworth Publishing.

Hunter, J. (2015). *Technology integration and high possibility classrooms: Building from TPACK*. New York: Routledge.

Krakower, B. & Plante, S. (2016). *Using technology to engage students with learning disabilities*. Thousand Oaks, CA: Corwin.

McJohn, S. (2015). *Examples & explanations: Copyright* (4th ed.). New York: Walters Kluwer.

Strong, W. (2014). *The copyright book: A practical guide*. Cambridge, MA: MIT Press.

Technology ad Economic Policy Board on Science (2014). *Copyright in the digital era*. Washington, DC: National Academies Press.

Online Resources and Apps

Edutopia

Edutopia is sponsored by the George Lucas Foundation and provides teachers current and archived access to special reports, blogs, and videos.

eSchool News

eSchool News is a convenient way to keep up to date electronically with what is going on in schools.

Sophia

Sophia is a source for tutorials, teacher tools, and professional development. The site holds many resources for teachers and students directed at helping students learn.

AECT.org

AECT Copyright Committee blog disseminates committee presentations, news, and announcements.

Gary Becker's Copyright Information Site

Gary Becker's copyright information site provides you with a quick reference to copyright issues.

Fair Use Guidelines for Educational Multimedia

The American Library Association is a valuable resource for questions about copyright issues.

U.S. Copyright Office

The U.S. Copyright Office offers expert and impartial information about copyright law. The website offers a variety of information and services related to the law.

Chapter 2
Designing Instruction and Assessing Learning

Learning Outcomes

This chapter addresses ISTE Standards for Teachers 2 and 5.

2.1 Describe the similarities and differences in learning theories.

2.2 List the eight principles of effective instruction for learners.

2.3 Describe the principles of effective technology utilization.

2.4 Describe why media literacy skills are vital in today's classrooms.

2.5 Describe the types of effective learning assessment.

Goal

Understand how to design instruction and assess learning.

Introduction

Learning is the development of new knowledge, skills, or attitudes as an individual interacts with information and the environment. Learning doesn't happen by magic. Rather, teachers must make important decisions to ensure learning, especially when integrating technology and media into a lesson. Foundational learning theories, the principles of effective instruction that integrate technology and media, and effective assessment of learning are all elements of designing and assessing learning.

Technology and media can be valuable resources to integrate into the assessment of learning. Learners need to be better educated to assume the challenges of continually evolving knowledge and skill requirements for the future (Partnership for 21st Century Skills, n.d.). What students are learning today needs to prepare them for an uncertain tomorrow, and lifelong learning is a cornerstone to guiding students toward understanding how to approach the shifting knowledge and skills of their future. By creating seamless access to the global community and opening new avenues for addressing how and what to learn, technology and media have become essential interfaces for learners as they move forward in their education.

Even as students are entering the classroom with greater understanding of worldwide issues, other learning challenges prevail. Many come into school speaking more than one language, and it is predicted that by 2025, nearly half of all classrooms will have students who do not speak English as their first language (Partnership for 21st Century Skills, n.d.). Students also have greater fluency with technology and media and have greater opportunities for exposure to different points of view and cultures. Even before today's children enter school, many have experience with technology as a learning tool through television programs designed to instruct young children. Many also understand how computers can be used for learning and for communicating. Another medium for communication and interactivity, the smart phone, has become the great equalizer for all students regardless of their social and ethnic backgrounds. How teachers view the role of technology and media in the classroom depends very much on their beliefs about how people learn.

Learning Theories

Over the past half-century there have been several dominant theories of learning. Each has implications for instruction in general and for the use of technology and media in particular. We briefly survey each of the major perspectives on learning and discuss their implications. Driscoll (2013) discusses learning theories and their impact on teaching decisions in greater detail.

Behaviorist Perspective

In the 1950s, B. F. Skinner, a psychologist at Harvard University and a proponent of **behaviorism,** conducted scientific studies of observable behavior. He was interested in voluntary behavior, such as learning new skills, rather than reflexive behavior as illustrated by Pavlov's famous salivating dog. He demonstrated that reinforcing, or rewarding, desired responses could shape the behavior patterns of an organism. Skinner based his learning theory, known as *reinforcement theory,* on a series of experiments with pigeons. He noted that when the pigeons were given a reward for a desired behavior, they tended to repeat it. When the pigeons did not receive any reinforcer, they tended to stop a particular behavior. Skinner reasoned that the same procedures could be used with humans. The result was the foundation for computer-assisted instruction. Unlike earlier learning research, Skinner's work was logical and precise, leading directly to improved instruction and learning.

Behaviorists refuse to speculate on what goes on internally when learning takes place. They rely solely on observable behaviors. As a result, they are more comfortable explaining relatively simple learning tasks. Because of this posture, behaviorism has limited applications in teaching higher-level skills. For example, behaviorists are reluctant to make inferences about how learners process information. Although most would argue that behavioral concepts are not necessarily applicable to the types of learners you are encountering in your classrooms, you may determine that some basic knowledge or skills require a behaviorist approach to instruction. For example, you might have a student who would benefit from completing a math program on the computer that guides him through a series of incremental steps to learning multiplication, with reinforcements integrated throughout, until he has mastered the multiplication table. The student will not be finished with the program until his work is considered to be acceptable and he can demonstrate his ability to complete multiplication facts.

Cognitivist Perspective

In the latter half of the twentieth century, cognitivists made new contributions to learning theory by creating models of how learners receive, process, and manipulate information. **Cognitivism,** based on the work of Swiss psychologist Jean Piaget (1977), explores the mental processes individuals use in responding to their environment—that is, how people think, solve problems, and make decisions. For example, behaviorists simply state that practice strengthens the response to a stimulus. Cognitivists, on the other hand, create a mental model of short-term and long-term memory. New information is stored in short-term memory, where it is rehearsed until ready to be stored in long-term memory. If the information is not rehearsed, it fades from short-term memory. Learners then combine the information and skills in long-term memory to develop cognitive strategies, or skills for dealing with complex tasks. For example, once students understand multiplication they are given opportunities to apply their knowledge and skills to solve practical application problems.

Cognitivists have a broader perception of learning than that held by behaviorists. Students are less dependent on the guiding hand of the teacher and rely more on their own cognitive strategies in using available learning resources. Many would suggest that the cognitivist approach to instruction is a good compromise between required **benchmarks,** those standards against which students are tested, and **metacognition,** thinking about one's own learning.

Constructivist Perspective

Constructivism is a movement that extends beyond the ideas of cognitivism, considering the engagement of students in meaningful experiences as the essence of experiential learning. Shifting from passive transfer of information to active problem solving and discovery, constructivists emphasize that learners create their own interpretations of the world of information. They argue that students situate the learning experience within their own experiences and that the goal of instruction is not to teach information but to create conditions in which students can interpret information for their own understanding. The role of constructivist instruction is to provide students with ways to assemble knowledge rather than the teacher dispensing facts. Constructivists believe that learning occurs most effectively when students are engaged in authentic tasks that relate to meaningful contexts (i.e., learning by doing). The ultimate measure of learning is, therefore, the ability of the student to use knowledge to facilitate thinking in real life. This approach fits with the needs of learners who must solve problems that not only capitalize on their existing knowledge, but also require them to seek additional information or skills in finding effective solutions.

Video Example 2.1: Constructivism

Watch this video to learn more about this teacher's view of constructivism. Why does she feel it is a valuable instructional strategy?

Social-Psychological Perspective

Social psychology is another well-established approach to the study of instruction and learning. Social psychologists look at how the social organization of the classroom affects learning. For example, what is the group structure of the classroom—independent study, small groups, or the class as a whole? What is the authority structure—how much control do students have over their activities? What is the reward structure—is cooperation rather than competition fostered?

Researchers such as Robert Slavin (1990) have taken the position that cooperative learning is both more effective and more socially beneficial than competitive and individualistic learning. Slavin developed a set of cooperative learning techniques embodying the principles of small-group collaboration, learner-controlled instruction, and rewards based on group achievement.

Today's learner enters your classroom with many skills developed from technology-based social networking. The ideas fostered in the social psychology perspective address such interdependent collaborative abilities that learners need to use as part of their learning.

Teachers need to develop an eclectic attitude toward the various schools of learning psychology. You are not obliged to swear allegiance to a particular learning theory. You want to use what works. If you find that a particular learning situation is suited to a behaviorist approach, then you should use behaviorist techniques. Conversely, if the situation seems to call for cognitivist or constructivist strategies, those are what you should use. When guiding the learners in your classroom, consider which learning theory best applies to the particular type of learning task at hand.

 Check Your Understanding 2.1

Principles of Effective Instruction for Learners

As a classroom teacher, your role is to establish learning experiences that foster the defined learner outcomes. At times those outcomes may be based on specific state or national learning standards; at other times they may be based on negotiated outcomes with individual learners. Whichever direction you take, you need to think about how to engage students in the learning process.

As an educator seeking ways to improve your practice, it is important to consider how to engage learners in their learning. Because one common feature across all classroom settings is the variety of learning levels and needs among students, it is also critical to determine the best ways to meet the needs of all students by becoming skilled at differentiating instruction to ensure that all learners are adequately and appropriately challenged in their learning. For example, you may offer in-depth reading materials for students who are reading above grade level for extended learning experiences, and worksheets with hints and answer keys for those who are struggling to understand the concepts of the topic.

Research-based classroom practices to engage learners have evolved over time. These principles of effective instruction offer ways to engage your learners regardless of their ability levels:

- *Assess prior knowledge.* Before you can properly provide instruction, you should gather relevant information about each student's knowledge and skill level. You need to know what knowledge your students already have acquired. To learn from most materials and activities, students must possess prerequisite knowledge and skills (Newby, Stepich, Lehman, & Russell 2010).

- *Consider individual differences.* Learners vary in terms of personality, general aptitude, knowledge of a subject, and many other factors. Be aware of the multiple learning needs of your students—for example, whether a language other than English is spoken in a child's home. You need to consider the technology and media experiences your students have had and what resources are essential to help your students learn. Effective instruction allows individuals to progress at different rates, cover different materials, and even participate in different activities.

- *State objectives.* For you and your students to know where instruction is going and what is to be accomplished, the goals must be specified. Learning objectives must match expected outcomes or standards.

- *Develop metacognitive skills.* The skills of selective monitoring, evaluating, and adjusting their approaches enhance students' learning and help to make them lifelong learners. Learners need assistance in understanding how they learn and what resources help in that process.

- *Provide social interaction.* Teachers and peers serving as tutors or group members can provide a number of pedagogical as well as social supports. Learners gain experience and expertise when collaborating with others in and beyond the classroom.

- *Incorporate realistic contexts.* Learners are most likely to remember and to apply authentic knowledge presented in a real-world context. Rote learning leads to "inert knowledge"; that is, learners know something but cannot apply it to real life. Students benefit from understanding how their knowledge and skills fit into the world around them.

- *Engage students in relevant practice.* The most effective learning experiences are those requiring learners to practice skills that build toward the desired outcome. Learner participation increases the probability of learning. Practice, especially in varying contexts, improves retention rate and the ability to apply the new knowledge, skill, or attitude. Practice promotes deeper, longer lasting learning (Morrison & Lowther, 2010).

- *Offer frequent, timely, and constructive feedback.* Student learning requires accurate information on misconceptions, misunderstandings, and weaknesses. Learners need to know if their thinking is on track. Feedback may come from a teacher, a tutor, a software program, the scoring system of a game, or oneself. In addition to knowing that responses are incorrect, students need to know why they have been unsuccessful and how they can improve their performance. Further, knowing details about their correct responses in terms of how and why they are accurate helps students understand more about what they have learned.

Information and Instruction

As educators, it is important to distinguish between information and instruction. **Information** is knowledge, facts, news, comments, and content. Information can be presented in the classroom, in a textbook, or through media such as television or online resources. Often the presentation, whether it is live, printed, or on the Internet, is general in content and its purpose is to give an overview of ideas or subject matter—to generate interest, to provide background information, or to give procedural details.

Learners should not be expected to be responsible for the retention or use of information they have only seen or heard. The information provided by a job aid (a short guide to help the user), like a phone book, is not meant to be memorized. It is assumed that you will look up the information when needed. With computers, it has become possible to give ever more rapid and detailed information in specific situations, to the point that the computer could be said to be helping or "coaching" the individual. Although with frequent use of a job aid or a computer help system a person might gradually internalize information, remembering more and more of the information provided, the learning is not an intentional part of the system, whose aim is only to provide just-in-time assistance or specific information.

Instruction, on the other hand, refers to any intentional effort to stimulate learning by the deliberate arrangement of experiences to help learners achieve a desirable change in capability. Instruction is meant to lead to learning. Active engagement with the information—questioning it, discussing it, applying it to practice situations—is the critical component of instruction. Meaningful understanding, retention, and application require instructional activities, including practice with feedback. Instruction, therefore, has as its goal a lasting change in the capability of the learner. This is a crucial point in distinguishing instruction from just providing information.

Instruction is also the arrangement of information and the environment to facilitate learning. By *environment* we mean not only where instruction takes place, but also the strategies, technology, and media needed to convey information and guide learning. The learner or the instructor may do this. Gagné (1985) describes instruction as a set of events external to the learner designed to support the internal process of learning.

Preparing the instructional environment is another critical role for teachers. As a teacher responsible for creating learning opportunities for your students, you will need to help them work within learning communities. By using collaborative learning tools such as classroom blogs, wikis, social networking resources, and learning management systems, you can help your learners move through the various levels of learning appropriate to their goals, the state learning standards, and expected outcomes.

Bloom's Digital Taxonomy and The "Four Cs"

Benjamin Bloom developed a learning taxonomy that he described as stages focused on cognitive learning skills ranging from knowledge through evaluation (Bloom and Krathwohl, 1984). His idea was that students progressed in an orderly fashion from simple to complex mental abilities. He suggested that students started at the knowledge stage by recalling specific content (e.g., reciting a poem from memory). Students then progressed to the comprehension stage, in which they would be able to paraphrase or summarize the content (e.g., using your own words, describe what the author meant in her poem). He assumed if students could understand meaning, then they were ready for the next step, application. At the application step, students could use the ideas or information in a meaningful way (e.g., using the author's ideas in her poem, relate those ideas to a similar topic). Finally, Bloom felt that when the student had progressed through these prior steps, it was now time to generate a new idea or example (e.g., using a similar poetry style, write your own poem about a similar topic). He called this highest step evaluation.

Over time, Bloom's Taxonomy has been revised and modified. While best known for his original work in the cognitive domain, Bloom added the psychomotor (manipulative or physical skills) and affective (attitudes or feelings) domains, which followed a similar pattern in a taxonomy. Bloom further expanded his cognitive taxonomy and divided it into lower-order thinking skills, such as requiring the ability to recall specific facts, and higher-order thinking skills, such as applying the facts to a unique task. His idea was that students needed the lower-order skills in order to be successful at the higher-order skills. In addition, he advocated that all students were to be guided through the steps into higher-order thinking. For example, a teacher would require students to learn multiplication tables, explain relationships between the number facts, use multiplication to solve a specific story problem, and finally to use their multiplication knowledge in a unique and different way, such as in an art project in which they discussed how they repeated certain design elements as a means to demonstrate their understanding of multiplication concepts.

The most recent modification to Bloom's original steps has been termed Bloom's Digital Taxonomy (Churches, 2008). What is significantly different about the new taxonomy is that it is not focused on only cognitive skills, but rather integrates action and resources into the stages. In the Digital Taxonomy, the interplay of use of resources with the cognitive process is an essential element to understanding how students learn. The premise of moving through each stage is not emphasized, but rather the intent is to capitalize on where the

Teachers guide students in their effective use of technology to support learning.

student is and what approaches will best help the student to learn the information and use it in meaningful ways. Also critical to the new taxonomy is a focus on collaboration and scaffolding of ideas. In the Digital Taxonomy, the teacher's role as a learning guide is emphasized, as is the idea that technology and media are essential tools to facilitate student learning. Now the teacher does not need to require prior knowledge of multiplication skills in order for students to gain that knowledge as they apply multiplication skills to a problems they generated as part of their explorations of a local problem to be resolved.

Fast forward several years, and the Partnership for 21st Century Skills identified skills that every student needs to have to be a successful learner. The focus is on those higher-order thinking skills that Bloom and Churches identified as critical to quality learning experiences. The Partnership identified four skills as the means by which children can acquire their academic knowledge: critical thinking, communication, collaboration, and creativity. Each of these skills requires that students have knowledge or can locate the information they need in order to be successful in the implementation of the knowledge as part of their active learning experiences. As a teacher, you would work with groups of students who share their knowledge and understanding to gain further knowledge as they resolve a creative and unique problem that has significant impact on a local setting.

CROSS-CULTURAL UNDERSTANDINGS.   Closely aligned to the four Partnership for 21st Century Skills are cross-cultural understandings through which students have opportunities to view their learning experiences in a global context. For the classroom teacher, these new views of Bloom's Taxonomy and the 21st century skills suggest new approaches of facilitating learning using media and technology outside the regular classroom to facilitate preparation of classroom activities. You can guide your students to work on larger issues across a greater span and learn more from students outside the classroom setting. The GlobalSchoolNet offers teachers opportunities to collaborate, plan, and conduct joint learning projects that engage students from varied locations in working together to solve a common problem. Teachers can also participate in topical discussions with groups focused on key educational issues. Other possibilities include the opportunity to manage or attend online courses, mentor other educators, or try out new ideas in a safe, supportive environment such as the New Tech Network (see Taking a Look at Technology Integration).

The teacher is no longer the source of knowledge, standing and delivering as in earlier school models. Rather, the teacher designs learning situations that focus on engaging learners in active learning experiences while developing their knowledge,

Taking a Look at Technology Integration

The New Tech Network

The New Tech Network is an international initiative to develop innovative schools. It started in California in 1996 and has grown to over 170 schools across the United States, Australia, and China. At its core is a philosophy that students should be empowered in their learning through alternative instructional approaches that will guide them to become creators, leaders, and tomorrow's productive citizens. New Tech Network advocates learning environments that provide student-centered settings in which

- Problem-based learning experiences engage learners.
- Students own their own learning and work with teachers to enhance their learning experiences.
- Technology is an integral component within the entire learning experience.

The goal is to provide students with an integrated curriculum that focuses on critical thinking, collaboration, and problem solving as vehicles to learning. The program takes a multiyear, hands-on approach to student learning experiences, ensuring that the students are immersed in their learning throughout their school experience.

They have the data to demonstrate that their ideas are working, with graduation rates that are significantly higher than the national averages across urban and rural and diverse settings. The students engage in college-ready learning experiences with assessments that call for students to apply knowledge and skills across the disciplines. College-ready assessments are embedded into the curriculum ensuring content knowledge, thinking skills, and verbal and written communication outcome standards are met.

The New Tech Network works with school districts that wish to provide rich learning experiences for their students. Students who graduate from New Tech Network programs are successful as life-long learners.

Source: newtechnetwork.org

understanding, and ability to use knowledge to generate new ideas. As a teacher, you will design lessons, considering the ISTE Standards for Teachers and ISTE Standards for Students and the resources available to students in order to facilitate moving them toward critical thinking, collaboration, and creativity. Technology and media provide the valuable resources that teachers and students can use to achieve the learning outcomes while engaging in those higher-order thinking arenas. In other words, you can "flip" your classroom by having your students explore the content through media and technology prior to coming to the classroom where you can engage them in applying that knowledge to real-world situations.

Application Exercise 2.1

Multiple Intelligences

It is important for teachers to be aware of the multiple types of student intelligences when planning lessons. Howard Gardner (2011), who was dissatisfied with the concept of IQ and its unitary view of intelligence, developed the concept of **multiple intelligences.** Noting that not everyone has the same abilities nor do they learn in the same way, he identified nine aspects of intelligence:

1. Verbal/linguistic (language)
2. Logical/mathematical (scientific/quantitative)
3. Visual/spatial (imagining objects in space/navigating)
4. Musical/rhythmic (listening/movement)

5. Bodily/kinesthetic (dancing/athletics)

6. Interpersonal (understanding other people)

7. Intrapersonal (understanding oneself)

8. Naturalist (relating to one's surroundings)

9. Existentialist (ability to reflect).

Gardner's theory implies that effective teachers need to consider the different learning abilities of their students, recognizing that students vary widely in terms of strengths and weaknesses in each of these areas. The best way to do this is by designing lessons that actively address the range of learning abilities, considering students' perceptual preferences and strengths, information processing habits, motivational factors, and physiological traits that influence their ability to learn. Your learners come into your classroom with abilities in varying states of development. Your responsibility is to determine how best to address their learning needs while also attending to their individual approaches to acquiring knowledge and skills.

Meeting Learner Needs

Your students are the focus of your instruction; everything you do in the classroom is designed to help your students meet the intended learning outcomes. The more you understand their levels of learning and their interests, the easier it will be for you to address ways to help them learn. When making instructional decisions your goal is to find ways to ensure success. Decide on the strategy or strategies you will use, the technology and media that will offer the best support, and how you will assess students' learning progress.

Most lessons can include a variety of technology and media that address the wide range of student abilities. For example, your lessons can include writing activities for students with verbal/linguistic strengths, use of graphics for visual/spatial abilities, or out-of-seat activities for students who prefer bodily/kinesthetic learning. Using Storymaker software allows your students to blend images with text and gives them the opportunity to practice both their verbal/linguistic and their visual/spatial intelligences.

 Check Your Understanding 2.2

Principles of Effective Technology Use

The National Education Technology Plan sets clear expectations for today's teachers to be competent in the use of technology in their teaching (U.S. Department of Education, 2010). This is especially true when working with today's learners and addressing the skills outlined for them. Teachers not only need to use technology effectively in their teaching, but they also need to guide students in using those tools to enhance their learning. The advent of newer technologies requires critical decisions related to the best tools to integrate into teaching. We will be addressing many of these newer technology resources throughout the remaining chapters of this textbook.

The **National Education Technology Standards for Students** summarized in the following list, specifically outline expectations for student use of technology to guide their learning (International Society for Technology in Education [ISTE], 2012).

- students are creative and innovative in technology use
- students effectively communicate and use technology collaboratively
- students use technology to gather information
- students use technology for critical thinking, problem solving, and decision-making
- students demonstrate good global citizenry
- students skillfully use technology resources

Many of these standards address the essential elements for success in acquiring knowledge and skills for successful careers. As a teacher, you will be expected to enhance students' abilities to engage in the use of technology to support their learning and address these six areas of competency, also known as **technology literacy** skills. In addition, you are expected to enhance learning by engaging students in activities requiring the "Four Cs" of critical thinking, collaboration, communication, and creativity and innovation. What you can note in looking at the two lists of skills to emphasize is that they are very similar and are not something to be considered as "add ons," but rather they can be integrated into the learning experiences you arrange for your students.

Video Example 2.2: Media Literacy Skills

Listen to Principal Chris Lehamnn as he shares his ideas about the importance of helping students understand media literacy skills. What are his main ideas?

You should combine knowledge and skills related to content areas and information literacy skills by using technology in ways that help students learn information and communicate knowledge. For example, in a science lesson on weather, you can present a problem to your students that will require them to search websites for data or information, use communication tools to collaborate with outside experts, generate solutions to the problem collaboratively, and present their ideas to classmates using creative resources. By approaching your instruction in that manner, you have addressed many of the standards by which your students will be measured and will have given them guided practice in developing their knowledge and skills.

Application Exercise 2.2

Check Your Understanding 2.3

Principles of Effective Media Use

Learning from multiple sources of media provides us with information and challenges our thinking. As users of these sources we need **media literacy** skills to know how to access them, how to understand and analyze the content, and how to create new media messages (Stansbury, 2009).

Text, television, video, and a host of other media sources covered within this textbook are all valid and vital sources of information. Your role is to guide your students to use these media as sources for their learning in ways that are wise, safe, and productive. For example, students need to learn to find multiple sources to verify facts they may have heard on the news or read in the newspaper. They need to learn to be critical users of these resources to ensure that they are well informed and their conclusions are accurate. As mentioned earlier, the ISTE Standards for Students and the "Four Cs" address many of the abilities learners need to be successful consumers of the media resources surrounding them.

Video Example 2.3: Using Online Resources

Diana Laufenberg talks with her students about using online resources. How does she guide them? What does she suggest they do?

Furthermore, your teaching approach should provide students with opportunities to explore how to use these media resources to communicate their knowledge. Later in this textbook you will see examples of how teachers guide their students to use a variety of media to express their knowledge and skills.

 Check Your Understanding 2.4

Principles of Effective Learning Assessment

The method of assessing achievement depends on the nature of the objective. Some learning objectives call for relatively simple cognitive skills—for example, stating Ohm's Law, distinguishing adjectives from adverbs, or summarizing the principles of the Declaration of Independence. Learning objectives such as these lend themselves to more traditional written tests.

Other objectives may call for process-type behaviors (e.g., diagramming a sentence, solving quadratic equations, or classifying animals), the creation of products (e.g., a sculpture, a written composition, a PowerPoint presentation, or a portfolio), or to exhibit attitudes (e.g., choosing to read during free-time activities, placing used paper in the recycle bin, or eating healthy snacks). This type of learning objective requires a more comprehensive, **authentic assessment,** such as a performance-based evaluation of a student's demonstration of learning in a natural context.

Authentic Assessment

Rising interest in authentic assessment of students is driven by commitment to a constructivist perspective. Authentic assessments require students to use processes appropriate to the content and skills being learned and to how they are used in the real world. It is the difference between learning science facts and doing what scientists do. How many people take paper-and-pencil tests as part of their occupation?

Authentic assessments can be applied to most types of performance or products that students develop to demonstrate their knowledge or understanding of the content. The most commonly used rating scales for authentic assessments include performance checklists, attitude scales, product-rating checklists, and rubrics.

When assessing basic process skills, a performance checklist can be an effective, objective way of recording student performances. Figure 2.1 shows a

Figure 2.1 Performance Checklist: Using an Audio Storybook

Performance Checklist: Using an Audio Storybook

Name _____ Class _____

Indicate Yes or No with an "X" in the appropriate column.

Did the Student	Yes	No
1. Locate the assigned audio storybook?	____	____
2. Complete the Material Checkout Form for the storybook?	____	____
3. Select the appropriate CD player?	____	____
4. Select the appropriate headphones?	____	____
5. Correctly insert the storybook CD?	____	____
6. Correctly connect the headphones?	____	____
7. Play the CD and follow along as the storybook was read?	____	____
8. Remove the CD and headphones when the story was finished?	____	____
9. Return the audio storybook, CD player, and headphones to the proper location?	____	____
10. Complete the Materials Return Form?	____	____

Teacher Name _____ Date _____

Figure 2.2 Attitude Scale: Biology

Attitude Scale: Biology

Each of the statements below expresses a feeling toward biology. Please rate each statement on the extent to which you agree. For each, you may select (A) strongly agree, (B) agree, (C) undecided, (D) disagree, or (E) strongly disagree.

A	B	C	D	E
Strongly Agree	Agree	Undecided	Disagree	Strongly Disagree

_____ 1. Biology is very interesting to me.
_____ 2. I don't like biology, and it scares me to have to take it.
_____ 3. I am always under a terrible strain in biology class.
_____ 4. Biology is fascinating and fun.
_____ 5. Learning biology makes me feel secure.
_____ 6. Biology makes me feel uncomfortable, restless, irritable, and impatient.
_____ 7. In general, I have a good feeling toward biology.
_____ 8. When I hear the word *biology* I have a feeling of dislike.
_____ 9. I approach biology with a feeling of hesitation.
_____ 10. I really like biology.
_____ 11. I have always enjoyed studying biology in school.
_____ 12. It makes me nervous to even think about doing a biology experiment.
_____ 13. I feel at ease in biology and like it very much.
_____ 14. I feel a definite positive response to biology; it's enjoyable.

primary-grade checklist for using an audio storybook. Notice the simple yes or no recording system.

Although attitudes are admittedly difficult to assess, measurement tools have been devised, such as attitude scales (see the biology example in Figure 2.2).

The five-point scale (strongly agree to strongly disagree) offers the opportunity to capture a range of attitudes. A number of other suggestions for attitude measurement can be found in Robert Mager's *How to Turn Learners On . . . without Turning Them Off* (see this chapter's Suggested Resources).

For product skills, a product-rating checklist can guide your evaluation of critical subskills and make qualitative judgments more objective, as in the rating form in Figure 2.3 for a student-created digital concept map.

This checklist provides more detailed information regarding student performance because each product component is rated from poor to excellent rather than on a yes/no scale.

Used to provide a more comprehensive assessment of student performance, a rubric is a set of assessment criteria for appraising or judging student products or performances (See Technology Resources). A rubric typically consists of a rating scale for performance criteria based on level-of-performance descriptors. The performance criteria are the key area of focus for the performance or the product (e.g., problem presentation, supporting graphics, appropriate labels). Rating scales to measure achievement of performance criteria normally range from three to six levels designated by names and/or numbers. A three-point scale might be shown as (1) needs work, (2) okay, (3) good. An example of a four-point scale might show the following levels: (1) beginning, (2) developing, (3) accomplished, and (4) exemplary. The descriptors for the

Figure 2.3 Product Evaluation Checklist: Digital Concept Map

Product Evaluation Checklist: Digital Concept Map

Name _____ Date _____

Rate the digital concept map on the basis of content and layout by checking the appropriate box.

Content	Poor	Fair	Good	Very Good	Excellent
• Key ideas are represented	☐	☐	☐	☐	☐
• Supporting ideas are logical	☐	☐	☐	☐	☐
• Information is accurate	☐	☐	☐	☐	☐
• Paraphrasing is appropriate	☐	☐	☐	☐	☐

Comments about the content:

Layout	Poor	Fair	Good	Very Good	Excellent
• Main idea shapes are appropriate	☐	☐	☐	☐	☐
• Supporting idea shapes are appropriate	☐	☐	☐	☐	☐
• Connecting lines are meaningful	☐	☐	☐	☐	☐
• Graphics support concepts	☐	☐	☐	☐	☐
• Use of colors is appropriate	☐	☐	☐	☐	☐
• Font is clear and easy to read	☐	☐	☐	☐	☐

Comments about the layout:

Overall Evaluation:

_____ Poor
_____ Fair
_____ Good
_____ Very Good
_____ Excellent

Overall Comments:

levels of performance describe the student performance or product at each level. By comparing an actual student product or performance to the descriptors, a teacher can give a numerical score. An example rubric for a multimedia product is presented in Figure 2.4. See "Technology Resources: Rubrics" for rubric resources.

Portfolio Assessment

If your assessment plan involves determining the overall individual performance of each student, traditional or electronic portfolio assessments can help achieve your goal. Portfolios are used to assess tangible products that exemplify student accomplishments in terms of analysis, synthesis, and evaluation. A key component of portfolios is their requirement for students to self-reflect on their own learning as demonstrated in the

Figure 2.4 Multimedia Product Rubric

Multimedia Product Rubric

Student's Name _____ Date _____

Category	4	3	2	1
Content	Covers topics in-depth with details and examples. Subject knowledge is excellent.	Includes essential knowledge about the topic. Subject knowledge appears to be good.	Includes essential information about the topic but there are 1–2 factual errors.	Content is minimal OR there are several factual errors.
Sources	Source information collected for all graphics, facts, and quotes. All documented in desired format.	Source information collected for all graphics, facts, and quotes. Most documented in desired format.	Source information collected for all graphics, facts, and quotes, but not documented in desired format.	Very little or no source information was collected.
Organization	Content is well organized, uses headings or bulleted lists to group related material.	Uses headings or bulleted lists to organize, but the overall organization of topics appears flawed.	Content is logically organized for the most part.	There was no clear or logical organizational structure, just lots of facts.
Requirements	All requirements are met and exceeded.	All requirements are met.	One requirement was not completely met.	More than one requirement was not completely met.
Originality	Product shows a large amount of original thought. Ideas are creative and inventive.	Product shows some original thought. Work shows new ideas and insights.	Uses other people's ideas (giving them credit), but there is little evidence of original thinking.	Uses other people's ideas, but does not give them credit.

portfolio products. For example, students are asked to select a piece of work that demonstrates achievement of a learning objective and then to explain why they chose the piece and how it shows the target knowledge and skills. The reflections can be extended to develop metacognitive skills by asking the students to describe what they would do differently to improve their learning.

To use portfolios, begin by deciding between traditional or electronic formats. Then identify the types of artifacts that will demonstrate student achievement of the standards and objectives and select or develop an appropriate rating scale (previously described). The rubrics should be given to students before they begin working on the products. The types of artifacts that a portfolio might contain include the following:

- Written documents such as poems, stories, or research papers
- Audio recordings of debates, panel discussions, or oral presentations
- Video recordings of skits, lab experiments, or 3-D models
- Computer multimedia projects such as animated timelines, podcasts, or WebQuests

TRADITIONAL VERSUS ELECTRONIC PORTFOLIOS. Traditional portfolios are physical collections of students' work, whereas electronic portfolios contain digital work. Traditional portfolios consist of paper documents, photos, video and audio recordings, or perhaps 3-D models. The portfolios are often kept in large three-ring binders and storage boxes, which are moved from teacher to teacher as the student progresses through school. As can be imagined, over time the portfolios can become quite large and hard to manage and store.

ELECTRONIC PORTFOLIOS (CALLED E-PORTFOLIOS). Electronic portfolios store all the students' work as digital files. For example, any computer-generated products, such as spreadsheets, word-processed reports, or WebQuests, can be directly added to the portfolio. Students' work created on paper, such as drawings, handwritten poems, or illustrated stories, can be converted to digital format with a scanner. For capturing actual student performances, digital audio and video are also important components of an electronic portfolio, including readings, skits or presentations, student-created 3-D models, or lab experiments conducted by students. The digital format also allows students to add their self-reflections as text or audio narration.

An e-portfolio provides the opportunity for a student to use artifacts in multiple ways. For example, if a student writes a paper on how the Mississippi River influenced the economy of the bordering communities that he feels is a good example of his language arts skills, he would place it in the e-portfolio for that purpose. If, later, that student realizes that the paper would also serve to demonstrate his insights into social studies knowledge, he can connect that same artifact to another aspect of his e-portfolio. The ability to move or connect the artifacts within the e-portfolio offers students more options in how they capitalize on the ways to demonstrate their success in learning outcomes. The Technology Resources feature provides a number of useful resources for you and your students.

Electronic portfolios can be created with specialized portfolio software, at online sites, or with combinations of basic software such as PowerPoint. Drawbacks for electronic portfolios include availability of equipment and time, as well as questions of access to the tools. Moreover, creating e-portfolios is initially time-consuming because teachers and students need to learn how to scan, save, and format documents in a useful and appealing manner. However, once the process is mastered, e-portfolios take less time to maintain and obviously require less storage space than traditional portfolios. Security is a concern when deciding who will have access to the files among parents, principals, counselors, teachers, and other students. For some practical tips on using Google Docs as an open source software solution for e-portfolios, visit Dr. Helen Barrett's ePortfolios website to find more information on this topic. Also check out the resources recommended in the Technology Resources feature box.

Technology Resources

Rubrics

Rubistar

Rubistar is a free online tool designed to assist teachers in creating a variety of rubrics. The website has numerous examples of rubrics that can be accessed through keyword searches. If you are new to rubrics, the site offers a rubric tutorial. When you are ready to try it out, Rubistar provides an easy-to-use template to create and print rubrics. If you complete the registration, you can save and edit rubrics online.

Assessment Focus

Assessment Focus offers a number of links to sites that will help you generate rubrics. The site includes links for ready-made rubrics, as well as sites that will allow you to build your own rubrics.

Teach-nology

The Teach-nology site offers a variety of rubric resources for teachers. Both samples and templates are available to use. The rubrics are developed for grades K–12 to include social studies, math, science, and reading and language arts.

Traditional Assessment

There are times when, as a teacher, you need to verify that students have specific knowledge or skills. Often, more traditional measures are used to demonstrate levels of knowledge. Such things as multiple-choice, fill-in-the-blank, true/false, or short-answer tests are ways to identify students who have mastered particular facts and to determine which students may need additional instruction (Waugh & Gronlund, 2012). Traditional tests tend to be used to measure lower-order learning, which is sometimes essential to ensuring students are meeting state and local learning standards.

Teachers can design traditional tests using learning objectives as their guide. Many instructional materials, such as textbook series, include tests as part of their teacher resource package. Teachers can use these types of tests as quick measures to determine which students need additional instructional assistance or to check on student progress on a particular topic or skill. Traditional tests can serve as a way to identify where students are in their knowledge about a topic prior to designing instruction; thus, you will not repeat content that students have already mastered.

In addition, each state is required to annually report the progress of students' learning. Statewide **standardized tests,** which are administered in a consistent manner and use the same scoring procedures, are a type of traditional assessment measure. In this instance, the tests are scheduled for a specific date across the state and the procedures are carefully orchestrated so that student learning is measured in the same way. Currently, state standardized tests are used to identify student learning that is meeting or exceeding state standards and to determine where there is a need for improvement.

 Check Your Understanding 2.5

Shared Writing Exercise 2.1

Summary

In this chapter we discussed issues related to learning theories, principles of effective instruction, technology and media utilization, and types of assessment.

- *Describe the similarities and differences in learning theories.* We presented four learning theories and gave examples of how they might be used in teaching. By knowing the theories of learning, as the teacher, you can make good decisions about the instructional approach to use.

- *List the eight principles of effective instruction for learners.* You learned about the characteristics of good instruction that will benefit all learners. The difference between information and instruction was clarified. And, you learned about the digital taxonomy, the four Cs, and multiple intelligences.

- *Describe the principles of effective technology utilization.* As the teacher, you will be expected to incorporate

technology use in ways that enhance and augment student learning. You learned about ways that can be effective when working with students.

- *Describe the principles of effective media utilization.* Media such as video, audio, and text are important to consider when selecting the appropriate medium for your students to use in their learning. You have learned about how you can make those selections effectively.

- *Describe the types of effective learning assessment.* There are a number of ways a teacher can measure student learning. The objectives serve as a guide to the teacher to determine the best approach to assess learning. Technology can be useful for capturing and storing student materials that document their learning outcomes.

Professional Development

Demonstrating Professional Skills

1. Prepare a 10-minute presentation on your reaction to a topic of interest in this chapter (ISTE Standards for Teachers 5.C).

2. Analyze an instructional situation (either real or hypothetical) and identify the psychological perspective on learning and the technology and media used (ISTE Standards for Teachers 5.C).

3. Prepare a position paper on the roles of technology and media in learning (ISTE Standards for Teachers 5.C).

4. Describe different instances in which you would use the types of assessment described in this chapter (ISTE Standards for Teachers 2.D).

Building Your Professional Portfolio

Reflecting on My Learning. Reflect on the different assessment processes described in the chapter. Discuss how these assessment strategies measure student learning and where they best fit into an instructional situation. Comment on the types of teacher feedback that might contribute to student understanding of the assessment results (ISTE Standards for Teachers 5.C).

Enhancing My Portfolio. Select a lesson from a source on the Web. Indicate how specific portions of the lesson illustrate, if present, the psychological perspectives addressed in this chapter (behaviorist, cognitivist, constructivist, and social psychology). Identify the assessment that is used to measure student learning. Discuss the value of the assessment being used. Cite the source of the lesson. Reflect on this analysis, providing strengths, weaknesses, and recommendations for teaching this lesson to a specific group of students (ISTE Standards for Teachers 2.C).

Suggested Resources

Print Resources

Anderson, R. & Mims, C. (2014). *Handbook of research on digital tools for writing instruction in K-12 settings.* Hershey, PA: Information Science Reference.

Cook, A. & Polgar, J. (2015). *Assistive technologies: Principles and practice.* St. Louis, MO: Elsevier.

Jonassen, D. H., Howland, J., Moore, J., & Marra, R. M. (2002). *Learning to solve problems with technology: A constructivist perspective* (2nd ed.). Upper Saddle River, NJ: Merrill/Prentice Hall.

Mager, R. (1997). *How to turn learners on . . . without turning them off.* Atlanta, GA: CEP Press.

Roblyer, M. & Doering, A. (2012). *Integrating educational technology into teaching* (6th ed.). Upper Saddle River, NJ: Pearson.

Online Resources and Apps

International Society for Technology in Education

ISTE is an association focused on improving education through the use of technology in learning, teaching, and administration. ISTE members include teachers, administrators, computer coordinators, information resource managers, and educational technology specialists.

eSchool News

This site offers a convenient way to keep up to date electronically with what is going on with technology in schools.

Partnership for 21st Century Skills

The Partnership for 21st Century Skills advocates for infusing 21st century skills into education. Working with leaders in business, education, and policy, the organization's goal is to work with schools to infuse 21st century skills into education and provides tools and resources to help facilitate and drive change.

Learning Styles Inventory

The Learning Styles Inventory has 70 questions that assess dominant and secondary learning styles concerning the following areas: aural, verbal, physical, logical, social, and solitary.

Learning Styles Inventory for Students with Learning Disabilities

This website offers an inventory to identify the preferred learning styles of students with learning disabilities. The inventory results provide educators and parents with a better understanding of students' learning preferences. This information will assist in adapting learning environments to better meet the needs of individual learners.

Chapter 3
Integrating Technology and Media into Instruction: The ASSURE Model

Learning Outcomes

This chapter addresses ISTE Standards for Teachers 2, 4, and 5.

3.1 Describe the ASSURE model.

3.2 State the three primary types of information used to analyze learners and describe the role of the information in the systematic planning process for learning.

3.3 Demonstrate how to go from national standards to learning objectives that include the audience, behavior, conditions, and degree of mastery.

3.4 Outline the procedures for selecting, modifying, and designing instructional strategies and resources.

3.5 Create examples of the five basic steps in utilizing resources (e.g., technology, media, and materials).

3.6 Describe and justify methods for eliciting student participation when using technology and media during instruction.

3.7 Compare and contrast the techniques for evaluating student achievement, strategies, and resources and for making database revisions.

Goal

Use the ASSURE model to systematically plan lessons that effectively integrate classroom use of technology and media.

ASSURE Classroom Case Study

The ASSURE model consists of six steps designed to help teachers plan lessons that effectively integrate use of technology and media for learning. To illustrate how to use the model, we provide you with an easy-to-understand description and a classroom case study to demonstrate implementation of each step. These steps taken together constitute a sample ASSURE lesson plan that describes the instructional planning of actual classroom teachers highlighted in the classroom case study.

Ninth-Grade English

This ASSURE classroom case study describes the instructional planning used by Tiare Ahu, a high school English teacher who wants to increase student learning and communication skills through the use of electronic portfolios, often referred to as *e-portfolios.* Tiare feels that her ninth-grade students often lack interest in improving their writing and oral communication

skills. Her students typically complete each class assignment without reflecting on past learning experiences, thus inhibiting their ability to grow and improve. She first addresses the concern by having students create paper-based portfolios of their writing. However, it proves difficult for students to revise and improve an existing paper-based assignment and equally difficult to add reflective comments without detracting from the original documents. Her solution is to use e-portfolios that allow students to easily update, modify, and add written or video reflections to their assignments. Throughout the chapter you can follow Tiare's use of the ASSURE model to design a lesson that integrates the use of electronic portfolios.

This ASSURE Classroom Case Study focuses on Tiare Ahu's ninth-grade English class working on their electronic portfolios. Video segments demonstrating Ms. Ahu's application of ASSURE model steps are provided throughout the chapter.

Introduction

Today's teachers have exciting opportunities for using technology and media to guide students' learning experiences in preparation for future careers. This chapter introduces you to the ASSURE model, which uses a step-by-step process to create lessons that effectively integrate the use of technology and media to improve student learning. Lessons created with the ASSURE model directly align with the Common Core State Standards, the International Society for Technology in Education Standards for Teachers (ISTE, 2008) and Students (ISTE, 2007) (hereafter referred to as ISTE-T and ISTE-S, respectively), as well as curriculum standards from the local to the national level. In addition, the ASSURE model utilizes a standard research-based approach to lesson design that easily aligns with school or district lesson plan templates.

The ASSURE Model

Effective instruction requires careful planning. Teaching with instructional technology and media is certainly no exception. This chapter examines how to plan systematically for the effective use of technology and media. We have constructed a six-step procedural model to which we have given the acronym ASSURE—it is intended to *assure* effective instruction. The six steps are: **A**nalyze learners; **S**tate standards and objectives; **S**elect strategies and resources; **U**tilize resources; **R**equire learner participation; and **E**valuate and revise. Some aspects of teaching and learning have stayed consistent over the years, such as the progressive stages or "events of instruction" that occur (Gagné, 1985). Research has shown that well-designed lessons begin with the arousal of students' interest and then move on to present new material, involve students in practice with feedback, assess their understanding, and provide relevant follow-up activities. The ASSURE model incorporates all these events of instruction, beginning with the analysis of learners.

Application Exercise 3.1

ASSURE A Model to Help Assure Learning

Analyze Learners

The first step in planning a lesson is to identify and analyze learner characteristics shown to be associated with learning outcomes. This information will guide your decision-making during the design of your lesson. The key areas to consider during learner analysis include (1) general characteristics of learners, (2) specific entry competencies (knowledge, skills, and attitudes about the topic), and (3) learning differences and needs.

State Standards and Objectives

The next step is to state the standards and learning objectives as specifically as possible. Begin with curriculum and technology standards adopted by your district, as these are based on state and national student performance criteria. Well-stated objectives name the learners for whom the objective is intended, the action (behavior) to be demonstrated, the conditions under which the behavior or performance will be observed, and the degree to which the new knowledge or skill must be mastered. For this text, the condition will include the use of technology and media to support learning and to assess achievement of the standard or learning objectives.

Select Strategies and Resources

Once you have analyzed your learners and stated the standards and objectives, you have established the beginning points (students' present knowledge, skills, and attitudes) and ending points (learning objectives) of instruction. Your task now is to build a bridge between these two points by choosing appropriate instructional strategies and resources to achieve the objectives.

Utilize Resources

This step involves planning your teaching role for utilizing the resources (technology, media, and materials) to help students achieve the learning objectives. To do this, follow the 5 Ps process: Preview the resources; Prepare the resources; Prepare the environment; Prepare the learners; and Provide the learning experience.

Require Learner Participation

To be effective, instruction should require learners' active mental engagement. Provide activities that allow them to practice the new knowledge or skills and to receive feedback on their efforts before being formally assessed. Practice may involve student self-checks, digital tutorials, Internet activities, or group exercises. Feedback can come from the teacher, digital devices, other students, or self-evaluation.

Evaluate and Revise

After implementing a lesson, evaluate its impact on student learning. This assessment not only examines the degree to which students achieved the learning objectives, but also examines the entire instructional process and the impact of using technology and media. Wherever there are discrepancies between learning objectives and student outcomes, revise the lesson plan to address the areas of concern.

 Check Your Understanding 3.1

Analyze Learners

The ASSURE model provides you with a systematic approach for analyzing learner characteristics that impact their ability to learn. The analysis information is used to plan lessons tailored to meet the needs of your students. The learner analysis examines three types of information: general characteristics, specific entry competencies, and learning differences and needs.

General Characteristics

It is critical to understand the general characteristics that may influence student learning. These characteristics range from constant variables, such as gender and ethnicity, to those that vary on a regular basis, such as attitudes and interest.

Review student records to identify the age differences of your students to better understand behavioral patterns or ability to focus during learning activities. When planning group work, consider gender differences that may impact student attention and willingness to participate. For example, mixed-gender groups may work well in early elementary classes but inhibit student learning for some middle school students. When students represent multiple ethnic groups, select instructional materials and examples that give high priority to cultural identity and values. For example, select digital images with children of the same ethnicity as your students to increase their connection to the lesson topic. Once you have this background understanding of your students' general characteristics, couple it with your observations of student attitudes and interest to design and implement meaningful lessons that address the unique needs of each student.

Specific Entry Competencies

Research reveals that students' prior knowledge of a particular subject influences how and what they learn more than does any psychological trait (Dick, Carey, & Carey, 2014). Therefore, a critical component of designing lessons is to identify the specific entry competencies of your students. You can do this informally (such as through in-class questioning) or by more formal means (such as reviewing standardized test results or giving teacher-made tests and assessments). **Entry tests** are assessments that determine whether students possess the necessary **prerequisites**, or competencies, to benefit from instruction. For example, if you are going to teach students to calculate the area of geometric shapes, the entry test should focus on multiplication skills to identify students who need remediation prior to the lesson. An important prerequisite skill for many lessons is reading ability. Therefore, you may want to test or arrange to have your students' reading abilities determined.

Once specific entry competencies are identified, list them in your lesson and include an **entry pretest** to identify students who need remediation prior to lesson implementation and also to identify those who have already mastered what you plan to teach.

Learning Differences and Needs

To ensure learning for all students, teachers must identify and analyze the unique differences and needs of individual learners. Research has shown that students have multiple intelligences, perceptual preferences and strengths, various information processing behaviors, a range of motivations, and differing physiological factors that influence learning. For example, Howard Gardner's (2011) foundational multiple intelligences research suggests a person can have varying abilities in eight areas:

1. Verbal-linguistic
2. Logical-mathematical
3. Visual/spatial
4. Body-kinesthetic
5. Musical
6. Naturalistic
7. Interpersonal/intrapersonal
8. Existentialist.

Teachers have access to several free online assessments to gather a variety of information regarding the learning preferences of her students. For example, does a student prefer to learn with visual materials, by listening to auditory recording, or with hands-on kinesthetic experiences (Hatami, 2012). The information you learn

ASSURE Classroom Case Study

Analyze Learners

Ninth-Grade English

General Characteristics

Tiare Ahu is teaching the basic ninth-grade English course geared toward the average learner. The students are 14 and 15 years old. Several students have learning disabilities, whereas others are above-average readers and writers. Her students come from primarily moderate- to low-income socioeconomic environments and represent an ethnic population common to an urban setting. Generally, the students are well behaved. However, some show lack of interest and apathy toward learning when activities are textbook and paper-and-pencil oriented.

Entry Competencies

The students in general are able to do the following:

- Create and save word processed documents
- Navigate the Internet
- Create and save digital video
- Respond via written and verbal communication that ranges from below to above grade-level proficiency.

Learning Differences and Needs

Tiare has found that her students appear to learn best from activities that incorporate technology and media. Using technology provides intrinsic motivation through the creation of personalized work and the careful reflection of learning. Tiare has also discovered that most of her students have difficulty working in a completely silent atmosphere and therefore she allows students to use headphones to listen to music when they work on their digital portfolios. Her students vary in their preferred forms of expression; some favor inputting their thoughts as written text, others choose to capture them with digital video, and still others prefer audio recordings.

Video Example 3.1: Analyze Learners

Observe how Tiare Ahu analyzes students in her ninth-grade English class. What learner characteristics influence her lesson design decisions?

from analyzing the general characteristics, specific entry competencies, and learning differences and needs of your students will guide your decision-making process as you design your ASSURE lesson (see the ASSURE case study for an example of the process).

 Check Your Understanding 3.2

State Standards and Objectives

The second step in the ASSURE model is to state the standards and learning objectives for the lesson. What new capability should learners possess at the completion of instruction? The learning objectives are derived from curriculum and technology standards—descriptions of expected student performance outcomes established at the school district, state, or national level. For this text, we focus on ISTE-S, Common Core State Standards, and other national curriculum standards, which provide general descriptions of expected student performance. As seen in Table 3.1, learning objectives, typically written by the teacher or school district, identify very specific outcomes.

It is important to note that a learning objective is a statement of what each learner will achieve, not how the lesson will be taught.

Importance of Standards and Objectives

It is important to state the standards and learning objectives for each lesson because they serve as the basis for the following three critical components of the ASSURE lesson plan: 1) strategies, technology, and media selection, 2) assessment, and 3) student learning expectations. The three components are described in more detail in subsequent sections of this chapter.

BASIS FOR STRATEGIES, TECHNOLOGY, AND MEDIA SELECTION. When you have clear statements of what students will know and should be able to do at the conclusion of the lesson, as stated in standards and objectives, you are better able to carefully select the strategies, technology, and media that will ensure learning.

BASIS FOR ASSESSMENT. Stating standards and learning objectives also helps ensure accurate assessment of student learning. The explicitly stated student outcomes serve as a guide when creating assessments to measure the targeted knowledge and skills that are directly aligned with standardized tests.

BASIS FOR STUDENT LEARNING EXPECTATIONS. Your students are better able to prepare for and participate in learning activities when they know the expected outcomes. The learning objectives may be viewed as a type of contract between teacher and

Table 3.1 Going from Standards to Learning Objectives: PK–4 and 9–12 Examples

Common Core (CCSS) and National Curriculum Standards	International Society for Technology in Education Standards for Students (ISTE-S)	Learning Objective Aligned to National Standards
GRADES PK–4 EXAMPLES		
CCSS: **English Language Arts** Students knowledgeably combine information on a topic from two or more sources. **National Center for History in the Schools** Students compare and contrast the history of people from their own state or region.	**ISTE-S:** Students are creative and innovative in technology use. Students effectively communicate and use technology collaboratively. Students skillfully use technology resources.	Given different storybooks that describe the lifestyles of Southwest Native Americans over the past 100 years, the third-grade students select two texts from which they will create a six-slide PowerPoint presentation for Parent Night that compares and contrasts the housing, diets, traditions, and work of today's Southwest Native Americans with those from 100 years earlier.
GRADES 9–12 EXAMPLES		
CCSS: **English Language Arts** Students locate and analyze information to develop valid, relevant, and well-supported arguments. **National Standards for Arts Education Visual Arts** Students meaningfully use media to create visual art that communicates the intended message.	**ISTE-S:** Students are creative and innovative in technology use. Students effectively communicate and use technology collaboratively. Students use technology for critical thinking, problem solving, and decision-making. Students skillfully use technology resources.	Given technology consisting of a digital camera and photo editing software, the tenth-grade student will (1) create a visual art product that includes at least three digital photos and two descriptive words to represent the concept of freedom, and (2) provide a written argument/rationale that supports their choice of media, techniques, and processes to demonstrate an understanding of freedom.

learner: "My responsibility as the teacher is to provide learning activities suitable to aid you to attain the objective. Your responsibility as the learner is to participate conscientiously in those learning activities."

The ABCDs of Well-Stated Learning Objectives

The ABCDs of well-stated objectives provide an easy-to-follow process for writing learning objectives: Specify the *Audience* for whom the objective is intended, the *Behavior* to be demonstrated, the *Conditions* under which the behavior will be observed, and the *Degree* to which the new knowledge or skill must be mastered.

AUDIENCE. Because learning objectives focus on what learners will know and be able to do after the lesson, it is important to clearly identify the targeted learners—for example, second-grade students. For students you will be teaching all year, you may choose the common audience identifier "The learner will . . . ," which is often abbreviated as TLW. For students who have individual education plans, the objectives will be targeted to students by name.

BEHAVIOR. The heart of the objective is the verb describing the new capability that learners will have *after* instruction. This verb is stated as an observable behavior, such as *define, categorize*, or *demonstrate*. Vague terms such as *know, understand*, and *appreciate* do not communicate observable performance. The Helpful Hundred list in Table 3.2 offers verbs that highlight the behavior or performance.

Strive to solicit student behavior or performance that reflects deep understanding and real-world capability. In other words, rather than having students "select the correct answers on a test about water conservation," have them "compare and contrast two water conservation systems to identify which is most eco-friendly." Or rather than selecting names of geometric shapes on a worksheet, have students identify shapes used in the Golden Gate Bridge.

CONDITIONS. Learning objectives should include the conditions under which the performance is to be assessed. In other words, what materials or tools will be allowed

Table 3.2 The Helpful Hundred

Suggested Behavior Terms				
Add	Alphabetize	Analyze	Apply	Arrange
Assemble	Attend	Bisect	Build	Categorize
Change	Choose	Classify	Color	Compare
Complete	Compose	Compute	Conduct	Construct
Contrast	Convert	Correct	Cut	Deduce
Defend	Define	Demonstrate	Derive	Describe
Design	Designate	Diagram	Distinguish	Draw
Estimate	Evaluate	Explain	Extrapolate	Finish
Fit	Generate	Graph	Group	Hit
Hold	Identify	Illustrate	Indicate	Install
Kick	Label	Locate	Make	Manipulate
Match	Measure	Modify	Multiply	Name
Operate	Order	Organize	Outline	Pack
Paint	Plot	Position	Predict	Prepare
Present	Produce	Pronounce	Read	Reconstruct
Reduce	Remove	Revise	Select	Sketch
Solve	Sort	Specify	Spell	Square
State	Subtract	Suggest	Swing	Tabulate
Throw	Time	Translate	Type	Underline
Verbalize	Verify	Weave	Weigh	Write

or not allowed for student use in demonstrating mastery of the objective? Thus, an objective might state, "Given a list of earthquake occurrences over the past 100 years, the student will generate a line graph to demonstrate trends over time." A language arts objective might say, "Without using reference materials, the student will write a 300-word essay on the relationship of nutrition to learning."

DEGREE. The final requirement of a well-stated objective is the degree of accuracy or proficiency by which minimally acceptable performance will be judged. Certainly students can exceed the stated expectations. A high school chemistry objective may read, "Given six unknown substances and testing equipment, students will identify five of the six unknown substances." When stating the degree or criterion for assessing student products that are more comprehensive in scope, a rubric rating scale that assesses several components of the product is appropriate. An average of the combined rubric scores can be used to provide an overall proficiency rating. For example, proficiency on a student product may be stated as follows: "Students are to achieve an overall rubric rating of 3 (on a four-point scale, where 4 = Exceeds Expectations)."

ABCD Objectives Checklist

Use the ABCD Objectives Checklist (Figure 3.1) to assess the degree to which your objectives communicate the intent of the learning.

Further guidelines for writing objectives are discussed in Gronlund's (2009) *Writing Instructional Objectives for Teaching and Assessment.*

You will find that learning objectives appearing in curriculum standards, textbooks, online lessons, and other instructional materials are written in a general format that

---

Figure 3.1 ABCD Objectives Checklist

ABCD Objectives Checklist			
Audience	**Appropriately Stated**	**Partly Stated**	**Missing**
Specifies the learner(s) for whom the objective is intended	☐	☐	☐
Behavior (action verb)			
Describes the capability expected of the learner following instruction • Stated as a learner performance • Stated as observable behavior • Describes a real-world skill (versus mere test performance)	☐	☐	☐
Conditions (materials and/or environment)			
Describes the conditions under which the performance is to be demonstrated • Equipment, tools, aids, or references the learner may or may not use • Special environmental conditions in which the learner has to perform	☐	☐	☐
Degree (criterion)			
States, where applicable, the standard for acceptable performance • Time limit • Range of accuracy • Proportion of correct responses required • Qualitative standards	☐	☐	☐

often lacks one or more of the ABCD components. Teachers can modify such objectives to meet the specific learning needs of their students; for example, a district standard may state: "The learner will be able to divide fractions." If you have students who struggle with math, you could adapt the objective by adding the following condition: "Given manipulatives, the learner will be able to divide fractions." The same objective for more advanced students would not include manipulatives.

Many curriculum standards also lack the use of technology to assist students in achieving the learning objective. This concern can be addressed by adding the appropriate ISTE-S (ISTE, 2007) to lessons. Include technology in the Condition component of the objective, as in the following examples:

- *Given spreadsheet software and data on population growth, natural resources, and global warming,* sixth-grade science students will use a spreadsheet to estimate the impact of population growth on natural resources from at least three perspectives.

- *Given digital images and presentation software,* first-grade students will construct a four-slide presentation with one student-selected clip art image per slide to demonstrate four student moods: happy, sad, angry, and bored.

- *Given access to word processing software and web-based resources on American wars,* high school students will generate *a word-processed table* that shows 25 similarities of and differences between World War I and World War II.

- *Given words and concept-mapping software,* students in seventh-grade language arts will create a concept map that arranges the words into six parts-of-speech groups.

Application Exercise 3.2

Learning Objectives and Individual Differences

The stated philosophy of most schools is to help students achieve their full potential. In a physical education class with students of mixed ability, for instance, the mid-semester goal might be for all students to complete a 100-meter run, with time standards that vary to show similarity of achievement. For a few, 12 seconds might be attainable; for many others, 16 seconds is doable; and for some, 20 seconds might be realistic. For a student with physical disabilities, it might be a major victory to move 10 meters in one minute.

Learning objectives are not intended to limit what students learn, but rather are intended to provide a minimum level of expected achievement. Incidental learning should be expected to occur (and should be encouraged) because learning takes different forms with different students. Class discussions and other kinds of student involvement in the instructional situation, therefore, should rarely be rigidly limited to a specific objective. Indeed, to foster incidental learning and provide for individual differences, it is sometimes advisable to have students specify some of their own learning objectives. (See a set of standards and learning objectives in the ASSURE case study.)

 Check Your Understanding 3.3

ASSURE Classroom Case Study

State Standards and Objectives

Ninth-Grade English

Standards

- **Curriculum**—National Council of Teachers of English: Students develop communication for a particular audience and purpose. *Common Core State Standards, ELA Literacy:* Students use clear and relevant reasoning in a structured approach applicable for the intended message.
- **Technology**—*ISTE-S*: Students use technology to gather information.

Lesson Objectives

1. Given the following questions, the ninth-grade English student will demonstrate ability to express reflective thinking by answering the following questions in a written or video reflection that meets the "Final Year Reflections" criteria listed on the assignment sheet.

- What did I learn about myself, reading, writing, learning, and overall during the past year?
- What do I hope to accomplish in these areas next year when I am a sophomore?

2. Using an application to create websites, the ninth-grade English student will create a new page titled "Final Year Reflections" that meets the formatting criteria for being included in the electronic portfolio reflections folder.

3. Using files of previously completed work, the ninth-grade student will be able to add the written reflection or upload a video reflection in an accessible format to the "Final Year Reflections" page in the electronic portfolio folder.

Review

Locate and review the Common Core State Standards, ISTE for Students, and other national curriculum standards appropriate to the area and grade level you teach or plan to teach.

Select Strategies and Resources

The next step in creating effective lessons that support learning through the appropriate use of technology and media is the systematic selection of instructional strategies and resources, which include technology and media, and lesson materials. The following guidelines discuss the selection process.

Select Strategies

All instructional strategies, whether teacher- or student-centered, should engage students in active learning. When identifying instructional strategies for a lesson, first consider where teacher-centered approaches should be used and where student-centered strategies might be more appropriate. The teacher strategies involve your own teaching activities, as when you present a concept by showing a video or reading a story, or when you use the interactive whiteboard to engage students in exploring the photosynthesis process. The student-centered strategies are those in which the teacher acts as a facilitator. Examples of student-centered learning include small groups discussing the pros and cons of a topic, pairs of students conducting an Internet search or taking digital photos of a process, or individuals listening to podcasts on a current news story. Most lessons include several teacher and student strategies.

Marzano and Heflebower (2012) propose that today's teachers need to implement instructional strategies that engage students in activities that build both cognitive and **conative** skills. The cognitive skills prepare students to (1) analyze and use information, (2) address complex problems and issues, and (3) create patterns and mental models in order to gain a deeper understanding and build new knowledge. On the other hand, the conative skills prepare students to (1) understand and control themselves, and (2) understand and interact with others (p. 9). These types of activities prepare students for future careers requiring similar application of knowledge and skills.

Another key consideration for selecting instructional strategies is keeping students motivated to learn. In other words, the strategies should be designed to encourage students to believe they have the *competence* to succeed and enough *control/autonomy* to make choices during the learning process. It is also important to provide students opportunities to interact with and receive recognition from teachers, family, and others of social importance to them (Usher & Kober, 2012).

Select Resources

When selecting resources for ASSURE lessons, decisions are made regarding the technology and media and the types of support materials needed to achieve the lesson outcomes. In addition to selecting support materials, teachers often need to modify existing materials or design new materials to meet specific lesson objectives. Guidelines and tools for making these decisions follow.

TECHNOLOGY AND MEDIA. Selecting appropriate technology and media can be a complex task, considering the vast array of available resources, the diversity of your learners, and the specific learning objectives to be pursued. Videos, for example, raise the issue of presentation pace, which varies for individual learners. In examining educational games, look for relevant practice and feedback. When selecting an audio storybook, look for functions such as embedded definitions and ease of returning to previously read sections. To help with this process, selection rubrics are provided for key technology and media presented in selected chapters, as noted in the Special Features of this text.

SELECTION RUBRICS. The selection rubrics provide a systematic procedure for assessing the qualities of specific technology and media. Each rubric includes a set of consistent selection criteria (as shown here) as well as criteria for the designated technology or media (e.g., application software, audio). You need to decide which criteria are most important for use in helping your students' achieve the stated learning objectives.

SELECTION RUBRIC CRITERIA.

- Alignment with standards, outcomes, and objectives
- Accurate and current information
- Age-appropriate language
- Interest level and engagement
- Technical quality
- Ease of use (for student or teacher)
- Bias free
- User guide and directions

The selection rubrics are templates with separate fields to enter the media title, source, and a brief description along with a predefined rating scale to assess the technology/media being reviewed.

Selecting, Modifying, or Designing Materials

When you have selected your strategies and the type of technology and media needed for your lesson, you are ready to select the materials to support lesson implementation. This step involves three general options: (1) selecting available materials, (2) modifying existing materials, or (3) designing new materials.

SELECTING AVAILABLE MATERIALS. The majority of instructional materials used by teachers are "off the shelf"—that is, ready-made and available from school, district, or other easily accessible sources. Many of these resources are free or inexpensive. Among many offerings, how do you go about making appropriate choices from available materials?

Involving the Library Media Specialist. You may want to begin by meeting with your library media specialist and discussing your learning objectives, instructional strategies, and desired media format(s). As the specialist gains a better idea of your needs, arrangements can be made to check out the appropriate materials from your school's library/media center or other media collections (public, academic, or regional).

Joining Other Teachers. Because evaluation of materials is time consuming and complex, it may be useful to involve other teachers, especially experienced teachers whose years of work with media and material alternatives have involved a lot of critical analysis about education resources. Working with other teachers allows a pool of shared ideas for using materials and a collective strength that may make it easier to acquire materials from museums or organizations.

Surveying Online Reviews. A variety of online reviews of educational resources are available to assist teachers with material selection. For example, Education World is a site that is updated on a daily basis and offers reviews of applications, websites, and technology products as well as lesson plans, classroom-ready resources, professional development articles, and social media tools to connect with other teachers. Another example is Kathy Schrock's Guide to Everything, which includes links to an alphabetized list of technology resource support sites such as iPads in the Classroom, Literacy in the Digital Age, and Twitter for Teachers. Also included are links to Apps for That, Authentic Learning, Video of the Month, and Kathy's Katch DEN Blog.

MODIFYING EXISTING MATERIALS. As you strive to meet the diverse needs of your students, you will find that "off-the-shelf" materials often need modifications to more closely align with your learning objectives. Technology provides several options for modifying existing materials.

Encouragingly, many educational resources are provided as copyright-free digital files or as paper copies. Digital materials are typically found on educational websites that provide downloadable resources. Example resources include lesson handouts, teacher PowerPoint presentations, and Excel spreadsheets formatted for easy data entry.

However, when materials are only available in PDF or paper format, modifications can be accomplished with digital scanning or creative use of a copy machine. For example, materials can be scanned and modified with editing software. Another approach is to modify a paper original and then make copies of the revised resource. For instance, if you want students to label 20 grasshopper features but have a handout based on 50, you can carefully cover the 30 unwanted features and then make copies.

A word of caution about using and modifying commercially produced materials is to be sure not to violate copyright laws and restrictions. If in doubt, check with your library media specialist, administrator, or legal adviser. General copyright guidelines are discussed earlier in the text.

DESIGNING NEW MATERIALS. When ready-made materials are not available or existing materials cannot be easily modified, you need to design your own lesson materials, which can range from hand printing a flip chart to using your laptop to create handouts, presentations, or an online blog. The remaining chapters provide guidance for developing meaningful materials involving a variety of technology and media. Remember to keep learner needs and learning objectives as the key considerations when designing your lesson materials (as in the ASSURE classroom case study).

ASSURE Classroom Case Study

Select Strategies and Resources

Ninth-Grade English

Select Strategies

Tiare Ahu selects teacher- and student-centered strategies for the electronic portfolio lesson. Teacher-centered strategies are chosen for reviewing the overall goals of using an electronic portfolio and to introduce student guidelines for completing the final reflections. The student-centered strategies are used for students' written or video reflections of their learning that are added to electronic portfolios. Tiare addresses student motivation by using the ARCS model (Keller, 2010) to consider how electronic portfolios gain student *attention*. To achieve *relevance*, students reflect on their personal growth over the year and set goals for next year. Their *confidence* is reinforced by the lesson's use of skills previously mastered in other electronic portfolio activities. Students gain *satisfaction* through personalizing their reflections with digital media such as colors, clip art, and photos.

Select Resources

Technology and Media: This lesson involves the continued use of Blackboard course management software and DreamWeaver software to create web-based portfolios. The lesson also calls for a digital video camera to record student reflections and the use of iMovie to edit the video. The following selection rubric guidelines help Tiare assess the appropriateness of her technology and media selections:

- *Alignment with standards, outcomes, and objectives.* The software provides the necessary tools for her students to meet the learning objectives.
- *Accurate and current information.* Not applicable for the chosen technology and media.
- *Age-appropriate language.* The software applications are written at a level appropriate for ninth-grade students.
- *Interest level and engagement.* The software applications provide features that enable the students to personalize their electronic portfolios.
- *Technical quality.* The software applications have superior technical quality.
- *Ease of use.* The applications require initial training and periodic review of functions for students to easily use the features.
- *Bias free.* The software applications are bias free.
- *User guide and directions.* The online help features of the software are moderately easy to use. Students most frequently ask each other, the teacher, or the technology assistant for help with technical difficulties.

Select Materials

This lesson includes a teacher-produced student assignment sheet that explains the details of creating and adding the final reflections to the electronic portfolio. Tiare was not able to use available materials or modify existing materials because the assignment sheet requires details very specific to the lesson.

Video Example 3.2: Select Strategies and Resources

Observe the strategies and resources Tiare Ahu uses in her ninth-grade English class. How will her selections help students gain confidence and achieve success in her classroom?

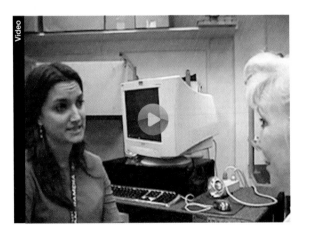

☑ **Check Your Understanding** 3.4

Utilize Resources

This step involves planning your role as a teacher for utilizing the lesson resources (e.g., technology, media, and materials). Follow the 5 Ps process: Preview and Prepare the resources; Prepare the environment; Prepare the learners; and Provide the learning experience.

Preview Resources

During the selection process you identified lesson resources appropriate for your learners. At this stage you need to preview the selected technology and media resources in relation to the learning objectives. The goal is to select the portions that directly align with your lesson. For example, if your lesson is on correct use of prepositions, preview several language arts software programs to find drill-and-practice activities that match your objectives. Then, design your lesson to include just the preposition sections of the software rather than the entire sequence. Similarly, if using a DVD video documentary, identify the segments that directly align with your lesson.

Even though your selection of materials may have already involved examining published reviews, distributor's blurbs, and colleagues' appraisals, it is critical for you to preview the materials yourself before using them. Not only will a thorough review enable you to use resources to their full potential, it will ensure that students are not exposed to inappropriate content or language found in some digital games, videos, and online or printed periodicals.

Prepare Resources

Next, you need to prepare the resources that will support your instructional activities. The first step is to gather all the materials and equipment you will need. Determine the sequence for using the materials and equipment and what you will do with each one. For example, you may want to change how an instructional game is used by preparing a new set of questions at a different level of difficulty or even on a new topic. Or, if the audio portion of a video doesn't align with the needs of your students, you can turn off the sound and provide the narration yourself.

Keep a list of the materials and equipment needed for each lesson and an outline of the presentation sequence of the activities. Finally, plan time to practice using the resources before implementing the lesson.

Prepare the Environment

Wherever the learning is to take place—in the classroom, in a laboratory, at the media center—the facilities will have to be arranged for effective use of the resources. Some media require a darkened room, a convenient power source, and access to light switches. You should check that the equipment is in working order. Arrange the facilities so that all students can see and hear properly. Arrange the seating so students can see and hear each other when cooperative or collaborative learning is included.

Prepare the Learners

Foundational research on learning tells us that what is learned from an activity depends highly on how learners are prepared for the lesson (Gagné, Wager, Golas, & Keller, 2004). We know that in show business entertainers are passionate about having the audience properly warmed up. Effective instruction also requires a proper warm-up, which can include one or more of the following:

- An introduction giving a broad overview of the lesson content
- A rationale telling how the content relates to real-world applications
- A motivating statement that creates a need to know the content
- Cues directing attention to specific aspects of the lesson

In most cases, you will also want to inform students of the learning objectives, introduce unfamiliar vocabulary, and review prerequisite skills needed for the lesson, including any new skills needed to use technology and media.

ASSURE Classroom Case Study

Utilize Resources

Ninth-Grade English

Preview Resources

Tiare Ahu previews the site map and selection properties of DreamWeaver and how to use the digital video camera and iMovie software.

Prepare Resources

Tiare creates a handout that explains what students should do to complete their "Final Year Reflections" in written or video formats. She also adds a "Final Year Reflection" to her sample electronic portfolio.

Prepare the Environment

The lesson will take place in the computer lab and in the video recording studio. Each computer in the lab needs to be checked to ensure that the DreamWeaver and iMovie software programs are functional and that all computers can save to the server and print. The studio needs to be arranged for recording student video reflections by setting up the tripod for the digital video camera and arranging the seating in a location with an appropriate background. Tiare also needs to check that the digital media storage device has enough space to store the student video reflections.

Prepare the Learners

To prepare the students, Tiare introduces the lesson and reviews the learning objectives. Students receive a handout about completing the "Final Year Reflection" for their electronic portfolios. In addition, the handout also includes the evaluation criteria for the reflection.

Provide the Learning Experience

Tiare guides student learning by reviewing how to add reflections to their electronic portfolios and by monitoring students as they create their written or video work.

Video Example 3.3 Utilize Resources

Watch how Tiare Ahu uses a variety of resources to implement the e-portfolio lesson in her ninth-grade English class. In what ways is Tiare Ahu using the "5 P" processes?

Provide the Learning Experience

Now you are ready to provide the instructional experience. A teacher-centered learning experience often involves a presentation, demonstration, drill and practice, or a tutorial. The provision of these learning experiences may require the use of various resources. (See the ASSURE case study for Tiare Ahu's approach to the stage of utilizing resources.)

Application Exercise 3.3

 Check Your Understanding 3.5

Require Learner Participation

As predicted by Bloom, Engelhart, Furst, Hill, and Krathwohl (1956) over 60 years ago, today's global economy will require students to have experience and practice applying, analyzing, synthesizing, and evaluating rather than just knowing and comprehending information. This follows constructivist views that learning is an active mental process built from relevant authentic experiences or **practice** for which students receive **informative feedback,** a response that lets them know the degree to which they have achieved the objective and how to improve their performance. National curriculum, Common Core State Standards, and technology standards have direct applicability when planning active student participation in meaning-ful activities in which students use a variety of technology, media, and resources to support learning.

Practice

The objectives for your lesson explicitly state what students are expected to know and do after instruction. Thus, it is critical to require learner participation through explicit practice with the new knowledge and skills. The ISTE-S supports this level of student participation through the use of a variety of technology and media (ISTE, 2007).

INSPIRING INNOVATION. One common way of requiring learner participation is through the student use of technology to express their creativity and innovative ideas. For example, young children can gain deeper understanding of new vocabulary words, when using software such as KidPix to locate images representing new words and add-ing personal definitions in their own words. Another example involves middle school students creating PowerPoint presentations depicting trends in American folk music over the past 100 years. The activity requires summarizing key ideas from historical documents, choosing the best photos and sound clips, and sequencing content in a meaningful way. At the high school level, social studies students can use spreadsheets to examine national population trends during the past century and make growth pre-dictions for the next 100 years.

SUPPORTING COLLABORATION. A key to preparing students for future careers is to engage them in collaborative activities in which they must communicate through various methods. For example, when using projected still pictures of students liv-ing in Alaska, you can engage students in a lively discussion in which they compare themselves with the students in the photos. Students can then exchange emails with Alaskan students to gain firsthand knowledge of life in Alaska. As another example, if the outcome is to increase student awareness of their right and responsibility to express opinions, student groups could write and submit their ideas to a public opinion section of a local news website.

BUILDING INFORMATION LITERACY SKILLS.   The Internet provides students with instant access to limitless resources. However, students need information literacy skills in order to identify, evaluate, and use information to "make informed decisions, apply knowledge to new situations, and create new knowledge" (ALA, 2007, p. 5). As a teacher, it is critical for you to plan activities that actively engage students in processing information and reporting results that are meaningful for the assigned task. Student research should also include information from books, periodicals, and people, because multiple resources will better ensure that students do not merely cut and paste web-based information into their work. For instance, if your students are to create a concept map of events influencing the rights of women, you want to set expectations for using multiple digital and non-digital resources, paraphrasing content, and providing appropriate citations.

DEVELOPING HIGHER-ORDER THINKING SKILLS.   Today's curriculum and technology standards require students to demonstrate application of critical thinking through activities such as planning and completing a successful project, solving problems, and drawing conclusions. It is important for students of all ages to regularly examine information through the use of tools such as electronic devices (e.g., science probes and microscopes), digital audio and video equipment (e.g., cameras and whiteboards), and a variety of applications (e.g., spreadsheets and databases). If students were addressing the question "Does the person with the most popular votes win a presidential election?" they could download election results into a spreadsheet to compare electoral votes to popular vote totals. To determine whether artificial ponds are as safe for fish as natural ponds, students could gather water samples and use a variety of electronic probes to collect data to compare in a spreadsheet. Young students learning colors could solve the following problem: "Can you find a rainbow in our room?" Student pairs would use a digital camera to photograph items matching each color of the rainbow for a "Rainbows in Our Room" activity book.

Technological tools specifically designed to engage students in problem solving include digital games and simulations. Games use competition, intrigue, and inquisitiveness as vehicles for students to gain content knowledge. An excellent example is Math Blaster, award-winning software that engages students in fast-action games to learn standards-based math content. Simulations use the similar features; yet allow learners great flexibility in making choices that affect outcomes in the games. SimCity is a well-known simulation game in which students design and manage a variety of systems for one or more cities. The design addresses a variety of systems required to support the citizens; for example power, water, taxes, education, transportation, hospitals, and police. The planning also needs to include identification of different zones within the city, such as residential, business, recreational, and industrial, while keeping in mind environmental and safety factors. The overall goal is to create a self-sustaining city with a balanced budget.

USING EDUCATIONAL SOFTWARE FOR PRACTICE.   Educational software provides excellent resources for engaging students with diverse abilities in individualized learning activities focused toward core content knowledge and skills. The programs allow students of lower-than-average abilities to move at their own pace completing practice activities while receiving immediate feedback and remediation. Many software programs provide suggestions for students to try more challenging activities after demonstrating mastery of previous skills.

USING OTHER MEDIA FOR PRACTICE.   Discussions, short quizzes, and application exercises can provide opportunities for practice and feedback during

ASSURE Classroom Case Study

Require Learner Participation

Ninth-Grade English

Student Practice Activities

Students individually write responses to the reflection question, "What did I learn this year about myself; about reading, writing, and learning; and about life generally?" Students have the option of using written or video reflections.

The students use computers and DreamWeaver software as a production tool to add reflection pages to their personal electronic portfolios. Students who choose to write their reflections add them directly to the page. Those choosing video meet with Tiare to record their reflections with a digital camera. The file is then transferred to students' computers for editing with iMovie before uploading to their electronic portfolios.

Feedback

Tiare uses the assignment criteria to review each student's electronic portfolio. She adds individualized comments to each student's file in the grade book section of Blackboard for the electronic portfolio assignment.

Video Example 3.4: Require Learner Participation

As you watch the video, notice various levels of student participation required to create electronic portfolios. Also watch as Tiare Ahu provides feedback to students about their work. In what ways do the activities require students to apply, analyze, synthesize, and/or evaluate information?

instruction. Teacher guides and manuals often suggest techniques and activities for eliciting and reinforcing student responses. However, many of these resources do not integrate the use of technology and media. Therefore, you will need to use applicable components of the ASSURE model to decide where student use of these tools is appropriate.

Feedback

In all cases, learners should receive feedback on their work. The feedback may come from the teacher, or students may work in small groups and give one another feedback. Feedback may also be part of a self-check activity done independently or with a mentor, often using technology. Brookhart (2008) describes various components of feedback for teachers to consider, such as when it is given, criteria used, clarity of feedback to students, and tone—is the feedback positive and will it encourage students to improve.

Check Your Understanding 3.6

Shared Writing Exercise 3.1

Evaluate and Revise

The final component of the ASSURE model, Evaluate and Revise, is essential to the development of quality instruction, yet this component of lesson design is often neglected. Without this step, it is often impossible to know whether instruction is successful or how to revise unsuccessful strategies. It also makes it difficult to judge the efficacy of different types of technology and media without taking the time to evaluate their use.

Evaluate Impact on Student Learning

The ultimate question regarding instruction is whether students have learned what they were supposed to learn. Can they demonstrate the capabilities specified in the stated standards and objectives? The first step in answering this question was taken near the beginning of the ASSURE model, when you formulated your learning objectives, including a criterion of acceptable performance. The next step is to develop assessment tasks that require students to demonstrate the behavior stated in the objective.

The method of assessing achievement depends on the nature of the objective. Some learning objectives call for relatively simple cognitive skills—for example, stating Ohm's law or summarizing the principles of the Declaration of Independence. Learning objectives such as these lend themselves to conventional written tests.

Other objectives may call for process-type behaviors (e.g., outlining a story, solving quadratic equations, or classifying animals), the creation of products (e.g., a sculpture, a written composition, a Prezi presentation, or a portfolio), or an exhibit of attitudes (e.g., choosing to read during free-time activities, placing used paper in the recycle bin, or eating healthy snacks). This type of learning objective requires a more comprehensive, **authentic assessment,** such as a performance-based evaluation of a student's demonstration of learning in a natural context.

Evaluate and Revise Strategies and Resources

Evaluation also includes assessment of your instructional strategies and the resources used to support the lesson. Were the instructional strategies effective? Could they be improved? Did the technology and media resources assist students in meeting the learning objectives? Were they effective in arousing student interest? Did they support meaningful student participation? A key component to the evaluation and revision of a lesson is learner input. You may solicit learner input on the effectiveness of specific media, such as a video, an activity, or on the entire lesson. A student survey similar to Figure 3.2 can be used to collect learner comments.

You can also obtain student feedback regarding your instructional strategies and use of technology and media through discussions and interviews. For example, you may learn that students would have preferred independent study to your choice of group presentation. Or perhaps students didn't like your selection of online resources and feel they would have learned more from watching a video. Your students also may let you know, subtly or not so subtly, that your own performance left something to be desired.

Figure 3.2 Sample Form Used by Students to Evaluate Their Teachers

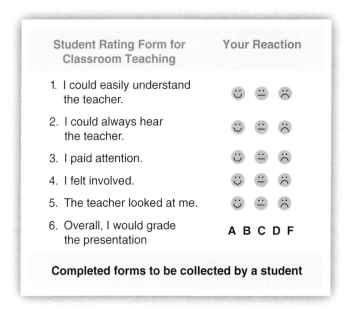

EVALUATION OF TEACHING. Although evaluation of your teaching may evoke some apprehension, the resulting information will provide excellent feedback for addressing areas of needed improvement—and for celebrating areas of high-quality teaching. There are four basic types of teacher evaluation: self, student, peer, and administrator.

1. For self-evaluation, you can create an audio or video recording of your instruction that you then listen to or view at a later time while using an evaluation form such as Figure 3.3.

2. Students, even in early grades, can provide valuable feedback through age-appropriate surveys. Students may be reluctant to "evaluate" their teacher in open-class discussions, but might share ideas in a group or submit comments anonymously.

3. You may ask a colleague, or peer, usually another teacher, to sit in the back of the room and observe your teaching skills. Feedback could be given in an open-ended evaluation (blank sheet of paper) or you may design a form that addresses areas for which you would like to receive feedback.

4. In most schools, administrators visit teachers on a scheduled sequence, often annually, semiannually, or more frequently due to increased teacher accountability. You may ask an administrator to visit more frequently on an "unofficial" basis. Many schools have a standard form that administrators use to observe teachers and provide feedback to them. You may also inform your administrator of other characteristics you would like her to observe.

Revision of Strategies and Resources

The final step of the instructional cycle is to sit back and look at your assessment and evaluation data. Examine discrepancies between your intentions and what actually happened. Did student achievement fall short on one or more of the learning objectives? How did students react to the instructional strategies and lesson resources? Are you satisfied with the value of the materials you selected?

Figure 3.3 Sample Presentation Evaluation Form for Self, Peer, or Administrator

Presentation Evaluation Form

Teacher _____ Evaluator _____ Date _____

SA = Strongly Agree   A = Agree   D = Disagree   SD = Strongly Disagree

1. Presenter appeared nervous.   SA   A   D   SD
    Comment...

2. Content was delivered well.   SA   A   D   SD
    Comment...

3. Movement enhanced presentation.   SA   A   D   SD
    Comment...

4. Voice was natural and conversational.   SA   A   D   SD
    Comment...

5. Vocal variety was used.   SA   A   D   SD
    Comment...

6. Presenter could be easily heard.   SA   A   D   SD
    Comment...

7. There were no distracting mannerisms.   SA   A   D   SD
    Comment...

8. Eye contact was established and maintained.   SA   A   D   SD
    Comment...

9. Natural gestures were used.   SA   A   D   SD
    Comment...

10. Overall, presentation was well done.   SA   A   D   SD
    Comment...

Strengths of presenter
....
....

Weaknesses of presenter
....
....

Overall comments
....
....

ASSURE Classroom Case Study

Evaluate and Revise

Ninth-Grade English

Assessment of Learner Achievement

Tiare Ahu uses the following rating form to evaluate students' Final Year Reflections:

Reflection Rating Scale

  1 = Response is minimal, primarily states facts

  2 = Response is adequate, reveals moderate reflection

  3 = Detailed response that demonstrates meaningful reflection

- At what level did the student write reflections for each item in question 1, "What did I learn about the following?"
  - Myself
  - Reading
  - Writing
  - Learning
  - Overall
- At what level did the student write a reflection for question 2, "What do I hope to accomplish in these areas next year when I am a sophomore?"

Technology Rating Scale

  1 = Did not complete task as describe

  2 = Completed task as described

- Did the student use DreamWeaver software to create a new page titled "Final Year Reflections" in his or her electronic portfolio folder?
- Did the student add a written or video reflection to the "Final Year Reflections" page in his or her DreamWeaver electronic portfolio folder?

Evaluation of Strategies and Resources

To evaluate the strategies and resources utilized, Tiare conducts debriefing activities with the students. In addition, she talks informally with students during the entire process. Tiare invites comments that address the importance of using an electronic portfolio to assess learning over time. The primary purpose of this debriefing session is to determine whether the students think creating electronic portfolios is worthwhile. In addition, they are asked to write their ideas for improving the lesson.

Revision

The students and Tiare complete a teacher-developed form for an overall evaluation of learner achievement, strategies, and resources. Tiare compares the student responses and overall average rating with her own perceptions. For items that appear discrepant, she will address the need for revision in her choice of learning activities, resource selections, and evaluation materials.

Video Example 3.5: Evaluate and Revise

Watch the Evaluate and Revise segment of Tiare Ahu's lesson and listen to her talk about her ideas and strategies for evaluating ninth grade students' electronic portfolios. What recommendation to other teachers do you find most helpful regarding implementing ePortfolios in your classroom?

Reflect on the lesson and each component of it. Make notes immediately following completion of the lesson, and refer to them before you implement the lesson again. If your evaluation data indicate shortcomings, now is the time to go back to the faulty part of the plan and revise it. The model works, but only if you constantly use it to upgrade the quality of your instruction (as in the ASSURE case study).

 Check Your Understanding 3.7

Summary

This chapter introduced you to the ASSURE model, which incorporates six critical aspects of instructional planning. The chapter placed key emphasis on seven learning outcomes:

- *Describe the ASSURE model.* The ASSURE model uses six steps to systematically plan lessons that effectively use technology and media to support and enhance student learning.

- *State the three primary types of information used to analyze learners and describe the role of the information in the systematic planning process for learning.* The key areas to consider during learner analysis include (1) general characteristics of learners, (2) specific entry competencies (knowledge, skills, and attitudes about the topic), and (3) learning differences and needs.

- *Demonstrate how to go from national standards to learning objectives that include the audience, behavior, conditions, and degree of mastery.* Begin with your district's curriculum and technology standards, which are based on state and national student performance criteria. Well-stated objectives name the learners for whom the objective is intended, the action (behavior) to be demonstrated, the conditions, or technology and media that supports learning, and the degree to which the new knowledge or skill must be mastered.

- *Outline the procedures for selecting, modifying, and designing instructional strategies and resources.* There are three primary steps involved in selecting, modifying, and designing instructional strategies: 1) Describe the instructional strategies and resources (e.g., technology, media, and materials) that are essential to the lesson; 2) Provide a rationale for each selection and any needed modifications; and 3) Use selection rubrics to evaluate the resources that best help students meet the intended outcomes.

- *Create examples of the five basic steps in utilizing resources (e.g., technology, media, and materials).* In order to plan your teaching role for utilizing resources intended to help students achieve the learning objectives, implement the 5 Ps process: Preview the resources; Prepare the resources; Prepare the environment; Prepare the learners; and Provide the learning experience.

- *Describe and justify methods for eliciting student participation when using technology and media during instruction.* To be effective, instruction should require learners' active mental engagement. It is critical to engage students in active learning that involves practice with the new knowledge or skills, use of technology and media, and provision of performance feedback. Feedback can come from the teacher, digital devices, other students, or self-evaluation.

- *Compare and contrast the techniques for evaluating student achievement, strategies, and resources and for making databased revisions.* After implementing a lesson, use traditional and authentic assessments to evaluate its impact on student learning. It is critical to also examine the entire instructional process and the impact of using technology and media. Wherever there are discrepancies between learning objectives and student outcomes, revise the lesson plan to address the areas of concern.

ASSURE Lesson Plan Template

Analyze Learners

- Describe general characteristics of the class as a whole—age, grade, and so forth.
- Describe entry competencies or types of knowledge expected of the learners before instruction.
- Describe the learning differences and needs of students.

State Standards and Objectives

- List curriculum and technology standards to be achieved.
- Describe the learning objectives using the ABCD format.

Select Strategies and Resources

- Describe the strategies and resources (e.g., technology, media, and materials) that are essential to the lesson.
- Provide a rationale for each selection and any needed modifications.
- Use selection rubrics to evaluate resources that best help students meet the intended outcomes.

Utilize Resources

- Preview resources (It is essential to know the technology, media, and materials prior to teaching with them.)
- Prepare resources (Practice using the technology, media, and materials prior to the lesson.)

- Prepare the environment (Arrange the facilities for effective use of the technology, media, and materials.)
- Prepare the learners (Knowing what is expected of them helps ensure learner involvement in the learning.)
- Provide the learning experience (Provide teacher-centered and student-centered learning experiences.)

Require Learner Participation

- Require active mental engagement by learners.
- Engage learners in practice of new knowledge or skills.
- Support learning with technology and media.
- Provide performance feedback prior to formal assessment.

Evaluate and Revise

- Use traditional and authentic assessments to determine learner achievement of stated standards and objectives.
- Examine the entire instructional process and the impact of using technology and media.
- If discrepancies between learning objectives and student outcomes are identified, revise the lesson plan to address the areas of concern.

Professional Development

Demonstrating Professional Skills

The Demonstrate Professional Skills activities in the remaining chapters are designed to address many of the ISTE Standards for Teachers (ISTE, 2008). Items aligned to ISTE Standards for Teachers are noted with the standard number in parentheses.

1. Write a learner analysis of your students or those you plan to teach. Describe their general characteristics, note their specific entry competencies for a topic of your choice, and discuss their learning differences and needs. If you are not yet a teacher, you may need to do some research on students in the grade level you plan to teach.

2. Write at least five learning objectives for a lesson you might teach and assess each objective with the Objectives Checklist (Figure 3.1).

3. Select a topic you might teach that would incorporate student use of technology and develop a set of learning strategies, resources, and associated assessment instruments (including traditional and authentic assessments) (ISTE Standards for Teachers 2.A, 2.C, and 2.D).

4. Locate a lesson, perhaps using the Internet, which does *not* provide learner practice and feedback. Design activities for the lesson that provide those elements.

Building Your Professional Portfolio

An important component for continuing your professional development is the creation of a professional portfolio to demonstrate the knowledge and skills gained from this text. Following the model shown in this section of each chapter you will have the opportunity to create, enhance, and reflect on lessons developed for each chapter.

- *Creating My Lesson.* Using the ASSURE model, design a lesson for a scenario from the Lesson Scenarios in the Appendix, from an example in the chapter; or use a scenario of your own design. You can do this by selecting a content area standard or topic you plan to teach. Be sure to include information about the learners, the learning objectives, and all other elements of the ASSURE model. When you have finished developing your lesson plan, reflect on the process you used and what you have learned about matching learners, content, strategies, technology, media, and materials.

- *Reflecting on My Lesson.* Reflect on the lesson you created for this chapter and on how you might enhance the lesson. Address the following in your reflections: How did use of the ASSURE model strengthen the lesson? What aspect of the ASSURE model do you consider the most critical for the lesson you created? How could your ASSURE lesson be improved? (ISTE Standards for Teachers 4.B and 5.C)

- *Enhancing My Lesson.* Enhance the lesson plan you created by describing how you would meet the diverse needs of learners in your class. Specifically, describe strategies you would include for students who already possess the knowledge and skills targeted in your lesson plan. Also describe strategies, technology, and media you could integrate to assist students who have not met the lesson prerequisites or who have disabilities that impact how they learn. For example, how would you meet the needs of students with visual or hearing limitations, or the needs of students who are reading below or above grade level?

Describe other types of technology and media that can be integrated into your instructional strategies for the lesson. If the lesson requires students to create a report, you might consider having students develop interactive presentations that embed digital photos, videos, and animations to depict what they learned. Or if students use drill-and-practice software to learn basic facts, you could have them create their own PowerPoint electronic flashcard practice set to achieve a higher level of student engagement (ISTE Standards for Teachers 2.A, 2.B, 2.C, 3.B, and 4.B).

Suggested Resources

Print Resources

Ambrose, S. A., Bridges, M. W., DiPietro, M., Lovett, M. C., & Norman, M. K. (2010). *How learning works: 7 research-based principles for smart teaching.* San Francisco, CA: Jossey-Bass.

Ribble, M. (2015). *Digital citizenship in schools: Nine elements all students should know.* (3rd ed.). Washington, DC: International Society for Technology in Education.

Baker, F. W. (2012). *Media literacy in the K-12 classroom.* Washington, DC: International Society for Technology in Education.

Brooks-Young, S. J. (2013). *Making technology standards work for you* (3rd ed.). Washington, DC: International Society for Technology in Education.

Carr-Chellman, A. A. (2015). *Instructional design for teachers.* (2nd ed.) New York: Routledge.

Gregory, G. H. & Kuzmich, L. M. (2014). *Data driven differentiation in the standards-based classroom* (2nd ed.). Thousand Oaks, CA: Corwin.

Stiggins, R. J. & Chappuis, J. (2012). *An introduction to student-involved assessment for learning* (6th ed.). Boston: Pearson Education.

Online Resources and Apps

Common Curriculum

Common Curriculum provides a browser-based environment that provides tools for teachers to create and save lessons and units and to collaborate and share materials with other teachers. The site is designed to support alignment of lessons with the Common Core State Standards.

Lessons Plans for Teachers

This site provides a variety of lesson plans organized by subject area and grade level and a Lesson Directories section with links to multiple sites focused on providing teacher resources to develop/modify lesson plans. Also provided is the Lesson Planning Help section that provides links to resources such as Lesson Plan Guidelines, Lesson Plan Software, and Finding Lessons Online.

Seesaw App

Seesaw is a free student driven digital portfolio app available for teachers to integrate into any grade level. The app enables students to capture and organize learning with photos and videos of physical work or digital creations.

Students can use built-in audio recording, drawing, and caption tools to add learning reflections. Teachers have immediate access to uploaded content from any device and can invite families to interact through their child's portfolio.

Digital Resources for Lifelong Learners of All Ages

This site offers links to educational materials for a range of learners on multiple topic areas and grade levels. The site includes sections for Social Media Connections, Course Website Materials, Personal and Professional Resources, and also maintains a Recent Updates section.

EdTechTeacher

The mission of EdTechTeacher is to support educators in their quest to enrich student learning experiences through emerging technologies. The site includes tutorials and helpful links, tech tools by subject and skill, innovative projects and lessons, live (free) webinars, assessments and rubrics, as well as recommendations for using Google and other educational apps. The site also hosts an active EdTechTeacher Blog that offers weekly resources as well as discussions on current topics of interest to teachers.

Education World

Education World provides current news, information, and online resources for teachers, administrators, and school staff. The site includes links for Teacher Essentials, Lesson Plans, and Technology. Teachers are provided with numerous classroom-ready resources and tips for using digital devices with students. Also available are reviews of apps, websites, and tech products as well as multiple professional development articles.

Kathy Schrock's Guide to Everything

Kathy Schrock has been actively involved with educational technology since the early 1990s, and is internationally known for her "practical presentations dealing with pedagogically-sound practices for the embedding of technology seamlessly into teaching and learning." Her site provides numerous workshop links, such as: Twitter for teachers, App for that, Information literacy, Digital storytelling, Google tools, and Video of the month.

Chapter 4
Designing Digital Learning Environments

Monkey Business Images/Shutterstock

Learning Outcomes

This chapter addresses ISTE Standards for Educators 1, 4, 5, and 6.

4.1 Describe 10 learning strategies used in the classroom.

4.2 Discuss how to integrate technology and media into learning strategies.

4.3 Differentiate between types of learning contexts.

4.4 Describe the value of integrating free and inexpensive materials into instruction.

Goal

Understand how to select appropriate learning strategies and integrate effective use technology and media to design digital learning environments.

ASSURE Classroom Case Study

The ASSURE Classroom Case Study for this chapter describes the instructional strategies used by teachers Lindsay Kaiser and Jena Marshall, who co-teach a fifth-grade social studies class at a school in a middle-income rural neighborhood. The students read at or above grade level and are experienced users of a variety of technology applications. Each student is equipped with a laptop with high-speed Internet access. The teachers are challenged by the students' lack of interest in U.S. history and try to address this concern by engaging students in a variety of activities about the Lewis and Clark expedition. A key activity includes designing a boat that could have been used by Lewis and Clark. The lesson begins with student pairs completing an interactive Lewis and Clark WebQuest to learn about the expedition and various "boat issues" they faced. To assist with the boat design, students conduct Internet searches to expand on information learned from the WebQuest. Students create an advertisement to sell their boat and write a letter to the president of a boat manufacturing company to seek interest in reproducing the Lewis and Clark boat. The students with the best design will receive an award.

Video segments throughout this chapter explore how Ms. Kaiser and Ms. Marshall design digital learning environments that enhance student learning.

Introduction

The explosion of available information requires teachers to create digital learning environments that engage this generation of students in authentic experiences to promote increased knowledge and skills and a better understanding of the world around them. As we explore a variety of instructional strategies and settings, such as the cooperative learning arrangement used by Ms. Kaiser and Ms. Marshall, we examine foundational components of a digital learning environment. First, we examine 10 commonly used learning strategies, discussing the advantages and limitations of each. Next are ideas for integrating technology and media when using the learning strategies. Following that is an overview of five learning contexts frequently used in PK-12 classrooms coupled with guidelines for how to use technology and media to support learning experiences within each context. The final section provides ideas for integrating free and inexpensive materials into instruction, their advantages and limitations, and suggestions for obtaining and evaluating them. As you will see, well-planned instructional strategies supported with appropriate technology and media not only promote student learning, but also better prepare students for future careers.

Types of Learning Strategies

There are 10 common types of instructional strategies used in classrooms: 1) presentations, 2) demonstrations, 3) drill-and-practice, 4) tutorials, 5) discussions, 6) problem-based learning, 7) cooperative learning, 8) gaming, 9) simulations, and 10) discovery. We provide an overview of each strategy and discuss the advantages and limitations of each.

Presentations

In a presentation, the teacher or students dramatize or otherwise disseminate information. Information sources include the teacher, guest speakers, textbooks, Internet sites, audio, video, or other students. Presentations can be highly interactive, involving questions and comments between the teacher and learners as a whole class or in small groups.

Technology can play a major role during a presentation, such as by including a live Internet broadcast from the International Space Station, a podcast of an author reading her poetry, or a concept map of bird migration that students build on an interactive whiteboard. However, classroom presentations can also involve non-digital support, such as reading a book or giving a lecture.

When planning presentations, Heick (2013) offers four suggestions for better ensuring effective outcomes. First, the presentation should be adaptive to meet the varying needs of students. Some students will need basic information, while some will be ready for more detailed descriptions. Second, focus on concepts and principles rather than factual information. Concepts and principles lead to better transfer of knowledge. The third recommendation is to consider student's individual learning profiles. This may involve providing information in different modes, visual, auditory, and tactile or including examples familiar to the different cultures represented by your students. The fourth suggestion is to collaborate with other teachers who are also teaching your students to identify areas in which it would be useful to provide consistent support and instruction across content areas.

ADVANTAGES OF PRESENTATIONS. The use of presentation learning strategies offers several advantages. Some key advantages include:

- *Present once.* You only have to present the information once for all the students.
- *Note-taking strategies.* Students can use a number of different note-taking strategies to capture the information presented.

- *Information sources.* Technology and media resources can serve as quality sources for the most current information.
- *Student presentations.* Students can present information they have learned to the whole class or a small group.

LIMITATIONS OF PRESENTATIONS. The use of presentation learning strategies also has some limitations, including the following:

- *Difficult for some students.* Not all students respond well to a presentation format to learn information; therefore, the lesson will need to include more than one way of presenting content (e.g., reading, listening, or viewing a video).
- *Potentially boring.* Without interaction, a presentation can be very boring. It is important to include ways to keep students interactive through questions and answers, check sheets to complete, or dialog.
- *Note-taking difficulty.* Students may need to learn how to take notes to benefit from a presentation. One solution is to provide a partially completed notes sheet to assist with note-taking skills.
- *Age appropriateness.* Younger students may have difficulty sitting for lengthy presentations, so it is important to adjust presentation time based on student age and attention level.

Demonstrations

During **demonstrations**, learners view an exhibition of a skill or procedure to be learned. Demonstrations can be used with a whole class, a small group, or an individual who needs a little extra explanation on how to do a task. With younger students, you can demonstrate basic procedures such as how to print letters, use a digital camera, or pronounce a word. When working with older students, you might demonstrate more complicated processes, such as how to solve an algebra problem, read tables of historical data, create interactive websites, or understand the way something works.

The purpose of the demonstration may be for your learners to imitate a physical performance, such as using a digital wind gauge, or to adopt the attitudes exemplified when you serve as a role model, such as how to ask questions when working in cooperative groups. In some cases, the point is simply to illustrate how something works, such as the effect of heat on a bimetallic strip. **Just-in-time peer demonstrations** often take the form of one-on-one sessions, with an experienced student showing a peer how to perform a procedure, such as using the copy/paste function in a word processing program. Demonstration allows your students to ask questions you can answer during active learning experiences.

ADVANTAGES OF DEMONSTRATIONS. As seen, demonstrations are a commonly used learning strategy due to advantages such as the following:

- *Seeing before doing.* Students benefit by seeing something done before they do it.
- *Task guidance.* A teacher can simultaneously guide a large group of students to complete a task.
- *Economy of supplies.* Only a limited number of supplies are necessary because not everyone will be handling materials.
- *Safety.* A demonstration allows the teacher to control the potential danger to students when using caustic materials or dangerous equipment.

LIMITATIONS OF DEMONSTRATIONS. Although demonstrations can yield beneficial outcomes, they can also include the following limitations:

- *Not hands-on.* Students do not get direct hands-on experience unless they are following along as the teacher demonstrates steps or skills.

- *Limited view.* Every student may not have an equal view of the demonstration, thus possibly missing some aspect of the experience. A technological solution involves using a document camera to project the demonstration.
- *Nonflexible pacing.* Not all students may be able to follow the demonstration's pace of presentation. Recording the procedure on video will allow students to review the demonstration as needed.

Drill-and-Practice

In **drill-and-practice**, learners complete practice exercises to refresh or increase fluency in content knowledge and skills, most commonly in mathematics, language arts, and second languages. Use of this strategy assumes that your learners have received some instruction on the concept, principle, or procedure they are practicing. To be effective, the drill-and-practice exercises should include feedback to reinforce correct responses and to remediate errors learners might make along the way. As seen in the Technology for All Learners: English Language Learners, digital drill-and-practice works well for students who are learning English.

ADVANTAGES OF DRILL-AND-PRACTICE.   Drill-and-practice is a commonly used learning strategy due to advantages such as:

- *Corrective feedback.* Students receive feedback on their responses.
- *Information chunking.* Information is presented in small chunks, allowing students to review the material in small bits.
- *Built-in practice.* Practice is built into the small chunks of information, giving immediate opportunities to try out the new knowledge in some positive way.

LIMITATIONS OF DRILL-AND-PRACTICE.   Along with advantages, there are also some limitations associated with the use of drill-and-practice, which include:

- *Repetitive.* Not all students respond well to the repetitive nature of drill-and-practice. It is important to limit the time spent or number of exercises to prevent monotony.

Technology for All Learners

English Language Learners

Nearly 10% of public school students are English language learners (ELLs) with approximately 75% of those speaking Spanish (NCES, 2017). Thus, teachers often need to help ELL students with learning English as well as content area knowledge and skills. Excellent digital resources are readily available to engage students in drill-and-practice activities to help students learn to speak, read, and write in English. Examples include:

- *Listen and repeat videos.* Free online videos, often on YouTube, provide vocabulary words in the student's home language and also in English, followed by the narrator pronouncing the word in English.
- *Alphabet Books.* Online books are organized by the English alphabet. For each letter, an English word that starts with the letter is provided (e.g., Flower) along with the same word in the student's home language (e.g., Flor for Spanish) and an image to help understanding (e.g., a daisy). Students can also create their own digital or paper alphabet books.
- *Matching Games.* Online matching games in which students must select the English word to match an image or a word in their home language. Free games are readily available for multiple topics, such as animals, family, shapes, fruit, transportation, etc.
- *Flashcards.* Digital flashcards are another option for teachers with ELL students. Free online ELL flashcards sometimes offer options for listening to the pronunciation of the word, using a timed setting for recognizing the name from three or four options, or using them in a traditional fashion for learning the new words.

- *Potentially boring.* Some drill-and-practice materials have too many items, which can lead to boredom. A solution is to review the content and only assign material that is relevant.

- *Non-adaptive.* If a student is making repeated errors, continued use of drill-and-practice material does not help the student learn. Keep track of student progress and use a different intervention if learning doesn't improve.

Tutorials

Tutorials involve learners working with an agent—in the form of a person, computer software, or special printed materials—that presents the content, poses questions or problems, requests the learner's responses, analyzes the responses, supplies appropriate feedback, and provides practice until the learner demonstrates a predetermined level of competency. Your students often work independently or with a partner as they are provided chunks of information designed to build knowledge. Students learn through practice with feedback after each small section. The difference between a tutorial and drill-and-practice is that the tutorial introduces and teaches new material, whereas the drill-and-practice focuses on content previously taught in another type of lesson (e.g., presentation).

ADVANTAGES OF TUTORIALS.   Tutorials are a time-honored learning strategy that yields key advantages:

- *Independent work.* Students can work independently on new material and receive feedback about their progress.

- *Self-paced.* Students can work at their own pace, repeating information if they need to review it before moving on to the next section of the material.

- *Individualization.* Computer-based tutorials respond to students' input by directing their study to new topics when content is mastered or to remediation activities when review is needed.

LIMITATIONS OF TUTORIALS.   In contrast, tutorials are also coupled with some limitations, including:

- *Potentially boring.* The repetition can become boring if the tutorial follows a single pattern that lacks variation.

- *Possibly frustrating.* Students can become frustrated if they do not seem to be making progress while working on the tutorial. Care needs to be taken to assign students to tutorials that are aligned with their abilities.

- *Potential lack of guidance.* The lack of a teacher's guidance can mean that a student does not move through the tutorial effectively. To avoid this, teachers must carefully select tutorials and provide ongoing support when they are used.

Discussions

As a strategy, **discussions** involve the exchange of ideas and opinions among students or among students and the teacher. Available at any time during instruction in small or large groups, it is a useful way of assessing the knowledge, skills, and attitudes of a group of students before determining instructional objectives, particularly when introducing a new topic or at the beginning of the school year when the teacher is less familiar with the students. Discussion can help you establish the kind of rapport within the group that fosters collaborative and cooperative learning.

Discussions can be an effective way to introduce a new topic or to delve more deeply into foundational concepts. You can lead discussions by introducing questions to elicit student responses or assign discussion topics to student groups. You may need to prepare your students for a discussion strategy when they are not familiar with the expectations for their participation. Be sure to focus questions on what you wish to have students learn. Also, use higher-level questions involving "What if . . . ?" and "How would . . . ?" to encourage deeper thinking about the topic or issue.

To encourage everyone to participate, you might begin with small groups of two to three students to share their ideas, which will then be shared with the class for further discussion. Other general guidelines for using discussions as a learning strategy include: involving a guest speaker, using fun props or other creative elements such as a game or debate format, establishing rules to keep the discussion fair and orderly, encouraging students to use examples, and keeping teacher input to a minimum (Gupta, 2016).

ADVANTAGES OF DISCUSSIONS.   When discussions are used as a learning strategy, advantages can include:

- *Interesting.* Students often find discussions more interesting than sitting and listening to someone tell them facts.
- *Challenging.* Discussions challenge students to think about the topic and apply what they already know.
- *Inclusive.* Rather than having only a few students answering teacher questions, discussion provides opportunities for all students to speak.
- *Opportunity for new ideas.* Discussions can be a way to bring in new ideas to the information presentation.

LIMITATIONS OF DISCUSSIONS.   Using discussions in the classroom can also present limitations, such as the following:

- *Potential for limited participation.* Not all students participate in discussions; therefore, it is important for the teacher to be certain that everyone has a chance to talk.
- *Sometimes unchallenging.* Sometimes students don't learn beyond what they already know and are not challenged to extend their knowledge during a discussion.
- *Difficulty level.* Some questions asked to elicit a discussion may be too difficult for students to consider based on their level of knowledge.
- *Age appropriateness.* Discussions may not be an effective strategy to use with younger students without teacher direction.

Problem-Based Learning

Lifelike problems can provide an excellent starting point for learning. In the process of grappling with real-world challenges, your students acquire the knowledge and skills needed for success in today's workforce. Through the use of **problem-based learning**, your students actively seek solutions to structured or ill-structured problems situated in the real world.

Structured problems present students with a clear sense of what might constitute an appropriate response. For example, math word problems are often structured applications of math computation skills students already possess. On the other hand, **ill-structured problems** can be solved in more than one way. For example, if your students are asked to propose solutions to increase student participation in school recycling, multiple responses will be submitted. Because there is more than one correct way to solve the problem, tools such as rubrics will be needed to assess whether your students have attained the stated objectives.

A variety of digital devices and apps provide the environment and tools students use to access, manipulate, and display information collected to solve problems. Use of these tools builds and supports student cognitive learning strategies and critical-thinking skills, while reinforcing and establishing stronger content knowledge.

ADVANTAGES OF PROBLEM-BASED LEARNING.   Multiple advantages are seen when students engage in problem-based learning. Examples include:

- *Engaging.* Students are actively engaged in real-world learning experiences.
- *Context for learning.* The relationship between knowledge and skill becomes apparent as students work toward a problem solution.
- *Levels of complexity.* Introducing additional problem issues over time can control the level of problem complexity.

LIMITATIONS OF PROBLEM-BASED LEARNING.   The limitations of problem-based learning should also be considered when selecting learning strategies, such as:

- *Difficult to create.* Creating quality problems for learning can be difficult. It can help to develop problem-based lessons with other teachers and to use web resources.
- *Age appropriateness.* Age and experience levels of students may mean that the teacher will need to adjust a problem to ensure that students will have a successful experience.
- *Time consuming.* Creating and using problem-based lessons can be very time consuming. Use the ASSURE evaluation step to refine and reuse lessons.

Video Example 4:1: Problem-Based Learning

Watch this video and observe how Ms. Kaiser and Ms. Marshall describe the Lewis and Clark lesson. What features of this lesson reflect the use of a problem-based learning strategy? In what ways did Ms. Kaiser and Ms. Marshall engage students during the problem-based learning?

Cooperative Learning

Cooperative learning is a grouping strategy in which students work together to assist each other's learning. There is long-standing and foundational research support regarding the effectiveness of students learning from each other when they work on projects as a team (Johnson & Johnson, 1999; Slavin, 1989–1990). Specifically, Johnson and Johnson (1999) suggest the following conditions need to be present for successful cooperative learning groups:

- Members view their role as part of a whole team
- Interactive engagement occurs among the members of the group

- Both individual and group share accountability
- Interpersonal and leadership skills are displayed
- The ability to reflect on personal learning and group function is engaged.

As a teacher, you can create formal cooperative groups designed to ensure that specific learning outcomes will be accomplished by assigning specific roles to each member of the group, such as secretary, time keeper, task director, and so on. Cooperative learning experiences can be informal as well. Students may determine their own learning needs and work with others to enhance their learning experiences. Informal groups will need to be monitored to ensure that all students in the group benefit from the interactions.

Many educators have criticized the competitive atmosphere that dominates many classrooms and interferes with students learning from each other. To instead allow students to gain knowledge from each other, you can engage them in cooperative learning situations. Cooperative learning has the additional benefit of equipping your students with the skills required for success in today's world of work.

ADVANTAGES OF COOPERATIVE LEARNING. Cooperative learning has a long history of providing several advantages to student learning, as seen in the following examples:

- *Learning benefits.* Mixing the ability levels of students within a group leads to learning benefits for all.
- *Formal or informal.* Groups can be informal or formal based on the learning requirements.
- *Learning opportunity.* Long-term groups can be developed, creating multiple learning opportunities.
- *Content areas.* Cooperative learning can be used with all content areas.

LIMITATIONS OF COOPERATIVE LEARNING. Even though cooperative groups can benefit learning, you will need to be aware of the following limitations when using this strategy:

- *Size limitation.* Groups need to be kept small (three to five students) to ensure equal participation.
- *Potential overuse.* If the strategy is overused, it can lose its effectiveness. Choose cooperative learning when student learning will be enhanced from discussion and sharing ideas.
- *Group member limitation.* Grouping members of the same ability level does not enhance learning opportunities for all students. Form groups carefully to ensure that multiple levels of ability are represented.

Gaming

Educational gaming provides a competitive environment in which learners follow prescribed rules as they strive to attain a challenging goal. Involving from one to several learners, games are highly motivating, especially for tedious and repetitive content. Games often require learners to use **problem-solving skills** in figuring out solutions or to demonstrate mastery of specific content demanding a high degree of accuracy and efficiency.

Use of games has been shown to increase learning as compared to traditional learning methods due to the added value of features such as challenge, interactivity, multimedia, feedback, fantasy, and realism (Graesser, 2017). Early research showed that by playing games, students begin to recognize patterns found in particular situations, take on participant roles within a game, and become immersed in the decision-making process as they search for solutions (Smutny & von Fremd, 2009). For example, young children playing a game of Concentration will learn to match patterns and increase their memory recall. Older students can learn French, German, Italian, or Spanish with Leonardo's Language Bridge game, in which students are taken on a fun adventure requiring use of the new language to build virtual bridges over a variety of obstacles. An online stock market game engages your students in determining how best to invest an imaginary sum of money. They need to make choices for their investments, deciding the best way to raise additional funds. Along the way, the game reinforces math and literacy skills and helps students develop an understanding of financial responsibility.

Challenging and fun to play, computer and traditional games add variety to learning experiences and offer opportunities to practice skills. Students like to play games and benefit by extending their learning experiences into challenging environments.

ADVANTAGES OF GAMING.   As seen, gaming offers several advantages, which include:

- *Engaging.* Students are quickly engaged in learning through games.
- *Match to outcomes.* Games can be adapted to match learning outcomes.
- *Variety of settings.* Games can be used in a variety of classroom settings, from whole-class to individual activities.
- *Gain attention.* Most games are colorful, interactive, and competitive, helping to gain student attention for learning specific topics or skills.

LIMITATIONS OF GAMING.   As with other learning strategies, the use of games also includes limitations, as described:

- *Competition concerns.* Because of the orientation to winning, games can become too competitive unless caution is used.
- *Levels of difficulty.* Less able students may find the game structure too fast or difficult. Provide alternate games to match student ability levels.
- *Expense.* Games, such as computer games, can be expensive to purchase. Often a similar game is available for free on the Web.
- *Misdirection of intention.* The learning outcomes may be lost because of the interest in winning rather than learning. Make sure to clearly state learning objectives before students use games.

Simulations

Simulations allow learners to confront a scaled-down version of a real-life situation. It permits realistic practice without the expense or risks otherwise involved. With the advent of newer technology, 3-D simulations are readily available on the Web or as educational apps experienced with mobile technology and viewing devices. Simulation may also involve participant dialog and manipulation of materials and equipment.

Simulations can be used as whole-class, small-group, or individual activities, offering experiences that might not otherwise be possible in the real world. For example, through role-playing your students can learn about the various aspects of voting by engaging in a class election process. They can create campaign information, determine voter registration guidelines, set up voting booths, and elect a counting commission to record and report the results.

Beyond role-playing, simulations can represent situations that may be too large or too complex to bring into your classroom. For example, in a science lesson about internal combustion, you can use two types of simulation resources. For direct hands-on experience, you can use a small color-coded automobile engine model that your students can manipulate to learn about internal combustion. Then your students can watch a 3-D simulation of an engine, such as the 4-Stroke Engine Simulator, to see it in action. By using the model engine and viewing the 3-D simulation, your students are able to get the inside look they need to help them understand the concepts being presented, while being protected from the hazards of operating a real engine.

Online simulations such as Gizmos provided by ExploreLearning, and other suggested websites at the end of this chapter, provide another type of simulated learning experience. The Gizmos site provides grade 3–12 numerous interactive simulations searchable by academic standard, grades and topics, and textbook. Additionally, lesson materials and teacher community comments and recommendations are included.

ADVANTAGES OF SIMULATIONS. Using simulations offers advantages such as:

- *Safety.* Simulations provide a safe way to engage in a learning experience.
- *Recreate history.* May be the only way to engage in the situation (e.g., role-playing ancient Roman history).
- *Hands-on.* Simulations offer opportunities for hands-on experience.
- *Variety of ability levels.* Students of all ability levels can be included in simulation experiences.

LIMITATIONS OF SIMULATIONS. Some limitations associated with use of simulations include:

- *Questionable representation.* May not be accurate representation of the actual event when the simulation is an artist's rendering rather than video or photos of an event.
- *Complexity.* May become too complex or intense for the classroom setting. Review all simulations before use and only integrate relevant sections.
- *Time factor.* May require too much time to complete. Search for a simulation that demonstrates targeted concepts in a shorter time frame.

Discovery

The **discovery** strategy uses an inductive, or inquiry, approach to learning that fosters a deeper understanding of the content through the learner's involvement with it. A common approach to discovery is the **scientific method**, which involves creating a hypothesis or question, trying out a possible solution, and analyzing the information learned to determine whether the approach worked. Various software applications, such as spreadsheets, databases, and concept-mapping, and digital devices, such as science probes and microscopes, assist students in organizing, analyzing, and reporting data and information needed to discover the answer to a question.

When using the ASSURE model or other lesson plans to design discovery lessons, ensure that the selected strategies include sufficient guidance and support when students are using digital devices to solve the problem. This will involve a carefully planned **scaffold** approach, building on prior knowledge as students move through the learning experience. For instance, you will need to consider what supports will be needed if students struggle to complete a step along the way as they move through the experience.

ADVANTAGES OF DISCOVERY. Discovery learning strategy provides advantages that include:

- *Engaging.* Discovery is very engaging for students at all levels of learning.
- *Repeated steps.* When using discovery learning, you can use procedures or steps that have been taught previously.
- *Student control of learning.* Discovery learning allows students the feeling of control over their own learning.

LIMITATIONS OF DISCOVERY.   Limitations to consider when implementing discovery include the following:

- *Time factor.* Discovery can be time consuming for design and implementation. An option is to adapt web-based discovery lessons.
- *Preparation is critical.* Discovery requires the teacher to think through all the possible issues that students might encounter. This becomes easier with practice.
- *Misunderstanding.* This strategy may lead to misunderstandings about a content area. Make sure to debrief students after a discovery lesson.

Application Exercise 4.1

  Check Your Understanding 4.1

Integration of Technology and Media into Learning Strategies

We provide recommendations, tips, and ideas for integrating a variety of technology and media into 10 instructional strategies commonly used in classrooms. The strategies discussed are: 1) presentations, 2) demonstrations, 3) drill-and-practice, 4) tutorials, 5) discussions, 6) problem-based learning, 7) cooperative learning, 8) gaming, 9) simulations, and 10) discovery.

Presentations: Integration of Technology and Media

The use of presentations is a core instructional strategy that has been successfully used for many generations. Today's teachers have the advantage of expanding on tried-and-true strategies by integrating digital resources to further engage students in deep-level thinking and processing to yield even higher levels of meaningful learning. In addition, a presentation is something that can last as long as necessary to help convey the information to students.

There are a number of technology resources that can enhance presentation of information. For example, you or your students can use an interactive whiteboard to seamlessly move from a video to a spreadsheet chart to notes recorded from student comments. For example, a high school social studies teacher could begin a lesson comparing New York City with Hong Kong by presenting a documentary highlighting key features of both cities. During the video, students take notes of similarities and differences, which are then summarized as a concept map on the whiteboard. After student notes are captured, the teacher opens a previously created spreadsheet comparing New York versus Hong Kong data such as: population density, unemployment, number of universities, median age of population, annual population growth, etc.

PowerPoint or *Prezi* slides are another very common way of presenting information. The slides can include hyperlinks to Internet information or animated diagrams to illustrate a concept, as well as summarized content and related images. These digital presentations work well when introducing mathematical concepts, such as estimation, number lines, patterns, etc. They also work well for presenting science related processes including simple machines, life cycles, erosion, and motion. To gauge learning during these presentations, consider using student "clickers," which are digital tools that immediately display student responses to questions. Use the results to determine if re-teaching is necessary.

Another way to integrate technology into a presentation is through the use of document cameras, which project printed materials and small 3-D objects. Examples of ways to use this technology might include closely examining an old photo of a landmark, displaying a storybook as it is read, or watching the metamorphosis of a caterpillar into a butterfly.

As you think about using this strategy, remember that a presentation can be an effective strategy if you do not overuse it and if you consider how to keep your students actively engaged during the presentation. Also ensure that you and your students follow copyright guidelines when adding information to presentations.

Demonstrations: Integration of Technology and Media

Demonstrations can be enhanced with the use of technological equipment such as digital cameras. The teacher, student, or small group of students can use digital video cameras to record a demonstration during or outside of class. If more than one camera is available to record the demonstration, the videos can be merged with editing apps. Creating videos is particularly effective with complex procedures or messy projects using actual objects for the demonstration. For example, groups of chemistry students can record steps used to identify an unknown compound, and then share recordings to discuss variations of applied problem-solving techniques. Younger students could record "talk aloud" processes to demonstrate how math problems are solved. Another example of a digital demonstration is an art teacher who records step-by-step ways for students to examine the style, genre, and form of different paintings. These teacher or student created recordings can be viewed with the class to further examine various aspects of the demonstration or used by small groups or individuals to review the process.

Other types of digital equipment used during demonstrations include devices that record specific phenomena, such as wind, temperature, moisture, speed, and pH, as well as magnification devices, such as digital microscopes. These devices are primarily useful in mathematics and science demonstrations in which the results are projected for whole-class or small-group viewing.

Another option used for integrating demonstrations with digital video from online sources is YouTube or TeacherTube. These demonstrations might include the basics of using an abacus app on a mobile device, how to divide integers, or how to test the pH of pond water. As expected, multiple examples emerge when searching for online videos, so review carefully before using them in class and remember to follow all copyright guidelines.

Drill-and-Practice: Integration of Technology and Media

Many computer applications offer students opportunities to review information and practice their knowledge or skill while enjoying a game-like experience. Other drill-and-practice apps follow more traditional approaches, such as online flashcards and interactive worksheets. Digital versions of drill-and-practice activities are available as downloadable apps and as free interactive online programs for core content areas such as math, language arts, science, and history facts and concepts. There are also many non-digital drill-and-practice resources with years of proven effectiveness that offer a tactile alternative to working on the computer. Most popular are items that your students can use individually or in pairs, such as flashcards, word cards, and worksheets in spelling, mathematics, and language instruction.

Tutorials: Integration of Technology and Media

Tutorial arrangements include instructor-to-learner (e.g., Socratic dialog), learner-to-learner (e.g., peer-tutoring), computer-to-learner (e.g., computer-assisted tutorial software), and print-to-learner (e.g., workbook) pairings. Tutorials are often helpful for students who have difficulty working in large-group situations or who need extra assistance as they learn new material.

As a teacher providing instructor-to-learner tutoring, you can work with an individual or a small group of students, guiding them carefully at their pace through the material being presented. Learner-to-learner tutoring needs oversight from you as a guide to ensure the students have clear instructions for the one-to-one sessions. Computer-to-learner tutoring apps are very popular in PK–12 classrooms due to the immediate, individualized feedback that can be provided in a patient and consistent manner. For example, **integrated learning systems (ILS)**, such as SuccessMaker, and Edmentum, offer computer- or Internet-based instruction. Your student is required to follow a log-on procedure, entering the specific name and password you have provided, to begin a new tutoring session or continue with a previously started session. Student progression through the tutorial is based on mastery of content. Because ILS systems can be expensive, they are typically purchased at the district rather than the school level.

Your **school media center** is an excellent source of tutorials. Most centers have a wide variety of tutorial formats, including apps, audio recordings, and printed materials that you can check out to use with your students.

Discussions: Integration of Technology and Media

Technology-supported discussions are becoming more popular as a method to extend learning conversations beyond the classroom. **Video conferencing**, or real-time virtual meetings with apps such as Skype or FaceTime, allows students from two or more locations to see and hear each other during discussions. For example, students at Amersfort School of Social Awareness in New York use video conferencing to engage in one of their regular conversations with students in the Netherlands. Students can also engage in online discussions that may allow others beyond the classroom to join in at certain times. These discussions can incorporate video, audio, and/or text as part of the exchange of ideas. Technology and media can also be used to support an in-class discussion. For example, concept-mapping software, such as Cmap, Edraw, and Coggle can help record key ideas and issues raised during the conversation to guide further input and archive the session.

As you and your students develop a concept map during the discussion, you are guiding them to consider options and ideas that they might not have otherwise identified. A discussion that incorporates your students' questions is a very effective way to engage them in higher-order thinking.

Problem-Based Learning: Integration of Technology and Media

Many computer applications are available to support problem-based learning. Cognitive mapping apps such as WiseMapping, MindMup 2, Popplet, and Tools4Students provide interactive tools to graphically represent information, with links between concepts to depict relationships needed to solve problems. Collaborative apps, such as Google Apps, also provide critical support when students are working together to solve problems. Students collectively work together to develop and explore data sets for answers. For example, students could create a database of endangered species in their state to address the following problems: "What are the commonalities among the species? In what areas are endangered species most common and least common? And, what interventions are helping?"

Teachers also have access to problem-based lessons developed by other teachers and professionals. For example, numerous example lessons are available on sites such as Pinterest as well as through **WebQuests**. The WebQuests provide step-by-step structured problems for students to follow, identify online resources, and provide instructions for students to share their solutions. Apps are available for teachers who want to create their own WebQuests. Topics for WebQuests cover an array of subject areas including social studies, science, math, and the fine arts. Although a WebQuest is an effective tool to use with children to guide them to discover the information, you will want to be selective in how often you use this type of resource with your students and how complex you make your WebQuests.

Video Example 4.2: Integrating WebQuests

Observe the ways Ms. Kaiser and Ms. Marshall facilitate student use of the Lewis and Clark WebQuest. In what ways does the WebQuest reinforce student learning of the lesson objectives? In addition to the WebQuest, how are other technology and media used to demonstrate student learning?

Cooperative Learning: Integration of Technology and Media

Students can learn cooperatively not only by discussing text material and viewing media, but also by producing media. For example, students can design and produce a podcast, video, or digital presentations. You will want to be a working partner with the students in such learning situations to serve as a guide in their learning.

If your classroom has a single computer, it is possible to establish cooperative groups to allow all students access. A team of students can easily use Google Apps that can accommodate cooperative grouping because of the **collaborative,** or sharing, nature of the programs.

You can have groups prepare presentations on topics for the rest of the class. Thus, each group becomes an expert on a portion of the total content. Preparing presentations as a group requires students to achieve a higher level of mastery than can be derived from studying individually. See an example in "Taking a Look at Technology Integration: Cooperative Learning."

Gaming: Integration of Technology and Media

Games used for educational purposes include digital and paper-based crossword puzzles, Sudoku, jigsaw puzzles, and logic or brainteaser puzzles. Puzzles can be used to practice information such as spelling words or state capitals. Students can build problem solving and logic skills with Sudoku games, or strengthen thinking skills with jigsaw puzzles.

The Web offers a multitude of free games for students of all ages across core content areas from highly reputable sources. Example providers include NASA's Space Place, Smithsonian Education, The Environmental Protection Agency's Environmental Kids Club Game Room, and PBS KIDS GO! from the Public Broadcasting Service. Teachers should carefully review games prior to use to ensure that the activity supports achievement of the stated standards and objectives. Also note that students should only complete the game activities that are directly associated with the lesson.

Taking a Look at Technology Integration

Cooperative Learning

Connie Courbat, a third-grade teacher, was aware of the various ability levels of her students and wanted them all to have a positive experience studying the westward movement of the 1800s. The lesson objectives were focused on helping students gain a better understanding of the impact of historical events on lifestyle choices. She introduced the topic by forming cooperative groups that used the Oregon Trail app on the one computer in her classroom to experience the adventures of a pioneer traveling the Oregon Trail. The app presented students with various scenarios as they worked their way through the trail, for example, equipment failure—losing a wagon wheel; managing supply shortages, and how to treat illnesses. She grouped the students to ensure that all ability levels were represented within each group, thus allowing all students to benefit from the experience. Ms. Courbat was careful to establish roles for each member of the group, such as team leader, recorder, and materials manager. She moved among the groups as they worked together, helping them to address questions and ensuring that they were accomplishing the tasks. Each group gave a presentation of their travels westward, explaining their successes and failures in achieving the goal of reaching Oregon.

The Stock Market Game, offered by the Simfa Foundation, is very effective in helping your students gain financial skills. This online, multiuser game requires that your students invest their online $100,000 portfolio, tracking their investments and working toward the goal of developing the highest performing portfolio among those who are participating. They work in teams, assuming leadership roles and building skills in cooperation and collaboration as they learn about investing. The game also provides your students with opportunities to practice their language arts and math skills as they work through their investment strategies.

Simulations: Integration of Technology and Media

Interpersonal skills and science experiments are popular subjects for simulations. In some simulations, learners manipulate mathematical models to determine the effect of changing certain variables, such as controlling the speed of a skier by changing the degree of incline.

Role-playing is another form of simulation to build communication and social skills needed in today's careers. As an example, the award winning simulation, Extreme Event, provides group-member roles in a simulated disaster situation that needs to be resolved through community efforts and information to help members as they move along in the process. The simulation is designed for students aged 14+ and focuses on building critical thinking skills associated with disaster resilience, while learning to prioritize resources and build coalitions to improve civic literacy.

You can simulate an event that occurred locally or a major event that occurred a century ago, like the sinking of the *Titanic*. One teacher engages her students in understanding the impact of the decisions made that eventful night by assigning roles of actual passengers to her students to reenact. While they are participating in "onboard" activities, such as playing card games, dancing, eating a meal, or taking a stroll along the deck of the boat, she guides the "crew" to begin their scurry to deal with the accident. Before the experience is over, she identifies who must leave the area because they have drowned. Her students better understand the devastating event as many of their classmates are escorted to a back section of the room. She shares implications of how an event such as this affects family members and what can be done to prevent such catastrophes.

When deciding which games or simulations will support your instructional goals, use the guidelines in the Selection Rubric: Games and Simulations to assist with the selection. For example, with the rubric you can assess the quality with which the game or simulation aligns with the lesson objective, provides accurate and current information, provides practice for relevant skills, and has the potential to hold the interest of your students.

SELECTION RUBRIC Games and Simulations

Complete and save the following interactive evaluation to reference when selecting Games or Simulations to integrate into lessons.

Search Terms

_____

_____

Title _____

Format

Source/Location _____

_____ Game

© Date _____ Cost _____ Length _____ Minutes _____

_____ Simulation

Subject Area _____ Grade Level _____

Instructional Strategies _____

Brief Description

Standards/Outcomes/Objectives

Prerequisites (e.g., prior knowledge, reading ability, vocabulary level, etc.)

Strengths

Limitations

Special Features

Name _____ Date _____

(Continued)

Rating Area	High Quality	Medium Quality	Low Quality
Alignment with standards, outcomes, and objectives	Standards/outcomes/objectives are addressed and use of simulation or game should enhance student learning.	Standards/outcomes/objectives are partially addressed and use of simulation or game may enhance student learning.	Standards/outcomes/objectives are not addressed and use of simulation or game will likely not enhance student learning.
Accurate and current information	Information is correct and does not contain material that is out of date.	Information is correct, but does contain material that is out of date.	Information is not correct and contains material that is out of date.
Age-appropriate language	Language used is age appropriate and vocabulary is understandable.	Language used is nearly age appropriate and some vocabulary is above/below student age.	Language used is not age appropriate and vocabulary is clearly inappropriate for student age.
Interest level and engagement	Topic is presented so that students are likely to be interested and actively engaged in learning.	Topic is presented to interest students most of the time and engage most students in learning.	Topic is presented so as not to interest students and not engage them in learning.
Technical quality	The material represents the best technology and media.	The material represents technology and media that are good quality, although they may not be best available.	The material represents technology and media that are not well prepared and are of very poor quality.
Ease of use (student or teacher)	Material follows easy-to-use patterns with nothing to confuse the user.	Material follows patterns that are easy to follow most of the time, with a few things to confuse the user.	Material follows no patterns and most of the time the user is very confused.
Bias free	There is no evidence of objectionable bias or advertising.	There is little evidence of bias or advertising.	There is much evidence of bias or advertising.
User guide and directions	The user guide is an excellent resource for use in a lesson. Directions should help teachers and students use the material.	The user guide is a good resource for use in a lesson. Directions may help teachers and students use the material.	The user guide is a poor resource for use in a lesson. Directions do not help teachers and students use the material.
Practice of relevant skills	The program offers much valuable practice of skills to be learned.	The program offers some practice of skills to be learned.	The program offers little or no practice of skills to be learned.
Game: winning depends on player actions	The actions of players determine their success in the game.	Success in the game is determined by both player actions and chance.	Winning or losing the game is determined by chance.
Simulation: realistic, accurate depiction of reality	The simulation is an accurate representation of actual situations.	There is some relationship between the simulation and actual situations.	There is little or no correlation between the simulation and the actual situations.

*Specific to rating Games and Simulation Resources.

From Smaldino, Lowther, & Mims, *Instructional Technology and Media for Learning*, 12th ed. Copyright © 2017 by Pearson Education, Inc. All rights reserved.

Recommended for Classroom Use: _____ Yes _____ No

Ideas for Classroom Use: _____

_____

Discovery: Integration of Technology and Media

There are a variety of ways that instructional technology and media can help promote discovery or inquiry. For instance, your students can set up a digital camera to take time-lapse photos of a plant during the day to discover that plants follow the sun, or they can examine a series of GPS images of the same location on a river to discover how landscapes change over time. Your students can use word processing tools to discover the reading level of well-known documents, such as the Bill of Rights and the Preamble to the Constitution, or to compare excerpts from classic books to discover whether fiction is easier to read than historical biographies.

Digital video may be used for discovery teaching in the sciences, allowing you to stop, enlarge, or slow down naturally occurring events to encourage the development of curiosity and student questions. You will guide student learning through probing inquiries and having them describe what they have "discovered" or learned.

When integrating discovery learning into your instruction, it is important to consider the instructional situation to identify appropriate technology and media to support learning. See the When to Use Learning Strategies for examples for presentations, demonstrations, problem solving, cooperative learning, and discovery learning strategies.

When to Use Learning Strategies

Instructional Situation	Strategy	Potential Technology/Media
The whole class needs to learn how to conjugate verbs.	Presentations	A PowerPoint presentation that interactively shows variations of a verb by clicking on key words. Using Camtasia or Captivate, the teacher creates a video that includes text showing the variations of each verb and video clips of students demonstrating the action noted in the verb.
Because of safety issues, students need to observe the teacher handling chemicals for an experiment.	Demonstration	Teacher models correct use of certain types of chemicals to ensure that safety measures are addressed in the classroom setting. Teacher shows a YouTube video about how to safely handle the chemicals.
The teacher wants to challenge students to think about what they know and need to know about a topic.	Problem solving	A forensic lab is created for students to "solve a crime" the teacher has created for them. Students are provided with handheld devices to collect local data to compare with data collected from students in a different state.
The teacher seeks to increase student learning by having the students work cooperatively to research, share, evaluate, and synthesize new content into a group product that demonstrates their learning.	Cooperative learning	Students meet using free online collaboration tools (NING, Google Docs, social bookmarking, etc.). Students use online apps (e.g., spreadsheets) to enter information about what they've learned together. Real objects can be used for the development of a final product.
The teacher wants students to discover key concepts in order to instill deeper levels of understanding.	Discovery	Students create digital concept maps to discover relationships among new information. Students download weather data sets into a spreadsheet to discover how weather is predicted.

Application Exercise 4.2

 Check Your Understanding 4.2

Learning Contexts in Today's Classrooms

The five learning contexts or situations most frequently encountered in PK–12 environments are: 1) face-to-face classroom instruction, 2) distance learning, 3) blended instruction, 4) independent study (structured), and 5) informal study (unstructured). Each of these contexts for learning represents a way in which you can engage your students in achieving their learning outcomes. It is up to you to consider the various options to determine which might best serve your students.

Face-to-Face Instruction

Although other learning contexts are gaining notoriety, face-to-face instruction remains the most prevalent type of instruction in PK–12 schools. Because the teacher and students are in the same room, the options for learning experiences in the classroom setting seem unlimited. Many of the types of technology and media you will be reading about in this textbook are easily used in the face-to-face setting. For example, teachers can use clickers to collect student opinions during presentations, use interactive whiteboards to show videos of historical events, play podcasts of mathematicians explaining how to solve a problem, or conduct live interviews with archeologists in Egypt using Skype. Face-to-face instruction can involve activities before instruction, use of learning centers and manipulatives, as well as exhibits.

BEFORE INSTRUCTION. As the teacher, you might assign a media-based task to be completed prior to the face-to-face learning experience. You would provide an instructional resource for your students to learn the content prior to the classroom experience, which might be a hands-on activity that guides your students as they apply that knowledge. By "flipping the classroom," you are giving your students more responsibility for their own learning while you are guiding them to the desired outcomes. For example, you might have your students review a video about the solar system as their evening assignment and then have them construct a model of the solar system as part of their classroom activity in a collaborative group. While they are busy with their model construction, you are providing them with hints and suggestions of ways to draw upon the knowledge they gained from viewing the video.

LEARNING CENTERS. Combining instructional materials into a **learning center**, a self-contained environment designed to promote individual or small-group learning, helps focus students to learn about a specific topic. A learning center may be as simple as some chairs and a table in an area where there might be an activity with audio instructions. Learning centers can also be an excellent location for digital devices. For example, a center can include just one laptop with a specific game that targets the lesson content, or as seen in Figure 4.1, it can include multiple devices. You may set up the learning center as a way of breaking the class into small groups so they can complete a set of tasks. Or, you could establish a series of learning centers that provide your students with a mix of learning activities throughout the day. In your design of the learning center, you will want to encourage active participation by your students. You will want to also be sure that your learning center is partially enclosed to reduce distractions while groups of your students are engaged in the center's learning activities.

Learning centers can take several forms. An interest center might be a way for you to stimulate new interests or encourage creativity. You might set up a center on an upcoming topic, like a unit on insects, to generate your students' curiosity. You could consider the possibility of a remedial center to help specific students who might benefit from additional assistance with a particular topic or skill. This could be a "safe

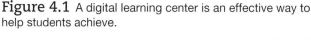

Figure 4.1 A digital learning center is an effective way to help students achieve.

place" for your students to practice their math computation skills. You can be creative in designing this type of center and be sure to include fun-to-do activities, use of digital devices, and other types of hands-on resources for your students. An enrichment center could offer stimulating learning experiences for those students who have completed their required work. You might, for example, allow students who have finished their geometry activities to go to a video center and view a DVD showing geometric shapes in bridges.

MANIPULATIVES.   When working with your students in the face-to-face setting, you might find it appropriate for your learners to use objects as part of their learning experiences. **Manipulatives** are the objects that can be viewed and handled by students. Manipulatives come in a variety of sizes and shapes and are generally categorized into three groups: real objects, models, and mock-ups.

The first manipulative category discussed are **real objects**, such as coins, tools, artifacts, plants, and animals, which are some of the most accessible, intriguing, and engaging materials used in education. Gerbils can draw a crowd of young children, the terrarium can help middle school students understand the concept of ecology, and a collection of colonial-era coins displayed in a high school social studies class are just a few examples of the potential of real objects that help students with obscure ideas or help stimulate their imaginations.

Next, are **models**, or three-dimensional representations of real objects. A model can be larger, smaller, or the same size as the object it represents. It can be complete in detail or simplified for instructional purposes. Indeed, models can provide learning experiences that real objects cannot offer. For example, when using a model of the human heart, important details are often accented with color, and most heart models are constructed to provide interior views that would not be possible with the real object. Models can be of almost anything and are often found in school media centers because of their size or costs to the school. You also can borrow models and artifacts from regional media centers and museums.

The final types of manipulatives are **mock-ups**, which are simplified representations of complex devices. By highlighting essential elements and eliminating distracting details, mock-ups help to clarify the complex. They are sometimes constructed as working models to demonstrate basic operations of the real device, allowing your students to manipulate the mock-up so they can comprehend how it operates. For example, a mock-up of a laptop computer might have the internal components labeled and spread out in a large container with a printed circuit diagram on a board. Your students' task is to put the components onto the diagram to "assemble" the internal workings of the computer. The most sophisticated type of mock-up, the simulator, is a device that allows learners to experience the important aspects of a real-life activity without undue costs or risk. Many young aviators learn about the complexities of flying by first experiencing how to fly in a simulator.

EXHIBITS. Also of value in your fact-to-face instructional situation is providing your learners with experiences seeing things. **Exhibits** are collections of various objects designed to form an integrated whole, examples or displays for instructional purposes. Any display surface can contribute to an exhibit. A **display** is an array of visuals and printed materials, often including real objects, with descriptive information included. For a lesson on your local region, a display could include a road map of the area, some pamphlets about points of interest, and some miniatures of types of vehicles that might be used for traveling around the region. A **diorama** is a static display consisting of a 3-D recreation of real scenes. Dioramas are usually designed to reproduce scenes and events from the past or present or to depict future scenarios. Your students can design their own dioramas as a follow-up activity after a lesson.

Video Example 4.3: Face-to-Face Learning Context

Observe the learning context used in the Lewis and Clark lesson. What features of the lesson align with those described for a face-to-face context? In what ways did Ms. Kaiser and Ms. Marshall provide support for student learning experiences?

Distance Learning

Although distance learning has been around for over 100 years, starting with correspondence study using the post office to exchange materials and assignments, recent technology innovations have made it more convenient and dynamic. As seen in Figure 4.2, students can be in one location while other members of the class and the teacher can be at other locations. You and a colleague may combine your classes at a distance to enhance their learning opportunities. For example, you might work with a teacher in California who has a class near the San Andreas fault line while your students are studying geology and causes of earthquakes. The California students could use mobile cameras to take your students on a field trip to the fault line without your students leaving their own seats.

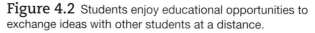

Figure 4.2 Students enjoy educational opportunities to exchange ideas with other students at a distance.

Learning at a distance may also be helpful if you have a small group of students who have a particular learning need and would benefit from additional tutoring not readily available at your school. Arrangements could possibly be made with a nearby college for individual or small group virtual tutoring opportunities. Regular meetings could be scheduled through video conferencing or online chats with a tutor who can provide them with additional help. The convenience of having the extra help without the hassle of trying to arrange transportation or locations makes it possible for your students to benefit from additional expertise.

Another time your students might benefit from a distance learning opportunity is when only a handful of students want to study a particular topic that isn't available at your school or not enough students are interested in the topic to form a whole class. This situation could offer a way for your students to participate in advanced placement or college-credit courses if they are eligible for this level of study. Thus, your students would be able to extend their learning opportunities.

Both public and private schools offer **online virtual schools**, comprised of various programs and courses that do not meet in a face-to-face classroom. Most online virtual programs are at the high school level; however, some course work targets middle school learners. Some states have initiated the requirement that all seniors must complete at least one distance or online course prior to graduation to better prepare them for post-secondary online learning. Although virtual schools are becoming increasingly common, this method of education needs further refinement as average graduation rates are lower than traditional public and charter schools (McLaughlin, 2016).

Blended Instruction

Another way to use distance learning experiences is through **blended instruction**, a mix of **synchronous settings** (e.g., face-to-face classroom or real-time video conferencing) and **asynchronous settings**, in which the teacher and students are not together at the same time. For example, high school students enrolled in a blended instruction Algebra 1 course might meet in a face-to-face classroom on Mondays and Wednesdays every other week. When not meeting in class, students use online courseware to work on assignments at times convenient for them. Students follow a schedule of due dates for uploading completed student products. The teacher would work with individuals and groups of students throughout the entire time, but the experiences would be varied.

As you design blended learning experiences, you want to be sure you know your students' content knowledge and their experiences with blended online learning settings. You may wish to start with your class having more synchronous meetings, such as in your classroom, or scheduled online video meetings before you move to more asynchronous types of experiences. You will be providing your students with the opportunity to become comfortable with the mixed schedule of class meetings and independent work time. If you find your students are familiar with a blended learning class, you will have more flexibility in arranging the course schedule.

Structured Independent Study

Structured independent study is based on the idea that your students can learn information and acquire skills without the teacher's direct instruction. However, you will have to prepare the independent study context using materials you have selected or developed yourself. The Web provides unlimited access to current and archived information that extends content covered in the text. Students will be able to work at their own pace and come to class ready to apply the knowledge.

Independent study can also occur during class through the use of learning centers. You can use a variety of technology, media, and materials, such as web resources, text, audio, video, and apps. Or you can develop remedial materials for students who are having difficulty with the topic being taught in class.

Nonstructured Informal Study

Students today have many opportunities to learn from their experiences outside of the classroom. You can prepare your students to successfully engage in informal study through the application of information and communication technology (ICT) literacy skills during class activities. At the same time, you can use techniques to help instill in them a love for learning and demonstrate through your own enthusiasm how to be a lifelong learner.

The nature of the study is what makes it informal. Many students seek information on the Internet and challenge themselves to learn about topics that might not be part of their in-class study. For example, student self-study may involve online discussions on how to "go green," searching for information about the history of pandas after visiting the zoo, or examination of sites about earthquakes to discover why they occur. Another example of informal learning occurs when students watch television shows on the History Channel, the National Geographic Channel, or the Public Broadcasting System. These experiences increase general knowledge without your directed instruction.

 Check Your Understanding 4.3

Shared Writing Exercise 4.1

Integrating Free and Inexpensive Materials

With the ever-increasing costs of instructional materials, teachers should be aware of the variety of materials they may obtain for classroom use at little or no cost. The types of free and inexpensive materials available online are almost endless. Of key importance to schools with limited technology budgets are **open source** websites that offer free productivity suites (e.g., word processing, spreadsheets, presentation software) similar to Microsoft Office. Among the most popular are Google Docs, Office 365, and Apple iWork.

In addition, by connecting to websites around the world, teachers and students can acquire digital video, audio, photos, and documents, such as books and news articles. The Web also offers free collaboration tools to facilitate cooperative learning and connections with classrooms around the globe. Many teachers post lesson ideas, media, and instructional materials, such as worksheets, for an array of subjects on their blogs, Pinterest, and personal and professional websites.

Free and inexpensive materials include all the types of media, with some being available in downloadable computer apps, and audio and video files. Other commonly available items include posters, games, pamphlets, brochures, reports, charts, maps, books, CDs, multimedia kits, and actual objects. The more costly items are usually sent only on a free-loan basis and must be returned to the supplier after use, while some DVDs and other materials will be donated to your school media center to be shared among many users.

Advantages of Free and Inexpensive Materials

In addition to the obvious advantage of low or no cost materials, other advantages include:

- *Up to date.* Free and inexpensive materials from online resources can provide current information not found in textbooks or other media.
- *In-depth treatment.* Subject-specific materials typically provide in-depth information on a topic.
- *Variety of uses.* Students can access open source applications outside of school. Audiovisual materials can be used for self-study or for presentation to the class. Posters, charts, and maps can be combined to create topical displays.
- *Student manipulation.* Materials that are expendable have the extra advantage of allowing learners to get actively involved with them. They can also scan printed information and visuals to import into digital products.

Limitations of Free and Inexpensive Materials

When selecting free and inexpensive materials to integrate into your instruction, consider the following limitations:

- *Bias or advertising.* Many free and inexpensive materials are produced and distributed by particular organizations. These organizations, whether private corporations, nonprofit associations, or government agencies, often have a message to convey. Carefully preview materials to ensure they are appropriate for classroom use.
- *Promotion of special interests.* Some materials do not contain advertising but do promote a special interest in a less obvious way. Soliciting materials on a topic from a variety of sources can help provide different points of view.
- *Limited quantities.* With the increasing expense of producing and shipping printed materials, your supplier may limit the quantities available at one time. You may not be able to obtain a copy for every student in the class.

Integration of Free and Inexpensive Materials

The materials that you obtain through free and inexpensive sources can be used just like you would use any classroom resource. Many times you will find that the types of materials you obtain can best fit into learning centers because they often have a distinct focus on a topic. Or you might find it better to use the materials in a presentation to the whole class at one time. For example, if a local fishing shop sends a video about fishing on a regional river, you might wish to show it one time to all your students.

When a vendor sends you items, you will need to be vigilant about what is appropriate for your students to handle and what might not be. You might obtain materials from the American Red Cross about caring for a cut or scratch. It might be ideal to have children work in small groups and use the materials to learn the steps involved. But, there may be some things included that are too mature for your students, so you might decide not to use them. Some of the materials sent might be fragile or subject to wear and tear, so you might display them but keep your students from handling them.

Sources for Free and Inexpensive Materials

There are local, state, national, and international sources for free and inexpensive materials, and many of these are now available online. Table 4.1 lists popular sources for these materials.

Table 4.1 Sources of Free and Inexpensive Materials

Source	Types/Topics of Materials
Business organizations	Businesses often provide guest speakers and materials associated with their line of business as well as entrepreneurship, investing, and budgeting. As an example, BP Global offers an Educational Service website with resources for primary and secondary students as well as Science Explorers and STEM Clubs and Challenges. The resources might include animations, videos, and interactive learning activities on topics such as geography, science, and design and technology.
Community–non-profit organizations	Community organizations focus on things such as sustainability, beautification, crime prevention, and zoning. PDF copies of brochures are made available on special interest topics (American Red Cross, League of Women Voters, Junior Achievement, Young Women's/Men's Christian Association)
Federal publications	The U.S. Government Publishing Office (GPO) provides digital copies of historical photos, books, and brochures available for download in several formats. The National Technical Information Services (NTIS) offers access to multiple data sets related to topics such as the nation's environment, economy, and population. The U.S. Department of Education (DOE) offers several digital resources for teachers such as the Kids.gov and Smithsonian Kids. They also support EDSITEment, which is focused on arts and culture, foreign language, history and social studies, as well as literature and language arts. Additionally, the DOE offers FREE.ED that provides teachers a regularly updated blog with resources and ideas for holidays, awareness months, anniversaries, and seasonal topics.
Foreign governments	Foreign government websites often provide PDF copies of posters, maps, travel booklets, as well as access to interactive government statistics (population density, economics, etc.). Many countries also offer virtual tours of national monuments and parks and live webcams, such as the Panda Cam from Sichuan, China.
Government agencies	Various government agencies provide downloadable classroom materials and apps on topics related to each service, and most offer updated Facebook, Twitter, and YouTube information. For example, Cooperative Extension Services provide content on topics such as agriculture, animals, biotechnology, and the environment. The Department of Public Health and Human Services offers information regarding health, aging, disability, financial, and safety/disaster assistance. Additionally, the National Park Service provides multiple digital resources such as virtual tours and webcams (e.g., Shiloh Eagle Cam; Oregon Caves Bat Cam; and Black Canyon's Grizzly Ridge). They also provide an Exploring Sound gallery with teaching materials for amphibians, birds, fish, insects, mammals, and reptiles as well as geological, and meteorological sounds. Additional cultural/historical sounds include things such as Native American music, harmonica, and battle sounds and the Human-Caused category has a boat, helicopter, siren, and snowmobile, plus others.
Museums	Local, state, regional and national museums typically provide PDF copies of booklets on culture, art, how to visit a museum, lesson plans—Smithsonian, Natural History Museum, National Gallery of Art (teaching packets with image CDs, DVDs, videos, online virtual tours and interactive materials, etc.). The Smithsonian website has a variety of digital tools to engage learners with inquiry-based activities such as the Science Game Center, Smithsonian Explorer X-3D models of a Woolly Mammoth skeleton, a Lincoln life mask, and the Wright Flyer (1903) plane.
News broadcasters	News broadcast websites have current and archived interview videos/audio podcasts and articles. ABC News provides a special link for students and teachers, Behind the News (BTN), with Pinterest feeds, weekly email updates and resources for key news stories that include discussion questions and full transcripts.
Police and fire departments	Police and fire departments will work with teachers and/or schools to provide safety presentations and materials. For example, the Los Angeles Fire Department teaches children about earthquake safety with their Shakey-Quakey program. The program uses a trailer set up like a classroom to simulate what happens during an earthquake. The students experience the shaking, sounds, and falling objects during the three-minute virtual earthquake. The students receive an earthquake preparedness booklet to read and share with their families.
Public broadcasting	Among the numerous resources available through PBS, the LearningMedia and PBS Kids are useful for Pk-12 teachers. The PBS LearningMedia website can be searched by grades, subjects, and media type (audio, video, interactive, lesson plan, etc.). Included are Teachers' Lounge blogs, Productivity Tools for Teachers, professional development, and PBS Digital Innovators. The PBS Kids provides videos and interactive games for teamwork, problem solving, Spanish, and core content areas. Also provided are Hard Games at three levels of difficulty for topics such as ecosystems, health, and natural disasters.
Public libraries	Most public libraries offer digital resources, including many books, photos, and scanned images of historical documents. The digital collection of the Library of Congress includes nearly 1,000 items from subjects such as American history, world cultures, performing arts, local history and folklife, sports and recreation, literature and poetry, and women's history.
Utility companies	Utility companies are often involved in educating students about energy conservation, going green, and safety. Some provide free classroom materials that include a teachers guide and student booklets, videos, and also on-site classroom presentations. In Texas, the Austin Energy Company uses School Outreach for this purpose. They host regional science fairs and provide classroom presentations for grades 3–5 to teach students the basics of electricity and how to use it safely.
Weather broadcasts and websites	The meteorologists from local TV stations may be available as guest speakers for your classroom or school. They often provide materials on severe weather, the difference between climate and weather, and so on. The Weather Channel website also provides numerous resources for teachers. In addition to providing weather data for any location across the nation, the site also provides preparedness guidelines for severe weather such as tornadoes, hurricanes, and flooding. Videos are available to view the latest weather trends and other popular topics such as Crazimals (e.g., Pelican on the Loose; Sheep Invasion), great outdoors, and extreme activities, (e.g., world's biggest swing in New Zealand).

There are a number of websites that serve as repositories for open source materials, or online products that are available for sharing. Among the websites are Curriki and Gooru, which are communities for sharing educational resources. Teachers, students, and families can use these sources for lessons, practice on specific topics, or to share resources they've designed themselves. Gooru uses a media-based format and actually includes the lesson's media, such as videos, as part of the lesson resources. Illustrative Mathematics is another website that provides games and activities to practice math concepts for grades 7 through 12. The Illustrative Mathematics author has years of experience teaching mathematics and offers many ideas for helping young people learn math concepts while enjoying the learning experiences.

Obtaining Free and Inexpensive Materials

Most classroom materials are available in a format that can easily be downloaded from the provider's website. For those resources that are not available online, you can submit your request via email, phone, fax, or mail. Some agencies may require the request to be submitted on school letterhead and signed by your principal, such as scheduling a police officer for a guest presentation. Any student requests should include your endorsement. When ordering hard copies of materials, ask for a preview copy before requesting multiple copies and, when appropriate, share the resources with other teachers. When obtaining online resources from sites with feedback options, respond with descriptions of how the materials were used along with student reactions. Be courteous, but be honest! Many suppliers attempt to improve free and inexpensive materials on the basis of user comments. When online feedback isn't possible, send a thank you note.

Evaluating Free and Inexpensive Materials

As with all types of materials, evaluate the educational value of free and inexpensive materials critically. Some are very "slick" (technically well presented) but not educationally sound. Use the appropriate selection rubric for the type of media (web resources, video, etc.) you are evaluating. All the selection rubrics in this book have the rating criterion "bias free." Use it judiciously when reviewing free and inexpensive materials.

Innovations in Teaching

Interactive Multitouch Desks

Classrooms of the future will no longer have desks and separate laptops. Interactive multitouch desks resemble the navigational interface used in science fiction movies, such as *Star Trek*. The screen serves as an individual workspace, an interactive whiteboard, and a collaboration tool for several students. Students use fingers or pens to interact with the desk and can define their own space with an icon or avatar. The desks are connected through a fully interactive classroom system, which is monitored with a teacher's console that can also be used to view student work on every screen or display example work.

 Check Your Understanding 4.4

Summary

This chapter discussed designing digital learning environments and placed key emphasis on the chapter's learning outcomes.

- *Describe 10 learning strategies used in the classroom.* The 10 most common learning strategies used in today's classrooms are: 1) presentation, 2) demonstration, 3) drill-and-practice, 4) tutorial, 5) discussion, 6) cooperative learning, 7) problem-based learning, 8) gaming, 9) simulation, and 10) discovery. Each strategy offers distinct advantages, which most frequently are related to enhanced student learning, as well as limitations, such as access and time issues that may impact classroom use of the strategy.

- *Discuss how to integrate technology and media into learning strategies.* Each of the 10 learning strategies can be enhanced and supported with different technology and media. Some strategies, such as drill-and-practice and tutoring have specifically designed media for implementation. The other strategies can involve the use of a wide variety of technology that ranges from productivity suites, social media apps, and specialized digital devices, such as science probes and digital microscopes.

- *Differentiate between types of learning contexts.* Five contexts for learning commonly found in PK–12 education include: face-to-face instruction, distance learning, blended instruction, structured independent study, and nonstructured informal study. The most frequent context is face-to-face instruction, which not only involves traditional teaching, but also can involve learning centers and use of manipulatives in the form of real objects, models, and mock-ups as well as use of exhibits.

- *Describe the value of integrating free and inexpensive materials into instruction.* Learning is enhanced when students interact with multiple resources, yet teachers often have no, or a limited, budget to obtain teaching materials. Free and inexpensive materials are available on the web for downloading, as apps on mobile devices such as tablet computers, or they may be hard copy materials that may be ordered from the web. These materials often help supplement instruction and are readily accessible from government, health, non-profit, and business/industry sources.

ASSURE Lesson Plan

This ASSURE Classroom Case Study is based on a social studies lesson co-taught by Ms. Lindsay Kaiser and Ms. Jena Marshall.

Ms. Kaiser and Ms. Marshall implement a lesson in which fifth-grade students complete a WebQuest to explore various aspects of the Lewis and Clark expedition. The lesson also involves a hands-on activity in which students design a Lewis and Clark boat.

Analyze Learners

General Characteristics

Ms. Kaiser and Ms. Marshall's fifth-grade students are of mixed ethnicities and from middle-income homes. They are fairly equally distributed with regard to gender and are all either 10 or 11 years old. All students are reading at or above grade level. Student behavior problems are minimal.

Entry Competencies

The fifth-grade students are, in general, able to do the following tasks required to complete the lesson activities:

- Conduct an Internet search
- Create and save word processing documents
- Create and save documents with publishing software (e.g., Microsoft Publisher)
- Use graph paper to draw images to scale

Learning Differences and Needs of Students

The fifth-grade students learn best when engaged in hands-on activities that are interesting and challenging. The students' level of interest and motivation increases when working as a team to win a competition. The students vary in the style with which they prefer to demonstrate their learning. For example, when creating the boat advertisement, some students prefer to write the content, whereas others choose to select and arrange photos and images to express their ideas.

State Standards and Objectives

Curriculum Standards

National Center for History in the Schools, United States Grades 5–12 Standards, Era 4 Expansion and Reform (1801–1861): Standard 1: United States territorial expansion between 1801 and 1861, and how it affected relations with external powers and Native Americans; Standard 1A: The student understands the international background and consequences of the Louisiana Purchase.

Technology Standards

ISTE Standards for Students–3. Students use research skills to locate and use relevant information. *5.* Students organize and evaluate data to solve problems.

(Continued)

Learning Objectives

1. Given Internet resources and drawing materials, pairs of fifth-grade students will design a boat appropriate for the challenges faced by Lewis and Clark during their expedition (e.g., able to withstand rough currents while portable enough for carrying across rugged terrain).
2. Using the student-created boat design, pairs of students will create an advertisement for their Lewis and Clark boat that clearly defines the reasons why it fulfills the requirements of suitability for the Lewis and Clark expedition.
3. Using the student-created boat design, pairs of students will write a persuasive letter to the president of a boat manufacturing company about why their Lewis and Clark boat should be produced by the company.

Select Strategies and Resources

Select Strategies

Ms. Kaiser and Ms. Marshall select four student-centered strategies: discussion, problem solving, discovery, and cooperative learning. Examples include working in cooperative pairs to complete a WebQuest, conducting Internet searches for information on boats used by Lewis and Clark, designing the boat, creating an advertisement to sell the boat, and writing a letter to the president of a boat manufacturing company.

Select Resources

This lesson involves student use of Internet-connected computers, the Lewis and Clark WebQuest, an Internet browser to locate information about boats, publishing software to create the advertisement, library resources, and word processing tools to write the letters. Students might also need access to a scanner to copy paper-based photos for their advertisements. The following guidelines were used to assess resource appropriateness.

- *Align to standards, outcomes, and objectives.* The WebQuest, Internet and library resources, and production software (publishing and word processing) provide the necessary tools for students to meet the learning objectives.
- *Accurate and current information.* Students will access multiple resources of Lewis and Clark information, which will allow the students to crosscheck content accuracy. Current information may be used for new ideas on building handmade boats with tools available at the time.
- *Age-appropriate language.* The WebQuest is written at an appropriate level for fifth-grade students. The teacher may need to assist with interpretation of some web-based resources.
- *Interest level and engagement.* The combined use of the WebQuest, the boat design, and the advertisement competition will keep student interest and engagement at a high level.

- *Technical quality.* The WebQuest and production software used by the students are of high technical quality.
- *Ease of use.* The WebQuest is designed for fifth-grade students. Students can easily use word processing software; however, the publishing application may require initial training and support.
- *Bias free.* The WebQuest and production software are bias free.
- *User guide and directions.* The online help features of the WebQuest and production software are fairly easy for fifth-grade students to use. However, students most frequently will ask each other, Ms. Kaiser, or Ms. Marshall for assistance with technical difficulties.

Utilize Resources

Preview Resources

Ms. Kaiser and Ms. Marshall preview the WebQuest and an online bookmarking site to list relevant Internet resources.

Prepare Resources

Ms. Kaiser and Ms. Marshall prepare the lesson instructions and rubrics for the boat design, letter, and advertisement. They add the WebQuest link and Internet resources links to Lewis and Clark information on the class webpage.

Prepare the Environment

Ms. Kaiser and Ms. Marshall check the classroom laptops to ensure the Internet connections are functional and that the publisher software is loaded on all machines. They retrieve the library cart with Lewis and Clark material and set out all instruction sheets and rubrics for the lesson.

Prepare the Learners

Ms. Kaiser and Ms. Marshall provide a brief overview of U.S. history studied up to the 1800s to provide a context for learning about the Lewis and Clark expedition. They also ask students to share personal boating experiences and projects in which they designed or built a model.

Provide the Learning Experience

Ms. Kaiser and Ms. Marshall begin the class by presenting a brief introduction to Lewis and Clark and the historical background of the time. They then present the boat competition challenge and explain how the lesson activities are structured.

Require Learner Participation

Student Practice Activities

The students in Ms. Kaiser's and Ms. Marshall's class use computers, the Internet, and word processing and publishing software to complete their work assignments. Each student individually completes the Lewis and Clark WebQuest. Students then join their partners and conduct research using

(Continued)

the Internet and resources from the library cart. The goal is to locate additional information about the Lewis and Clark boats and boat construction. This research allows students to crosscheck information learned in the WebQuest. The students use the information to design their boat, create the advertisement, and write their letter. All the activities provide opportunities for the students to engage in practice and re-learning of Lewis and Clark information.

Feedback

Ms. Kaiser and Ms. Marshall provide ongoing feedback to students as they conduct Internet and library information searches, draft beginning boat designs, and write the first drafts of their letters to the boat manufacturer. Students use the rubrics (see next section) for these three products to check progress and focus of the work.

Evaluate and Revise

Assessment of Learner Achievement

Ms. Kaiser and Ms. Marshall use the rubrics to assess each team's final boat design, advertisement, and letter. The rubrics assess demonstration of content knowledge, as seen in the students' advertisements and letters and in their

technology skills. Ms. Kaiser and Ms. Marshall assess these skills by evaluating the final student advertisements and letters according to the assignment criteria.

Evaluation of Strategies and Resources

Ms. Kaiser and Ms. Marshall evaluate the strategies, technology, and media. Evaluation of the lesson strategies involves reviewing the students' final products to determine the degree to which students have met the learning objectives. They also engage in continuous communication with the students to learn what is working and identify areas of needed improvement. Ms. Kaiser and Ms. Marshall regularly communicate with the school's technology support staff regarding technology upkeep and problems.

Revision

Ms. Kaiser and Ms. Marshall review the information collected from evaluation of the lesson strategies, technology, and media. The evaluation shows that the Lewis and Clark WebQuest was an excellent source of information to guide the remaining boat design activities. However, students struggled with writing the persuasive letter. Ms. Kaiser and Ms. Marshall revised the lesson to include a review and practice for writing persuasive letters.

Professional Development

Demonstrating Professional Skills

1. Develop a table that lists the 10 types of instructional strategies in the first column. In the second column, write a brief description of how you could use each strategy in an ASSURE lesson (ISTE Standards for Educators 5.A and B).

2. Using the table developed for Item 1, add a third column that describes how technology can be used to support each of the 10 learning experiences (ISTE Standards for Educators 5.A and B).

3. Design an ASSURE lesson for one of the learning contexts and settings (ISTE Standards for Educators 5.A and B).

4. Using the district or state curriculum guide from the grade level and subject area that you teach or plan to teach, create an annotated list of free and inexpensive resources you could integrate into your teaching and describe how you could use the resources (ISTE Standards for Educators 1.C).

Building Your Professional Portfolio

- *Creating My Lesson.* Using the ASSURE model, design a lesson for one of the Lesson Scenarios in the Appendix or use a scenario of your own design. Incorporate into your lesson one or more of the instructional strategies

and technology and media ideas described in this chapter. Choose a learning context appropriate for your lesson. Carefully describe the audience, the objectives, and all other elements of the ASSURE model. Be certain to match your intended outcomes to state or national curriculum and technology standards for your content area.

- *Reflecting on My Lesson.* Reflect on the process you have used in the design of your lesson and your efforts at enhancing that lesson to meet student needs within your class. How did information from this chapter about instructional strategies, learning contexts, and free and inexpensive materials influence your lesson-designing decisions? In what ways did the technology and media you selected for your lesson enhance the learning opportunities for your students?

- *Enhancing My Lesson.* Using the lesson you created in the previous activity, consider how to meet the needs of students with varying abilities. What adaptations are needed to keep advanced learners actively engaged while helping students who struggle with reading? What changes are needed to ensure that students transfer knowledge and skills to other learning situations? You might look for free and inexpensive resources to enhance the lesson. How can you integrate additional use of technology and media into the lesson?

Suggested Resources

Print Resources

Bates, A. W. (2015). *Teaching in a digital age: Guidelines to designing teaching and learning for a digital age.* Tony Bates Associates, Ltd. Retrieved from https://opentextbc.ca/teachinginadigitalage/

Marcus, A. S., Stoddard, J. D., & Woodward, W. W. (2017). *Teaching history with museums: Strategies for K-12 social studies.* New York: Routledge.

Marcus-Quinn, A. & Hourigan, T. (Eds.) (2017). *Handbook on digital learning for K-12 Schools.* Switzerland: Springer International Publishing.

McKnight, K., O'Malley, K., Ruzic, R., Horsley, M. K., Franey, J. J., & Bassett, K. (2016). Teaching in a digital age: How educators use technology to improve student learning. *Journal of Research on Technology in Education, 48*(3), 194–211.

Nugent, G., Kohmetscher, A., Namuth-Covert, D., Guretzky, J., Murphy, P. & Lee, D. (2016). Learning from online modules in diverse instructional contexts. *Interdisciplinary Journal of e-Skills and Lifelong Learning, 12,* 113–121.

Veletsianos, G. (2016). Digital learning environments. In N. Rushby & D. W. Surry (Eds.), *The Wiley Handbook of Learning Technology.* West Sussex, UK: John Wiley & Sons.

Online Resources and Apps

Common Sense Education: Teacher Rated Apps

Common Sense Education offers teacher reviews and ratings of educational apps sorted by six categories: platform, subject, grade, price, skills, and purpose. Also included are teacher tips and suggestions for successful classroom use.

Creative Commons

Creative Commons is a resource for you to "license" your own work using the open source options that are available. Creative Commons provides you with instruction about open source materials, gives you directions for assigning a license to your own work, and helps you locate other materials you might like to use.

Federal Reserve Education

The Federal Reserve Education website provides educational resources for K through adult learners. The content focuses on various topics associated with the Federal Reserve, such as banking, economics, government, monetary policy, and personal finance. A wide variety of resources are available, including activities, blogs, comic books, games, and videos.

Fermilab

The Fermilab Education Office provides teachers with STEM (science, technology, engineering, and mathematics) classroom resources. For example, life science resources include activities focused on prairie flora and fauna, one-day physics activities, and physical science interactive field-studies programs.

PhET Interactive Simulations

PhET provides over 100 interactive simulations to engage students in meaningful, yet fun inquiry-based science and mathematics activities. The simulations help make invisible concepts visible as students manipulate variables with easy-to-use virtual tools.

Science Bank Online Dissections

The Science Bank provides animal-friendly dissection resources in an online format. Many are available free of charge. Students can interact with several virtual dissections such as earthworms, grasshoppers, crayfish, frogs, sharks, fetal pigs, and rats.

Share my Lesson

This site has access to more than 400,000 free lesson plans and activities that are searchable by grade (early childhood to high school) and subject areas. It also includes resources on current news from around the globe. The American Federation of Teachers funds the free lesson sharing.

Chapter 5
Engaging Learners with Digital Devices

This chapter addresses ISTE Standards for Educators, 2, 5, 6, and 7.

5.1 Describe strategies for and examples of using digital devices in the classroom.

5.2 Discuss the advantages of using digital devices to support learning.

5.3 Discuss the limitations of using digital devices to support learning.

5.4 Discuss ideas related to integrating technology for learning support.

5.5 Describe the types of applications that might be selected for use in the classroom.

5.6 Describe the basics of hardware elements you will find in learning settings.

5.7 Discuss how you might configure the digital classroom to support student learning.

 Goal

Select and integrate computer resources into instruction to promote learning.

ASSURE Classroom Case Study

The ASSURE model consists of steps designed to help teachers plan lessons that effectively integrate use of technology and media for learning. We provide a classroom case study to illustrate the implementation of the model into an elementary classroom setting.

The ASSURE Classroom Case Study in this chapter describes the instructional planning of Kerry Bird, an elementary teacher for nearly 30 years, and one of the first in his school to embrace technology. Kerry, who views the advent of computers as one of the biggest changes in education during his career, is currently teaching fourth grade, where he strives to integrate a variety of computer projects into instruction. He has found that student motivation and learning increase during active hands-on engagement with computers. As one of his projects, he is considering how to upgrade his presentation of the water cycle, a concept with which his students have struggled. He currently teaches this process by having students create water cycle posters. He would like his students to use computers to demonstrate their understanding of the water cycle.

Video segments within the chapter explore how Mr. Bird develops a lesson about the water cycle, how he selects the activities and instructional strategies, and chooses the materials, multimedia, and technology that will promote learning.

Introduction

Digital devices have become one of the key instructional technologies in education, especially in light of what we know about today's learner. These devices, including the computer, play multiple roles within the curriculum, ranging from tutor to student creativity resource. Teachers can use the computer as an aid to collect student performance data, as well as to manage classroom activities.

As educators, we need to begin thinking of ways to apply these extended mobile capabilities as learning tools. Examples include field-based learning experiences where students can take photos of events or phenomena, such as demonstrating the carbon footprints they find within their community. Students can then upload the images to a classroom website and write a blog entry about their observations. Experts on the topic of carbon footprinting can provide additional information or guide approaches to the topic. The classroom can be moved outside the school building and beyond the limits of the school day. To make informed choices on technology use, you need to be familiar with the various applications—word processing, graphics, and presentation software; games and simulations; tutorials; and teacher resources. Software applications designed for mobile devices, **mobile apps**, enable many of these devices to take photos and short videos, email, surf the Web, play games, provide location-based services (GPS), and use calendars and other personal management tools.

It is extremely important to develop critical skills for appraising instructional software because there are so many available programs and apps. The hardware, too, becomes much less intimidating when you know some of the basic technology. Whether you teach with a single computer in the classroom or a room full of digital devices, you can learn to make optimal use of the technology to support student learning.

This chapter focuses on the types of digital resources available for the classroom, as well as on how to go about selecting applications to support student learning. To help understand how computers operate, there is information on the components of the computer, as well as classroom setup options to optimize technology use.

Using Digital Devices in the Classroom

When the International Society for Technology in Education (ISTE) first developed standards for students, they started their list of knowledge and skills with the ability to operate the equipment. In 2007, ISTE reordered the list for students and changed the importance of computer operations and concepts from the first skill (ISTE, 2017). Although determining that it was still important for students to know about and be able to operate the computer efficiently, ISTE decided that knowing how to use tools to support learning was more important than being able to label the parts of a computer or select and use applications.

ISTE also developed a set of standards for teachers that parallel those for the students. The teacher standards also do not place much emphasis on the operations of the tools but rather emphasize the ability to create learning opportunities for students with computers and technology. Teachers are expected to model appropriate use of the resources and to guide students as part of their learning experiences. The decisions teachers make about using digital tools to support learning are considered more important than knowledge of basic operations. Digital literacy helps teachers understand how the integration of technology can enhance instructional practice and increase student performance.

Video Example 5.1: Planning Digital Lessons

Observe how Mr. Bird reflects on his planning strategies for student use of digital devices. Why did Mr. Bird choose to integrate use of technology into the water cycle lesson? What did he describe as the primary digital features students will use when working with computers?

Desktop to Mobile Continuum

Today's classrooms have changed considerably since the first desktop computer was introduced into educational settings. The desktop computer was considered to be the innovation that changed our views of how teaching was transformed from the teacher standing in the front of the classroom to the teacher moving among the students as they worked on individual or small group learning projects. More recently as the technology has evolved into smaller and more transportable devices, the computer has shifted from something that was connected by wires to something that can be easily moved around locations both inside and outside the classroom and can access information wirelessly (Adams, Becker, Freeman, Giesinger, Hall, Cummins, and Yuhnke, 2016).

This shift from the desktop computer device to the smaller and agile digital device is not due only to changes in size, but also to shifts in the capacity and speed of access to software applications and information. Further, the shift in the movement toward using the smaller and more efficient devices includes the ways in which the user can interface with the device. With a desktop computer, using the device required a keyboard and mouse or graphics tablet to interface with the device. With the advent of the tablet and smart phone, the interface became more intuitive, relying on the individual's touch and movement, and it became easier to access the resources stored within or to access information through wireless technologies.

In today's classrooms you will still find the desktop computer with appropriate auxiliary devices available to use. In addition, you will also find the use of mobile devices such as tablets and smart phones. Students will be expected to be able to use all the devices as appropriate for their learning experiences. As a teacher, you will decide which of the devices that you have in your classroom will be most effective in providing your students with quality learning experiences.

Strategies and Approaches

Educating today's students has shifted from providing information to opening doors for them to explore topics and create meaningful learning experiences for themselves. Technology has been incorporated as a central feature of this process. The implication is that educators are moving away from the idea of school as a place to *get knowledge* to the view that school is a place to *learn how to learn*. The challenge for you as a teacher is to provide opportunities for all students to use technology in meaningful ways to accomplish learning tasks. This may mean selecting specific software for individual students—for example, to practice math skills or to search online databases. This may mean changing your entire approach to a lesson. Student projects, such as working on an ecology report, are not new within the school curriculum, but the approach certainly can be.

You should be a model user of technology for your students. Students will quickly notice if the teacher makes illegal copies of programs and apps and doesn't follow copyright guidelines. Remember, actions speak louder than words. Check with your technology coordinator, library media specialist, or principal for the specific guidelines and licensing agreements that you should follow. See Copyright Concerns.

Students can interact directly with various technologies as part of their instructional activities in a variety of ways, from working with material presented by the computer or mobile device in a controlled sequence, such as a drill-and-practice program, to a student-initiated creative activity, such as a digitally published book of student poems. Learners may take tests on the computer or a mobile device or input information into personal e-portfolios. Students can use the e-portfolio to demonstrate specific learning or to create a catalog of their work over time to record their educational progress. The technology can help both the teacher and students in maintaining information about their learning and in guiding instruction. That is, the digital device can organize and store easily retrievable

Copyright Concerns

Software

Congress amended the Copyright Act to clear up questions of fair use of copyrighted programs. The changes defined the term *computer program* for copyright purposes and set forth rules on permissible and nonpermissible use of copyrighted computer software. According to the amended law, you are permitted to do the following with a single copy of a program:

- Make one backup or archival copy of the program.
- Use a "locksmith" program to bypass the copy-prevention code on the original to make the archival copy.
- Install one copy of the program onto a computer hard drive.
- Adapt a computer program from one language to another if the program is not available in the desired language.
- Add features to a copyrighted program to make better use of the program.
- Adapt a copyrighted program to meet local needs.

Without the copyright owner's permission, you are prohibited from doing the following:

- Making multiple copies of a copyrighted program.
- Making additional copies from an archival or backup copy.
- Making copies of copyrighted programs to be sold, leased, loaned, transmitted, or given away.
- Selling a locally produced adaptation of a copyrighted program.
- Making multiple copies of an adaptation of a copyrighted program even for use within a school or school district.
- Putting a single copy of a program onto a network without permission or a special site license.
- Duplicating the printed copyrighted software documentation unless allowed by the copyrighted software company.

information about each student and about relevant instructional materials. Many programs and apps can generate reports and graphs detailing the progress of an individual student or an entire class. Many computer programs and mobile apps can also diagnose the learning needs of students and prescribe optimal sequences of instruction for each student.

Traditionally, computers were used to reinforce classroom instruction. Software was designed to provide direct instruction or practice for students, often programmed to branch to other segments of the lesson based on student responses. Many of these designs are still in use today. Based on the constructivist view of learning, current instructional strategies try to engage students in ways that allow them to develop, or construct, their own mental structure in a particular area of study. To engage students in this type of learning, the environment must provide them with materials that allow them to explore. Early research by Papert serves as the foundation for digital "microworlds"—environments that permit students to freely experiment, test, and invent (Papert, 1993a, 1993b). These environments reinforce learning and career development skills by allowing students to focus on a problem area and create solutions that are meaningful to them.

Jonassen, Howland, Moore, and Marra (2003) have expanded the idea that technology can engage and support students in their learning. They have suggested that students learn from the digital environment because it encourages students to use cognitive learning strategies and critical-thinking skills. Students control how and when the computer provides them with the information they need. Part of your responsibility as the teacher is to choose from among the many possible technologies, software programs, and mobile apps available to create such learning environments and to assist your students in constructing their own mental models.

Types of Digital Resources

Digital technologies provide virtually instantaneous response to student input, have extensive capacity to store and manipulate information, and are unmatched in their abilities to serve many students simultaneously. Technology's role in instruction is to serve as a resource for rich learning experiences, giving your students the power to influence the depth and direction of their learning. Technology makes it possible to control and integrate a variety of media—still and motion pictures, graphics, and sounds, as well as text-based information. Digital devices can also record, analyze, and react to student responses typed on a keyboard, selected with a mouse or touch screen, or activated by voice. As your students begin to work with information, they find the digital resources available to them help make the process easier and more fun. Students can use the technology to gather information and to prepare materials that demonstrate their knowledge and understanding of that information.

Besides providing information, digital devices are also tools for creativity and communication. Because these technologies allow sharing and collaboration with others around the world, students often strive to achieve their "best" artifacts of learning because their work can be seen by an audience outside the classroom.

Computers and mobile devices can be used for word processing and desktop publishing. Most students have access to word processing programs to produce papers and assignments. Some students create multimedia projects, integrating graphics, sound, and video for presentations to their classmates or other groups. Presentation software, which can be connected to a digital projector, allows students to share and discuss their work.

WORD PROCESSING AND DESKTOP PUBLISHING.   Using concept-mapping software and mobile apps such as Inspiration and SimpleMind+, students can gather their ideas into concept maps. They can then begin to develop those ideas into connected text from outlines generated by the concept-mapping programs. These outlines can be imported into a word processing program, which makes it easy for students to edit their work. The word processor makes it possible for students to work with their ideas and to quickly make changes as they explore various ways to present them. Spelling and grammar checking are available to assist your students in identifying and correcting errors in draft versions of their papers.

In many programs, an integrated thesaurus helps students find the right word for a specific situation. Editing, a process children are not prone to enjoy, suddenly becomes easier. Students are more willing to make changes when editing is simplified.

Students enjoy putting their ideas onto paper. They especially enjoy seeing their work in finished copy. Desktop publishing allows students to design layouts that are creative and enjoyable to read. Using a desktop publishing program, students can add graphics to their pages. They can see how the pages will look before they print them or publish them on the Web. Students of all ages like to produce their writings in formal documents, such as small books and newsletters. Class newsletters are also very popular, as students work together to produce a document they are proud to share with family and friends.

CALCULATORS AND SPREADSHEETS.   Most computers and mobile devices include calculators as one of the basic tools built into the operating system, with newer equipment offering graphing calculators as a more robust option. Learners can use these calculators to solve complex mathematical problems. Students can also learn to use a spreadsheet program to prepare sets of data collected as part of a project. The technology can also facilitate data gathering when connected to laboratory equipment. The collected data are downloaded to a spreadsheet program for analysis and to prepare tables or graphic displays of the results.

TEXT-BASED COMMUNICATIONS.   Today's students frequently communicate via email, text messaging, or online chatting. This can be accomplished from a computer, mobile phone, tablet, or through online platforms such as Google+, Edmodo, and Facebook. This type of message format is quick and easy to use. In the classroom, you may wish to engage students with email messages as a means for connecting with classmates or students from a distant location (e-pals). As communications through these technologies continue to increase, you may want to take some time to teach your students when it is appropriate to use formal (traditional) versus informal (textspeak and shorthand) writing techniques.

AUDIO- AND VIDEO-BASED COMMUNICATIONS.   Communication in your class is not limited to text-based communications. You can encourage students to incorporate audio files they create to enhance their communication with others. Many types of audio resources are available for learners to create exciting representations of their learning. For example, students can add narration, music, and sound effects for a presentation, create an audio podcast in which they reflect on issues associated with the topic of climate change, or practice their diction and articulation as they learn a foreign language. Students who enjoy music or have musical talent can create interesting vocal and instrumental music with programs like GarageBand and incorporate their music into slideshows and multimedia presentations.

Students are very creative and can use images captured on their mobile devices or digital cameras to enhance their messages or as substitutes for words. In addition, you and your students can interact with each other, as well as experts around the world, using teleconferencing tools such as Skype and Google+ Hangouts.

GRAPHICS.   Drawing and creating graphics is a fun activity for students. Computer software such as KidPix 3D, and mobile apps such as Doodle Buddy can make drawing even more pleasurable. These programs and apps provide a variety of engaging effects, with special tools such as a rubber stamp that makes noise as it marks on the screen or a path animation tool that makes characters come to life with walking, running, and flying. It is also possible to import a photo and then customize it by drawing on it, editing it, or adding special effects and filters to it. Computer technology thus changes the dynamics of art for children.

As students gain skill with drawing software, they can learn more complex drawing and drafting programs. High school students can use computer-aided design (CAD) and graphics programs to prepare complex visuals. Many of the skills associated with these types of software are easy for students to learn. As another example, an art program such as Photo Deluxe allows your students to develop complex projects with an array of tools ranging from basic drawing tools for lines and shapes to advanced tools for editing and redesigning. They may create their own pictures or begin with commercially designed clip art available from many suppliers. A simple picture can be developed into a very artistic piece with only a few keystrokes.

PRESENTATIONS. Presentations have become a popular format for teachers and students. With the computer connected to a digital projector, it is possible to share information and ideas using colorful slides and animations. Many students enjoy preparing presentations for their classmates using programs and online services such as PowerPoint, Keynote, and Prezi. These programs can also be used to create other forms of media, such as e-portfolios, digital storybooks, and interactive games that allow students to demonstrate their understanding or to challenge other learners. You should supervise your students carefully; they can be distracted by the "bells and whistles" and spend more time deciding the color scheme, the transitions, or the font style than they do thinking about and preparing the content of the presentation.

Video Example 5.2: Preparing Students to Create Digital Presentations

Observe how Mr. Bird reflects on how he prepares students to create digital presentations. In what ways does Mr. Bird prepare students before they go to the computer to create their digital presentations? Describe why Mr. Bird felt it was important to engage students in pre-planning?

GAMES AND SIMULATIONS. Games and simulations are instructional tools that support students in learning knowledge and skills and involve the use of problem-solving strategies and techniques. Computer games, mobile apps, and electronic simulations incorporate many important learning principles, such as interactivity, challenge, problem solving, systems thinking, distributed knowledge, and performance related to competency (Gee, 2013). In short, games and simulations provide learners with multiple opportunities to practice solving structured or ill-structured problems, engaging students in complex, higher-order thinking. Students are asked to analyze a task, determine the conditions needed to address that task, identify cues, and engage in self-monitoring and evaluation. Problems can be introduced to students as a way to have them practice skills in practical applications. Providing students with rich and varied problems challenges them to integrate knowledge and skills into their learning strategies while they are engaged in a meaningful activity within a virtual world (Shute, Rieber, & Van Eck, 2011).

COMPUTER-ASSISTED INSTRUCTION. Students benefit from practice on basic skills or knowledge. **Computer-assisted instruction (CAI)** helps students learn specific knowledge and skills. Technology can be used to reinforce classroom instruction. The variety of instructional tools across all content areas is vast. Possibilities range from basic drill-and-practice and tutorials to more extended and complex learning problems. For students who need review or practice, drill-and-practice programs can help them acquire the specific steps needed to complete a task. For example, Math Blaster's computer games and mobile apps assist students in learning math facts (addition, subtraction, multiplication, and division) through drill-and-practice using an arcade game format, giving students the opportunity to practice what they have learned. You will want to use caution not to over-use the drill-and-practice types of activities when using computer resources with your students. It is important to provide them with a wide spectrum of learning opportunities.

Software is capable of providing students with complex tasks that engage them in real-world problems. Programs such as Neighborhood MapMachine engage students in activities related to geography in which they create and navigate maps of their own neighborhoods and other communities while learning challenging navigation concepts, such as using scale to determine the distance between places on maps. Video technologies can easily be incorporated, focusing attention on tangible examples of geographic distances and how they impact travel, trade, and more. Word processing, graphics, and a host of computer software programs help students organize and communicate their ideas.

COMPUTER-MANAGED INSTRUCTION. Computer-managed instruction (CMI) is a label for a broad category of applications designed to assist in the management of the instructional process. CMI aids you in the management of instruction without actually doing the teaching. CMI can provide you with learning objectives, learning resources, and assessment of learner performance. For example, you can use a mobile device to collect information on how students are completing tasks. You can also use the computer to assist you in preparing instructional materials such as handouts or presentations.

Application Exercise 5.1

 Check Your Understanding 5.1

Advantages of Using Digital Devices

There are advantages to using digital devices with your students. As you plan your lessons, you will find that these devices can provide richer learning experiences.

- *Learner Participation.* Students engage in learning activities when using digital materials. These materials help to maintain students' attention.
- *Individualization.* Digital resources allow students control over the rate and sequence of their learning, giving them more control over outcomes. High-speed, personal-ized responses to learner actions yield immediate feedback and reinforcement.
- *Special needs.* Digital technologies are effective with special learners, gifted and at-risk students, and students with diverse physical or demographic backgrounds, such as second language learners. Their special needs can be accommodated to ensure that instruction proceeds at an appropriate pace.
- *Monitoring.* The recordkeeping ability of the software, mobile apps, and online services makes instruction more individualized; you can prepare individual lessons for all your students and monitor their progress.
- *Information management.* Electronic resources can cover a growing knowledge base associated with the information explosion. They can manage all types of

information—text, graphic, audio, and video. More information is easily accessible by you and your students so they can monitor their own progress as well.

- *Multisensory experiences.* Digital devices provide diverse learning experiences. These can employ a variety of instructional strategies that use audio, visual, and tactile approaches at the level of basic instruction, remediation, or enrichment.

 Check Your Understanding 5.2

Limitations of Using Digital Devices

There are some issues associated with using digital devices that need to be considered. As you plan to integrate the technology into your lessons, you should consider some of those issues.

- *Copyright.* The ease with which software and other digital information can be duplicated without permission has inhibited some commercial publishers and private entrepreneurs from producing and marketing high-quality instructional software. For additional information regarding copyright, refer to the "Copyright Concerns" feature in this chapter.
- *High expectations.* You and your students may have unrealistic expectations for technology. Many view computers and mobile devices as magical and expect learning to happen with little or no effort, but in reality, users derive benefits proportional to their investments.
- *Complex.* More advanced programs may be difficult to use, especially for student production, because they require the ability to use complex skills.
- *Lack of structure.* Students whose learning preferences require more structured guidance may become frustrated. Students may also make poor decisions about how much information to explore.

 Check Your Understanding 5.3

Integrating Technology for Learning

The ultimate value of technology in education depends on how fully and seamlessly it is integrated into the curriculum. Technological devices in the classroom are not additional "things" that you must include, but rather are integral to the support and extension of learning for all your students (ISTE, 2017). You need a framework for using technology that covers a variety of learning characteristics and accommodates varied teaching strategies. Most important, results need to be measurable to align with a clear set of objectives—the second step in the ASSURE model. In classrooms where technology is integrated successfully, students use it with the same ease with which they use pencils, books, rulers, and maps. In technology-rich classrooms, you and your students engage in problem solving, cultivate creativity, collaborate globally, and discover the value of lifelong learning.

With increasing ease of use, technology is becoming more natural to use in problem-solving and cooperative learning strategies. Software, telecommunications, and social media can provide students with experiences in working together to solve complex problems. Often, students incorporate several different types of applications to explore a problem situation. For example, when assigned to prepare a report on ecology, a group of your students might use computer databases to search for information resources to

Taking a Look at Technology Integration

Testing the Waters

A community was being bothered by an odor from a stream in a small park next to a middle school property. A trio of science teachers decided to combine their classes and presented students with the problem of the smelly stream to guide them in the process of learning how to apply the scientific method. The teachers introduced the scientific inquiry model and provided an array of technologies that included probes, magnifiers, and data analysis spreadsheets that the students could use at the nearby stream. Students gathered water samples from the stream, tested the water, analyzed the data, and hypothesized about factors that might be producing the identified odor problem. Groups of students worked together to exchange their data, analysis, and ideas. Together the three classes decided on a course of action and communicated their ideas to the community and helped them take action to alleviate the smell. Reorganizing the science classes and integrating technologies to successfully solve real problems demonstrated to their school administration that problem-based learning is a constructive and beneficial way for students to learn. It also was an activity that guided the students in understanding how to apply their knowledge toward improving their community.

include in their report. They might connect with people in different locations around the world through email, texting, teleconferencing, or social media to request information. They might use spreadsheet programs to store, sort, analyze, and share their information (see Taking a Look at Technology Integration).

The use of multimedia can be helpful for information and tasks that must be shown rather than simply told. Printed material and lecture alone cannot adequately present some instruction (see When to Use Technology). Your students who want to interact with the instruction may need to find an appropriate software choice. Many newer versions of software now come with interactive media demonstrations. For example, The Ellis Island Experience is an interactive documentary with a wealth of information about the role this primary immigration station played in U.S. history from 1892 to 1954. Designed for middle-level and high school students, the software lets them explore five modules filled with images, audio, and video to learn more about the experiences of immigrants as they entered the United States. An artifact viewer resource lets students look at images, memorabilia, and documents in detail.

When to Use Technology

Guidelines	Examples
Practicing what they have just studied in class	Students who need extra help with a skill or task can play a drill-and-practice game to practice skills or reinforce their understanding.
Learning independently	Technology can be part of a kindergarten classroom learning center. Young students can complete learning tasks by using digital tutorials from software, mobile apps, or multimedia to advance their knowledge.
Creating learning opportunities for gifted students	Gifted students can be challenged to expand or enhance their learning by using more complex programs and apps or by extending classroom activities with challenging problems.
Working collaboratively with other students	Students can work together to navigate through instructional materials to help each other understand the information.
Reaching a student who is having difficulty in learning	Students can use the material in personally meaningful ways, navigating through the material as appropriate to their learning characteristics.
Challenging students to present information in a new way	Students can create their own materials to share their knowledge with others in the class or school.

Check Your Understanding 5.4

Application Selection

NOTE: For the purposes of this discussion, the term *software* includes computer software, mobile apps, and online services. Therefore, PowerPoint, Creationary, and Google Docs would all be considered software in this context.

There are several factors associated with selecting software (see Selection Rubric: Software). It is very important to examine the software within the context of learning outcomes. Other factors that should be considered include how the software stimulates creativity, fosters collaboration, and provides feedback. You should also consider your **operating system,** which is the computer's underlying system software, such as Mac OS, Windows, or Unix, that functions as the computer's interface with the user. Specific software programs, also called **applications,** or **apps**, are written to run on different operating systems, which determine precisely how the user, computer, and application interact to produce the desired results. You must ensure that software you select is designed to run on your available operating system and that it will function properly with your specific hardware configuration (See Technology for All Learners).

When you are evaluating instructional software, you should consider how information is presented to be certain it is done in a clear and logical manner to ensure learning (see Selection Rubric: Software). You need to examine the intent

Technology for All Learners

Software and Apps

Computer software and mobile apps can help with a variety of learning needs. The following examples demonstrate ways that learners can use technology to help with specific learning difficulties.

Students can work on improving their problem-solving abilities with The Factory Deluxe, software that highlights different strategies for problem solving, such as working backward, analyzing a process, and determining a sequence. Learners are given a square on the computer and four types of machines to shape it as they work through a series of levels that build their knowledge of geometric attributes in order to prepare a product. The "rotator" machine can be programmed to rotate the square from 30 to 180 degrees. The "puncher" machine can punch square or triangular holes in the square. The "striper" machine paints thin, medium, or thick stripes of various colors. And the "cutter" cuts off and discards parts that are not needed. Learners must apply problem-solving strategies in order to successfully manufacture a product with the machines.

For students with visual impairments who need to use computer software, email, or the Internet, adaptive software programs called *screen readers* use speech synthesizers to read aloud the text and names of icons. Learners can navigate using the keyboard, hitting the tab button to move from icon to icon. Nontext items, such as graphics and photos, are labeled with alternative textual descriptions, called *alt-tags*, which allow learners with visual impairments to hear descriptions of these items. These software programs are available on both PC and Mac operating systems in the settings of the operating software called "universal access." Some learners with visual impairments may be able to avoid the necessity for screen readers by using increased font sizes and modified display settings that provide higher contrast. These modifications can be made in the operating system's general settings under "universal access."

Students with advanced learning skills can be challenged to put on their thinking caps and create interesting solutions by completing complex puzzles. Puzzles are an interactive way to engage students in finding alternative ways to examine an issue or problem. For example, using inquiry and imagination, students link their knowledge of facts to the resolution of the puzzles presented in the Jewel Quest game. Students are given clues along the way to help them find the golden path. In the process, students learn some information about archeology. Jewel Quest is only one of many types of puzzle-based games available to challenge students.

SELECTION RUBRIC **Software**

NOTE: For the purposes of this discussion, the term software includes computer software, mobile apps, and online services.

Complete and save the following interactive evaluation to reference when selecting online software to integrate with learning.

Title _____

Hardware Required _____

Source/Location _____

© Date _____ Cost _____ Length _____ Minutes _____

Primary User(s) _____

Subject Area _____ Grade Level _____

Instructional Strategies _____

Brief Description

Standards/Outcomes/Objectives

Prerequisites (e.g., prior knowledge, reading ability, vocabulary level)

Strengths

Limitations

Special Features

Name _____ **Date** _____

(Continued)

SELECTION RUBRIC **Software**

Rating Area	High Quality	Medium Quality	Low Quality
Alignment with standards, outcomes, and objectives	Standard/outcome/objective addressed and use of technology should enhance student learning.	Standard/outcome/objective partially addressed and use of technology may enhance student learning.	Standard/outcome/objective not addressed and use of technology will likely not enhance student learning.
Accurate and current information	Information is correct and does not contain material that is out of date.	Information correct but does contain material that is out of date.	Information is not correct and does contain material that is out of date.
Age-appropriate language	Language used is age appropriate and vocabulary is understandable.	Language used is nearly age appropriate and some vocabulary is above/below student age.	Language used is not age appropriate and vocabulary is clearly inappropriate for student age.
Interest level and engagement	Topic presented so that students are likely to be interested and actively engaged in learning.	Topic presented to interest students most of the time and engage most in learning.	Topic presented so as not to interest students and not engage them in learning.
Technical quality	The material represents best available technology and media.	The material represents technology and media that are good quality, although there are some problems.	The material represents technology and media that are not well prepared and are of very poor quality.
Ease of use (user may be student or teacher)	Material follows easy-to-use patterns with nothing to confuse the user.	Material follows patterns that are easy to follow most of the time, with a few things to confuse the user.	Material follows no patterns and most of the time the user is very confused.
Bias free	There is no evidence of objectionable bias or advertising.	There is little evidence of bias or advertising.	There is much evidence of bias or advertising.
Stimulates creativity	Most students can use the software to create original pieces that represent learning.	Some students can use the software to start original pieces that begin to show their learning.	Most students cannot use the software to create original pieces that represent their learning.
Fosters collaboration	Students are able to work in collaborative groups when using the software with little problem.	Students are able to work in collaborative groups when using the software most of the time.	Students are not able to work in collaborative groups when using the software.
Practice and feedback	Software provides students with skill or knowledge practice and information that helps them complete their learning tasks.	Software provides students with some skill or knowledge practice and information that sometimes helps them complete their learning tasks.	Software does not provide students with skill or knowledge practice, nor information that helps them with their learning tasks.

Recommended for Classroom Use: _____ Yes _____ No

Ideas for Classroom Use: _____

_____

of the lesson and its relation to your intended outcomes, the curriculum, and the pertinent achievement standards. The information needs to be presented in a manner designed to maintain student interest and involvement in the learning tasks. Additional aspects to consider are accuracy, age appropriateness, and ease of use.

It is important that instructional software follows sound educational techniques and principles and also provides your students with **feedback** on their efforts. In a drill-and-practice program, it is important that students have frequent informative feedback in order to improve their skills. When using software designed to challenge higher-order thinking, students will need feedback to determine the quality of their choices. If your goal is to provide students with collaborative learning opportunities, many programs are designed so that groups of students can work together to achieve the intended outcomes. Several of these types of programs are designed with the one-computer classroom in mind.

Sometimes software has special effects or features that may be essential for effective learning. Often, however, special effects are only window dressing that adds no value to the learning. In fact, they may interfere with learning. Color, graphics, animation, and sound should be a part of quality software only if they contribute to student learning. Text should be presented in a consistent manner, using size, color, and location to reduce the cognitive burden of deciphering meaning. Keystroking and software interface techniques should be intuitive for students. The manner in which students interact with software needs to be transparent, allowing them to focus on content.

✓ **Check Your Understanding** 5.5

Hardware

Regardless of type of computer or complexity of the system, computing devices have a number of standard components. The physical equipment that makes up the computer is referred to as the **hardware.** A computer's specific combination of hardware components is called its **configuration**. The basic hardware components are diagrammed in Figure 5.1.

Input devices transmit information to the computer; **output devices** display the information to the user. The most commonly used input device is the keyboard.

Figure 5.1 Basic Elements of a Desktop or Laptop Computer

Others include the mouse, stylus, joystick, graphics tablet, probe, scanner, microphone, and camera. Both students and teachers can use graphics tablets to incorporate drawings into their programs. Science laboratory monitoring devices, such as temperature probes, can also be connected directly to a computer with the proper interface device.

Monitors are the standard output device. Another output device, which allows large-group viewing, is the digital projector. Connected to the computer, the digital projector can be used as part of class instruction, such as in a PowerPoint display or to show slides outlining steps for students to follow when using specific software in a computer lab. Other output devices include speakers, printers, and peripherals, such as Lego Mindstorms, remote controlled vehicles, and flying drones.

The **central processing unit (CPU)** is the core element, or "brain," that carries out all the calculations and controls the total system. In a personal computer, the CPU is one (or more) small chips (microprocessors) inside the machine.

The computer's memory stores information for manipulation by the CPU. The memory contains what is termed the *control function*—that is, the programs written to tell the CPU what to do and in what order. In computers, control instructions and sets of data are stored in two types of memory:

- *Read-only memory (ROM).* The control instructions that have been "wired" permanently into the computer's memory make up the ROM, which the computer needs constantly to read programming language and perform internal monitoring functions.

- *Random access memory (RAM).* The more flexible part of the memory makes up the RAM. The particular program or set of data being manipulated by the user is temporarily stored in RAM, only to be erased or transferred to storage after use to make way for the next program.

A computer's memory size is usually described in terms of how many bytes it can store at one time. A **byte** is the number of bits required to represent and store one character (letter or number) of text. A **bit** is a single unit of data, coded in binary form as either 0 (off) or 1 (on). A byte is usually made up of 8 bits of various combinations of 0s and 1s (Figure 5.2) A **kilobyte (KB)** refers to approximately 1,000 bytes (1,024 to be exact), a **megabyte (MB)**, or "meg," indicates 1,000 KB or approximately a million bytes, and a **gigabyte (GB)**, or "gig," is equal to 1,000 MB or approximately one billion bytes. Megabytes are the units used to measure the RAM storage capacity of a computer. Thus, if a computer can process 1,024,000 bytes, it is said to have 1 "meg" of memory capacity. We now talk about RAM storage in terms of **terabytes (TB),** which is a million megabytes or a trillion bytes. More powerful machines are capable of processing more bytes simultaneously, thus having more computing capacity.

A computer's memory is one of its limiting factors. You need to be sure that the computer has enough memory to run the software you will be using. If you plan to use more than one application at a time, it is recommended you have a minimum of 1 GB. Although 1 MB of memory can hold approximately 2,000 single-spaced pages of text, many graphics and animations require several megabytes to display properly. The computer's operating system, application programs, and data files are usually stored on the computer hard drive, which is inside the computer. The hard drive provides a "permanent" place within the computer for these types of programs and documents to reside. But a hard drive is vulnerable and can crash, so it is often best to keep backups of programs and data files separately from the CPU. Portable flash drives (discussed further in the following paragraph) and external hard drives are common ways to store programs, and recordable DVDs may also be available. Storage capacity (measured in MB, GB or TB) has expanded to keep pace with the rapidly growing memory demands of today's software and the ever-increasing size of graphics- and animation-laden data files.

Figure 5.2 Representation of the Letter A in ASCII (American Standard Code for Information Interchange)

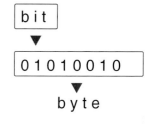

High-capacity removable media devices serve as the portable storage format of choice. Generally termed **removable storage devices,** they are small, portable, and used primarily for backing up and archiving data files. **USB** (universal serial bus) is a hardware interface technology that allows the user to connect a device without having to restart the computer. A USB mini-drive, more commonly called a **flash drive** (or jump drive), is a form of removable storage device that lets you store files in a portable unit. The capacity of a flash drive can range from a few megabytes to a gigabyte or more. Some mini-drives have removable flash memory cards, allowing the user to increase the memory capacity of the mini-drive by changing the memory chip. This same memory chip might also fit into a digital camera or a hand-held device, thus making the interchange of visual and text information very flexible. The USB mini-drive does not require any special wiring and can fit into your pocket. One additional feature is its suitability for either Windows or Mac computers, permitting users to switch between platforms with ease. Removable storage devices have many uses, including:

- Archiving old files that you don't use anymore but may want to access someday
- Storing unusually large files, such as graphic images, that you need infrequently
- Exchanging large files with someone
- Moving your files from one computer to another, perhaps from your desktop to your laptop computer or from your home computer to a classroom computer
- Keeping certain files separate from files on your hard disk (e.g., old test files)

Application Exercise 5.2

 Check Your Understanding 5.6

The Digital Classroom

There has been a trend in schools toward the multiple-device classroom, in particular, toward the use of laptop carts and carts of mobile devices. Some schools are focused on the use of a "one-to-one" initiative where all students have access to a device throughout the school day. In earlier days, when schools had a limited number of computers, they often resided in a computer laboratory. As more computers became available, single computers were assigned to individual classrooms. Teachers soon discovered how to successfully use multiple computers in their classrooms. Some schools, therefore, dismantled the laboratories and distributed the computers to individual classrooms, thereby increasing the number of classrooms with multiple computers.

Single-Device Classroom

In some schools, access to technology is still limited. Often there is just a single technology lab where you can take your whole class of students to work on computers or mobile devices as part of a lesson. However, increased interest by many teachers in incorporating technology into lessons limits the availability of the technology lab. One solution has been to place a single computer or mobile device in each classroom that the teacher and students can use throughout the day.

It is possible for you to use a single computer or mobile device in creative ways with a whole class of students. Although some software is intended to be used by single students for work on specific tasks, other software is designed for group activities. For example, with the series Decisions, Decisions, groups of students interact with the technology to get specific information before they can proceed with their group activity. Your students do not need to work on the device during the entire lesson. While one group interacts with the computer or mobile device, the remaining groups are working at their desks.

The single-device classroom allows several formats for use of the equipment:

- *Large group.* With a digital projector, you can demonstrate to a whole class how to use a particular software program or how to manage a particular set of data.

- *Small group.* A small group of students can work together on the computer or mobile device. Each group has a turn using the software to gather or present data and then returns to their seats, allowing the next group to have their turn.

- *Learning center.* Individual students or small groups can go to a learning center anchored by the computer or mobile device. By integrating a specific software program, you create an interactive learning center on that subject.

- *Personal secretary.* The computer or mobile device can assist you with maintaining grades, communicating with parents, and preparing instructional materials.

Multi-Device Classroom

Many classrooms have several computers and/or mobile devices available. This can be helpful when groups of students need to use the same software simultaneously (Figures 5.3 through 5.5). Student groups of two or three can share one device. You may also have a projector to display information for your students on one screen.

Figure 5.3 Elementary Classroom with Four Computers Used for Individual and Small-Group Study

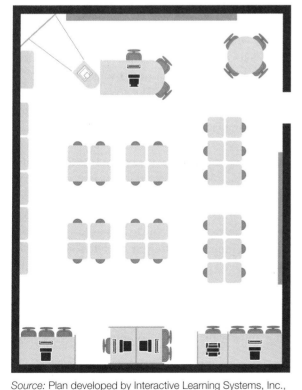

Source: Plan developed by Interactive Learning Systems, Inc., Cincinnati, OH.

Figure 5.4 High School Classroom with 12 Computers and 2 Printers Used Individually

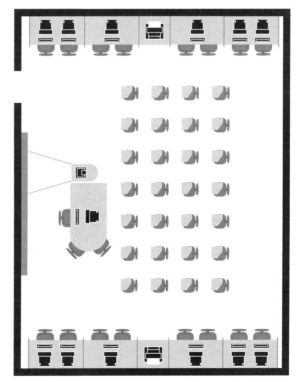

Source: Plan developed by Interactive Learning Systems, Inc., Cincinnati, OH.

Figure 5.5 Middle School Classroom with Chairs Arranged at Computers for Collaborative Learning

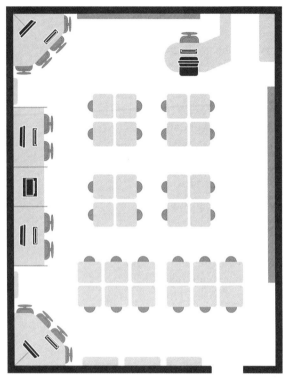

Source: Plan developed by Interactive Learning Systems, Inc., Cincinnati, OH.

Figure 5.6 Computer Lab Computers around the wall in a laboratory allow one teacher to monitor all student activity.

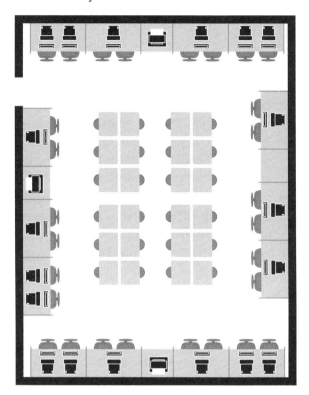

A popular variation of the multi-device classroom is the mobile technology cart. Many schools provide a laptop cart or a cart of mobile devices as a way to offer devices for the classroom without the major expense of permanent installations. The carts allow you access to a set of computing devices when needed. You share the cart with other teachers and benefit from technology in classroom settings when you need it, rather than having to leave the classroom to go to a technology laboratory, which might not be available at a time you wish to use it. In addition, the carts take advantage of wireless technology, thus providing access to the Internet or to software available on the central school server. Most schools have wireless available throughout the building for easy access to the Internet.

On occasion you may want each of your students to be working on a computer or mobile device during a lesson; it may be necessary for the whole class to have access to the same technology simultaneously. Schools often place 20 to 30 networked computers or mobile devices together in a single room shared by all. The technology laboratory or "lab" is appropriate if you want your students to be working independently or in small groups on different programs and different activities. To monitor student activity and keep them on task, as well as to prevent students from viewing inappropriate or irrelevant material, the devices can be arranged around the walls of the computer lab with the monitors facing the center of the room (see Figure 5.6), allowing you to quickly see what each student is doing and respond to student questions individually. In some networks, the teacher can control and monitor what is shown on each student computer.

Video Example 5.3: Multiple Device Classroom

Listen to Mr. Bird's comments regarding student use of computers in a multiple device classroom. How does computer use benefit student learning? In what ways does Mr. Bird better ensure that the needs of individual students are met?

There are advantages to using a technology lab. A group of students can be taught the same lesson simultaneously, which might be more efficient for you. Also, software can be located in one place conveniently. Supervision and security are often easier when all the computers are located in a single room. Labs are often structured to facilitate ease of use by putting all the computers on one network, sharing software stored on a central server. This allows connected computers to be placed throughout the school building so students can connect to the network from the technology lab, their classrooms, or the media center.

The foremost limitation with the technology lab is access. If there are no other computers or mobile devices available to students outside the lab, then students will have to wait until the lab is not scheduled to use the facilities. If one class is scheduled to use the lab, the other classes will have to wait. Also, because of scheduling problems, some classes may not have access to the lab at all. Creative use of school-wide networks can ease some of the congestion problems so that classroom computers and mobile cart devices can be connected to the resources. Thus, if the lab is not available, then the students can use the classroom technology to do what they needed to do in the lab.

Innovations in Teaching

Digital Fabricator: A Printer for Real Objects

Three-dimensional printers or rapid prototyping machines, also known as "fabbers" (short for fabricators), are a relatively new form of computer output device that can build 3-D objects by carefully depositing materials drop by drop, layer by layer. Using a geometric blueprint from a CAD program and the proper type of fast-setting liquid, you can create complex objects that would normally take special tools and skills when using conventional manufacturing techniques. A fabber can allow you to explore new designs, email physical objects to other fabber owners, and most importantly, set your ideas free.

Traditional 3-D printers are room-sized and cost thousands of dollars. The Fab@Home digital fabricator printer is designed to be the size of a desktop printer and cost about the same as a home computer system. It uses common materials to create the 3-D objects. Silicon caulk, fast-drying liquid resin, and even Cheez Whiz work well in the fabricator. The one thing the printer cannot print is paper! If you can imagine it, you can build it on your fabricator.

These printers are appearing in schools around the world where students are learning to use CAD programs. Now students can design their ideas with the CAD program and then actually print or "fab" them on the spot. They can hold the object and view it from all directions, permitting 21st century learners to move literally into new dimensions of learning.

> ✓ **Check Your Understanding** 5.7

Shared Writing Exercise 5.1

Summary

- *Describe strategies for and examples of using digital devices in the classroom.* In the digital classroom there are a number of ways in which devices can be used to augment the curriculum. There has been a shift from the desktop computer to hand-held tablets and smart phones along with an array of devices that extend the access to resources.

- *Discuss the advantages of using digital devices to support learning.* An important consideration is engaging the learner and digital devices offer that opportunity. The multisensory aspects of the information provide for individualization and meeting the learning needs of all students.

- *Discuss the limitations of using digital devices to support learning.* A major issue is that of copyright, both in the software use and in the attribution of resources. Some students require a more structured approach to their learning experiences, which may not be offered by some digital resources. Software needs to be age appropriate in order to ensure that the complexity of the software does not frustrate the learner.

- *Discuss ideas related to integrating technology for learning support.* Digital devices are not add-ons, but are useful components of any learning experience. The hardware and applications offer multiple opportunities for students to engage in developing basic skills, creativity, and problem solving.

- *Describe the types of applications that might be selected for use in the classroom.* There are a number of different types of applications available for use and the selection depends on learner needs. Student interactions with software need to be considered for optimal learning experiences.

- *Describe the basics of hardware elements you will find in learning settings.* Even though the standards emphasis is on use, there is still a need to understand the basics of hardware elements. As devices continue to change, the basics remain the same.

- *Discuss how you might configure the digital classroom to support student learning.* With the shift from the desktop device to mobile resources, the classroom setting for using digital devices changes. There are a number of ways a teacher can arrange a classroom setting to accommodate learning and use of the variety of devices available.

ASSURE Lesson Plan

This ASSURE Classroom Case Study is based on the "The Water Cycle" by teacher Kerry Bird, who shares teaching tips and ideas for implementing a lesson in which fourth-grade students complete a PowerPoint project to demonstrate their knowledge of the water cycle.

This ASSURE Lesson Plan describes the instructional planning used by Kerry Bird, a fourth-grade teacher who wanted to increase student learning and interest in science through the use of computers. To address this challenge, his students created PowerPoint presentations of the water cycle. Following is Kerry Bird's ASSURE lesson plan for the water cycle project.

Kerry Bird
Fourth Grade
Topic: Water Cycle

Analyze Learners

General Characteristics

The students in Kerry Bird's class are of mixed ethnicities and from low- to middle-income homes. They are fairly equally distributed by gender and all are 9 or 10 years old. The majority of the students are reading at grade level, with four reading above grade level and three struggling with reading. Generally, the students are well behaved, but tend to become restless when required to complete traditional seatwork.

Entry Competencies

The students are, in general, able to do the following:

- Create and save PowerPoint presentations
- Locate and download digital files from the server
- Insert graphics into presentations
- Enter and edit presentation text

Learning Differences and Needs

Mr. Bird's students learn best when engaged in hands-on activities. Their level of motivation increases when using computers because they can personalize their work. Some students prefer to express their creativity through written narratives or drawn images, whereas some choose to create or find existing images to express their ideas. Students' learning styles also vary in their preference for working independently or with other students.

State Standards and Objectives

Curriculum Standards

National Science Education Standards—Content Standard D: As a result of their activities in grades K–4, all students should develop an understanding of changes in earth and sky.

Technology Standards

ISTE Standards for Students 4.A—Deliberate Use of Deign Process, 4.b – Select and Use Digital Tools, and 4.c – Develop and Refine Prototypes: Students use a variety of technologies to identify and solve problems by creating new, useful, or creative solutions.

Learning Objectives

The learning objectives for this lesson are as follows:

1. The students will illustrate and accurately label the four stages of the water cycle in a hand-drawn storyboard.
2. The students will create a PowerPoint presentation meeting the following criteria: contains five slides, with first slide as title slide; each slide includes a graphic, text, and sound; transitions are used between each slide; and the presentation uses a design template that supports the water cycle theme. The PowerPoint presentation illustrates and provides an accurate text explanation of each of the four phases of the water cycle.
3. The students will verbally describe each of the four phases during their PowerPoint presentations of the water cycle.

Select Strategies

Kerry Bird selects teacher- and student-centered strategies. The teacher-centered strategies involve a review of the water cycle process by the use of a wall poster and a student question-and-answer session. Mr. Bird also guides students through the beginning stages of producing their water cycle storyboards to ensure they understand the process. The student-centered strategies occur in three stages. First, students complete their water cycle storyboards by writing descriptions of each phase and sketching images to illustrate the concepts. Next, students go to the computer lab to create PowerPoint presentations of the water cycle. The final strategy involves how students present their water cycle projects.

Select Resources

This lesson involves student use of computers and PowerPoint software to create water cycle presentations. Mr. Bird uses the computer lab for the lesson because each student is required to create an individual PowerPoint presentation. The lab also has a digital projector and screen for the student presentations. Students download digital photos of local areas and insert audio files of weather sounds and music to their PowerPoint presentations. Mr. Bird uses the following guidelines to assess the appropriateness of his technology and media selections:

- *Alignment with standards, outcomes, and objectives.* PowerPoint provides the necessary tools for students to meet the learning objectives.
- *Accurate and current information.* Not applicable for the chosen technology and media.
- *Age-appropriate language.* PowerPoint is written at a somewhat advanced level for fourth-grade students; however, the icons assist with understanding.
- *Interest level and engagement.* PowerPoint provides features, such as inserting graphics and sound and

(Continued)

personalizing backgrounds and color, that increase student interest level and engagement.

- *Technical quality*. PowerPoint has superior technical quality.
- *Ease of use.* Use of PowerPoint requires initial training and support when using some features, such as inserting graphics from a server or the Web.
- *Bias free*. PowerPoint is bias free.
- *User guide and directions.* The online help features of PowerPoint are difficult for fourth-grade students to use. Students most frequently ask each other or the teacher for assistance with technical difficulties.

Utilize Resources

Preview Resources

Mr. Bird previews the PowerPoint software to ensure it has the features needed for the lesson. He previews the water cycle poster to ensure it has content that matches the lesson standards and objectives. He also previews the digital photos saved on the school server to ensure that images accurately reflect water cycle stages.

Prepare Resources

Mr. Bird prepares two sets of materials for the lesson. The first is a hand-drawn storyboard of the water cycle that will serve as a model for the student products. The second is a Power-Point presentation of the water cycle that not only serves as a model for the students, but also ensures that the planned activities are workable. In other words, students will be able to access and download files from the server, students will be able to insert and listen to audio files, and the presentations will be viewable with the digital projector.

Prepare the Environment

The lesson takes place in the classroom and the computer lab. Computers in the lab should be checked to ensure that PowerPoint software is functional and that all computers have access and can save to the school server. The projector needs to be tested to ensure that it projects clear images, is properly connected to the appropriate computer, and displays PowerPoint presentations with full functionality.

Prepare the Learners

To prepare the students, Mr. Bird introduces the lesson and reviews the learning objectives. When in the computer lab, he reviews the basics of using PowerPoint software, downloading files from the server, and operating the digital projector.

Provide the Learning Experience

The learning experience occurs in the classroom and the computer lab. It involves both teacher-centered and student-centered activities and the use of computers to produce and present student-created PowerPoint presentations of the water cycle.

Require Learner Participation

Large-Group Activities

Mr. Bird introduces the lesson, reviews the learning objectives, and asks students questions about the water cycle as he completes the first two stages of a "class-size" storyboard. Mr. Bird uses the questions to check for student understanding of previously learned content.

Independent Student Activities

Following the large-group activity, the students individually complete their water cycle storyboards. Taking the storyboards to the computer lab, the students use computers and PowerPoint software to create water cycle presentations. Students produce the basic five-slide presentation and add text to each slide as it is written on their storyboards. They then review images saved on the server and select one or more for each water cycle stage. When the text and images are in place, students can add audio, change the backgrounds and color schemes, and add transitions between slides. For the final activity, students present their water cycle PowerPoint products to the class.

Evaluate and Revise

Assessment of Learner Achievement

Mr. Bird assesses learner achievement in two ways. He first assesses demonstration of content knowledge from the information in students' PowerPoint displays and in their oral narrations during the presentations. The second part of his assessment considers the technology skills shown, which Mr. Bird assesses by evaluating the final student presentations according to the assignment criteria stated in the learning objectives: five slides, the first of which is the title slide; each slide containing a graphic, text, and sound; transitions used between each slide; presentation based on a design template that supports the water cycle theme.

Evaluation of Strategies and Resources

Mr. Bird evaluates the water cycle lesson strategies, technology, and media by continually checking with students during lesson implementation and by also conducting a whole-class discussion of the process at the conclusion of the lesson. His goal is to determine student impressions of this use of technology and to solicit their ideas for improving the process. Also, because Mr. Bird keeps notes for each lesson, he can review past water cycle lessons and compare the current lesson to identify strengths and weaknesses.

Revision

The evaluation reveals that the students really enjoyed creating the PowerPoint presentations but were uncomfortable presenting them to the class, primarily due to feeling unprepared and from lack of student interest in the presentations. Mr. Bird revises the lesson by providing instruction on how to give an oral presentation. He also introduces the use of a peer evaluation form that includes student ideas about what an "excellent" presentation would include.

Professional Development

Demonstrating Professional Skills

1. Create a list of topics you would include if you were to conduct a one-day computer implementation workshop for teachers in your content area (ISTE Standards for Educators 2.C).

2. Describe how you can use a computer resource as a learning tool within your content area (ISTE Standards for Educators 5.B).

3. Select at least five computer programs suitable for your content area. Critique each program using the Selection Rubric: Software found later in this chapter (ISTE Standards for Educators 5.A).

4. Select a topic or standard that can be used in a classroom setting of your choice. Describe three ways to use computer software to address the diverse learning needs of students and three ways to develop students' higher-order thinking skills and creativity (ISTE Standards for Educators 5 & 6).

Building Your Professional Portfolio

- *Creating My Lesson.* Using the ASSURE model, design a lesson for one of the case studies presented in Appendix A or use a scenario of your own design. Incorporate into your lesson one or more of the instructional strategies and technology and media ideas described in this chapter. Be sure to include information about the audience, the objectives, and all other elements of the ASSURE model. Be certain to match your intended outcomes to state or national learning standards for your content area (ISTE Standards for Educators 5.A, 5.B, 5.C).

- *Reflecting on My Lesson.* Reflect on the process you have used in the design of your lesson and your efforts at enhancing that lesson to meet student needs within your class. What have you learned about matching audience, content, instructional strategy, and materials? What could you have done to develop your students' higher-order thinking or creativity skills? In what ways did the materials you selected for your lesson enhance the learning opportunities for your students (ISTE Standards for Educators 7.A)?

- *Enhancing My Lesson.* Using the lesson you have just designed, assume that some of your students have special needs, such as physical or learning impediments. Also assume that several students are identified as gifted. How will you adapt or change your lesson design to ensure that these students are recognized and supported, to allow them to succeed in your lesson (ISTE Standards for Educators 5.A, 5.B, 5.C)?

Suggested Resources

Print Resources

Dell, A., Newton, D., & Petroff, J. (2017). *Assistive technology in the classroom: Enhancing the school experiences of students with disabilities* (3rd. ed.). Boston: Pearson.

Dowd, H. & Green, P. (2016). *Classroom management in the digital age: Effective Practices for technology-rich spaces.* Irvine, CA: EDTechTeam Press.

Hamilton, B. (2015). *Integrating technology in the classroom: Tools to meet the needs of every student.* Eugene, OR: ISTE.

O'Bannon, B. & Puckett, K. (2010). *Preparing to use technology: A practical guide to curriculum integration* (2nd ed.). Boston: Allyn & Bacon.

Roblyer, M. & Doering, A. (2015). *Integrating educational technology into teaching* (7th ed.). Boston: Pearson.

Online Resources and Apps

Kathy Schrock's Guide to Everything

This directory of educational resources offers classroom teachers an array of links, lesson plans, and professional development suggestions.

Awesome Library

A resource for technology use in the classroom at all levels and for helping schools with technology decisions.

InTime

Watching teachers use technology in their teaching and following along as they describe what they do. InTime provides many different types of examples of using technology in learning.

Best Kids Apps

This website provides reviews of educational apps for Apple and Android mobile devices.

Chapter 6
Connecting Learners Using Web 2.0

Learning Outcomes

This chapter addresses ISTE Standards for Educators 3 and 5.

6.1 Describe key functions of Web 2.0 that have implications for learning.

6.2 Identify ways to integrate Web 2.0 resources into instruction.

6.3 Discuss advantages of using Web 2.0 resources to support learning.

6.4 Discuss limitations of using Web 2.0 resources to support learning.

Goal

Understand the use of Web 2.0 resources to facilitate learning.

ASSURE Classroom Case Study

Vicki Davis is a high school technology teacher who incorporates Web 2.0 tools into her teaching. The ASSURE Classroom Case Study for this chapter describes the planning process she uses to create a lesson. Her primary goals are to engage her students to organize their thoughts, to communicate clearly, and to plan for the implementation of their project.

Throughout the chapter you will find video segments that explore how Ms. Davis integrates Web 2.0 activities and strategies that engage students in discussion and sharing of ideas while promoting enhanced learning.

Introduction

Schools of today are changing. No longer are they limited to the existing structure or resources of the building. It is possible to reach beyond the traditional school setting to design learning opportunities with global reach to engage today's learners. By dynamically integrating Web 2.0 resources into instruction, student learning is transformed while requiring new perspectives on teaching. This chapter discusses the key functions of Web 2.0 resources and provides integration examples for common tools that can actively engage students in learning. Also discussed are advantages and limitations of using Web 2.0 for instruction as well as information on ways to address social-ethical issues associated with online learning.

Web 2.0 Functions

The term **Web 2.0** refers to websites that are more than static webpages, or Web 1.0 resources. A Web 2.0 site typically allows users to interact with and publish data and information, while a Web 1.0 website limits users to passively viewing content. YouTube, Twitter, Facebook, Wikipedia, and Pinterest are among the numerous examples of frequently used Web 2.0 resources.

Most of the resources available as Web 2.0 tools are the products of the **open source** concept, meaning that software developers from around the globe can collaboratively create and maintain stable, yet innovative products (Pickett, 2017). One emerging direction for open source tools is called **cloud computing**, in which files and applications can be synced to and used on multiple devices across a network. Cloud-based resources can be free or very low cost and include substantial capabilities for sharing files and information with others across the Web. The software and files are not stored on individual computers but rather are stored in the cloud, or network of computers supporting the software application being used. As an example, students in the U.S. working with students in Ireland can use cloud computing to collaboratively contribute to a blog comparing family culture.

Collectively, Web 2.0 is comprised of online apps, or applications, designed to support user-generated content. Although Web 2.0 applications often include a wide variety of capabilities, notable functions include: 1) collaborative contributions, 2) social networking, and 3) mashups. Most Web 2.0 resources provide two or more of these functions.

Collaborative Contributions

Web 2.0 sites that support real-time **collaborative contributions** are those in which users build the site with content added and edited by more than one contributor. Among the examples are productivity apps such as Google docs, sheets, etc.; blogs; wikis; and social bookmarking.

Social Networking

Social networking is provided through mobile and web-based applications such as Facebook and Twitter that enable users to interact, collaborate, co-create, share, and publish information, ideas, and multimedia. The focus of social networking sites can be educational, professional, or personal, such as those designed for family and friend networking. Popular examples include Edmundo as a global education network, LinkedIn as a professional social networking site focused toward individuals or groups, and Facebook, which supports education, professional, and family/friends. For example, Facebook hosts many groups of teachers who collaborate in communities based on grade level, subject areas, and also areas of interest, e.g., technology integration, math competitions, and so on.

Mashups

A web **mashup** uses applications that bring together content from a variety of resources, creating websites that are new and different from the original sources. For example, online news media sites combine text, video, audio, and real-time information updated about every 15 minutes. This combination of information provides current data for you and your students to use in reports or as part of classroom activities.

Application Exercise 6.1

 Check Your Understanding 6.1

Integrating Web 2.0 Resources into Instruction

With Web 2.0 resources, students can connect to share ideas, engage in inquiry, and search for additional information. Sometimes called **learning communities**, collaboration among students and teachers expands educational possibilities through interactive digital connectedness. Students can engage in critical thinking and problem solving while collaborating and communicating with others in and beyond their classrooms. There are a number of ways that Web 2.0 tools can support learning. Your role as a teacher is to find the best means of optimizing the learning opportunities for your students using these types of resources.

Online Web 2.0 resources that are often used to enhance student learning include blogs, wikis, productivity apps, social bookmarking, multimedia sharing, social networks, and mashups. These types of Web 2.0 tools provide learners different ways of accessing information and sharing their thinking and understanding. As their teacher, you can integrate these resources into your lessons to ensure students are able to communicate and share their knowledge and creativity with others.

Video Example 6.1: Students Learning to Use Web 2.0

Observe how Ms. Davis' students discuss learning how to use Web 2.0 tools. In what ways did Ms. Davis encourage students to use Web 2.0 tools? How did students react to the methods used by Ms. Davis to increase their comfort level with using the online tools?

Blogs

Blogs, short for *web logs*, were initially designed to be a set of personal commentaries about a specific topic. Many teachers have adapted blogs and use them for class websites, weekly newsletters to parents, daily homework communication, writing journals, and much more. Blogs can contain text, visuals, multimedia, and links to websites, and they allow learners to share information with each other, with the teacher, and with the world. A blog can also be a dialog with a group of people around the world that share an interest in a common topic or issue. The structure of a blog is arranged so that the most recent posting is first, allowing easy access to the most recent comments. Any reader who wishes, however, can easily scan through the blog postings to see earlier entries.

INTEGRATION OF BLOGS INTO INSTRUCTION.   As an educator, you can engage students with blogs created by others or start a blog to support student learning by using a site such as Wordpress, EduBlogs, or Blogger. Blogs are available in most content areas for elementary through high school students. Content experts often write blogs, giving students a chance to be informed about a topic with the most up-to-date information. Examples include, NASA's Space Station Blog, Tanya Khovanova's Math Blog, Mike Anderson's Ancient History Blog, and landscape artist, Brad Teare's Thick Paint Blog. Among content area blogs are Science Buddies Blog, which provides teachers and students an ongoing supply of fun and interactive science projects, and the StoryCenter Blog, a site for sharing stories on themes like family, identity, relationships, community, and environment. The Math-Only-Math Blog offers regular posts on basic math topics like: Standard Units of Length and Estimating a Sum. When integrating blogs created by others into your lessons, carefully review the content and focus of current and archived contributions to determine the appropriateness for your lessons.

You may also want to create your own instructional blogs that can be kept private or a class blog for your students or made public to share with others. You may wish to start with a class blog, giving your students a chance to learn how to use good writing skills successfully in a familiar blogging environment before you engage them with public blogs. Blogs you create can be used for many instructional purposes, including discussions of books, current news, local culture, or sharing student poetry within and beyond your class. An idea for science might be to create a weather blog for middle school students to regularly share and compare stories about their local weather with students from different states.

Blogs are also useful for collaboration with other teachers to remain current and share teaching ideas. You can create a blog for professionals in your building or district to explore topics of interest and develop new ideas to use in your teaching. As part of your exchange with other educators, you can build in professional development opportunities such as special guests who can provide insights that may prompt additional discussion among your colleagues. There are national blogs that include a larger community of educators such as TeacherLingo, which invites teachers to share ideas and exchange resources. Additionally, the TeachersFirst Edge blog provides current information on safe-for-classroom-use Web 2.0 resources. By exploring your educational endeavors through a blog, you are providing opportunities for other educators to advance their ideas and to share in improving educational options for students.

Wikis

Wikis are web-based applications that support collaborative writing and editing of online content. Wiki translates to "quick" in Hawaiian, as the browser-based app provides simple-to-use writing and editing tools that enable users to quickly create a Wiki site. In comparison with blogs, which do not allow users to edit posts, wikis allow users to write new information and edit information posted by others on a collaborative website. Content changes whenever a user interacts with the page. Wikipedia, a free, collaborative encyclopedia, is a well-known type of wiki. The content on Wikipedia is frequently created, updated, and changed by users to keep it current, unlike commercial encyclopedias that are often costly and outdated.

INTEGRATION OF WIKIS INTO INSTRUCTION.   Wikis provide teachers and learners with a tool for creating and sharing online information and media with others. This shifts the role of students to producers rather than consumers of knowledge, thus developing higher-order thinking skills. Teachers can use apps such as Wikidot or Wikispaces Classroom, a free wiki host that lets teachers create online spaces with visual editing easy for most students to use. Students access Wikis using any digital device with a web browser. In addition, students can work together while one student is at home and the other is in a nearby library.

When planning to integrate wikis into instruction, it is important to consider the following: How will students be grouped? Will students create a new wiki or contribute to an existing one? What content will be added or edited? Where will students obtain new content? How will student contributions be monitored for correct and appropriate content, spelling, and grammar? How will wiki creation and/or editing support student achievement of learning objectives?

Wikis can have a wide range of topics and purposes. For example, a student-created wiki can focus on book reviews of autobiographies, historical landmarks, ideas for entrepreneurship, how to go green, staying healthy, ways to stop cyberbullying, and so on. To help elementary students learn about dinosaurs, they can create a dinosaur wiki with student-created descriptions and drawings of popular species. Other students who visit the dinosaur wiki are invited to add their own drawings and additional facts. A high school English teacher can have students publish their reactions to historical readings such as *To Kill a Mockingbird* or *Macbeth*. Additionally, wikis work well when engaging students in debates. The TMHS Climate Change Debate involves

Video Example 6.2: Integrating Web 2.0

Observe how Ms. Davis and her ninth-grade students discuss plans to use Web 2.0 collaboration tools to communicate with a seventh-grade class. In what ways did Ms. Davis guide student thinking with regard to achieving successful online interactions? How did students contribute to the lesson design?

students in creating pages in which they research and define the issue, defend their position, describe an action plan, and provide support data. Numerous examples of existing educational wikis are available on Internet sites such as Educational Wikis and Wikiversity.

Teachers also use wikis to create learning resources for their students. These sites include things such as digital copies of teacher created materials, a calendar of assignments, and links to support materials. Teachers often create topic-specific wikis to provide enrichment activities and information beyond what is in the textbook. Spanish and French teachers use wikis to offer vocabulary practice and links to videos with native language students discussing cultural aspects of their country. Social studies lessons are supported with wikis that include historical photos of famous people, settings, and documents. The teacher-created wikis can be private or open for others to contribute ideas and comments.

Productivity Apps

Online **productivity apps**, also known as online office tools, are Web 2.0 apps for common tasks such as word processing, presentations, spreadsheet calculations and graphing, and concept mapping. These types of productivity tools allow users to create and edit documents online while collaborating in real time with other users. Cloud computing is used to save files, making them available across any device with an Internet connection. Many of these tools make it possible to also save the files to a local computer or mobile device using a variety of common file formats. Most of these online productivity tools are free or far less expensive than their competitors. It is common for schools and districts to choose to use productivity apps, such as Google Docs or OpenOffice, rather than expensive traditional software suites such as Microsoft Office.

INTEGRATION OF PRODUCTIVITY APPS INTO INSTRUCTION.   Web 2.0 productivity apps offer similar functionality as traditional ones. Word processers support writing, formatting, and editing of written documents; spreadsheets perform calculations and create charts; and presentation apps enable creation of slides with text, images, and animations. The key difference with Web 2.0 apps is the ability for two or more students to simultaneously work on one document while each student uses a different digital device. This makes it possible for small groups of high school students to enter data from their chemistry experiments into a shared live spreadsheet. Differences in these data sets can serve as the basis for a classroom discussion on possible reasons for different outcomes. Pairs of younger students in a one-to-one laptop class can collaboratively create vocabulary tables where one student contributes a photo to represent evenly numbered new words and the other contributes an image for odd numbered words. They then write a rationale for why they think their partner chose the images added to the table.

Prezi is a Web 2.0 productivity tool that is commonly used for presentations and storytelling. Ideas, information, and media are organized on the *canvas*, and the presentation interface allows users to navigate by zooming in and out of the presentation content. Prezi can be used collaboratively, with multiple users having the ability to edit presentations. A social studies lesson for middle school students can involve students from different locations across the U.S. who share digital stories of family culture, e.g., how we celebrate birthdays, our favorite meals, homeland of my grandparents. See Taking a Look at Technology Integration for another example of using the productivity app, Prezi for a cross-grade science lesson.

Integrating Web 2.0 productivity apps supports thinking, engagement, and social interaction. These tools also help prepare students for future careers in which collaboration and good communication skills are necessary to achieve success.

Taking a Look at Technology Integration
Productivity App

When Ms. Paszotta's kindergartners were starting their study of insects, she wanted to capitalize on the school's philosophy of integrating arts and technology into their learning experiences. And, when talking with Ms. Mullins, a fourth-grade teacher, she learned that the fourth graders were studying insects as well. The two teachers collaborated on their lessons and decided on the culminating activity in which students worked together to create an interactive presentation with the Prezi app to demonstrate what they learned.

Each kindergarten student selected an insect to study, then he or she worked with a fourth-grade partner to investigate the insect and to prepare a short Prezi presentation about what they learned together. The kindergarteners drew images of their selected insects and their fourth-grade partner worked with them to write informational text about the insect to be included in the presentation. When completed, each pair of students shared their insect presentation during a joint kindergarten and fourth grade class session. The final student presentations were linked to a teacher-created Insect wiki shared with other elementary classes via the district website.

Social Bookmarking

Social bookmarking enables users to organize, store, manage, and search for bookmarked resources online. **Bookmarking** uses an aggregation or collection tool to save web page addresses. Social bookmarks from hosts such as Diigo or Delicious provide users with links to online resources they want to remember and share, with Diigo being one of the most robust social bookmarking tools. In addition to bookmarking useful web resources, Diigo users can also organize, highlight, annotate, and share webpage collections. These bookmarks are usually public, but it is possible to save them privately, or share them with only specified groups, such as your students. Typically, bookmarks can be viewed chronologically, by category or tags, or found using the bookmarking service's search engine. As these services have grown, additional features have been included. These include the addition of ratings, commenting, importing and exporting bookmarks from browsers, emailing of bookmarks, and other social networking features.

INTEGRATION OF SOCIAL BOOKMARKING INTO INSTRUCTION. Social bookmarking features make it a useful research tool to support student projects. The highlighting and annotation tools enable students to identify and share specific web content rather than emailing web links to group members who would have to carefully review the website to find specific information. For example, social bookmarking would support a high school lesson involving student groups creating a wiki on notable women scientist. When searching for online information about Rosalind Franklin, noted for her DNA research, group members bookmark, highlight, and add notes to content useful for their wiki. Group members engage in ongoing review and editing to finalize the collection of bookmarked resources needed to complete their portion of the wiki about notable women scientists.

Social bookmarking can also be integrated as a tool to help middle school students improve mathematics knowledge and skills. As new math topics are introduced, students can bookmark websites with tips, ideas, and practice that help them learn the skill. The bookmarks are categorized by the math skills, for example, algebraic expressions, polynomials, absolute value, and so on. Students add notes to share how the information helped them understand the concepts or how to better solve related problems. The bookmarks are readily available to students for review and practice when at school or home.

To prepare students for social bookmarking, it is important to provide guidelines for conducting online searches. Teach students how to select appropriate search terms related to the topic, check validity of the content, how to identify relevant content to highlight, and how to add useful notes.

Multimedia Sharing

Many Web 2.0 apps support the sharing of multimedia such as audio, video, and images. Popular apps that support multimedia sharing are podcasts for audio, video, and text, YouTube for video, and pinboards, like Pinterest for images and web resources.

AUDIO SHARING.   **Podcasts** are online digital multimedia files that can be downloaded or accessed online with a player app. Numerous podcasts are available for use in PK-12 instruction in the form of lectures, music, storytelling, sounds of nature and science, and other sounds such as traffic or construction equipment. Additionally, teachers and students can create and share podcasts with others using apps such as Podcast Generator or VoiceThread.

VIDEO SHARING.   Web 2.0 sites that support **video sharing** typically offer users the opportunity to not only upload and view video, but also to add comments and ratings, as well as to report inappropriate videos to the site administrators. YouTube is a widely used free video sharing Web 2.0 resource. Other options include Vimeo, Veoh, and Vine—designed to accept 6-second videos that are looped for repeated watching. Of importance to educators is TeacherTube, a free site for teachers to upload, view, and review instructional videos on classroom content as well as teaching tips and ideas.

PINBOARDS.   Online **pinboards** enable users to organize photos, videos, and other information onto digital boards by topic areas. Pinterest is a free popular Web 2.0 pinboard app in which users "pin" Web content on theme-specific boards that they or others created. Boards can be private or public. Although Pinterest includes many teacher boards, there are also pinboards specifically for educators, such as eduClipper that enables registered users of the free app to "clip" content from any website while automatically recording source information for citation purposes. Education focused pinboards organize content by areas such as lessons, units, grade-levels, or subject areas.

INTEGRATION OF MULTIMEDIA SHARING INTO INSTRUCTION.   The use of Web 2.0 multimedia for sharing audio, video, and images can foster an atmosphere of excitement, motivation, and learning by engaging students and capturing their attention. See When to Use Web 2.0 for example Web 2.0 integration ideas.

When to Use Web 2.0

Use when student learning will be enhanced by . . .	Examples
Reading and writing about shared learning experiences	Middle school students post information on a classroom blog site.
Practicing English as a second language	High school English learners listen to podcasts to help them with their classroom studies.
Sharing information with classmates	Elementary students post their digital stories on Storybird to share both their visual and written stories with others.
Exchanging information about a carbon footprint class project	Middle school students post video captured on their cell phones to a classroom blog site and write about what they have seen.

Integrating Audio Sharing.   Online audio files are available for all grade levels and subjects. Teachers of young students can integrate podcasts of stories being read by a variety of readers to offer new voices beyond the teacher. Free weekly stories are provided with subscriptions to podcasts such as Children's Fun Storytime and Storynory. Science lessons for middle through high school students can be enhanced with podcasts from sites such as Tumble Science, Astronomy Cast, and This Week in Science.

Audio podcasts are an excellent addition when teaching social studies and history lessons as they enable students to listen to actual recordings of historical figures. For example, Greatest Speeches of the 20th Century, a public domain site with 56 original recordings which include U.S. presidential inaugural and farewell speeches, as well as presidential comments on the significant events such as the Cuban missile crisis and the signing of the Civil Rights Bill. Also included are Amelia Earhart's, "The Future of Women in Flying," and Neil Armstrong's, "The Moon Landing." English/Language Arts teachers also have multiple opportunities to integrate podcasts into their instruction. Popular sites include Classic Poetry Aloud, It's All Journalism, and Audio Literature Odyssey, which offers podcasts of biographies, children's stories, novels/novellas, poetry, and short stories.

Integrating Video Sharing.   Similar to audio, numerous online videos are available for lesson integration. Video sites with Web 2.0 features enable users to add comments and ratings, and may enable uploads of user-created video. The WatchKnowLearn site offers over 50,000 free, teacher recommended videos that are categorized by subject and grade level. As an example, French teachers have access to over 300 videos, which include basic conversations in French, e.g., showing gratitude, asking questions, and accepting invitations. NeoK12 offers videos with associated teaching materials to support core content areas. Geography has videos for Deserts, Ecosystems, Ice Age, Rivers, Volcanos, and others. Teachers can add ideas and comments for each resource. The OpenEd site provides free educational videos that are searchable by grade, subject, and learning standards. Sample titles are Sing a Song of Synonyms; Zero Gravity and the Circus; Fractions are Division; and The Dust Bowl Episode.

A highly popular Web 2.0 video sharing site is YouTube, which provides numerous educational videos. However, these videos are among all the other videos and require the use of general search terms to locate resources that may support student learning. Thus, you may want to use TeacherTube, which is designed to provide a variety of digital resources for educators. The videos are grouped by a combined list of subject areas and grade levels and include professionally prepared as well as student and teacher created videos with varying levels of quality, as may be noted in viewer comments and ratings.

Integrating Pinboards.   Collections of digital images and resources are publically available on pinboards such as Pinterest and EduClipper for teachers to integrate into lessons. When searching Pinterest for "middle school literacy," multiple tabbed categories of resources are generated at the top of the page. Among the categories are: activities, centers, strategies, and graphic organizers. Each tab offers numerous teacher- and student-created pinboards that then link to further examples related to the topic. The EduClipper site offers access to Clips, Boards, and Portfolios created by others and tools to create similar resources. Free accounts are offered for students and teachers.

When integrating pinboard resources, you may select boards created by others that align with your lesson, such as linear equations, D-Day Allies, or teaching irony, or create your own pinboard of resources to fit your specific lesson requirements. Pinboards are also an excellent tool for students to demonstrate their understanding of a topic. For example, small groups of upper elementary students can create pinboards of resources that depict life during the Roman Empire. Each group would include a concept map showing how the resources represent the time period. Similar student boards could focus on science concepts, themes represented in literary works, or student drawings of engineering innovations.

It is important that you and your students are mindful when using images that do not belong to you. Be sure that you and your students use these images with attribution and in accordance with each image's copyright or creative commons license. A creative commons license will provide you with specifics as to how the resource can be used and what types of attribution will be necessary.

Social Networks

A **social networking service,** or site, facilitates online connections and interactions of users who typically have shared backgrounds, interests, and experiences. Users are able to share ideas, messages, information, and multimedia with people in their network. Google+, Facebook, Twitter, and Tumblr are examples of social networks. Social networks offer ways for users to join others interested in similar topics or issues through community groups. Groups can be open to anyone with similar interests or can be set up as "closed" groups that require an invitation before an individual can join. Because "open" groups are shared across the Internet, information on these sites is available to anyone around the world.

Some social networking sites limit the amount of text a user can use in each post, encouraging brief communications when exchanging information. For instance, Twitter, an online network for sharing current, up-to-the-minute status reports in very brief messages, limits posts, or "tweets," to 140 characters. In response to the concept of quick notes, users created a type of shorthand to communicate their ideas. For example, a user would type the letter u for the word *you*, the numeral 2 for the word *to,* or BRB for *be right back.* You need to help your students know when it is appropriate to use the shortcuts and when they need to use formal writing skills.

INTEGRATION OF SOCIAL NETWORKS INTO INSTRUCTION.   The widespread and global use of social networks, such as Facebook, results in many sites containing inappropriate content for educational use. Therefore, school systems often restrict access to social networking sites, which may mean that even if you create an educational application, you may not be able to use it with your students. However, there are social networking sites that provide a classroom friendly and safe environment for students. Edmodo is a social learning platform that is frequently used as a social network connecting teachers, students, and parents within a class, school, or district (see Figure 6.1). Edmodo can be used to post assignments, create student polls, share multimedia clips, create learning groups, post a quiz, and share a calendar of events and assignment deadlines. Students can submit assignments and teachers can grade and annotate the assignments directly within Edmodo.

Figure 6.1 Edmodo
As a teacher, you can create your own class social networking site.

Source: Reprinted by permission of Edmodo.

Another option is Biblionasium, which is a reading-focused social network for elementary and middle school students. Teachers create and add students to a classroom, which includes a virtual bookshelf of required and recommended books for the students to read. The site logs student reading and tracks progress towards reading challenges. Students share their personal book reviews with others in the class and beyond, if the site is open to other classrooms. Parents can also join to encourage reading at home and during the summer.

Many teachers are integrating Twitter into their instruction as the short posts of 140 characters requires students to write in a concise, yet informative manner. The real-time nature of the "tweets" add a sense of accountability—thus increasing student engagement and interactions (Tang & Foon Hew, 2017). Twitter can be used to support discussions and debates among group members regarding current or past issues, such as climate change, endangered species, civil rights, and so on. Your lessons can also integrate information from existing Twitter sites. When searching in Twitter or other social media sites, use **hashtags** (#) before the search term. For example, if wanting to connect students with experts from around the globe who regularly share thoughts, ideas, and data on their tweets, you can use the following: #BillNye to find tweets from the "Science Guy," #Christiane Amanpour for tweets from a CNN Chief International Correspondent, or #J.K. Rowling, author of the Harry Potter series. Among the numerous Twitter options that offer information to support learning are: #Congress, #Nasa, #Smithsonian, #Archaeology Magazine, #Shakespeare's Globe, and #NEH to see Tweets from the National Endowment for the Humanities.

Mashups

Mashup websites provide current, real-time data from different applications and websites to meet the purpose of the website and the needs of users. Common mashup sites include information from an interactive map, such as Google Maps, combined with concurrent data from different sources, which include the National Weather Service, restaurants, hotels, crime reports, or traffic. Other popular mashups are online news sites focused on world, national, or local news. These sites offer live broadcasts and text stories of up-to-date news as well as archived video and stories. Many news sites also cover topics such as health, politics, entertainment, science, and technology.

INTEGRATING MASHUPS INTO YOUR INSTRUCTION. The integration of mashup resources works well when the use of current, real-time data will enhance and deepen student learning. For instance, your students can take advantage of mashup sites to learn more about geography or mapping skills. They can use a mashup site that combines mapping and satellite information to identify specific locations in cities around the world. The assignment might be to locate particular types of buildings or specific monuments using a site like Google Maps, in which students can easily pinpoint specific places, get directions, or view the maps to identify the location's proximity to surrounding areas.

A problem-solving lesson might involve students in planning an imaginary trip to a historical city, such as Rome, Egypt, or Washington, DC. The students could be tasked with finding the shortest route through the city as they "visit" targeted historical sites. The "street view" tool on Google Maps enables students to experience 3-D imagery as if they were walking through the streets. Also available are 3-D photos of key monuments and buildings taken from within and around the sites. Students can explore Rome's Trevi Fountain, Egypt's Great Pyramid at Giza, or take a stroll through the National Mall in Washington, DC. Students then communicate their thinking and understanding through a variety of modalities using multimedia in mashups.

You can integrate mashups to support students' learning in mathematics, geography, and science. For example, if you are working on estimation in math, you can have your students estimate the walking distance between home and school. Once

Figure 6.2 Students can communicate their thinking and understanding through a variety of modalities using multimedia in mashups

they have guessed the distance, they can use an online map, such as Google Map, that provides routed directions from one point to another and the option to choose walking as the method of travel. The outcome shows distance and approximate time for two or three routes. A geography or science lesson can be based on information from the United States Geological Survey (USGS) mashup site that provides real-time data and interactive maps showing location and scale of events such as earthquakes, volcanos, flooding, and landslides. Also included are archived data searchable by location, year, and topic. You can guide students to compare that data with geology information they have on global fault lines and plate tectonics.

Students can also create their own mashup using software such as Glogster to create digital posters and timelines that are comprised of information and multimedia from a variety of sources. Glogster makes it possible for students to combine photos, audio and video clips, slideshows, text-based information, links to other websites, and animations into online posters. Glogster projects can be completed to demonstrate student written and illustrated stories, student depiction of the Tea Party, or examples of erosion in their home state. As seen in Figure 6.2, these learning artifacts can be media rich and provide opportunities for students to engage multiple learning modalities.

Selecting Web 2.0 Resources

When selecting Web 2.0 resources to integrate into your instruction, use the ASSURE model to determine how the resource will support your instructional goals. To assist with the selection, use the guidelines in the Selection Rubric: Web 2.0 Resources. For example, with the rubric you can identify the format of the resource (blog, wiki, production app, etc.) and record information useful for lesson planning, such as where the resource is located, subject area, grade level, as well as standards, strengths, limitations, and special features. Additionally, the Rubric can be used to assess the quality of the Web 2.0 resource with regard to how well it aligns with the lesson objective, provides accurate and current information, provides practice for relevant skills, has the potential to fosters collaboration among your students, and so on.

Selection Rubric Web 2.0 Resources

Complete and save the following interactive evaluation to reference when selecting
Web 2.0 Resources to integrate into lessons.

Search Terms

_____

_____

Format

_____ Blog

_____ Wiki

_____ Production App

_____ Social Bookmarking

_____ Pinboards

_____ Audio/Video

_____ Mashup

_____ Others

Title _____

Source/Location _____

©Date _____ Cost _____ Length _____ minutes

Subject Area _____ Grade Level_____

Instructional Strategies _____

Brief Description

Standards/Outcomes/Objectives

Pre-requisites (e.g., prior knowledge, reading ability, vocabulary level, etc.)

Strengths

Limitations

Special Features

Name _____ Date_____

(Continued)

Rating Area	High Quality	Medium Quality	Low Quality
Alignment with standards, outcomes, and objectives	Standards/outcomes/objectives addressed and use of app or resource should enhance student learning.	Standards/outcomes/objectives partially addressed and use of app or resource may enhance student learning.	Standards/outcomes/objectives not addressed and use of app or resource will likely not enhance student learning.
Accurate and current information	Information is correct and does not contain material that is out of date.	Information is correct, but does contain material that is out of date.	Information is not correct and contains material that is out of date.
Age-appropriate language	Language used is age appropriate and vocabulary is understandable.	Language used is nearly age appropriate and some vocabulary is above/below student age.	Language used is not age appropriate and vocabulary is clearly inappropriate for student age.
Interest level and engagement	Topic is presented so that students are likely to be interested and actively engaged in learning.	Topic is presented to interest students most of the time and engage most students in learning.	Topic presented so as not to interest students and not engage them in learning.
Technical quality	The resource represents the best technology and media.	The resource represents technology and media that are good quality, although they may not be the best available.	The resource represents technology and media that are not well prepared and are of very poor quality.
Ease of use (student or teacher)	Resource follows easy-to-use patterns with nothing to confuse the user.	Resource follows patterns that are easy to follow most of the time, with a few things to confuse the user.	Resource follows no patterns and most of the time the user is very confused.
Bias free	There is no evidence of objectionable bias or advertising.	There is little evidence of bias or advertising.	There is much evidence of bias or advertising.
User guide and directions	The user guide is an excellent resource for use in a lesson. Directions should help teachers and students use the resource.	The user guide is a good resource for use in a lesson. Directions may help teachers and students use the resource.	The user guide is a poor resource for use in a lesson. Directions do not help teachers and students use the resource.
*Reading level	Most students can use the web tools to create original pieces that represent learning.	Some students can use the web tools to start original pieces that begin to show their learning.	Most students cannot use the web tools to create original pieces that represent their learning.
*Fosters collaboration	The resource is presented at an appropriate level so that most students can share information.	The resource is presented at a level so that some students can share information.	The resource is presented at a level so that few students can share information.
*Clarity of organization	The resource is presented in such a way that most students are able to use the information.	The resource is presented in such a way that some students are able to use the information.	The resource is presented in such a way that few students are able to use the information.

*Specific to rating Web 2.0 Resources.

From Smaldino, Lowther, & Mims, *Instructional Technology and Media for Learning*, 12th ed. Copyright © 2017 by Pearson Education, Inc. All rights reserved.

Recommended for Classroom Use: _____ **Yes** _____ **No**

Ideas for Classroom Use:_____

✓ **Check Your Understanding** 6.2

Shared Writing Exercise 6.1

Advantages of Using Web 2.0 for Instruction

Collectively, Web 2.0 offers users opportunities to contribute, interact, respond, and learn from real-time and archived information and multimedia that is often reflective of interconnected communities (Greenhow & Askari, 2017). The Web 2.0 tools described in this chapter target these skills and provide students with learning opportunities beyond simple information access. Teachers have multiple Web 2.0 resources readily available to support and enhance learning of students with varying levels of ability and needs, as seen in Technology for All Learners.

Although there is a wide variety of Web 2.0 resources that range from blogs, wikis, social networks, podcasts, and mashups, the resources share some common advantages, which include the following.

- *Portability.* Information can be accessed and used anywhere on mobile devices such as laptops, tablets, and cell phones as well as desktop computers.
- *Easy to produce.* The Web 2.0 apps provide user-friendly tools for creating and sharing digital content such as podcasts or online videos.
- *Authentic audience.* When developing literacy and communication skills, interactive Web 2.0 tools such as blogs and wikis offer opportunities to reach an authentic audience of readers beyond the classroom who can provide valuable feedback.
- *Connectedness.* Web 2.0 communication among students facilitates, encourages, and supports collaboration.
- *Social awareness.* Students become more sensitive to others through social networking sites where they have access to information to learn about each other.
- *Free.* Many Web 2.0 tools are available for educational uses at no charge.

Technology for All Learners

Web 2.0 Tools

Students may have difficulty expressing themselves in class due to limited language skills from a learning disability or because their first language is not English. They frequently tend to be quiet or not participate in class or group discussions. Gifted learners may want more challenges for their own learning. There are many resources for helping all students access information to increase their learning.

Audio podcasts allow students to hear the teacher's instruction after class so that they can review the information, follow directions that might have been presented, or prepare for a test about the material covered in class. Video podcasts provide visual information, along with the audio, to help students follow along using multiple modes of learning. These tools may help learners who benefit from seeing visual depictions of concepts or strategies to be applied. It is also helpful for students who may need to review a process more than once to gain the full benefit of the demonstration.

When writing is a challenge for students, a wiki or productivity app such as word processing can be a way to let them improve their skills in sharing information with classmates or other audiences. These tools allow everyone to offer and exchange ideas. It also allows others to provide ideas about how to express those ideas in writing, thus influencing writing skills.

Challenging students with a wide range of skills and abilities is often difficult. By using Web 2.0 resources, such as the DIY collaborative social networking site, gifted students can engage in challenges in which they create and share their solutions with other students around the world. These types of exchanges provide students with opportunities to express themselves and to learn from others.

Application Exercise 6.2

 Check Your Understanding 6.3

Limitations of Using Web 2.0 for Instruction

When deciding which Web 2.0 tools to integrate into your instruction, it is important to carefully consider noted limitations of these online resources to help you make informed decisions. Extra caution is needed with regard to using Web 2.0 to support your teaching, as many of the resources, such as Facebook, YouTube, and Twitter are extensively used for non-educational purposes. This substantially increases the possibility of students accessing inappropriate content or users, which throws into question the following.

- *Access to necessary sophisticated hardware.* Some interactive Web 2.0 tools require hardware capabilities not available on less expensive mobile technology models.

- *Instability of open source apps.* Because many Web 2.0 apps are open source (free) and thus not purchased and licensed, teachers may plan to use a particular application, only to find that it is no longer available or is now only usable if you pay a fee.

- *Quality of messages.* Because they are easy to produce and free, many types of Web 2.0 postings are of poor quality and not well prepared.

- *Credibility.* Just because something appears on the Web does not make it an authentic or authoritative source. Web 2.0 tools make it very easy to post information that may be inaccurate.

- *Bias.* Blogs may be highly subjective in nature, written by individuals as a way to express their ideas and positions to an audience.

- *Safety issues.* Because of the open nature of the resources, it is essential that teachers ensure students understand the need for caution and obtain parental or guardian approval before sharing personal information.

- *The possibility of cyberbullying.* Cyberbullying can range from annoying an individual online to far more dangerous situations, if not handled properly. The Cyberbullying Research Center provides examples of actual incidents and contact information for seeking assistance.

Video Example 6.3: Issues of Web 2.0 Use

Observe how Ms. Davis' students reflect on issues related to Web 2.0 use. What issues related to the use of Web 2.0 for online interactions did Ms. Davis' students consider important? How did students respond regarding the need for safe interactions when collaborating online?

Application Exercise 6.3

Innovations on the Horizon

Semantic-Aware Applications

Using a current search engine like Google, you type in a keyword and may get a large number of hits. Semantic-aware applications actually work with your computer to help it "understand" what you want to know and guide the search for an answer that addresses the question you've posed. Rather than searching on a group of keywords, the computer makes connections based on working with your input to focus on what you wish to know. In this innovative way to engage in Internet searches, your digital device recognizes the meaning of the word or question you've provide. The semantic-aware applications can even use images instead of words for some of the information pulled from various sites. These applications will gather the information you seek quickly and make browsing through multiple pages a thing of the past.

Semantic technology is making it much easier to pose questions and locate answers, saving you valuable time. Your computer understands more about you and tries to make the work of searching easier, helping you be more efficient and successful in a wide range of Internet activities such as searching and sharing your knowledge with others. Your computer could also learn to connect dates, places, and people and use that information to keep your calendar, places of interest, and contacts list up-to-date without you having to do it yourself. Semantic-aware applications are making it easier to find and connect information, making learning and discovering new information much easier for everyone who has access to the Internet.

 Check Your Understanding 6.4

Summary

This chapter discussed ways to connect learners through the use of Web 2.0 tools. The chapter was structured to emphasize the following learning outcomes.

- *Describe key functions of Web 2.0 that have implications for learning.* Most Web 2.0 applications include a variety of capabilities, among which are three notable functions. First are collaborative contributions, which involves Web 2.0 content being added and edited by more than one contributor. The next is social networking that enables users to interact, collaborate, co-create, share, and publish information, ideas, and multimedia on sites such as Facebook. The third is Web 2.0 mashups, which bring together content from a variety of resources, creating websites that are new and different from the original sources.

- *Identify ways to integrate Web 2.0 resources into instruction.* Popular online Web 2.0 resources that are often integrated into instruction include:

  - *Blogs:* Blogs allow learners to share information with each other, with the teacher, and with the

world. Teachers can engage students with blogs created by others or one created by the teacher or students. Blogs are available in most content areas for elementary through high school students.

- *Wikis:* Wikis are web-based applications that support collaborative writing and editing of online content. Wikis provide teachers and learners with a tool for creating and sharing online information and media with others.

- *Productivity apps:* Web 2.0 productivity apps include word processing, presentations, spreadsheets, and concept mapping. A main difference between traditional productivity apps and Web 2.0 apps is the ability for two or more students to simultaneously work on one document while each student uses a different digital device. Integrating Web 2.0 productivity apps supports thinking, engagement, and social interaction.

- *Social bookmarking:* Social bookmarking enables users to organize, store, manage, and search for bookmarked resources online. The highlighting and annotation tools enable students to identify and share specific web content, which make social bookmarking a useful research tool to support student projects.

- *Multimedia sharing:* Popular apps that support multimedia sharing are podcasts for audio, video, and text, YouTube for video, and pinboards, such as Pinterest for images and web resources. Numerous podcasts are available for use in PK-12 instruction in the form of lectures, music, storytelling, sounds of nature, and other sounds. Web 2.0 video sharing sites typically support uploading and viewing of videos, and adding comments and ratings. Education focused pinboards typically organize content by lessons, units, grade-levels, or subject areas and may automatically record source information for citation purposes.

- *Social networks:* Social networks, such as Google+ Facebook, Twitter, and Tumblr facilitate online connections and interactions of users. Teachers can integrate student use of social networks to support discussions and debates among class members or with experts from around the globe.

- *Mashups:* The integration of mashup resources works well for mathematics, geography, and science as these areas often require the student to use current, real-time data to enhance and deepen student learning. Integration of student-created mashups demonstrates learning through the collection of information and multimedia from a variety of sources.

- *Discuss advantages of using Web 2.0 resources to support learning.* Advantages of using Web 2.0 resources to support learning include: the resources are portable, easy to produce, and engage learners with an authentic audience. Additionally, they support connectedness among users and help in creating a sense of social awareness of others. And, of importance to teachers, who are often on a limited budget, most Web 2.0 resources are free.

- *Discuss limitations of using Web 2.0 resources to support learning.* Among the noted limitations of using Web 2.0 resources to support learning are the following: some require sophisticated hardware; the instability of open source apps; poor quality of messages; poor credibility of content; biased content; safety and cyber-bullying concerns due to the open nature of Web 2.0.

ASSURE Lesson Plan

This ASSURE Classroom Case Study is based on a lesson that integrates Web 2.0 resources. Ms. Vicki Davis collaborates with her ninth-grade students to create lessons for seventh graders in a virtual world.

This ASSURE Lesson Plan describes the instructional planning used by Vicki Davis, a ninth-grade teacher who wanted her students to develop lesson plans for seventh graders with whom they connected virtually. To address this challenge, Ms. Davis collaborated with her students to create these lessons. Below is Vicki Davis' ASSURE lesson plan for the project. Vicki Davis Ninth Grade Topic: Web 2.0

Analyze Learners

General Characteristics

The students in Vicki Davis' high school class are primarily rural students with a variety of interests in technology. They are fairly equally distributed with regard to gender and range in age from 13 to 15 years old. Student reading ability is at or above grade level, although there are several students with diagnosed learning disabilities in the class. Student behavior problems are minimal.

Entry Competencies

The students are, in general, able to do the following:

- Demonstrate competency in keyboarding, document editing, and general computer skills.

- Prepare written materials, such as narratives, for the lessons they are going to teach to the seventh-grade students, including wiki and blog entries.
- Use Web 2.0 apps to participate in blogs and wikis and to develop and interact in virtual world settings (primarily using OpenSim) with their own avatars.

Learning Styles

Vicki Davis' students learn best when engaged in activities that are relevant and include lively discussions of meaningful topics. Her students vary in comfort level when speaking with the seventh graders, but are very comfortable in the virtual world created for their class to help the younger students learn about "digital citizenship" and Internet safety. Vicki guides her students through their use of technology, building on their prior experiences and skills. When working in groups, her style of coaching facilitates their teamwork abilities.

State Standards and Objectives

Curriculum Standards

The following **Common Core Standards for Technology and Career Education** are addressed in this lesson: (2) Communicate thoughts, ideas, information, and messages in writing and technologically create documents: Students collaborate using blogs, wikis, and preparation of instruction for younger students; (5) Organize ideas and communicate orally in a clear, concise, and courteous manner: Students convey their

(Continued)

ideas within group discussions and in presentations; and (8) Implement a plan of action making modifications as needed to achieve stated objectives: Students arrange their presentations to ensure that the seventh-graders are able to learn the important elements of digital citizenship and Internet safety.

Technology Standards

ISTE Standards for Students: 2—Students understand societal issues related to technology and practice ethical behavior; 4—Students use digital tools to design innovative products and processes; and 5—Students use digital tools to collect and analyze information to solve problems.

Learning Objectives

The learning objectives for this lesson are as follows:

1. Develop virtual worlds that engage students in scenarios in which they apply digital citizenship and safety guidelines.
2. Select appropriate technology tools to accomplish team objectives.
3. Participate in authentic research and use appropriate attribution for ideas.
4. Communicate strategies for using Web 2.0 tools to solve problems.
5. Write avatar scripts that demonstrate knowledge of digital citizenship and safety.

Select Strategies and Resources

Select Strategies

Vicki Davis selects teacher- and student-centered strategies to plan the lesson for seventh graders. The teacher-centered strategies involve engaging the students in discussion through questions and feedback that lead to additional ideas. The student-centered strategies consist of students initiating design ideas for the lessons they plan to develop for the seventh graders and utilizing Web 2.0 tools to share information and create interesting learning experiences.

Select Resources

This lesson involves students' work with computers and Web 2.0 software to post their ideas to a wiki and a blog. They also use software to develop a virtual world environment that will serve the younger students' learning needs. Vicki applies the following guidelines to assess the appropriateness of her technology and media selections:

- *Alignment with standards, outcomes, and objectives.* The Web 2.0 tools provide the necessary support for Vicki Davis' students to meet the learning objectives.
- *Accurate and current information.* Students use both text-based and Internet resources to conduct their research on digital citizenship and safety.
- *Age-appropriate language.* Ms. Davis' students consider how to instruct the seventh graders about virtual worlds, digital citizenship, and safety in language that will help them understand the concepts in the lessons.

- *Interest level and engagement.* The ninth-grade students are excited about sharing their knowledge of digital citizenship and safety with the seventh graders through their virtual world environment. They are very engaged with developing their lessons to help the younger students gain skills in navigating virtual worlds and learning about digital citizenship and safety.
- *Technical quality.* The technical quality of the Web 2.0 tools allows the students to engage in online interactions and communication beyond the school day and setting.
- *Ease of use.* The Web 2.0 tools are fairly easy for high school students to understand, especially as they are using them regularly in their learning.
- *Bias free.* Web 2.0 tools are bias free.
- *User guide and directions.* The online help features of some Web 2.0 tools are moderately easy for students to use. Students most frequently ask each other or use the help option within the software for assistance with technical difficulties.

Select Materials

Vicki Davis provides her students with different types of Web 2.0 tools to use for their interactions, research, and design ideas.

Utilize Resources

Preview Resources

Vicki Davis previews the Web 2.0 software to ensure that it has the features needed for her students to be successful. She previews selected technology resources to ensure students can use them in the school setting, as well as making certain the tools will meet their needs.

Prepare Resources

Vicki prepares starter questions for the group discussion following the presentation the ninth graders completed for the seventh graders.

Prepare the Environment

Vicki tests the lab computers and ensures that the software needed is accessible from each computer. She also tests the capability of the technology to connect the lab classroom to the nearby school media center.

Prepare the Learners

Students in Vicki's class have been involved in group discussions previously, and learner preparation, therefore, primarily focuses on the topics to be covered during the live lesson and follow-up discussion.

Provide the Learning Experience

The learning experience occurs in three formats: live presentation to a group of seventh-grade students, interactions within the discussion following the presentation, and their online discussions on the blog and wiki for this project.

(Continued)

Require Learner Participation

Student Practice Activities

The students in Vicki Davis' class use computers, the virtual world they created, and Web 2.0 software to prepare for and participate in the presentation to the seventh-grade students. Her students use information from their observations and discussion to generate ideas to improve their next presentation and to develop a series of lessons about virtual worlds, digital citizenship, and safety. During the discussion, students practice and test their knowledge and skills by asking and answering student-created questions. They post their ideas to the class blog for further exploration and discussion beyond the class period. Furthermore, they work collaboratively on the class wiki in the planning and design of their instruction for seventh-graders on digital citizenship and Internet safety.

Feedback

Vicki provides continuous feedback as students participate in their discussion and guides them in their decisions on the best ways to interact with the seventh-grade students. She encourages them to provide feedback to each other through their online discussions.

Evaluate and Revise

Assessment of Learner Achievement

Vicki reviews the discussion notes posted to the wiki. She examines the materials that are prepared for the school blog and looks at the materials her students have developed for their next seventh-grade lesson. She also reviews the video that the students have located to see whether it is appropriate for the seventh graders. Vicki uses rubrics to assess both student ability to apply technology for creativity and their communication skills by evaluating student comments and their posted notes. She also uses a rubric to assess the accuracy of the digital citizenship and student safety information included in the virtual world scripts prepared by the ninth graders.

Evaluation of Strategies and Resources

Vicki evaluates the effectiveness of the lesson strategies, talking about the process with the students in her class. Evaluation of the technology and media involves examining the functionality of the Web 2.0 software and the virtual world environment created by her students.

Revision

The evaluation results revealed that student interactions could benefit from assigning students to work in design pairs to increase interactions and information exchange. Furthermore, teacher notes and edits of student work on the wiki provided improved documentation of the lesson. Another revision that emerged from the evaluation results was to limit teacher-directed questions to encourage more student-to-student discussion.

Professional Development

Demonstrating Professional Skills

1. Prepare a 10-minute presentation on how you might use one of the Web 2.0 tools in your teaching (ISTE Standards for Educators 5.C).

2. Locate resources online that provide guidance for ensuring student safety when working with Web 2.0 tools (ISTE Standards for Educators 3.B).

3. Locate and critique a lesson plan that describes an actual use of Web 2.0 tools (ISTE Standards for Educators 5.A).

Building Your Professional Portfolio

- *Creating My Lesson.* Using the ASSURE model, design a lesson for one of the Lesson Scenarios in the Appendix or a scenario of your own design. Integrate into your lesson a Web 2.0 tool that will facilitate student learning. Carefully describe the audience, the objectives, and all the other elements of the ASSURE model. Be certain to match your intended outcomes to state or national curriculum and technology standards for your content area.

- *Reflecting on My Lesson.* Reflect on the process you have used in the design of your lesson and your efforts at enhancing that lesson to meet student needs within your class. How did information from this chapter about Web 2.0 tools influence your lesson design decisions? In what ways did the technology and media you selected for your lesson enhance the learning opportunities for your students?

- *Enhancing My Lesson.* Using the lesson plan you created in the previous activity, consider how to meet the needs of students with varying abilities. What adaptations are needed to keep advanced learners actively engaged while helping students who struggle with reading? What changes are needed to ensure students transfer the knowledge and skills to other learning situations? You might look for additional Web 2.0 resources to enhance the lesson. How can you integrate additional use of technology and media into the lesson?

Suggested Resources

Print Resources

Greene, K. (2017). Teacher blogs and education policy in a publicly private world. Filling the gap between policy and practice. *Learning, Media and Technology, 42*(2), 185–197.

Gwee, S. & Damodaran, S. (2016). Using Web 2.0 Tools to Support Student Writing. *Proceedings of the Mobile Learning Futures–Sustaining Quality Research and Practice in Mobile Learning*, Sydney, Australia, 105–111.

Karlin, M., Ozogul, G., Miles, S., & Heide, S. (2016). The practical application of e-portfolios in K-12 classrooms: An exploration of three Web 2.0 tools by three teachers. *TechTrends, 60*(4), 374–380.

Powell G. (2017) Blogging as a form of Web 2.0 technologies for reflective practice. In A. Marcus-Quinn & T. Hourigan (Eds.), *Handbook on Digital Learning for K-12 Schools* (pp. 271–291). Switzerland: Springer International Publishing.

Online Resources and Apps

Web 2.0: Cool Tools for Schools

This site offers many types of Web 2.0 tools that teachers have used in their classrooms. Organized by category, such as presentation tools, and by content areas such as math and reading, a number of resources are suggested for classroom use.

Pablo

Teachers and students can use the Pablo app to create annotated images using those provided in the app or uploaded images. Pablo provides templates and editing tools to adjust image size, color, and brightness as well as placement options for annotations. This software would be useful when having students find images to represent different concepts presented in a poem. The annotation could describe why the image was chosen.

Pindex

Pindex is a Web 2.0 pinboard for teachers. The site supports searching teacher created boards by core subject areas and popular topics, such as TED talks and creative writing with Pixar. Teachers can create pinboards to help students learn new vocabulary by including representative images for each term. Students can use various Pindex tools and representative photos and quotations to demonstrate their understanding and personal interpretation of a historical event.

Verse

Verse is an app to create interactive videos. The Web 2.0 tools enable students to embed hotspots within a video to further demonstrate concepts; to combine photos and videos into a slideshow; and to embed menu-driven decision points to enable viewers to personalize the path to learning. Teachers could use this app to develop interactive videos to help students learn foundational concepts of science, mathematics, and language arts.

Chapter 7
Teaching at a Distance

Learning Outcomes

This chapter addresses ISTE Standards for Teachers 1, 2, 3, and 4:

7.1 Identify elements that are important to the design for teaching at a distance.

7.2 State strategies that are effective when teaching at a distance.

7.3 List advantages to using distance education.

7.4 List limitations to using distance education.

7.5 Identify distance resources that can be integrated into learning.

7.6 Identify network resources that are used in distance education.

Goal

Understand design characteristics and teaching strategies that facilitate student learning in a distance learning setting.

ASSURE Classroom Case Study

The ASSURE model consists of six steps designed to help teachers plan lessons that effectively integrate use of technology and media for learning. To illustrate how to use the model, we provide a classroom case study to demonstrate implementation of the model in a distance learning setting.

The ASSURE case study for this chapter describes the instructional planning of Jimmy Chun, a high school teacher in Hawaii, who incorporates distance education into his social studies course. His primary goal is to build connections between his students and students on the mainland, specifically in New Hampshire, to increase

their understanding of pre-1770 U.S. history. This particular time frame includes direct connections between the Hawaiian Islands and key historical events involving New Hampshire. Mr. Chun works with a fellow teacher located in a New Hampshire high school. Together they develop a lesson in which students exchange historical as well as current information from their states.

Video segments throughout the chapter explore how Mr. Chun uses strategies, technology, and materials to engage his students in the use of distance education to advance their social studies knowledge.

Introduction

One of the greatest advantages offered by modern electronic technology is the ability to instruct without the teacher's direct presence in the classroom. That is, we can both **time shift** our instruction—experienced at a time selected by the student—and **place shift** our instruction—experienced at some place away from the classroom. The book was the first invention that made it possible to time shift and place shift instruction, a use that continues to the present day.

For more than a century, people in all parts of the world have been able to participate in guided independent study through correspondence courses, originally using the traditional mail system. Learners receive printed lessons, do written assignments, send them to the remote instructor, and get feedback. However, today's technologies now make it possible to experience place-shifted instruction with a stunning array of auditory and visual resources that far exceed text-based materials and extend the experience with a rich range of interaction, not only with the instructor but also with other learners. This chapter introduces the foundation of distance-learning concepts and provides general information about designing and delivering instruction at a distance.

As a teacher, you need to be aware of the variety of options discussed in this chapter for facilitating instruction at a distance. Distance education encompasses a broad array of learning opportunities incorporating a selection of technologies to promote learning. You need to be able to select the best technology and media to support your students' learning. You can use the suggestions in this chapter to help you prepare to guide your students who are learning at a distance.

Designing Learning at a Distance

Distance learning has become the popular term to describe learning via telecommunications. The term **telecommunications** embraces a variety of technology and media configurations, including audio, video, and text-based resources. What they all have in common is implied in the Greek root word *tele,* which means "at a distance" or "far off"; that is, they are systems for communicating over a distance. As we explore the broad topic of distance learning, we will focus on designing student learning in distance settings. Desmond Keegan (2016) identified key elements of a formal definition of distance education, which have not changed with the advent of newer technologies for delivery:

- Physical separation of learners from the teacher
- Organized instructional program
- Telecommunications technology
- Two-way communication

The emphasis on student learning is as important in a distance education setting as it is in a traditional classroom. Successful instructional strategies apply to the same degree in distance settings as they do in the regular classroom. Regardless of the technology used, from live video interactions to text-based discussions, an instructional telecommunication system must perform certain functions to be effective.

It is necessary for you to think about the instructional setting in a new light. Your classroom is now a series of "rooms" connected electronically. Your role may shift to that of facilitator of the learning rather than directly leading the class. You must also keep a watchful eye on the students' activities to be sure no one is falling behind.

With the latest technological advances, your students can become more engaged in learning through interactions, yet it remains your responsibility to organize the instructional experience to encourage interactivity (Simonson, Smaldino, & Zvacek, 2014). Students, for their part, need to know how to use the distance education technology to communicate with you and with each other using proper communication etiquette.

As you look at these elements of distance education, you begin to see that content and technology standards relate to the type of knowledge and skill you will need to bring to learning experiences within a distance learning setting. You will need to be prepared to engage your students by:

- Facilitating learning experiences that engage your students
- Modeling and promoting learning and responsibility for independent and collaborative work
- Engaging learners in active participation with you and with each other

When teaching at a distance, many elements need to be considered. Teachers have learned that it involves more than simply taking an existing lesson and teaching it online. There are many aspects that need to be adjusted or changed. You will need to organize and sequence content as it relates to intended outcomes, know what resources are available, know what experiences your students have had with the distance learning system being used, and know what students need to do to ensure quality learning experiences. These are all essential for you to consider when you are engaging your students in learning experiences, whether they are **blended**, in which some of the time your students are in the classroom with you and other times they are at a distance, flipped, in which you have your students work online prior to coming to class for guided learning activities, or **online**, where your students are always at a distance, even though you might have scheduled meeting times.

Application Exercise 7.1

Video Example 7.1: Blackboard Design

Watch this video segment to see how Mr. Chun reflects on how he changed the design of his instruction for using Blackboard discussions after he observed student performance. What was Mr. Chun's solution to earlier problems with use of the discussion boards and why was it successful?

Student Access to Resource Materials

One element often overlooked in distance learning is the access students have to resource materials. If you wish to have your students engaging in research or working together in a problem-solving or collaborative activity, it is critical that they have access to related materials, for example, books in the media center or access to online resources. You may need to change particular types of hands-on activities or make special arrangements for materials to be sent to your students. Your students at a distance location should not be at a learning disadvantage because of limited resources. You can work closely with your school library media specialist to ensure that your students have equal access to the materials essential for the learning experience. By working together you can be certain that your students will have the technology they can use to be connected to the class and to the available resources. Many schools offer technology loan programs or extra after-school hours so that students can use the resources at school. It is important to ensure that your students have the technology and resources they need to be successful.

Although the Web has a wealth of materials, there are still some courses in which resources for students are not readily available online or copyright issues do not allow using the Internet to provide those resources. Your school library media specialist should be aware of the copyright issues and be able to help you provide access to materials. See Copyright Concerns: Distance Learning.

 Check Your Understanding 7.1

Copyright Concerns
Distance Learning

In 2002, Congress revised the distance learning aspects of the copyright law by passing the Technology, Education and Copyright Harmonization (TEACH) Act. It extended **fair use**, an exception to the copyright laws that allows limited use of copyrighted materials in teaching, into the digital world and acknowledged that the boundaries of teaching space extend beyond the walls of a classroom. The act allows greater liberty to teachers in their use of materials in an online environment, permitting the display and performance of nearly all types of materials (visuals, sculpture, art, music, video, etc.) meeting the following conditions.

- The transmission is an integral part of a systematic, ongoing instructional activity mediated by an instructor.
- The transmission is directly related to and of material assistance in the teaching of content.
- The transmission is solely for and limited to students officially enrolled in the course.
- The teacher informs students that materials used may be subject to copyright protection.
- The institution employs measures to prevent retention of the materials in accessible form by the students for longer than the duration of the course.
- The institution employs measures that limit the transmission of the material to students enrolled in the course and precludes unauthorized student retention and/or redistribution to the extent technologically feasible.
- In order to facilitate digital transmissions, the TEACH Act permits scanning of some materials, but only if the material is not already available in digital form.

Certain specific restrictions are spelled out for use of copyrighted material in distance education.

- There is a time limit on use, comparable to the time the materials would be used in a face-to-face class. One may not continue to use the copyrighted materials beyond the duration of the semester the course is offered nor may the materials be used during another semester without prior permission.
- Teachers may not transmit textbooks, printed materials, or other media that are typically purchased or acquired by students.
- Off-air recordings may not be altered from their original content. They may not be combined or merged (physically or electronically) to constitute teaching anthologies or compilations.

Teaching at a Distance

The emphasis on student learning, whether in a teacher-led or student-centered environment, is as important in a distance education setting as it is in a traditional classroom.

Strategies and Approaches

When designing instruction for distance learning settings, whether blended, flipped, or online, you will need to consider the setting and the technology available. Regardless of the technology used or whether the lesson takes place in actual time by computer conferencing or through time-delayed interactions, an instructional telecommunication system must perform certain functions to be effective:

1. *Information presentation.* A standard element for any lesson is presentation of information involving not only teacher-led strategies, but also procedures within student-centered approaches. Common examples include the following.

   - *Teacher presentation and demonstration, such as a prepared video on how to complete a specific task that students can view on their own.* In a blended or flipped learning setting, you could assign the instructional video in preparation for the hands-on class activities when your students meet in class.

   - *Student presentation or small-group work, which might be a small group of students who report their solution to a case study they investigate.* Your students can lead a topic discussion with the rest of the class and, as facilitator, you can provide support and guidance while they prepare their questions or discussion points.

   - *Class resources (e.g., handouts, correspondence, study materials), like a set of articles you have put on e-reserve with the school's library media center.* Your students can use these materials to provide them with the background they need for a live "chat" or illustrations that will help them see the images about the topic within an audio teleconference.

   - *Live or recorded voice, music, and other sounds.* For example, you might have an author or content expert prepare a podcast about why she wrote the story, to which your students can listen before they have an online discussion with that person.

   - *Full-motion images which might be archived videos for students to use in their study of historical events.* Your students can create their own video to share an idea with the rest of the class or as a means to demonstrate to you that they have learned the concept you are assessing.

2. *Practice with feedback.* We know that the most learning takes place when learners are participating actively and mentally processing the material. Teachers induce activity in various ways, such as the following.

   - *Question-and-answer activities (carried out during or after the lesson).* You will want your questions to engage your students at a critical thinking level of inquiry. You can help your students improve their ability to think critically and creatively through additional questions you might provide following the instruction. Your students can generate questions they can use with an expert or to prepare for an in-depth inquiry into a topic.

   - *Discussion activities (during the class or as homework).* You will want your discussions to be engaging and allow your students to bring in additional information from resources they have located. In an online discussion, you can observe the discussion and add comments or redirect your students as the discussion proceeds.

   - *Testing.* A test can help your students recognize areas where they need to delve into the topic more to understand the details of the issue. Or, a test can help you assess the level of understanding your students have about the topic. By seeing how they are doing with the content, you can make adjustments in your instruction and help them see where they need to focus.

- *Structured group activities (e.g., role-playing or games).* When you design online activities, you want to be certain that everyone understands what is expected of him or her. Keeping the instructions clear will help your students get started. Your observations of their progress will help you guide them when necessary.

- *Group projects.* You can facilitate learning by bringing students together in groups to complete designated tasks or projects. At times you might let them form their own groups, other times you might organize the groups based on what you have learned about them. You can make yourself part of each group to check their progress, helping them in their work by adding comments as they work together.

- *Peer tutoring.* Your students can help each other to understand concepts and, in the process, learn the information better themselves. You can observe the tutoring and see how well students are learning the material.

3. *Access to learning resources.* Lessons and courses are usually structured with the assumption that learners will spend time outside class working individually or in small groups with the material, doing homework, projects, papers, and the like. You will need to be certain your students can get to the resources in order for them to be successful in their learning experiences. External learning resources include the following.

- *Text materials (e.g., textbooks, supplementary readings, worksheets).* Text materials are assets in any learning experience; they provide your students with the information to help guide them in their learning. In an online instructional setting, providing additional readings or worksheets will help your students as they gain confidence in working independently.

- *Audiovisual materials (e.g., DVDs, podcasts, online resources).* Similar to printed materials, these materials support students' learning experiences. For example, you could have the author of the textbook provide a short video presentation of the book at the beginning of the learning experience.

- *Online resources (e.g., for online searches).* You can find quite an array of online materials for your students to use. Some online resources are interactive and can give your students additional learning experiences. Other online resources contain detailed up-to-date information that supplements your instruction.

- *Kits (e.g., for laboratory experiments or to examine specimens of real objects).* Subjects such as science are complicated without the necessary hands-on experiences. Providing your students with the appropriate materials to use for an experiment or the specimen to examine closely provides your students with the opportunity to gain in-depth knowledge of the topic.

- *Library materials (e.g., original source documents).* It is essential for you to consider your students' access to library materials. You want to be certain that all your students will have the ability to find the materials that will assist them in completing tasks and assignments. Federal Resources for Educational Excellence provides a wealth of information from a number of public agencies at no cost (www.free1.ed.gov).

As in a regular classroom, various technology, media, and materials can be employed in a distance learning setting (Figure 7.1).

Application Exercise 7.2

Types of Technology Resources

There is an assortment of distance learning resources used to support student learning: audio, video, and text-based resources, which we will describe briefly for you. All three types of resources can be used both **synchronously**, when all the participants are

Figure 7.1 Examples of Media Used in Distance Education

Each of the various telecommunication systems used in distance learning has strengths and limitations. The characteristics of the systems are discussed at greater length in the following sections of this chapter.

Audio	Video	Text
Audio teleconference	Television	Bulletin board posting
Podcasting	Vidcasting	Correspondence (email/mail)
Audio recordings (tape or digital)	Online video	Blog/wiki

together at the same time, and **asynchronously**, when the participants are not working on the activities at the same time. When using any of these resources, you should consider copyright issues, which you can read more about in the "Copyright Concerns" feature in this chapter.

AUDIO-BASED TECHNOLOGY.   Audio has a rich history of facilitating instruction at a distance. Radio was one of the first technologies used to deliver education remotely. Although not used in the United States today, there are still instructional applications of radio in some international settings, often in rural areas where Internet connections are very limited resources.

The key to successful use of audio in instruction is to consider what resources are available to students at various locations and to be aware that sometimes audio may be sufficient to convey the learning experience. To use audio as a viable option for delivery of information, resources such as podcasts can be available to students for individual use or a conference call can be established among members of a class as a means for two-way communication.

An **audio teleconference**—a live, interactive conversation using telephone lines, satellites, or the Internet—connects people at different locations via audio. One issue

Video Example 7.2: Online Academic Discussion

Watch this video segment to see how Mr. Chun prepares his students for their online discussion task with the students from New Hampshire. What suggestions does he offer to his students to help them become comfortable interacting with the other class?

associated with relying only on audio transmissions is the lack of visual information. However, audio can be supplemented by providing visual information such as handouts that can be attached to emails, or a PowerPoint presentation provided within a course management tool such as Blackboard, Edmodo, or Moodle.

VIDEO-BASED TECHNOLOGY.   Similar to audio, video has been available in many formats for distance education use for years. There are two primary types of video transmissions. **One-way video** is in use when the visual and auditory information is delivered to learners with limited opportunities for immediate connections with the teacher or source of the information. You might prepare a presentation using Power-Point or Prezi to send to your students and then engage with them in an online chat at a different time. Or, you might have your students watch a National Geographic special on earthquakes and have them prepare a paper on what they learned. In both cases, the information is provided with little exchange between the students and the source of the information at the time of the presentation. And, because it is one-way, the students do not have to view the video at the same time or in the same location. In the example of the PowerPoint presentation, students can view it when they have time. For the television special, your students might be at home watching it with family.

Two-way video is in use when visual and auditory information are exchanged across the system between learners and the teacher synchronously. This is also referred to as **videoconferencing**. Two-way video is often preferred, because everyone can see each other and the interactions among the participants are easier and more immediate. When learners are new to distance learning experiences, two-way video makes it easier to become familiar with learning in a setting in which the teacher and students are separated. You might decide that your students will benefit from engaging with the author of a novel they are reading. You can help them prepare by guiding them to think about what they would like to know about the author and more specifically about the book and the characters. At the time of the exchange, your students can prompt the author with their questions and share their views of the book. Because everyone can see and hear each other, the experience is enriched for all the

Video Example 7.3: Video Discussion

Observe Mr. Chun's students engage in a discussion about how the Hawaiian Islands were established using the school's video conferencing system. How does Mr. Chun guide his students to consider the historical elements that are part of the history discussion?

participants. Or, you might want to share the instruction of a topic with a colleague from another region of the state. Together you plan your session, you bring the classes together in the two-way video setting, and you offer a new learning experience for all your students.

TEXT-BASED TECHNOLOGY. Text-based technology is instruction delivered electronically using computer-based, or online, media. For online learning, students need to access the Internet to obtain the materials through a network. However, online learning involves not just accessing information (e.g., locating webpages), but also assisting learners with specific outcomes (e.g., meeting objectives). In addition to delivering instruction via online resources, the teacher can monitor performance and report learner progress.

The uses of online learning in education are increasing. Your students no longer need to rely only on textbooks; they now have access to educational materials located far beyond the walls of the school building. You and your students can obtain information housed in many distant, physically inaccessible libraries around the world! Resources once beyond the dreams of all but the most affluent are readily available to everyone.

You and your students can enhance classroom learning by accessing information from an array of sources (databases, libraries, special interest groups) and by communicating via computer with other students or with experts in a particular field of study and exchanging data. Activities such as the Monarch Butterfly Journey North conducted by the Annenberg Foundation and the GeoBee Challenge of the National Geographic Society make it possible for your students to reap the benefits of connecting to a national network of students, teachers, and scientists to investigate a variety of topics.

Your students can also access electronic documents to enrich their study. Students can actively participate because online learning provides an interactive learning environment. Your students can hyperlink digital information to their papers and projects, making them "living" documents connected to other segments of their work or to additional documents or visual resources.

Because computers have the ability to deliver information in any medium (including text, video, and audio recordings of voice and music), the computer has become a boundless library. Your students are able to communicate instantly with text, picture, voice, data, and two-way audio/video, and the resulting interactions are changing the roles of both students and teachers. You can now be separated geographically from your students, and students can learn from other students in classrooms all over the world.

You might recognize that the content to be studied is very complex, but you feel that you don't need to meet daily with your students. You schedule specific class times during the week. For the other times during the week, you prepare activities online for your students to complete between class meetings. You will want to be certain to engage your students in challenging online learning experiences or collaborative experiences, such as small-group work, to facilitate their learning. You could use the non-class time for your students to learn about aspects of the topic online and use the class time when they are together for active hands-on activities in which your students apply their knowledge. You might be teaching a topic that allows your students to complete their learning in an authentic setting. For some of the time, you meet with your students online via video or audio or engage in a text-based discussion. And, part of the time, your students are engaged in an authentic activity in a setting in which you can observe them at a distance, communicate with the person supervising them, and connect classroom knowledge with the actual application. Your role is to facilitate their active learning during that face-to-face time and to connect their knowledge with applications.

Video Example 7.4: Video Class

Watch how the two classes are guided in their videoconference discussion based on their Blackboard exchange about Calvinism in New Hampshire in the 1700s. How does the earlier online discussion influence the students in their videoconference discussion?

Critical Issues

There are many important issues associated with distance learning, especially when online. They include security, monitoring student use, acceptable use policies, and netiquette.

SECURITY. Your students should be instructed not to give out information such as their phone numbers, addresses, or other personal information over the Internet. Students have been contacted and even harmed by unscrupulous individuals. It may be wise for your students to give their school's address for correspondence if they need to provide such information. Also, you must have parental permission to post children's photos and written work, such as essays, poems, and artistic creations, on the Web.

The Center for Education and Research in Information Assurance and Security (CERIAS) focuses on multidisciplinary research and education about information security. The organization is concerned with supporting educators on issues of privacy, ethics, and management of information. Exploring issues such as confidentiality of student records, privacy of information, and protection of students while they work online are important considerations. This organization provides guidelines for educators to establish policies within their schools to protect students, teachers, and the school community.

Any time your students encounter an inappropriate contact while working online, they should inform you quickly. Your school should have a policy in place about addressing such an interaction. You will want to spend some time with your students to help them understand what it means to be bullied or approached by someone. Just as you would discuss such actions that might happen on school grounds or on the way to school, you will want to ensure your students understand cyberbullying and cyberstalking.

MONITORING STUDENT USE. Teachers and parents must monitor students' Internet use to ensure that their behavior is appropriate and to discourage them from exploring inappropriate material either deliberately or accidentally. The amount and level of monitoring is often based on the age of the students—younger students *might* need more monitoring than older students. Your final decisions about monitoring should be made in conjunction with parents and school administrators. Also, if one of your students encounters information or visuals that are inappropriate, that student should feel comfortable letting you know about it. Software can assist with monitoring student access to information. For example, WebWatcher software allows you to prevent students from going to sites that are "off limits." Schools and libraries are required to have an Internet filtering system installed on their networks. Sometimes it is difficult for your students to access a particular type of website and if it is appropriate for your students to use you will need approval from your building administrator. Then, you can request a limited time access to a particular site through the district technology services.

Close supervision is essential. There is no organization or agency controlling activity on all computer networks. It is important for you to work with your students' parents to understand their responsibilities regarding student access to information outside the school setting. Control is in the hands of individuals; consequently, students may access questionable materials. Software such as Net Nanny or ContentBarrier is available for home use to prohibit access to topics specified by a parent.

ACCEPTABLE USE POLICIES.   Agreements among students, parents/guardians, and the school administration outlining what is considered proper use of the Internet by all parties involved, called **acceptable use policies (AUPs)**, have been developed by most schools. Check to see if your school has such a policy.

The policy usually includes a statement that the school will do what it can to control access to inappropriate information, that students will accept responsibility for not accessing such information, and that parents understand the possibility that children may access such information in spite of the school's efforts. All parties sign the document agreeing that they have read and will abide by the policy. Most states' departments of education have generated resources to assist educators in developing AUPs for their schools.

DIGITAL CITIZENSHIP.   There are informal rules for appropriate behavior on the Internet. If the Internet is the information superhighway, these are the rules of the road. Referred to as **digital citizenship**, the following rules apply to email, texting, and to other interactions on the Web.

- Keep your message short and simple. Try to limit the length of your message. Think before you write. Make it brief, descriptive, and to the point.

- Identify yourself as the sender somewhere in the communication, including your name and school address. Not all devices clearly identify the sender.

- Double check the address or URL before sending a message.

- When replying to a message, include the pertinent portions of the original message.

- Don't write anything you would not want somebody other than the receiver to read as your message can be intercepted or forwarded.

- Check spelling, grammar, and punctuation. Use lowercase letters except for proper names and beginnings of sentences. When texting, use common conventions where appropriate. When you use all capital letters the receiver may interpret this as you shouting.

- Be sensitive to others. Treat other people with respect and courtesy, especially in reference to social, cultural, and ethnic differences. Be aware of cyber bullying and do not engage in that form of inappropriate behavior.

- Don't use sarcasm. It often falls flat and doesn't come across as you intended.

- Be careful with humor. It is a double-edged sword. The reader doesn't always have the benefit of your facial expression, body language, or tone of voice. You can use **emoticons**, those little pictures of faces or things, but this type of humor doesn't communicate as well as being face-to-face.

- Cooperate and share. Consider yourself a guest on the system just as if you were a guest in someone's home. Make an effort to share only pertinent information. In exchange for help and information you receive, be willing to answer questions and to share your resources.

- Carefully consider copyright. Just because something can be copied electronically doesn't mean it should be distributed without permission. Unless stated otherwise, *all* material on the Internet is copyrighted (see Copyright Concerns in this chapter).

- Be alert for obscenity. Laws governing obscenity apply to messages on the Internet. Moreover, even material that is not deemed legally obscene may still be inappropriate for school-age children!

 Check Your Understanding 7.2

Shared Writing Exercise 7.1

Advantages of Distance Learning

When you offer your lessons at a distance, your students receive many benefits. And, with the requirement of many states that all students must have at least one distance learning experience prior to high school graduation, your students can be better prepared for their future.

- *Variety of media.* Distance learning is a versatile means of delivering information to learners around the world with a variety of media, including text, audio, graphics, animation, video, and downloadable software.

- *Up-to-date information.* Until recently, students were limited to the resources in their school buildings. Now, however, with the ability to connect to resources in the community and around the world, students can access current information.

- *Idea exchange.* Students can engage in "conversation" with experts in specific fields of study. Special speakers who can augment a class discussion or provide access to an area of study help students advance their learning.

- *Convenient communication.* Students in various locations can share ideas. They can "speak" to each other at different times and respond at their own convenience, based on the electronic record of their exchanges.

- *Interactive.* All participants get the same message, and the same interactivity in talking to the instructor or the other learners.

- *Extra/advanced resources.* Distance learning expands the opportunities for smaller schools, as well as for individuals participating in home schooling. Students who need additional challenges in their study or have moved beyond what is available in their school can access extra coursework that allows them to continue to advance in their learning.

- *Remediation/course recovery.* Distance learning expands the opportunities for students who are in need of supplementary instruction. Students who have fallen behind due to illness or other factors can enroll in distance education courses to continue their education.

 Check Your Understanding 7.3

Limitations of Distance Learning

Of course, as the teacher, you must design your distance learning lessons well. You need to consider the resources and technology available, as well as your students' experiences with learning at a distance.

- *Inappropriate material.* One concern is that some of the topics, especially online, are *not* appropriate for students. For example, tobacco and alcohol ads appear on the Internet along with games and music kids enjoy. Students can find their way, innocently enough, into topics that are inappropriate or into unsafe environments.

- *Copyright.* Because information is so readily accessible, it is easy for an individual to quickly download a file and illegally appropriate it. Thus, students may turn in a paper or project that is "cut and pasted" and is not their own work. See Copyright Concerns, Online Learning.

- *Finding information.* It is estimated that several thousand new websites are added online every day. Because this growth makes finding information more difficult, teachers need to work with the school media specialist to help students learn effective search strategies. To assist in information retrieval, several commercial companies and universities provide search engines that follow web links to return results matching your query.

- *Support.* Without good technical support and thoughtful management, distance learning can be frustrating for the learner and the teacher. The teacher may have designed quality instruction, but if the technology is not working properly, the learner will find it difficult to access the information. It would be beneficial to have technical support as part of the delivery options for students at a distance.

- *Lack of quality control.* Students need to be critical thinkers and readers who know how to evaluate information. Everything posted online is not fact. Anybody can post anything on the Web, including unsubstantiated, erroneous, or untruthful information.

- *Cost.* It is expensive to establish a quality distance learning program. For the learner, many of the costs for Internet access are not apparent. To be effective, a program requires a large-capacity computer connected to the Internet as a file server. The design of the instruction requires not only the instructor's knowledge of content, but also the hardware and software for delivery and the technical support that is necessary to ensure success.

- *Intimidation.* Lack of experience with this type of communication technology may make some learners less willing to participate.

- *Limited experience using the systems.* Many teachers and students are unfamiliar with interactive learning systems.

Copyright Concerns
Online Learning

Frequently, unauthorized copies of copyrighted works are posted on a website without the knowledge of the copyright owner. Recently the authors found the ASSURE model on five websites without attribution to its source. The casual observer would assume it was developed by the organization on whose website it was found. Instead, each of the cases involved a serious violation of copyright law!

Observe the following guidelines for online use of copyrighted materials:

- Contrary to popular opinion, *all* material on the Internet is copyrighted unless stated otherwise. It is copyrighted even if it does *not* display the copyright symbol.
- Email is considered an original work, fixed in a tangible medium of expression that is covered by copyright. It can legally be read, but not legally forwarded or copied for instructional purposes, except under fair use. You can make one copy for your personal use. It is recommended that you not forward any email without permission, in consideration of both copyright and the Privacy Act. However, you may quote excerpts and report the "gist" of the message. For example, if a teacher has sent you an original poem, which is automatically copyrighted, and you forward it to a friend, then you have definitely violated *both* copyright law and the Privacy Act (adapted from Becker, 2003).
- Downloading an article from a newspaper's website, making copies, and distributing them to your students prior to a class discussion on the topic is permissible following the current photocopying guidelines, which permit making multiple copies for classroom use. The exception would be individually bylined, copyrighted articles, or articles from a source specifically designed for the educational market (e.g., *Scholastic Magazine*). Such articles *cannot* be copied legally for class distribution (adapted from Becker, 2003).
- You cannot post students' essays, poems, or other works on the school website unless you have the permission of the students and their parents or guardians.
- Always link to the home page rather than a location within a website. In general, linking to another website is not viewed as a copyright infringement. However, it does offer the potential of becoming a copyright issue. If the link takes the user to the body of an author's work, and the initial website does not inform users they are being taken to another site, this may falsely give the impression that one is still on a page within the original website being viewed, thereby not giving credit to the linked site (Becker, 2003).
- Downloading and/or file sharing of video, audio, and other works is considered copyright infringement unless authorized by the copyright law or the owner of the work.

Educators should treat copyrighted materials from the Internet the same way they do print formats. Because the copyright law is still muddled in the area of online resources, the best guideline is to always obtain permission. It is usually not that difficult. When in doubt, ask!

Application Exercise 7.3

 Check Your Understanding 7.4

Integrating Distance Resources into Learning

Distance learning options continue to expand, from whole courses or programs to enhanced classroom activities, as does the amount of information about topics of interest.

Virtual Public Schools

There are a number of **virtual public schools (VPS)** using the Internet for delivery of instruction, offering courses or whole programs of study. The VPS are typically offered as state-level initiatives in which students can access courses that might not be available to them at their local schools or take advanced placement classes from other high schools or from colleges and universities anywhere in the world. It is possible to obtain a high school or college diploma without ever setting foot in a classroom. Many software applications (e.g., Blackboard or Moodle) provide both ease of access to the instruction and resources for the instructor and students for successful study online.

The following issues need to be addressed by anyone wishing to venture into this area of academic study:

- Credentials of the institution offering the degree
- Quality and rigor of the courses
- Costs associated with online courses, such as equipment requirements, online charges, and tuition

Connecting with Text

Text communication between individuals through electronic mail (email) or mobile texting can be integrated into lessons and used by students to gather information from and ask questions of individuals beyond the school walls (e.g., other students and experts). For example, during a unit on weather, your students can gather weather data (temperatures, rainfall, and wind direction) from students in other geographic areas. They can also request weather maps from the local TV meteorologist, which can be sent as attachments to email, or use the NOAA website for recent satellite photos. Experts from the National Weather Service can be contacted for the answers to specific questions. Of course, you should always make any necessary arrangements in advance.

Your students can also use email to gather information for individual projects. For example, middle school students investigating careers can contact individuals in those professions for answers to their questions. The products of the students' investigation can be job reports to be shared with the class either as oral presentations or written documents.

One growing use of electronic learning at the PK–12 level promotes writing skills by connecting students with electronic pen pals or "key pals." For example, one teacher connected her elementary students with students in a language arts methods class at a university across the state (see Taking a Look at Technology Integration: Key Pals).

Systems have also been set up that allow students from different countries, even those speaking different languages, to learn about each other's cultures through computer-mediated communications. To address any language barriers, the computer can be set up to provide language translations.

Your students can participate in projects conducted with classes in other locations, allowing them to plan and produce projects collaboratively. Examples include sharing local history with students in other geographic locations and collaborating with students in different classes to solve complex mathematical problems.

Integrating WebQuests

Although students can access a rich array of information on the Web, their searches often use random or low-level thinking skills. With **WebQuests** you can help your students access the Web effectively for gathering information in student-centered learning activities within the classroom (Dodge, 2015). Developed by Bernie Dodge at San Diego State University, WebQuests have been a longtime teacher favorite for

Taking a Look at Technology Integration

Key Pals

Rick Traw, a professor at the University of Northern Iowa, wanted to extend the experiences of his elementary education teacher candidates in language arts applications. He felt the need to have his students work with actual writing examples from young children. Because of scheduling difficulties, it was impossible to arrange a visit for his teacher candidates to work on writing skills with students in a nearby urban elementary school. With the aid of the Internet, however, it was possible for the elementary students to send their stories to their university "key pals" for review. The teacher candidates were able to work individually with each of the elementary children to improve their writing. And, Dr. Traw was able to provide his teacher candidates an authentic teaching experience for his language arts course. The elementary children had an exciting new audience for their writing, and the university teacher candidates had an opportunity to learn about working with emerging writers. Dr. Traw and the classroom teacher collaborated to provide guidance to the college teacher candidates in techniques for assisting the young children with their writing.

Her students exchanged email in which the university teacher candidates helped the younger ones with their writing. Both groups benefited from this experience. The younger students learned ways to improve their writing, and the college teacher candidates learned about working with children. This is an example of how mentors can be linked with students to help them learn about a variety of topics.

infusing Internet resources into the school's curriculum to make a **hybrid**, or mixed, learning environment. A WebQuest is an inquiry-oriented simulation activity designed with specific learning outcomes in mind, in which some or all of the information that students interact with comes from resources on the Internet. Students follow a series of steps to gather information meaningful to the task:

1. *Introduction.* A scenario points to key issues or concepts to prepare the students to ask questions.

2. *Task.* Students identify issues or problems and form questions for the WebQuest.

3. *Process.* In groups, students assume roles and begin to identify the procedures they will follow to gather information to answer their questions.

4. *Sources.* Resources that will be investigated in the WebQuest are identified by the teacher and students. This is one area where the teacher helps to provide the links to websites and to ensure students have access to other support materials. Your school media specialist can also be of help in gathering the resources for students to use.

5. *Conclusion.* This is the end of the WebQuest, but it invites students to continue to investigate issues or problems. WebQuests often end with an evaluation of the process students used, along with benchmarks for achievement.

WebQuests can be applied to many types of lessons and information sources.

- Monitoring current events for social studies
- Science activities, such as tracking weather and studying space probes to other planets
- Databases of information for expository writing assignments
- Mathematics puzzles, which require logical thinking
- Discussion groups with online exchange of information
- Job banks and résumé services for practice in job-seeking activities

Read Taking a Look at Technology Integration: Extending Knowledge through Webquests for an example of how one teacher uses webquests in her classroom.

Taking a Look at Technology Integration
Extending Knowledge through WebQuests

Sherri Wright wanted to give her fifth graders a chance to practice their literacy, technology, and research skills, along with being able to augment her social studies lessons. Because of the daily schedule, it was difficult for her to develop an extensive series of social studies units, but her idea was to engage her students in their expanded inquiry into social studies topics. She decided a set of WebQuests was the way to make it possible for her students to investigate important concepts and give them opportunities to practice their research skills. With the students, she generated a set of what, how, and why questions they would use as they gathered information about their topic. These questions served as the foundation for her students' inquiry. She gave the students four topics: slavery, the Revolutionary War, the Louisiana Purchase, and the moon mission. Her students decided which of the topics to study, thus forming their collaborative groups. Ms. Wright and the school's library media specialist provided the students with print and Internet resources to investigate their topic. During the 4-week period she allowed for this activity, Ms. Wright met with her student groups to discuss their progress and to help guide them in their search for information. At the end of the 4 weeks, each group presented to their classmates the results of their inquiry, using Prezi and handouts. One requirement that Ms. Wright insisted upon was that their presentations had to be interactive and engaging for the rest of the class with activities and questions. Because they were so successful in their inquiry, the students asked if they could "show off" to their parents and repeat their presentations for them. In addition, Ms. Wright required her students to complete a set of reflection questions that focused on their collaboration, communication, inquiry and literacy skills, and their use of technology. Because she provided opportunities and resources to her students, guiding them through the experience with a WebQuest, Ms. Wrights' students were able to expand and extend their knowledge of their chosen topic, learn about the other topic studies, and gain a sense of confidence in their ability to research using text and online resources.

Connecting with Computer Conferencing

You can establish opportunities for your students to learn from experts or to engage in collaborative activities with other students in a variety of settings. An example of the depth of this type of experience is the STEM Teen Read program at Northern Illinois University that introduces K–12 students to science fiction literature and then brings them together to explore the science that was introduced in the stories. The project brings together students of all grade levels and reading abilities who are interested in exploring the science behind the stories they are reading. After completing online interactions, the STEM Read program staff bring together the author of the novel and experts in the science used in the story to connect electronically with the participating students to discuss the story and the science and ethics behind the issues within the novel. You can engage your students in studies of literature, mathematics, social sciences, and the arts through similar types of activities.

Connecting with Parents

Communications with parents can be enhanced if they have Internet access. You can send general information to the parents of your students or specific information or questions can be addressed to an individual student's parents or guardians. Class webpages can inform parents of homework assignments, parent meetings, or materials needed for a special project. If you do post any student photos or student work on your class webpages, you must have permission from the parents or guardian. For those parents without Internet access, you will need to employ written correspondence or use the telephone.

Connecting with Other Teachers

You can also use email to share ideas with other teachers in your content area or who teach the same grade level. Lesson plans can be sent as attachments or placed on the school's or district's server. Questions can be asked of an individual teacher or a group of teachers (e.g., all physics teachers in a state). Another means for electronic sharing of ideas is a **blog**, which looks a lot like an online discussion board. Blogs written by experts can provide teachers and students with access to information. Teachers can also assist students in developing personal blogs to enhance their ability to exchange ideas. One word of caution when beginning this type of electronic community: As stated throughout this book, you need to prepare your students regarding their online safety, advising them not to reveal personal information in any communication. In addition, your school's acceptable use policy will also assist you in ensuring your students will engage in ethical use of the online resources.

Connecting with Communities

A number of cities have created websites that involve a broad cross section of the community, including schools, businesses, local government, and social agencies. This is another example of how the artificial wall between the classroom and the world beyond is dissolving, making it possible for students and teachers to access information and people from every imaginable source (see Taking a Look at Technology Integration: GLOBE).

You can take your students on a virtual field trip to the local zoo or botanical garden. They can meet with a specialist in waste management as part of their study of their carbon footprint. You will want to explore your community and region to identify resources that will blend into your curriculum.

Also, many museums and zoos are creating online "tours" of their exhibits. Your students can visit the Guggenheim and view the collections while learning more about the artists. They can visit the Natural History Museum or the Smithsonian National Zoological Park and participate in activities designed to help them learn. In addition, an increasing number of online journals and magazines are being published, either as supplements to existing print versions or as entirely new efforts. Moreover, most major publishers have put their catalogs on the Web, making it easy to locate and order books, software, and other products. Many publishers are willing to make their actual products available online, usually as trial packages that "dissolve" within a certain period of time (usually 30 days). However, the continuing prevalence of illegal copying and distribution of materials makes some publishers wary of providing complete and unlimited access to software and files.

Course Connections

School districts or schools often purchase or develop instructional modules that can be sent over a restricted school-only network. This method of delivery is used to provide students with remediation or to enhance learning opportunities with the latest version

Taking a Look at Technology Integration

GLOBE: Networking Students, Teachers, and Scientists

The GLOBE program (www.globe.gov) is a program that uses technology to promote scientific inquiry and environmentalism. To participate, students send scientific data they collect over the Internet to the GLOBE network. In return, the class receives information about the data they sent, as well as how those data fit into the larger global picture. Students from over 100 countries participate in GLOBE projects. Scientific professionals from many disciplines participate and use collected GLOBE data to advance scientific knowledge of environmental issues. For example, scientists use the valuable student-collected data to research global changes. Students benefit as well, learning about data collection, scientific protocols, and databases, in addition to having opportunities to chat with scientists and other experts worldwide.

The GLOBE project provides teachers with grade-level appropriate interactive materials that match state and national content standards. One focus of the GLOBE project is to provide hands-on opportunities for students who may not have shown an interest in science. The project provides teacher professional development and online collaboration with other teachers worldwide. Globe also has developed a mentoring program for teachers and students.

Technology for All Learners

Distance Learning Resources

Students in our classrooms have a variety of learning needs. The following examples show ways that your learners can use distance learning resources to help them with their learning.

For students who have visual disabilities or difficulty reading information on a webpage, various design guidelines can be helpful. When including graphics or images, text descriptions can be a resource. For example, along with the image of a feline, add the word *cat* nearby. Avoid using complex tables with many columns. Computer text readers read across one entire line at a time instead of reading each column separately. On hyperlinks, use meaningful terms rather than a graphic or "click here" link that tells nothing about the link. Additional information about how to make webpages accessible to all students is available at the World Wide Web Consortium (W3C) Accessibility Initiative. PowerMapper offers a website accessibility analysis tool to ensure your website materials can be used by all students, including those with disabilities.

Young students who would like to learn more about using the Internet safely can play the Internet Safety Game on Kids.com. Through games and activities, students are guided through protocols that advise them about being safe when engaging in pursuits on the Internet. There are many sites with guidelines, lessons plans, and types of activities available to teachers. Many of these sites also offer materials for parents about how they can teach and maintain online safety at home. Most of the materials for teachers about online safety are free.

of materials. Updating these materials is relatively easy because the core set of digital material can be electronically modified and made immediately available, whereas in the past, revisions often required shipping printed materials or computer disks to schools. Electronic learning provides flexibility for students as well because they may study materials at any time and at any location. Students can also take tests over the intranet. Once the answers are in the database, they are scored and the results are made available immediately to students and the teacher. Online learning is very useful when learners are geographically dispersed and instruction is updated frequently (see Technology for All Learners: Distance Learning Resources to learn about ways to meet the needs of all your students).

Video Example 7.5: Blackboard Benefit

Mr. Chun talks about the benefits of using online discussion boards with his students. What did he learn about guiding students in their online discussions?

Network Resources

It is common knowledge that computers can be used to connect students to people and resources outside of the classroom. Once you connect computers in ways that enable people to communicate and share information, you have a **network**. Networks connect schools, homes, libraries, organizations, and businesses so that students, families, and professionals can access or share information and instruction instantly in several ways.

Types of Networks

There are a number of networks that connect individual computers to one another to permit exchange of files and other resources.

LAN. The simplest of all networks is a **local area network (LAN)**, which connects computers within a limited area, normally a classroom, building, or laboratory.

A LAN relies on a centralized computer called a **file server** that "serves" all the other computers connected to it. A computer lab is often itself a LAN because all the computers in the lab are connected to a single file server, usually tucked away in a closet or other out-of-the-way space. Whole buildings can also be connected to a local area network, usually with a single computer that is located in the office or media center, which serves as the school's file server. Through a LAN, all of the classrooms in a school can have access to the school's collection of software. Many schools also allow teachers and students to save their computer work in personalized folders on the server, which is very useful when multiple students use one computer. It also allows teachers access to their materials, such as PowerPoint presentations, while in the computer lab.

Within a school, LANs can also reduce a technology coordinator's workload, which might otherwise include installing programs, inventorying software, and other such tasks. Coordinators can then spend more time working with teachers and students rather than with machines and software. For example, the media center can store its catalog of materials on the file server, giving teachers and students easy access to the information available on a certain topic.

WAN. Networks that extend beyond the walls of a room or building are called **wide area networks (WANs)**. A campus or district-wide network connecting all buildings via a cable or fiber system is one such example. In this arrangement, the buildings are linked to a centralized computer that serves as the host for all the software used in common. Even though a WAN can connect computers over a wide geographic area (across a city, state, or even a country), it is most often used for smaller configurations, such as connecting the buildings within a school system.

As the name implies, a **wireless network** connects computers without wire. Instead it relies on radio frequency, microwave, or infrared technology that depends on a base station for connection to the network. Such networks use transmitters placed inside the room, throughout the building, or across a campus area and operate in the same manner as hardwired networks. Some cities have installed wireless networks in their downtown areas. Wireless networks omit the need for cabling, which can be costly to install, particularly in older buildings. Computers are no longer bound to workstations. Laptops may be used anywhere within the room, building, or campus area and still have access to the Internet.

INTRANET.   A special type of network called an **intranet** is used internally by a school or organization. It is a proprietary or closed network that connects multiple sites across the state, within the country, or around the world. Systems connected to an intranet are private and accessible only by individuals within a given school or organization.

Intranets provide internal networks for schools. Intranets are a way of increasing communication, collaboration, and information dissemination within schools where divisions, departments, and workgroups might each use a different **computer platform** (hardware and operating system), or where users work in geographically distant locations. Even though an intranet may be connected to a larger network (the Internet, for example), a software package called a **firewall** prevents external users from accessing the internal network, while allowing internal users to access external networks. The intranet allows the school to keep student and employee records and data confidential.

INTERNET.   The **Internet** is a global interconnection of computer networks with a broad collection of millions of computer networks serving billions of people around the world. Any individual on the Internet can communicate with anyone else on the Internet. Users can access any information, regardless of the type of computer they have, because of standard protocols that allow all computers to communicate with each other. Most information is shared without charge except for whatever access fee is required to maintain an account with an **Internet service provider (ISP)**. Many schools provide Internet access to teachers and students at no charge.

Many educational and commercial organizations' networks are developing connections to the Internet called **gateways** or **portals**, designed to provide access to many Internet services. The maze of connections is largely "transparent" to the user. Users just log on to their computer (enter the computer system, often with a special password for privacy), connect to their networking service or ISP, and begin to exchange information.

Complicating information retrieval is the fact that the Internet does not operate hierarchically. There are no comprehensive directory trees or indexes for Internet resources. There is no Library of Congress cataloging scheme or Dewey Decimal system. You can consider the Internet a library where every shelf is labeled "Miscellaneous." Finding one interesting service or item of information is no guarantee that you're on the right track to others. In fact, most of the Internet's resources are in little cul-de-sacs on the network, not linked in any predictable way to other, similar resources. To find information on the Internet you must use **search engines**, programs that identify websites containing user-entered keywords or phrases (see Technology Resources: Search Engines for Kids).

The World Wide Web

The **World Wide Web (the Web)** is a network of networks that allows you to access, view, and maintain documents that can include text, data, sound, and video. It is not separate from the Internet. Instead, it rides on top of the Internet, in the same way that an application such as PowerPoint runs on top of an operating system such as Windows.

The Web is a series of communications protocols between client and server. These protocols enable access to documents stored on computers throughout the Internet while allowing links to other documents on other computers. The Web protocol **hypertext transfer protocol (HTTP)** ensures compatibility before transferring information contained in documents called **webpages**. Each individual collection of pages is called a **website**, which users access by entering its address or **uniform resource locator (URL)** into a browser (see the list of websites at the end of this chapter).

The URL incorporates the name of the host computer (server), the domain, the directory on the server, and the title of the webpage (actual filename). Navigation within and among webpages relies on hypertext links that, when selected, move users to another location on the same page, another website on the same host computer, or to a different computer on the Web.

To use the Web for online learning, webpages have to be designed and written, and a host computer must be available to house them. Universities and large companies are usually directly connected to the Internet and run the necessary web-hosting (server) software. A popular resource in online distance education, the **Learning Management System (LMS)**, is software designed to make it easier for the teacher to design and deliver instruction and to use the resources that are part of the system, such as the discussion board, test options, and grade book. When using an LMS program such as Blackboard or Moodle, the teacher can concentrate on the instruction and not have to be concerned with computer programming issues.

Evaluating Online Resources

There are so many resources available for students and learners on the Web that it can be difficult to determine which are the best to support learning. You can start with those provided in Technology Resources: Search Engines for Kids.

See the **Selection Rubric: Online Resources** provided to guide you in identifying online resources that will benefit your professional development or support your students' learning. You can even ask students to use the rubric to evaluate sites they find while exploring new resources for their learning experiences.

Technology Resources

Search Engines for Kids

KidRex.org

This is a colorful, fun, and safe search site for kids that is designed by kids. KidRex searches the Internet for kid topic sites and employs the Google SafeSearch technology.

GoGooligans.com

This is an advanced academic and educational search engine for kids and teens. The search engine site offers additional resources for children with disabilities. For older teens, there is an advanced search engine, GoogleScholastic.com. Both search engines use Google SafeSearch technology to ensure that children are guided to sites that are appropriate for them.

FactMonster.com

FactMonster offers text, video, and other resources on many topics. A reference desk with access to a dictionary, atlas, and encyclopedia is included. A Homework Center is available with ideas about how to develop homework habits and skills and how to use the available resources. It is available for grade levels K–12 and includes topics covering math, language arts, social studies, and science.

Askkids.com

This is a student version of Ask.com that uses age-appropriate content, filtering, and search terms to help kids narrow their searches by asking questions.

Kidsclick.org

Librarians created this site to help students conduct searches. Main topic menus and helpful links make it a kid-friendly search engine.

SELECTION RUBRIC   **Online Resources**

Complete and save the following interactive evaluation to reference
when selecting online resources to integrate into lessons.

Search Terms when
selecting online

_____

_____

_____

Title _____

Source/Location _____

© Date _____   Cost _____

Primary User(s)

Subject Area _____   Grade Level _____

_____ Student

Learning Experiences _____

_____ Teacher

Brief Description

Standards/Outcomes/Objectives

Prerequisites (e.g., prior knowledge, reading ability, vocabulary level)

Strengths

Limitations

Special Features

Name _____   Date _____

(Continued)

Rating Area	High Quality	Medium Quality	Low Quality
Alignment with standards, outcomes, and objectives	Standards/outcomes/objectives are addressed and use of online resource should enhance student learning.	Standards/outcomes/objectives are partially addressed and use of online resource may enhance student learning.	Standards/outcomes/objectives are not addressed and use of online resource will likely not enhance student learning.
Accurate and current information	Information is correct and does not contain material that is out of date.	Information is correct, but does contain material that is out of date.	Information is not correct and does contain material that is out of date.
Age-appropriate language	Language used is age appropriate and vocabulary is understandable.	Language used is nearly age appropriate and some vocabulary is above/below student age.	Language used is not age appropriate and vocabulary is clearly inappropriate for student age.
Interest level and engagement	Topic is presented so that students are likely to be interested and actively engaged in learning.	Topic is presented to interest students most of the time and engage most students in learning.	Topic is presented so as not to interest students and not engage them in learning.
Technical quality	The material represents the best technology and media.	The material represents technology and media that are good quality, although they may not be the best available.	The material represents technology and media that are not well prepared and are of very poor quality.
Ease of use (student or teacher)	Material follows easy-to-use patterns with nothing to confuse the user.	Material follows patterns that are easy to follow most of the time, with a few things to confuse the user.	Material follows no patterns and most of the time the user is very confused.
Bias free	There is no evidence of objectionable bias or advertising.	There is little evidence of bias or advertising.	There is much evidence of bias or advertising.
User guide and directions	The user guide is an excellent resource for use in a lesson. Directions should help teachers and students use the material.	The user guide is a good resource for use in a lesson. Directions may help teachers and students use the material.	The user guide is a poor resource for use in a lesson. Directions do not help teachers and students use the material.
Clear directions	Navigation is logical and pages are well organized.	Navigation is logical for main use, but can be confusing.	Navigation is not logical and pages are not well organized.
Stimulates creativity	Use of online resources gives students many opportunities to engage in new learning experiences.	Use of online resources gives students some opportunities to engage in new learning experiences.	Use of online resources gives students few opportunities to engage in new learning experiences.
Visual design	The online resource is designed with appropriate use of graphics and text to ensure student understanding.	The online resource is designed with graphics and text that are of average quality.	The online resource is designed with graphics and text that are of poor quality and distract students from understanding.
Quality of links	The online resource links facilitate navigating the material and finding additional information.	The online resource links are not easy to navigate and make it difficult to find additional information.	The online resource links make it very difficult to navigate the material and to find additional information.

Recommended for Classroom Use: _____ Yes _____ No

Ideas for Classroom Use: _____

Innovations in Teaching

Mobile Learning

Mobile Learning, also known as M-Learning, is described as personal, spontaneous, and informal learning experiences that are available using personal mobile devices such as tablets or smart phones. The focus of the learning experience is that it is learner-centered and learner-initiated. It is beyond the idea of just-in-time learning which is tied to a formal educational setting because it includes the idea that the learning experience is also viewed by the learner as "just-for-me." Mobile learning does rely on the use of mobile devices and the ability of the learner to seek the information using the resources on the devices. The search for information is not limited to text but includes such things as performance arts as a means to gain knowledge. The learner assumes responsibility for gathering information using mobile devices to expand knowledge and understanding of content that may be aligned with the school curriculum. But, with the idea of "just-for-me" as a theme of mobile learning, the search for knowledge may be more personal in nature. And, while the technology is an element of the idea of learning mobility, m-learning is about the ability of the learner to gather information at any point in time in a way the is meaningful to the individual and serves to advance the learner's knowledge.

 Check Your Understanding 7.6

Summary

- *Identify elements that are important to the design for teaching at a distance.* Designing distance learning experiences requires a different way of thinking about engaging learners in the class. Teachers need to consider the learners and where they are located. We presented ideas about how to use the ASSURE model to develop distance learning activities for your students.

- *State strategies that are effective when teaching at a distance.* Most regular classroom instructional strategies can be used in distance education settings, although they may need to be modified to ensure that students will have engaging learning experiences.

- *List advantages to using distance education.* Among the advantages are that teachers can augment student study and bring additional resources into the classroom through distance education. The blending of the regular classroom and distance learning resources has made it possible for students of all ability levels to enjoy an enhanced educational experience.

- *List limitations of distance education.* With technology there are some considerations to be made. For example, there are expenses to consider when establishing a distance education program in terms of the cost of technology and software necessary for a complete course of study. There is also the time to develop the course and teacher professional development that are considerations.

- *Identify distance resources that can be integrated into learning.* Teachers are no longer limited to the materials in their classrooms or in the school media center; they can now access resources from around the world. They can provide their students with experiences such as WebQuests that help them learn to use the Internet as a source of information. Students can reach out to other students and to experts for exchanges of ideas.

- *Identify network resources that are used in distance education.* From LANs to WANs, which include wireless networks, connection to online resources has become much easier for those involved. Teachers and students can now access learning resources from any location and at any time. This opens up multiple learning opportunities for students.

ASSURE Lesson Plan

This ASSURE Classroom Case Study is based on the lesson Mr. Chun created for his high school social studies class in collaboration with another teacher in New Hampshire.

Mr. Chun wants his students to review their state's history and to consider the current status of the state. He plans to use the interactive distance learning resources to provide his students with opportunities to meet with high school students in New Hampshire who are engaged in a similar lesson.

Analyze Learners

General Characteristics

The students in Jimmy Chun's high school class are primarily Hawaiian and from low- to middle-income homes. They are fairly equally distributed with regard to gender and range in age from 15 to 17 years old. Student reading ability is at or above grade level. Student behavior problems are minimal.

Entry Competencies

The students are, in general, able to do the following:

- Conduct online research
- Use Blackboard software to participate in discussion boards and exchange digital documents

Learning Differences and Needs of Students

Jimmy Chun's students learn best when engaged in activities that are relevant and include lively discussions of meaningful topics. His students vary in comfort level with speaking to students in the distance education (New Hampshire) class. Some students prefer live audio to using the text-based discussion boards.

State Standards and Objectives

Curriculum Standards. **National Council for the Social Studies, Dimension 2 (9–12)—Historical Thinking: Change, Continuity, and Context**—Evaluate how historical events and developments were shaped by unique circumstances of time and place as well as broader historical contexts.

Technology Standards. **National Educational Technology Standards for Students 2**—Students communicate and work collaboratively to support learning; **3**—Students gather, evaluate, and use information.

Learning Objectives

1. Using content from conducting Internet and library research of pre-1770 U.S. history regarding Hawaiian and New Hampshire culture, religion, government, economy, and social structure, the students will write questions and give written responses during an online discussion.
2. Using the questions and information gained during discussion board dialog, the students will ask New Hampshire students questions regarding their pre-1770 society with respect to culture, religion, government, economy, and social structure.
3. Using the information gained during discussion board dialog and personal knowledge, the students will answer questions posed by the New Hampshire students regarding Hawaiian pre-1770 society with respect to culture, religion, government, economy, and social structure.

Select Strategies and Resources

Select Strategies

Jimmy Chun selects teacher- and student-centered strategies for the pre-1770 U.S. history lesson. The teacher-centered strategies involve providing a detailed description of the lesson objectives and how students should prepare for the video teleconference with New Hampshire students. Mr. Chun also provides feedback to his students as they complete their work. The student-centered strategies consist of students' Internet research on the pre-1770 history of both their states, posting their questions on the discussion board, and participating in the two-way audio/video distance education teleconference with the New Hampshire students.

Select Resources

This lesson involves student use of computers, distance education equipment, and Blackboard software to post to the discussion board and exchange documents. Mr. Chun applies the following guidelines to assess the appropriateness of his technology and media selections:

- *Alignment with standards, outcomes, and objectives.* The Internet sites, Blackboard software, and distance education video teleconference provide the necessary support for Jimmy Chun's students to meet the learning objectives.
- *Accurate and current information.* Students use both text-based and Internet resources to conduct their research on pre-1770 U.S. history.
- *Age-appropriate language.* Mr. Chun has his students access websites that are appropriate for high school students. When needed, he provides assistance for student use of Blackboard.
- *Interest level and engagement.* The Hawaiian and New Hampshire students are very excited to "meet" and discuss important pre-1770 U.S. history and current topics of interest to them on the discussion boards and during the live two-way audio/video sessions.
- *Technical quality.* The technical quality of the two-way audio/video interactions is consistent with current standards in that the video is slightly delayed. Discussion board interactions and Internet searches have consistently high technical quality due to high-speed access at both schools.
- *Ease of use.* Blackboard requires initial training and support but is fairly easy for high school students to use after basic skills training.

(Continued)

- *Bias free.* Students find multiple references for their research to better ensure the content is bias free. Blackboard software is bias free.
- *User guide and directions.* The online help features of Blackboard are moderately easy for students to use. Students most frequently ask each other or Mr. Chun for assistance with technical difficulties.

Jimmy Chun also provided a list of Internet sites for students to reference when conducting online research on pre-1770 U.S. history.

Utilize Resources

Preview the Resources

Jimmy Chun previews Blackboard software to ensure it has the features needed for the lesson. He previews selected resources to verify that students can find Internet and text-based information on pre-1770 U.S. history. He also previews the video teleconferencing system to make certain students will be able to see and hear each other.

Prepare the Resources.

Mr. Chun prepares an assignment sheet that describes the lesson requirements and criteria that will be used to assess the final student products. He adds starter questions to the Blackboard discussion area.

Prepare the Environment.

Jimmy Chun tests the Internet connections on the lab computers and ensures that Blackboard is accessible from each computer. He also tests the distance education equipment by connecting to the classroom in New Hampshire and practicing with the cameras, microphones, and lighting.

Prepare the Learners.

Students in Mr. Chun's class have conducted Internet research and have participated in previous video teleconferences with the students in New Hampshire. Therefore, learner preparation primarily focuses on the topics to be covered on the discussion board and during the live session.

Provide the Learning Experience.

The learning experience occurs in two distance education formats: text-based exchanges via discussion boards and live two-way audio/video interactions between the Hawaiian and New Hampshire students.

Require Learner Participation

Student Practice Activities.

The students in Jimmy Chun's class use computers, the Internet, and Blackboard software to prepare for and participate in the online discussions of pre-1770 U.S. history of Hawaii and New Hampshire. The students apply information from their research and discussion board topics to generate questions to ask during the live video teleconference. During the live session, students practice and test their knowledge by asking and answering student-created questions.

Feedback.

Jimmy Chun provides continuous feedback as students conduct their research, participate in discussion boards, and interact with students from New Hampshire.

Evaluate and Revise

Assessment of Learner Achievement.

Mr. Chun reviews the discussion board posts of each individual student to assess knowledge of pre-1770 Hawaiian and New Hampshire society. He also reviews recordings of the video teleconference to assess student oral responses to questions asked by the New Hampshire students. Mr. Chun assesses student ability to use technology for communication and research by evaluating student Blackboard posts.

Evaluation of Strategies and Resources.

Mr. Chun evaluates the effectiveness of the lesson strategies, talking about the process with the New Hampshire teacher and students and with the students in his class. Evaluation of the technology and media resources involves examining the functionality of the Blackboard software, the Internet browser, and the two-way audio/video distance education session.

Revision.

The evaluation results revealed that student interactions could benefit from arranging students in cross-state pairs to increase interactions and information exchange. Another revision that emerged from the evaluation results was to limit teacher input during the live two-way audio/video sessions to encourage more student-to-student discussion.

Professional Development

Demonstrating Professional Skills

1. Interview a teacher who regularly uses audio or television for distance learning in the classroom. Prepare a brief written or recorded report addressing the objectives covered, techniques utilized, and problems encountered. An example might be elementary students using a two-way audio/video system to investigate a community issue (ISTE Standards for Teachers 1.B, 3.B).

2. Develop a lesson incorporating a WebQuest to engage learners. What changes did you need to make in the design of the lesson to incorporate the WebQuest? What Internet safety issues have to be confronted? What learner skills and assessment considerations do you need to address when including a WebQuest in a lesson (ISTE Standards for Teachers 1.B, 2.A, 2.C, 3.D, 4.A, 4.B)?

3. Develop an Internet acceptable use policy for your school (either where you attended or where you teach) (ISTE Standards for Teachers 4.A, 4.C).

4. Observe or participate in a class taught at a distance. Describe how the teacher and students interact with each other. Also, describe the types and uses of media within the lesson (ISTE Standards for Teachers 1.D, 3.D).

Building Your Professional Portfolio

- *Creating My Lesson.* Using the ASSURE model, design a lesson for a scenario from the Lesson Scenarios in the Appendix, from an example in the chapter; or use a scenario of your own design. Apply one of the instructional strategies described in Chapter 4 and information from this chapter related to incorporating online learning into your instructional setting. Be sure to include information about the audience, the objectives, and all other elements of the ASSURE model. Be certain to match your intended outcomes to state or national learning standards for your content area (ISTE Standards for Teachers 2.A, 2.B, 2.C).

- *Reflecting on My Lesson.* Reflect on the process of designing your lesson and your efforts at enhancing that lesson to meet student needs in your class. What have you learned about matching audience, content, instructional strategy, and materials? What could you have done to develop higher-order thinking or creativity skills or to engage students more deeply in active learning at a distance? In what ways did the strategies you selected for your lesson enhance learning opportunities for your students? What considerations do you need to better address when planning another lesson for a distance setting (ISTE Standards for Teachers 2.A)?

- *Enhancing My Lesson.* Enhance your distance lesson to address any of your students who have special needs, such as physical or learning impediments. Also assume that several students are identified as gifted. How will you change your lesson design to ensure that these students are recognized and supported to allow them to succeed? Also consider the options available to your students at a distance related to resources and technology. How might that affect your lesson design (ISTE Standards for Teachers 2.A, 2.B, 2.C)?

Suggested Resources

Print Resources

Conrad, R. M. & Donaldson, J. A. (2011). *Engaging the online learner: Activities and resources for creative instruction, Updated Edition.* San Francisco, CA: Jossey-Bass.

Lipinski, T. A. (2005). *Copyright law and the distance education classroom: Working within the information infrastructure.* Lanham, MD: Scarecrow Press.

Moore, M. G. & Anderson, W. G. (2008). *Handbook of distance education* (2nd ed.). Mahwah, NJ: Lawrence Erlbaum.

Palloff, R. M. & Pratt, K. (2007). *Building online learning communities: Effective strategies for the virtual classroom.* San Francisco, CA: Jossey-Bass.

Shank, P. (2011). *Online learning idea book: 95 proven ways to enhance technology-based and blended learning* (2nd ed.). San Francisco, CA: John Wiley & Sons.

Simonson, M., Smaldino, S. E., & Zvacek, S. (2014). *Teaching and learning at a distance: Foundations of distance education* (5th ed.). Charlotte, NC: Information Age Publishing.

Online Resources and Apps

Creative Commons

Creative Commons is a nonprofit organization to share and use through the use of free legal tools. They provide a simple, standardized way for you to give the public permission to share and use the web-based materials you develop. Creative Commons licenses are not an alternative to copyright, but they give you the tools to modify the copyright terms for your work.

The Adventures of Cyberbee

This site is filled with helpful ideas and activities for using the Internet in education.

CNN Interactive

CNN is an up-to-the-minute source for world news and information about weather, sports, science, technology, show business, and health.

Public Broadcasting Service (PBS)

A nonprofit consortium of the nation's public television stations, PBS makes noncommercial television available to the public. Its website includes resources related to quality programs and services for educators and parents.

San Diego Zoo and Wild Animal Park

This site provides a virtual tour of the San Diego Zoo and includes information about the zoo, its inhabitants, and endangered species.

Sesame Workshop

A nonprofit educational organization that creates entertaining and educational radio and television programming, the Sesame Workshop focuses on providing learning opportunities for children, while assisting teachers, daycare providers, and parents in developing quality learning experiences and curricula in a variety of media formats.

Chapter 8
Enhancing Learning with Multimedia

Learning Outcomes

This chapter addresses ISTE Standards for Teachers 2 and 5:

8.1 Compare and contrast multimedia literacies for audio, video, text, and visuals.

8.2 Explain how to use audio recordings to enhance learning for students.

8.3 Give examples of how the four types of educational videos support student learning.

8.4 Describe strategies to increase student comprehension of text resources.

8.5 Explain how use of each of the six types of visuals will enhance student learning.

Goal

Utilize a variety of multimedia materials to enhance PK–12 student learning.

ASSURE Classroom Case Study

This chapter's ASSURE Classroom Case Study describes the instructional planning used by Scott James, a fifth-grade teacher in a school with students coming from low- to middle-income homes. Mr. James realizes that students learn best when lessons reflect real-world situations. He has also seen increased student motivation and interest when computers are integrated into his lessons. Scott's school recently purchased a digital video camera and iMovie software for the lab computers. To take advantage of these resources, Scott designs a lesson on natural disasters that is multidisciplinary, incorporates the use of the new digital video camera, and builds his students' expository writing skills. During the lesson, student pairs create digital videos of natural disaster "news broadcasts" they have scripted. One student assumes the role of news anchor, while the other is the on-the-scene news reporter.

Video segments throughout this chapter explore how Mr. James engages students in the use of digital audio and video and discusses the benefits, limitations, and suggestions for using multimedia tools to improve student learning.

Introduction

Today's PK–12 students are experiencing an explosion of enhanced learning through the use of multimedia resources. At the click of a mouse, a swipe of a trackpad or with the touch of a tablet or other mobile device, teachers can select from a vast array of digital audio, video, text, and visual materials to support and enrich instructional experiences. In addition, multimedia production equipment and apps are readily available in most PK–12 schools. Thus, students can use these tools to demonstrate a depth of understanding and application beyond traditional testing. In this chapter, we explore how to enhance learning with audio, video, text, and visuals.

Incorporating Multimedia Literacies into Teaching

The longstanding theory of multimedia learning proposes that actively learning from both auditory and visual resources results in deeper levels of understanding (Mayer, 2012). However, effective design and use of multimedia require you, as a teacher, to understand the advantages, limitations, and strategies needed to integrate multimedia, or as presented in this chapter, audio, video, text, and visuals into your instruction. You will need to understand the variables that affect how learners interpret multimedia resources, how the multimedia enhances learning, and key strategies for you and your students to create meaningful audio, video, text, and visual resources. In other words, the actual benefit to student learning is dependent upon the teacher's ability to design multimedia lessons that build students' audio, video, text, and visual literacy knowledge and skills.

Audio and video literacy are key factors required of today's students to interpret and produce multimedia. **Audio literacy** requires attentive listening and deciphering important message components to connect with prior knowledge, as well as to produce meaningful audio communication. Whereas, **video literacy** encompasses the knowledge and skills needed to "consume" or meaningfully view video, as well as to produce video to demonstrate knowledge and skills. Collectively, today's teachers should help students "develop a wider set of literacy skills . . . to both comprehend the messages we receive and effectively utilize these tools to design and distribute our own messages." (National Association for Media Literacy, 2016, Resources, para. 8).

Rowe (2012) advocates that today's student must be able to locate, understand, and use informational text to fully participate in our society. These skills are foundational components of **text literacy**. There are two aspects to a student becoming literate in the use of text as part of the learning process. One aspect is that of comprehending text, or the ability to understand and evaluate the message. The other is producing text, which is the ability to synthesize and write about what they read or experience. In both cases, the technology and media you use as a teacher can help to facilitate the development of text literacy skills in your students (Handsfield, Dean, & Cielocha, 2009).

Visual literacy refers to the learned ability to interpret visual messages accurately and to create such messages. Visual literacy can be developed through two major approaches: helping learners to interpret, or **decode**, visuals proficiently by practicing visual analysis skills, and helping learners to create, or **encode**, visuals to express themselves and communicate with others. Seeing a visual does not automatically ensure that one will learn from it. Many variables affect how a learner decodes a visual; for example, young children tend to interpret images more literally than do older children. Additionally, interpreting visuals may be affected by the student's cultural background and experiences. Another aspect of visual literacy is student creation of visuals. Just as writing can spur reading, producing visuals can be a highly effective way of promoting visual understanding. You should encourage students to include carefully selected or created images with their assignments to enhance the demonstration of knowledge.

 Check Your Understanding 8.1

Shared Writing Exercise 8.1

Enhancing Learning with Audio

Audio adds a dimension to classroom environments that expands and deepens students' learning experiences. Imagine your students listening to Abraham Lincoln presenting his inaugural address, Einstein explaining relativity, Ernest Hemingway reading a passage from one of his novels, or Picasso interpreting one of his paintings. Also imagine a third-grade student being recorded as she reads a story for her digital portfolio, then comparing that recording with stories she recorded in first and second grade.

Advantages of Audio

Using audio in the classroom offers advantages to consider when planning integration of audio into your instruction. You will discover that both teachers and students can use various types of audio to enhance learning opportunities, and you will discover ideas for accessing and producing audio. Some advantages include:

- *Readily available, simple to use, and portable.* Most students have been using CD and MP3 players since they were young. These types of players are easy to operate. Audio players are portable and can even be used in the field. Portable audio devices are also ideal for home study; many students already have their own players.

- *Inexpensive.* Once the storage devices and equipment have been purchased, there is no additional cost because the storage devices are erasable and reusable. Many MP3 files are available on the Internet for free or at low cost.

- *Reproducible.* You can duplicate digital files when using the appropriate software and equipment. You can easily duplicate audio materials in whatever quantities you need, for use in the classroom, in the media center, and at home. Remember to observe copyright guidelines.

- *Stimulating.* Audio media can provide a stimulating alternative to reading and listening to the teacher. Audio can enhance text messages through the addition of dramatic voice intonations and sound effects. With a little imagination, you and your students can create very versatile audio recordings.

- *Provides oral message.* Students who have limited reading ability can learn from audio media. Students can listen and follow along with visual and text material. In addition, they can replay portions of the audio material as often as needed to understand it.

- *Provides current information.* Web-based audio often consists of broadcasts of live speeches, presentations, or performances.

- *Supports second language learning.* Audio resources are excellent for teaching second languages because they not only allow students to hear words pronounced by native speakers, but they also allow them to record their own pronunciations for comparison.

- *Easy to store.* MP3 files can be stored on a computer hard drive, USB drive, or MP3 player.

Limitations of Audio

Along with the advantages that audio integration offers teachers and students, it also has some limitations, including the following:

- *Copyright concerns.* Commercially produced audio can easily be duplicated, which might lead to copyright violations.

- *Doesn't monitor attention.* Some students have difficulty studying independently, so when they listen to recorded audio their attention may wander. They may hear the recorded message but not listen attentively and comprehend. Teachers can readily detect when students are drifting away from teacher-directed learning, but an audio player cannot do this.

- *Difficulty in pacing.* Determining the appropriate pace for presenting information can be difficult if your students have a range of attention spans, abilities, and experiential backgrounds.

- *Fixed content.* The content of audio media presentation segments is fixed, even though it is possible to hear a recorded segment again or select a different section.

When to Integrate Audio into Instruction

The uses of audio are limited only by the imaginations of you and your students, as it can be used in all phases of instruction—from introduction of a topic to evaluation of student learning. As seen in the When to Use Audio box, integration of audio resources can enhance the learning of all students.

Multiple levels of higher-order thinking are required for students, working individually or in groups, to create their own recordings. In addition, these activities provide opportunities for students to express their innovative and artistic abilities. Also important, foundational knowledge and skills can be reinforced for students with learning disabilities through the use of digital recordings to go back and repeat segments of instruction as often as necessary because the "playback" capability is a very patient tutor.

When integrating audio, teachers can prepare their own recordings or use commercially available or free digital recordings to supplement instruction. For example, a second-grade teacher can record directions for students to create sentences with word cards or a teacher of ninth-grade students with learning difficulties, but average

When to Use Audio

Use audio when student learning will be enhanced by . . .	Examples
Text being read out loud	High school students with limited reading ability listen to a recording of a Shakespeare sonnet being read.
Listening to key political speeches	Middle school students prepare for a debate by listening to podcasts of speeches given by candidates for mayor of their city.
Recording impressions	Students create a digital journal of their learning by recording weekly impressions of the most important things they learned.
Easy access to verbal examples	Students use an online French translation app to listen to correct pronunciation of new vocabulary words.
Listening to an author-read story	As a story is being projected on a screen, elementary students listen to a recording of the author as she reads the story that is streamed from a children's storybook website.
Hearing the sounds of nature	Intermediate-grade students use a bird website to practice identifying the sounds of different birds from their local area to prepare for a nature trail field trip.
Listening to an expert	Students in a music class listen to a recording of two successful musicians sharing tips for creating vocal harmonies.
Listening to current events	A high school social studies class listens to an Internet radiobroadcast of a United Nations General Assembly opening session.
Recording personal reading	Elementary students create a digital reading journal that contains yearly recordings of the students reading a favorite story.

intelligence, can provide instruction on how to listen to lectures, speeches, and other oral presentations. The students practice their listening skills with digital recordings of stories, poetry, and speeches.

Application Exercise 8.1

How to Integrate Audio into Instruction

There are multiple ways to integrate audio for student use. A popular project in social studies classes is the recording of **oral histories.** The students interview local citizens regarding the history of their community. This project serves the dual purpose of informing students and residents about local history as well as collecting and preserving information that might otherwise be lost.

Audio recordings are an excellent way for students to prepare book reviews. The recordings can be posted on a classroom or library website that includes a brief annotation added by the student. These recorded reviews present classmate perspectives that serve to encourage other students to perhaps expand their areas of reading interests. Plus, similar to online product reviews, multiple reviews can be submitted for one book and a rating scale can be added to obtain overall opinions.

Students can also use mobile devices to record information gleaned from a field trip. Upon returning to the classroom, students can play back the recording for discussion and review. Many museums, observatories, and other public exhibit areas now supply visitors with prerecorded messages about various items on display, which may, with permission, be downloaded or rerecorded for playback in the classroom.

Another use of audio is for students to record themselves reciting a poem, presenting a speech, performing music, and so on. They listen to the recording privately or have the performance critiqued by the teacher, other students, or family members. Small-group projects can include recorded reports of procedures and processes used to achieve a final outcome. Audio recordings are an excellent addition to a student's electronic portfolio.

More traditional uses of audio remain viable integration options to enhance learning; for example, using learning centers for primary students to listen to favorite storybooks. The students follow along in the book to associate letter combinations with sounds. The technique encourages reading and promotes literacy. Additionally, audio recordings of music and exercise instructions engage elementary students in fun and energizing physical exercises. The goal of the experience is to promote lifelong good health through daily exercise. See Technology for All Learners: Audio for examples of using audio for hearing-impaired learners, English language learners, advanced learners as well as all learners.

Learning becomes fun when integrating audio into instruction. Students love to hear and tell stories. Stories can be entertaining and informative. Storytelling is an important skill to develop in students of all ages. The goal should be teaching students to express ideas through verbal communication. To capture and edit audio recordings, students can use one of the free apps, such as Audacity, which provides special sound effects or elements of music to enhance presentations. Apps are also available that enable students to use a keyboard or other instrument connected to a computer to "compose" their own music. They can "see" the music on the screen and

Technology for All Learners
Audio

We have students in our classrooms with a variety of learning needs. Here are some examples of how to use audio resources to support learning.

- *Audio for hearing-impaired learners.* The most familiar technique to assist hearing-impaired learners is closed captioning (CC) for television and video programs. Closed captioning displays text narratives of the audio portion of a program. Online multimedia presentations and audio materials use this feature as an option that needs to be selected. This technology is also useful for students who are learning a second language, those listening to content in a noisy environment, and students learning to read who need additional practice.
- *Audio for all learners.* Some students enjoy listening to stories and will often benefit from reading along with an audio recording of a book. Students who select books beyond their regular reading levels also benefit from the audio presentation of the story. The audio book option allows students to practice their vocabulary pronunciation and enhance their reading experiences as part of their independent reading.
- *Audio for English language learners.* When working with English language learners, the addition of audio cues can help them understand the text that they are reading.
- *Audio for gifted learners.* Students who wish to challenge their learning experiences can delve deeper into history by using audio to explore famous speeches or to enhance their experience of a particular time period. For example, students who wish to explore the speeches of Martin Luther King to develop a presentation for their classmates on his themes and timeline might listen to his speeches and incorporate audio clips into their digital presentations for the class.

hear what they have composed through headphones to keep them from disturbing other students in the room. Students then write stories around the music or sounds they have created.

An often-overlooked use of audio materials is for evaluating student attainment of lesson objectives. For example, you may prerecord test questions for members of the class to use individually. You may ask students to identify the composer of a particular piece of music. Students in social studies classes could be asked to identify the speaker and the relevance of the speech after listening to historical speeches. Testing and evaluating in the audio mode is especially appropriate when teaching and learning have also been in audio mode.

Selection of Audio Resources

When selecting audio to support your instructional goals, use the guidelines in the Selection Rubric: Audio Resources to assist with the selection. For example, is the audio recording bias free, of high technical quality, and accurate? Additionally, with the rubric you can assess the quality with which the audio aligns with lesson objective, uses appropriate language and pacing, and has the potential to hold the interest of your students.

Types of Digital Audio

Digital audio has multiple PreK-12 uses. The common types of digital audio recordings include music, voice, sound effects, nature, and other sounds. The most common formats for digital audio are MP3, MP4, and AAC. MP3 is the most compatible audio format that can be played on almost any digital device, while MP4 is a format used to store audio and/or video. AAC (Advanced Audio Coding) is a streaming audio format (see below) that generally results in better sound with files being the same size or smaller. AAC is the standard audio format for many common games and smartphones. Digital audio can be created for or accessed through traditional CDs, as well as streaming, podcasts, and Internet radio.

STREAMING AUDIO. **Streaming audio** files are sent in packets to the user, which provides the opportunity to listen to portions of a file as it is being downloaded. Streamed MP3 files are available to anyone who has access to the Internet. The required software to play MP3 audio files, like Windows Media Player and iTunes, is free and typically comes installed on most digital devices.

PODCASTS. **Podcasts** (from the words "iPod" and "broadcasting") are recorded audio files typically in MP3 or AAC formats that are distributed over the Internet. These audio files can be sent automatically to "subscribers" and stored for listening at their convenience. Podcast Alley provides a variety of audio resources to support student learning. With podcasting software, students and teachers can create their own newscasts or documentaries and have subscribers download and listen to them on their digital devices. Podcasting offers teachers and students remarkable opportunities for their voices to be heard in their local communities or around the world. One could think of podcasting as blogging in an audio rather than text format.

INTERNET RADIO. **Internet radio** uses the Internet to offer online radio stations consisting of a variety of programming—music, sports, science, weather, as well as local, national, and world news. Live and recorded programming from around the world can enhance language, social studies, science, and current events lessons. Any Internet-connected device can play Internet radio stations. Visit Internet-Radio for an extensive list of stations.

Selection Rubric   Audio Resources

Complete and save the following interactive evaluation to reference when selecting Audio Resources to integrate into lessons.

Search Terms

_____

_____

Format

Title _____

_____ CD

Source/Location _____

_____ Podcast

©Date _____ Cost _____ Length _____ minutes _____

_____ Streamed

Subject Area _____ Grade Level_____

_____ Other

Instructional Strategies _____

_____

Brief Description

Standards/Outcomes/Objectives

Pre-requisites (e.g., prior knowledge, reading ability, vocabulary level, etc.)

Strengths

Limitations

Special Features

Name _____ Date _____

Selection Rubric   Audio Resources

Rating Area	High Quality	Medium Quality	Low Quality
Alignment with standards, outcomes, and objectives	Standard/outcome/ objective addressed and use of audio should enhance student learning.	Standard/outcome/objective partially addressed and use of audio may enhance student learning.	Standard/outcome/objective not addressed and use of audio will likely not enhance student learning.
Accurate and current information	Information is correct and does not contain material that is out of date.	Information is correct but does contain material that is out of date.	Information is not correct and does contain material that is out of date.
Age-appropriate language	Language used is age appropriate and vocabulary is understandable.	Language used is nearly age appropriate and some vocabulary is above/below student age.	Language used is not age appropriate and vocabulary is clearly inappropriate for student age.
Interest level and engagement	Topic presented so that students are likely to be interested and actively engaged in learning.	Topic presented to interest students most of the time and engage most in learning.	Topic presented so as not to interest students and not engage them in learning.
Technical quality	The material represents best available technology and media.	The material represents technology and media that are good quality, although there are some problems.	The material represents technology and media that are not well prepared and are of very poor quality.
Ease of use (student or teacher)	Material follows easy-to-use patterns with nothing to confuse the user.	Material follows patterns that are easy to follow most of the time.	Material follows no patterns and most of the time the user is very confused.
Bias free	There is no evidence of objectionable bias or advertising.	There is little evidence of bias or advertising.	There is much evidence of bias or advertising.
User guide and directions	The user guide is an excellent resource for use in a lesson. Directions help students use the material.	The user guide is a good resource for use in a lesson. Directions may help students use the material.	The user guide is a poor resource for use in a lesson. Directions do not help students use the material.
*Appropriate pacing	The audio material is presented so most students can understand and process the information.	The audio material is presented so some students start to understand and process the information.	The audio material is presented so most students cannot understand and process the information.
*Use of cognitive learning aids (overviews, cues, summary)	The audio material is well organized and uses cognitive learning aids.	The audio material is fairly well organized and uses some cognitive learning aids.	The audio material is not well organized and does not use cognitive learning aids.

*Specific to rating Audio Resources.

Recommended for Classroom Use: _____Yes _____No

Ideas for Classroom Use: _____

Producing Audio

Digital audio recorders are easy-to-use, small devices that allow students to create news broadcasts, listen to and practice foreign language speaking, conduct interviews, record bird songs, or manipulate any other sounds needed for educational experiences. It is important for students to carefully plan audio products by writing and editing the narration prior to producing the audio recording. Notes can be added for the types of special effects or music to include as well as timing suggestions for when to add the music and for how long. Specialized software enables students to add music and sound effects to their digital creations as designated on their notes. It is important to follow copyright guidelines when working with music, as seen in the Copyright Concerns box. Two audio recording software examples are musical instrument digital interface (MIDI) and digital synthesizer software.

MUSICAL INSTRUMENT DIGITAL INTERFACE (MIDI).   **MIDI** is a longstanding software that enables MIDI-equipped instruments to interact with synthesizer software to compose music. MIDI not only transmits which notes are played, but also the length of time and velocity or intensity with which they are played. This technology allows students to create music by focusing on musical ideas rather than the mechanics of playing an instrument or learning musical notation. The technology is relatively inexpensive and can be plugged into most computers. Gardner (2011) identifies "musical/rhythmic" as one of his nine foundational aspects of intelligence. MIDI technology can be used to develop and support the musical/rhythmic aspect of intelligence.

Copyright Concerns
Audio—Music

The use of music is a highly regulated activity in the realm of copyright law. It is also heavily policed and enforced by the music industry.

Permitted copying of music includes the following:

- For academic uses other than performances, teachers and students may make copies of up to 10 percent of a musical work, provided the excerpt does not comprise a part of the whole that would constitute a performable unit such as a section, movement, or aria.
- Single copies of a recording of student performances may be made for rehearsal purposes or evaluation.
- Single copies of a recording of copyrighted music may be made from a recording owned by a school or teacher for the purpose of constructing aural exercises or assessments.

The following are not allowed:

- Compiling a collection of recordings.
- Making copies of printed music scores. Additional copies must be purchased or duplication rights must be negotiated.
- Making an arrangement of a copyrighted musical work without permission of the copyright holder. This falls into the category of creating a derivative work.
- Performing a musical work publicly without the copyright owner's permission.
- Copying music from a website. You must also pay for the use of music you download from the Internet. The copyright owners of sound recordings have rights set forth in the Digital Performance Right in Sound Recordings Act of 1995 and the Digital Millennium Copyright Act of 1998. These laws give sound recording copyright owners rights to online performances of their recordings.

Internet transmissions may involve the reproduction and distribution of musical works and the copying of a copyrighted musical work or sound recording onto your digital device. Unauthorized copying constitutes exploitation of the reproduction rights. You must contact the copyright owner of the sound recording (usually the distributor) for authorization to copy the sound recording. Even though some online sites advertise music free from copyright, it is critical to carefully review the licensing agreements regarding approved uses of the material, as it is better to ask than to be caught with illegal copies of music.

MIDI technology allows students to create music as easily as word processing facilitates writing. Rather than using conventional musical notation, this technology uses lines of sound on a grid whose height corresponds to pitch and whose length corresponds to duration. MIDI and music composition software like Apple's GarageBand provide creative learning opportunities for students.

SYNTHESIZER SOFTWARE.   Students use synthesizer software, sometimes referred to as *softsynth*, to create original music, radio programs, and other audio materials to demonstrate their learning. Features of the software give student productions a professional polish. For example, creating podcasts using digital synthesizer software puts your students in the control room of their own full-featured radio station. The software includes sound effects and jingles from an audio library. An example of this software is Acoustica's Mixcraft. Students can browse and select from sound effects including sounds of people, animals, and machines. They can then drag these sounds into their podcast to sync up with their vocal track.

Video Example 8.1: Audio in Learning

Watch this video and observe how Scott James describes benefits derived from students conducting research to write audio narration scripts and how he supports students during a recording session. In what ways is student learning enhanced by conducting research to write an audio script? How do the narration notes assist students during recording?

 Check Your Understanding 8.2

Enhancing Learning with Video

There are multiple benefits for integrating student production of video into instruction. Understandably, increased student engagement and motivation are at the top of the list as most students think it is fun to create videos. Additional benefits include student development of multimodal literacy and problem-solving skills as well as furthering content knowledge (Morgan, 2013). Student creation of video also aligns and supports achievement of the ISTE Standards for Students and builds real-world skills required for 21st century careers.

Videos can be an excellent addition to classroom instruction, but you must consider its advantages and limitations. Video can be used in all instructional environments with whole classes, small groups, and individual students. Videos are available on almost any topic for all types of learners in all the domains of instruction—cognitive, affective, psychomotor, and interpersonal. They can take the learner almost anywhere and extend students' interests beyond the walls of the classroom. Objects too large to bring into the classroom, as well as those too small to see with the naked eye, can be studied. Events too dangerous to observe, such as an eclipse of the sun, are studied safely. The time and expense of a field trip can be avoided, as many companies and national parks provide video tours to observe assembly lines, services, and the features of nature. It is important for you, as a teacher, to know the types of video available, how to locate and evaluate them, as well as guidelines for producing videos.

Advantages of Video

It is a commonly known that most students become excited when the opportunity to watch a video arises during class. However, there are other learning advantages besides student engagement when video is integrated into instruction.

- *Motion.* Moving images have an obvious advantage over still visuals in portraying concepts and processes in which motion is essential to learning (such as Newton's Laws of Motion, erosion, metamorphosis).
- *Risk-free observation.* Video allows learners to observe a variety of events in a safe environment, such as a volcanic eruption, demonstrations, or a chemical reaction.
- *Dramatization.* Dramatic recreations bring historical events and personalities to life. They allow students to observe and analyze human interactions.
- *Affective learning.* Because of its great potential for emotional impact, video can be useful in shaping personal and social attitudes. Documentary and propaganda videos have often been found to have a measurable impact on viewer attitudes.
- *Problem solving.* Open-ended dramatizations are frequently used to present unresolved situations, such as a growing homeless population in the United States, leaving it to the students to discuss various ways of dealing with the problem.
- *Cultural understanding.* Seeing depictions of everyday life in other societies helps develop an appreciation for other cultures. The genre of ethnographic video serves this purpose, as seen in *The Hunters, The Tribe That Hides from Man, The Nuer,* and *River of Sand.*
- *Establishing commonality.* By viewing video programs together, a dissimilar group of students can build a common base of experience to more effectively discuss an issue.

Limitations of Video

Although instructional use of video can have an initial increase in student interest, it is important to understand the limitations of video. Knowledge of these factors enables teachers to address the issues when selecting videos and planning lessons that integrate video.

- *Fixed pace.* Although videos can be stopped for discussion, this is not usually done during group showings. Because the program runs at a fixed pace, some students may fall behind while others are waiting impatiently for the next point.

- *Talking head.* Many videos, especially local productions, consist mostly of head-shots of people talking. Video is not a great oral medium—it is a visual medium. Use audio recordings for strictly verbal messages.

- *Still phenomena.* Although video is advantageous for concepts that involve motion, it may be unsuitable for other topics for which detailed study of a single visual is involved (e.g., a map, a wiring diagram, or an organization chart).

- *Misinterpretation.* Documentaries and dramatizations often present a complex or sophisticated treatment of an issue. A scene intended as satire might be taken literally by a young or naive student. The thoughts of a main character may be interpreted as the attitudes and values of the producer.

- *Abstract, nonvisual instruction.* Video is poor at presenting abstract, nonvisual information. The preferred medium for words alone is text. Philosophy and mathematics do not lend themselves well to video unless the specific concepts discussed lend themselves to illustration using historical footage, concrete or graphic representation, or stylized imagery.

Integration of Video

The use and creation of video can greatly enhance student learning. As emphasized in the ASSURE model, student viewing or production of videos should directly support achievement of the lesson objectives and build video literacy knowledge and skills.

There are several options for viewing educational videos, including whole-class viewing with a digital projector or a large-screen TV, small group viewing on laptops or tablets, and individual or paired viewing on smartphones. When teaching students to "critically" view video, you can guide the viewing process by asking questions that require students to think critically about core concepts (Jolls, 2008). For example: Why do you think this video was created? Who is the intended audience for this video and why? What would you do differently to enhance the purpose of the message and why?

Another consideration when integrating video is to strategically integrate video segments that align with the lesson rather than an entire video. Keep in mind that students have grown up with TV programs that utilize short segments to teach educational content. For example, *Curious George*, *Wild Kratts*, and *Dinosaur Train* change topics every few minutes. Many educational videos are formatted into short segments in order to provide you maximum flexibility to promote learning specifically related to student needs.

Also important is the adaptation of lessons to meet the special needs of students. Video-based courses with multiple sound tracks can be aimed at different types of learners. Text can be displayed in multiple languages and used to subtitle or annotate video content. Quick Response (QR) codes are often added to text materials to access specific video segments from online resources or on a DVD. Some videos offer the ability to view an object from different angles selected in real time during playback. See Technology for All Learners: Video for examples of using video for hearing-impaired learners, English language learners, and advanced learners as well as all learners.

When planning lessons, keep in mind the prominent features of video that will help to enhance student learning. These include the ability to depict motion, show processes, offer risk-free observations, provide dramatizations, and support skill learning. Videos also portray scenarios to build affective learning, introduce open-ended problem-solving vignettes, and develop cultural understanding and establish commonality. See When to Use Video for examples of each guideline.

Technology for All Learners
Adapting Video

Video offers different options for meeting the needs of diverse learners.

- *Video for visually impaired learners.* Audio descriptions are available on some educational videos. The United States Access Board (2015) defines audio description as

    Narration added to the soundtrack to describe important visual details that cannot be understood from the main soundtrack alone. Audio description is a means to inform individuals who are blind or who have low vision about visual content essential for comprehension. Audio description of video provides information about actions, characters, scene changes, on-screen text, and other visual content. Audio description supplements the regular audio track of a program. Audio description is usually added during existing pauses in dialogue. Audio description is also called "video description" and "descriptive narration." (Rehabilitation Act: Section 508 Standards: E103.4)

- *Video for gifted students.* Gifted students can be challenged to explore videos for higher-order concepts, generate questions for further research, or present summary points to share in groups of mixed ability students. In addition, students gifted with different aspects of video production can provide peer tutoring to build the skills of all students.

When to Use Video

Use video when student learning will be enhanced by . . .	Example
Motion	High school students watch video clips of various chemical reactions to determine the environmental impact of using gasoline engines.
Processes	Elementary students watch a video that shows each step of the recycling process to learn how aluminum cans are recycled.
Risk-free observation	Middle school students view a video of a Hawaiian volcano eruption.
Dramatization	Elementary children watch a video showing the evolution of transportation.
Skill learning	Art students in a middle school view a video that shows step-by-step techniques used to draw shadows.
Affective learning	Kindergarten students watch a video to better understand the feelings and challenges of children with disabilities.
Problem solving	Middle school students in an interdisciplinary gifted class view documentaries explaining the overpopulation concerns of some large U.S. cities, and then discuss possible solutions.
Cultural understanding and establishing commonality	High school students in a school with a growing population of English language learners from multiple ethnic backgrounds view videos that highlight the commonalities between ethnicities.

Types of Educational Videos

Although there are vast numbers of commercially produced educational videos appropriate for use in PK–12 classes, most videos can be grouped into four common types: documentary, dramatization, storytelling, and virtual field trips.

DOCUMENTARY. Video is the primary medium for documenting actual or reenactments of events and bringing them into the classroom. The documentary deals with fact, not fiction or fictionalized versions of fact. Documentaries attempt to depict essentially true stories about real situations and people. Many nonprofit organizations, such as the Public Broadcasting System (PBS), regularly produce significant documentaries available at PBS Video. For example, the video *To the Ends of the Earth* allows students

Taking a Look at Technology Integration

Video

StoryCenter, previously named the Center for Digital Storytelling, " . . . has worked with nearly a thousand organizations around the world and trained more than fifteen thousand people in hundreds of workshops to share stories from their lives ... to transform the way [people] think about the power of personal voice, in creating change" (StoryCenter, 2016, About). StoryCenter offers numerous free digital stories on topics such as family, identity, relationships, health, healing, place, environment, education, work, social justice, human rights, and youth voices. An interesting story within Youth Voices is "My Write to Draw" by Max Bessesen, a middle school student who describes how he used cartooning to build his writing skills. A Community story, "Remaking El Rancho," created by Dulce Alonso recalls how the making of tortillas reminds her of stories she heard while visiting her grandparents during the summer. Tatiana Stroud's, "If You Really Knew Me," Youth Voices story reflects her personal views of her characteristics and strengths that may be overlooked by others. The StoryCenter offers teacher workshops to assist educators with integrating digital storytelling into their instruction.

to "experience" the story of a perilous sea voyage based on William Golding's novel of the same name. *The Civil War* miniseries is a documentary of a critical period in U.S. history. Programs such as *Nova* and National Geographic specials offer outstanding documentaries on science, culture, and nature, many of which are available for viewing on the Internet. Virtually all television documentaries are available for purchase.

DRAMATIZATION.   Video has the power to hold your students spellbound as a drama unfolds before their eyes. Literature classics available on video, such as *Anne of Green Gables, Hamlet,* and *Moby Dick,* expand student learning opportunities as they compare and contrast the differences between the text and video. Historical fiction classics, such as *Shogun* and *War and Peace,* use a combination of fiction and facts to dramatize historical events. Dramatization is also an excellent venue to build positive student character and attitudes concerning such areas as multiculturalism, disabilities, self-esteem, and working cooperatively.

STORYTELLING.   From childhood, we have learned to love stories because they are entertaining and informative. Stories can be incorporated into instruction through videos, such as NetSmartz's "Real-Life Stories" of teenagers involved with Internet safety issues such as cyberbullying (NCMEC, 2016). Storytelling is an important skill to develop in students of all ages. Digital storytelling allows students to be creative while developing their visual literacy skills, writing skills, and video production skills. The goal is to teach students to express ideas, concepts, and understandings through stories. In the process, students can both teach and learn from each other. See Taking a Look at Technology Integration: Video for additional information on video storytelling.

VIRTUAL FIELD TRIPS.   Videos can take students to places they might not be able to go otherwise. You can take your students to the Amazon rainforest, the jungles of New Guinea, or the Galápagos Islands. Students can also go on a virtual tour of the Egyptian pyramids, the Great Wall of China, or the Acropolis in Athens, Greece. Video field trips enhance and build upon knowledge gained from reading textbooks, Internet descriptions, or listening to presentations.

Selection of Video Resources

After you have located some potentially useful videos, use an evaluation tool to assess alignment with your lesson. A good appraisal form is brief enough not to be intimidating but complete enough to help teachers choose materials that will enhance student learning. In some cases, the evaluation results help justify the purchase or rental of specific titles. The Selection Rubric: Video Resources includes the most commonly used criteria, particularly those that have research-based evidence of effectiveness. The specific areas of importance for evaluating video are pacing and the use of cognitive learning aids, such as an overview, cues, and a summary. Cues are features that

Selection Rubric   Video Resources

Complete and save the following interactive evaluation to reference
when selecting Video Resources to integrate into lessons.

Search Terms

_____

_____

Format

Title _____   _____ CD

Source/Location _____   _____ Podcast

©Date _____ Cost _____ Length _____ minutes _____   _____ DVD

Subject Area _____ Grade Level_____   _____ Streamed

Instructional Strategies _____   _____ Other

_____

Brief Description

Standards/Outcomes/Objectives

Pre-requisites (e.g., prior knowledge, reading ability, vocabulary level, etc.)

Strengths

Limitations

Special Features

Name _____   Date _____

Selection Rubric   Video Resources

Rating Area	High Quality	Medium Quality	Low Quality
Alignment with standards, outcomes, and objectives	Standard/outcome/objective addressed and use of video should enhance student learning.	Standard/outcome/objective partially addressed and use of video may enhance student learning.	Standard/outcome/objective not addressed and use of video will likely not enhance student learning.
Accurate and current information	Information is correct and does not contain material that is out of date.	Information is correct but does contain material that is out of date.	Information is not correct and does contain material that is out of date.
Age-appropriate language	Language used is age appropriate and vocabulary is understandable.	Language used is nearly age appropriate and some vocabulary is above/below student age.	Language used is not age appropriate and vocabulary is clearly inappropriate for student age.
Interest level and engagement	Topic presented so that students are likely to be interested and actively engaged in learning.	Topic presented to interest students most of the time and engage most in learning.	Topic presented so as not to interest students and not engage them in learning.
Technical quality	The material represents best available technology and media.	The material represents technology and media that are good quality, although there are some problems.	The material represents technology and media that are not well prepared and are of very poor quality.
Ease of use (student or teacher)	Material follows easy-to-use patterns with nothing to confuse the user.	Material follows patterns that are easy to follow most of the time.	Material follows no patterns and most of the time the user is very confused.
Bias free	There is no evidence of objectionable bias or advertising.	There is little evidence of bias or advertising.	There is much evidence of bias or advertising.
User guide and directions	The user guide is an excellent resource for use in a lesson. Directions help students use the material.	The user guide is a good resource for use in a lesson. Directions may help students use the material.	The user guide is a poor resource for use in a lesson. Directions do not help students use the material.
Appropriate pacing	The video material is presented so most students can understand and process the information.	The video material is presented so some students start to understand and process the information.	The video material is presented so most students cannot understand and process the information.
Use of cognitive learning aids (overviews, cues, summary)	The video material is well organized and uses cognitive learning aids.	The video material is fairly well organized and uses some cognitive learning aids.	The video material is not well organized and does not use cognitive learning aids.

*Specific to rating Video Resources.

Recommended for Classroom Use: _____ Yes _____ No

Ideas for Classroom Use: _____

help point learners to important aspects of the video, such as a flashing arrow pointing to parts of a flower as each is being presented. Evaluating videos also provides you the opportunity to make notes for class discussion of the key topics and areas that need further explanation or emphasis to enhance student learning.

Producing Video

Producing video requires students to engage in the higher-order thinking skills of planning a video that will "tell the story," recording key scenes, and editing the content to ensure the intended message is conveyed. Use your teacher facilitation skills throughout the video production process to help students keep work aligned to their planning documents.

PLANNING. As with all media production, preproduction planning is necessary. Actively involve students in planning videos they are to produce. This planning involves storyboarding, scripting, and planning for recording, editing, and revising their video productions. To provide each student with a variety of experiences, involve them in rotating roles of writers, editors, camera operators, and on-camera talent. Students begin the process of video production by creating a series of storyboards to facilitate planning and production of video. The storyboards include a rough sketch of the scene, script, and any notes for the camera operator, such as "zoom in for close-up of object." Free storyboard or graphic organizer software, such as Kidspiration and Inspiration, provide useful tools for creating storyboards. When a group of students are cooperatively involved in designing a video, storyboarding is particularly helpful to organize and represent multiple viewpoints.

RECORDING. Digital videos can be recorded with smartphones, tablets, or digital cameras. The built-in microphone on these devices has an automatic level control that adjusts the volume to keep the sound at an audible level. However, the problem is that these microphones amplify all sounds within their range, including shuffling feet, coughing, street noises, and equipment noise, along with the sounds you want. You may, therefore, want to bypass the built-in microphone by connecting to an external microphone such as a lavaliere, or neck mike when recording a single speaker. A desk stand may be used to hold a microphone for a speaker or several discussants seated at a table. For situations in which there is unwanted background noise or the speaker is moving, a highly directional microphone is best. When recording video ensure you have proper lighting, clear clutter from areas to be recorded, show what is being talked about, and coach those being recorded to speak clearly, look at the camera, and remain on topic (Harris, 2014).

EDITING. After recording video, the next step is to use a video-editing app to produce the final product. Most digital devices come with a free app, such as Apple's iMovie or Windows' Movie Maker. The editing app provides tools not only to delete and rearrange content, but also to add titles, music, photos, and special transitions. Remind students to refer to their planning storyboards during the editing process, keeping in mind that changes will be necessary as recording often includes unexpected outcomes. Also important, you and your students must follow copyright guidelines when producing video, as described in the Copyright Concerns: Video.

Application Exercise 8.2

Copyright Concerns

Video

The Copyright Act of 1976 did not cover educational uses of video recordings of copyrighted broadcasts. A negotiating committee composed of representatives from industry, education, and government agreed on a set of guidelines for video recording of broadcasts for educational use. The following guidelines apply only to nonprofit educational institutions.

You may do the following:

- Ask your media/technology specialist to record the program if you lack the equipment or expertise. The request to record must come from a teacher.
- Retain the recording of a broadcast (including cable transmission) for a period of 45 calendar days, after which you must delete the program.
- Use the recording in class once per class during the first 10 school days of the 45 calendar days, and a second time if instruction needs to be reinforced.
- Have professional staff view the program several times for evaluation purposes during the full 45-day period.
- Make a limited number of copies to meet legitimate needs, but you must delete these copies when deleting the original recording.
- Use only a part of the program if instructional needs warrant.
- Enter into a licensing agreement with the copyright holder to continue use of the program.

You may *not* do the following:

- Record premium cable services, such as HBO, without express written permission.
- Alter the original content of the program.
- Exclude the copyright notice on the program.
- Record a program in anticipation of use.
- Retain the program, and any copies, after 45 days.

Remember that these guidelines are not part of the copyright act but are rather an agreement between producers and educators. You should accept them as guidelines in good faith.

Video Example 8.2: Video in Learning

Observe how Scott James facilitates the video-editing process. Describe how Mr. James works with students as they edit their natural disaster video. What are key benefits for students when producing video to demonstrate their learning?

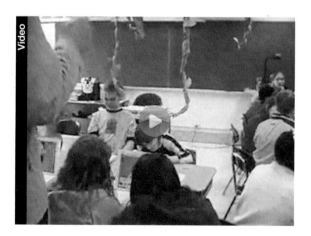

Check Your Understanding 8.3

Enhancing Learning with Text

Text is everywhere in students' learning experiences. Students encounter text through print and digital materials such as textbooks, fiction and nonfiction books, newspapers, booklets, pamphlets, magazines, study guides, manuals, and worksheets, as well as word-processed documents prepared by students and teachers. As with other resources, use of text materials for instruction has advantages and limitations.

Advantages of Text

Text resources are an integral component of instruction for students of all ages. The benefits of providing written information to support and enhance learning are well established. Specific advantages for integrating text into PreK–12 instruction are briefly outlined below.

- *Availability.* Text materials are readily available on a variety of topics and in many different formats.
- *Flexibility.* Text resources are adaptable to many purposes and may be used in any environment.
- *Portability.* Most text materials in print form or viewed with a mobile device are easily carried from place to place.
- *User friendly.* Properly designed text materials are easy to use, not requiring special effort to "navigate" through them.
- *Personalization.* Digitized text often includes tools to personalize content to reader preferences, such as adding highlights, bookmarks, comments, links to associated resources, or modifying font size and color to improve readability.

Limitations of Text

When planning lessons that integrate text resources, teachers should address issues related to possible limitations of the available resources. Considerations for review include the following.

- *Reading level.* The major limitation of text materials is that they are written at a certain reading level that may not align with all students in your class.
- *Vocabulary.* Some textbooks introduce a large number of vocabulary terms and concepts in a short amount of space. Readers sometimes lack the prerequisite knowledge to comprehend the vocabulary and terminology.
- *One-way presentation.* Because most text materials are not interactive, they tend to be used in a passive way, often without comprehension.
- *Curriculum determination.* Sometimes textbooks dictate the curriculum rather than being used to support the curriculum. Textbooks are often selected to accommodate the curriculum guidelines of particular states or provinces rather than specific needs in local school districts.
- *Cursory appraisal.* Selection committees might not examine textbooks carefully. Sometimes textbooks are chosen by the "five-minute thumb test"—whatever catches the reviewer's eye while thumbing through the textbook.

Integration of Text

Text materials are integrated into lessons through reading and project-based assignments in which they are shared during class discussions, in student products, and on assessments. Lessons frequently integrate student use of supplementary text materials on a specific topic not covered in their textbook. As a teacher, you will not only be responsible for locating text resources that support and enhance student learning and achievement of learning outcomes, but you will also need to ensure that students comprehend the intended message of the resources. The International Reading Association (IRA) Common Core State Standards (CCSS) Committee (2012) offers three recommendations for teachers to increase student comprehension:

1. Engage students in closely and critically reading high-quality texts.
2. Teach research-proven reading comprehension strategies using gradual release of responsibility approaches.
3. Guide students to apply strategies when reading particularly challenging texts. (p. 2)

In addition, it is important for students to engage in opportunities to steadily increase their level of understanding when reading literary or complex informational text. Thus, you should assist students in "making an increasing number of connections among ideas and between texts, considering a wider range of textual evidence, and becoming more sensitive to inconsistencies, ambiguities, and poor reasoning in texts" (NGA Center & CCSS, 2010, p. 8). These skills will also better enable students to create or produce text that meaningfully demonstrates their learning.

Types of Text Resources

Text materials are divided into two primary types, **literary** and **informational text.** Examples of literary text include stories, dramas, poetry, and myths, whereas informational texts include textbooks and other nonfiction resources. The Common Core State Standards (CCSS) for English Language Arts (ELA) and Literacy in History/Social Studies, Science, and Technical Subjects emphasize that "to build a foundation for college and career readiness, students must read widely and deeply from among a broad range of high-quality, increasingly challenging literary and informational texts" (NGA Center & CCSSO, 2010, p. 10). However, as students progress in grades, a greater emphasis is placed on consuming and producing informational texts. The foundation for this shift is found in "extensive research establishing the need for college and career ready students to be proficient in reading complex informational text independently in a variety of content areas" (NGA Center & CCSS, 2010, p. 4). This increased emphasis is also seen on the 2015 National Assessment of Educational Progress (NAEP) Reading Framework that includes equal distribution of literary and informational passages on the grade 4 assessments, but shifts to 30% literary and 70% informational passages on the grade 12 assessments (NCES, 2015).

As a teacher, you will want to consider all types of text-based materials available to enhance your lessons, keeping in mind the limitations mentioned above as well as student literacy levels. It is important to assess the reading ability of each student and work with a special education coordinator to identify needs of students with learning disabilities. See Technology for All Learners: Text for information on text readers and digital books.

Technology for All Learners

Text

Text Readers and Digital Books

Students who are poor readers because of dyslexia and other learning disabilities frequently have to reread passages, struggle to decode unfamiliar words, and may suffer from fatigue and stress. While, gifted learners often find the text materials in the classroom too simple or boring to challenge them. There are many resources for helping students access a variety of text information for all learners.

- *Text for all learners.* Digital books allow instant access to any page, chapter, or subheading. Most provide the option to have the text read by one or more narrators. They also provide definitions and pronunciations when a word or selection is highlighted.

- *Text for visually impaired learners.* Learning Ally, formerly Recordings for the Blind and Dyslexic, is a non-profit organization that provides a wide collection of digitally recorded educational titles, including an expansive collection of accessible textbooks. A moderate subscription fee is charged.

- *Text for struggling learners.* Kurzweil provides literacy technology tools to support reading and writing. Tools include a text-to-speech program in over 30 languages, a multimedia approach to digital text that provides additional visual and audible cues, a picture and talking dictionary, as well as other support tools for struggling learners.

Selection of Text Resources

When selecting literary or informational text during lesson planning, it is important to consider the guidelines on the Selection Rubric: Text Resources before making the final decision. The Selection Rubric includes a rating scale to help you determine the quality (high, medium, or low) of various aspects of the text materials under review. Included among the aspects are: alignment with lesson objectives, accurate and current information, age appropriate language, and interest level and engagement. The rubric also includes two areas specific for text resources: reading level and clarity of organization. It is important to record notes regarding strengths and limitations of the text during lesson implementation.

Producing Text

Most students begin producing simple forms of text during early primary grades and continue communicating with text throughout their years of education and while in the workforce. As a teacher, you will be challenged to prepare your students to produce text that meets three primary goals that are components of most curriculum standards: (1) *to persuade,* in order to change the reader's point of view or affect the reader's action; (2) *to explain,* in order to expand the reader's understanding; and (3) *to convey experience,* real or imagined, in order to communicate individual and imagined experience to others (NAGB, 2010, p. 3). States and school districts frequently require the use of a specific writing process. Common steps in a writing process are prewriting, drafting, revising, editing, and publishing. Revising and editing can be repeated, as needed, to produce a quality product.

As technology is increasingly available at school and home, text materials created by students are often in a digital format. Most commonly, text is produced with a word processing app that easily supports revisions such as rewriting or moving content, changing font styles, adding features such as bullets, and inserting images, charts, and hyperlinks to online resources. Students also produce digital text materials with apps for presentations, graphic organizers, blogs, wikis, and discussion boards.

Selection Rubric **Text Resources**

Complete and save the following interactive evaluation to reference
when selecting text resources to integrate into lessons.

Search Terms

_____

_____

Format (Digital or Print)

Title _____   _____ Textbook

Source/Location _____   _____ Novel/Story Book

©Date _____ Cost _____ Length _____ minutes _____   _____ Periodical

Subject Area _____ Grade Level_____   _____ Other

Instructional Strategies _____   _____

Brief Description

Standards/Outcomes/Objectives

Pre-requisites (e.g., prior knowledge, reading ability, vocabulary level, etc.)

Strengths

Limitations

Special Features

Name _____ Date_____

Selection Rubric   **Text Resources**

Rating Area	High Quality	Medium Quality	Low Quality
Alignment with standards, outcomes, and objectives	Standard/outcome/objective addressed and use of text should enhance student learning.	Standard/outcome/objective partially addressed and use of text may enhance student learning.	Standard/outcome/objective not addressed and use of text will likely not enhance student learning.
Accurate and current information	Information correct and does not contain material that is out of date.	Information correct but does contain material that is out of date.	Information is not correct and does contain material that is out of date.
Age-appropriate language	Language used is age appropriate and vocabulary is understandable.	Language used is nearly age appropriate and some vocabulary is above/below student age.	Language used is not age appropriate and vocabulary is clearly inappropriate for student age.
Interest level and engagement	Topic presented so that students are likely to be interested and actively engaged in learning.	Topic presented to interest students most of the time and engage most in learning.	Topic presented so as not to interest students and not engage them in learning.
Technical quality	The material represents best available technology and media.	The material represents technology and media that are good quality, although there are some problems.	The material represents technology and media that are not well prepared and are of very poor quality.
Ease of use (student or teacher)	Material follows easy-to-use patterns with nothing to confuse the user.	Material follows patterns that are easy to follow most of the time.	Material follows no patterns and most of the time the user is very confused.
Bias free	There is no evidence of objectionable bias or advertising.	There is little evidence of bias or advertising.	There is much evidence of bias or advertising.
User guide and directions	The user guide is an excellent resource for use in a lesson. Directions should help students use the material.	The user guide is a good resource for use in a lesson. Directions may help students use the material.	The user guide is a poor resource for use in a lesson. Directions do not help students use the material.
Reading Level	The material is presented at an appropriate reading level so that most students can understand the information.	The material is presented at a reading level so that some students can understand the information.	The material is presented at a reading level so that few students can understand the information.
Clarity of Organization	The material is presented in such a way that most students are able to use the information.	The material is presented in such a way that some students are able to use the information.	The material is presented in such a way that few students are able to use the information.

*Specific to rating Text Resources.

From Smaldino, Lowther, & Mims, *Instructional Technology and Media for Learning*, 12th ed. Copyright © 2017 by Pearson Education, Inc. All rights reserved.

Recommended for Classroom Use: _____Yes _____No

Ideas for Classroom Use: _____

Video Example 8.3: Text in Learning

Observe how Scott James uses a text-based handout to prepare students for the natural disaster lesson. What components of the lesson are included on the handout? How does Mr. James ensure students are familiar with the lesson criteria?

 Check Your Understanding 8.4

Enhancing Learning with Visuals

Visuals are an integral component of instruction and learning. This section discusses the advantages, limitations, and integration of visuals in the classroom and information regarding the selection and types of visuals, as well as guidelines for producing visuals.

Advantages of Visuals

There is a long history of using visuals to help students learn a variety of content and skills. Some key advantages of using appropriately selected visuals that are effectively integrated into instruction are discussed below.

- *Readily available.* Visuals are pervasive. They are in almost all print and digital educational materials.
- *Range of materials.* Visuals cover the complete range of curriculum areas and grade levels.
- *Ease of preparation.* You can easily prepare your own visuals and visual displays as described in this chapter.
- *Inexpensive.* Visuals are available at little cost. Many are free.
- *Ease of use.* Visuals are very easy to use. Even young children can effectively use them for presentation of ideas.
- *Interactivity.* Visuals are ideal for "what if" displays of spreadsheet data or brainstorming activities using a graphic organizer app. This becomes an interactive medium when students' decisions or ideas are entered into the app and the outcome is displayed on the screen.

- *All students have equal view.* Visuals permit everyone to have an equal opportunity to easily view the same material at the same time.

Limitations of Visuals

Even though the advantages of using visuals can offset the limitations, it is important to understand possible restrictions. When planning lessons that integrate visual resources, teachers should select resources that minimize the limitations or include instructional supports to compensate for the limitations.

- *Two-dimensional.* Visuals are two-dimensional and show only one view of the object or scene. Using multiple views or software that provides a three-dimensional perspective to images can compensate for this limitation.
- *Too many words on one visual.* Some people put too many words on one visual. Limit the number of words on each.
- *Bulky hardware.* Digital visuals require a large monitor, which can be bulky, heavy, and cumbersome to transport, or a digital projector, which requires a laptop/computer and a screen on which to project.
- *Expense.* Although prices steadily decrease, many teachers may not have the funds to purchase high-quality digital cameras, scanners, and projectors. Lower-priced equipment may lack the capability to meet your instructional needs.

Integration of Visuals

Every teacher can integrate visuals effectively to promote learning, as visuals can serve a multitude of purposes in the classroom. When planning lessons, consider integrating visuals when student learning will be enhanced with the provision of a concrete reference, or seeing a concrete example of an abstract idea. Visuals also help to motivate students, direct their attention to important concepts, provide a way to repeat information from a different perspective, assist in recalling prior learning, and, importantly, reduce the effort required to learn.

PROVIDE A CONCRETE REFERENT FOR IDEAS. Words don't look or sound like the thing they stand for but visuals are **iconic**—that is, they have some resemblance to the concrete thing they represent. Just like icons on a digital device are used to represent different apps (mail, messages, music, etc.), visuals serve as a more easily remembered link to the original idea (see Figure 8.1).

In the classroom, a teacher uses visuals to help students more easily remember the content being taught. For instance, a geometry teacher may bring in a bag of grocery items to teach shapes (e.g., orange = sphere, can = cylinder).

Figure 8.1 The Concrete-Abstract Continuum.

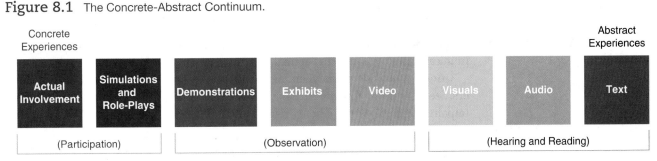

Source: Adapted from Paul Saettler, *The Evolution of American Educational Technology.* Copyright © 2004 Information Age Publishing. Reprinted by permission.

MAKE ABSTRACT IDEAS CONCRETE. Teachers use multiple methods to help make abstract ideas concrete. These include using photographs of people voting to represent freedom, a series of connected beads to show a model of DNA, or a diagram of word endings to assist beginning readers. Concrete visuals, such as blocks or tiles, are used as manipulatives to help students understand abstract mathematical concepts. It is also useful for students to select visuals to represent abstract ideas and then provide a rationale for their selection choice.

MOTIVATE LEARNERS. Interest enhances motivation. Visuals can increase interest in a lesson and motivate learners by attracting and holding their attention, thus generating engagement in the learning process. Visuals draw on the learners' personal interests to make the instruction relevant. For example, when teaching a history lesson, show "then" and "now" photos, such as buttons used before zippers, crank telephones before cell phones, or butter churns before margarine tubs.

DIRECT ATTENTION. Use a visual pointer to draw the learner's attention and thinking to relevant parts of a visual. Visual pointers may be color, words, arrows, icons, shading, and animation. Use these signals to focus attention on important points within complex visual content.

REPEAT INFORMATION. When visuals accompany spoken or written information, they present that information in a different modality. This option of "dual coding" in both visual and verbal or text format provides learners the opportunity to comprehend visually what they might miss in verbal or text format, which results in deeper understanding (Paivio, 1971).

RECALL PRIOR LEARNING. Visuals can be used to activate prior knowledge stored in long-term memory and to summarize the content from a lesson. These same visuals can be used at the beginning of the next lesson to remind the learners of what should have been learned.

REDUCE LEARNING EFFORT. Visuals can simplify information that is difficult to understand. Diagrams can make it easy to store and retrieve such information. They can also serve an organizing function by illustrating the relationships among elements, as in flowcharts or timelines. Often, content can be communicated more easily and effectively with visuals (Mayer, 2014). As a teacher, you want to convey your message in such a way that students expend little effort making sense out of what they are seeing and are free to use most of their mental effort for understanding the message itself.

Selection of Visual Materials

Considering the vast number of visual resources available for use in your lessons, the selection of appropriate visuals will be easier when following the guidelines on the Selection Rubric: Visual Materials. The easy to use rubric provides space for you to rate the quality (high, medium, or low) of the important components of the visual you are reviewing. Among those components are: alignment with standards, outcomes and objectives, accurate and current information, bias free, and technical quality. The rubric also has five components specific for visuals: legibility, simplicity, use of color, communicates clearly, and visual appeal.

Another consideration when selecting visuals is how they meet the needs of learners. See Technology for All Learners: Visuals for examples of using visuals for visually impaired learners, struggling learners, and gifted learners.

Types of Visuals

The visual selected for a particular situation should depend on the learning task. The types of visuals can be described on the basis of the key function they are to serve. Six types of visuals are often used to support and enhance learning: representational, mnemonic, organizational, relational, transformational, and interpretive (Clark & Lyons, 2010).

Selection Rubric Visual Resources

Complete and save the following interactive evaluation to reference
when selecting Visual Resources to integrate into lessons.

Search Terms

_____

_____

Format (Digital or Print)

Title _____   _____ Still Picture

Source/Location _____   _____ Drawing/Cartoon

©Date _____ Cost _____ Length _____ minutes   _____ Chart/Graph

Subject Area _____ Grade Level_____   _____ Poster

Instructional Strategies _____   _____ Other

_____

Brief Description

Standards/Outcomes/Objectives

Pre-requisites (e.g., prior knowledge, reading ability, vocabulary level, etc.)

Strengths

Limitations

Special Features

Name _____ Date_____

Selection Rubric   Visual Resources

Rating Area	High Quality	Medium Quality	Low Quality
Alignment with standards, outcomes, and objectives	Standard/outcome/objective addressed and use of visual resource should enhance student learning.	Standard/outcome/objective partially addressed and use of visual resource may enhance student learning.	Standard/outcome/objective not addressed and use of visual resource will likely not enhance student learning.
Accurate and current information	Information correct and does not contain material that is out of date.	Information correct but does contain material that is out of date.	Information is not correct and does contain material that is out of date.
Age-appropriate language	Language used is age appropriate and vocabulary is understandable.	Language used is nearly age appropriate and some vocabulary is above/below student age.	Language used is not age appropriate and vocabulary is clearly inappropriate for student age.
Interest level and engagement	Topic presented so that students are likely to be interested and actively engaged in learning.	Topic presented to interest students most of the time and engage most in learning.	Topic presented so as not to interest students and not engage them in learning.
Technical quality	The material represents best available technology and media.	The material represents technology and media that are good quality, although there are some problems.	The material represents technology and media that are not well prepared and are of very poor quality.
Ease of use (student or teacher)	Material follows easy-to-use patterns with nothing to confuse the user.	Material follows patterns that are easy to follow most of the time.	Material follows no patterns and most of the time the user is very confused.
Bias free	There is no evidence of bias or advertising.	There is little evidence of bias or advertising.	There is much evidence of bias or advertising.
User guide and directions	The user guide is an excellent resource for use in a lesson. Directions help students use the material.	The user guide is a good resource for use in a lesson. Directions may help students use the material.	The user guide is a poor resource for use in a lesson. Directions do not help students use the material.
Legibility for use (size and clarity)	The visual is presented so that most students can see and understand the information.	The visual is presented so that some students can see and understand the information.	The visual is presented so that most students cannot see and understand the information.
Simplicity (clear, unified design)	The visual is well organized; students are able to understand the information.	The visual is fairly well organized; students are mostly able to understand the information.	The visual is poorly organized; students are unable to understand the information.
Appropriate use of color	Colors are appropriate and enhance the learning potential.	Colors are somewhat appropriate and may enhance the learning potential.	Colors are not appropriate and do not enhance the learning potential.
Communicates clearly and effectively	The visual communicates clearly and effectively.	Visual communicates somewhat clearly and effectively.	Visual does not communicate clearly and effectively.
Visual appeal	The visual attracts the attention of most students.	The visual attracts the attention of some students.	The visual attracts the attention of few students

*Specific to rating Visual Resources.

Recommended for Classroom Use: _____ Yes _____ No

Ideas for Classroom Use:_____

REPRESENTATIONAL.   Representational visuals show the actual object under study. They can translate abstract ideas into a more realistic format. They allow instruction to move from the level of abstract (verbal) symbols on the concrete–abstract continuum (refer to Figure 8.1) to a more concrete (visual) level. For example, the color photograph of a covered wagon in Figure 8.2 is a representational visual. Using natural colors can heighten the degree of realism. No representation, of course, is totally realistic. The real object or event will always have aspects that cannot be captured pictorially, even in a three-dimensional, color motion picture.

MNEMONIC.   Mnemonic visuals help learners recall factual information through the use of graphic cues. For example, one way to help students use the correct spelling of "their" versus "there" is by replacing the "i" in "their" with a standing person and the "r" in "there" as a directional sign post. The use of mnemonics has been shown to be most effective when combined with additional learning strategies, such as retrieval practice and spacing (Putnam, 2015). The use of a visual mnemonics app, *Picmonic*, has been shown to increase retention of scientific factual knowledge (De Moll, Routt, Heinecke, Tsu, & Levitt, 2015). One way of using mnemonics is to have student groups create their own visual representations. Students enjoying seeing differences in mnemonics created for the same factual information.

Technology for All Learners

Visuals

Presentation Software

Teachers can do several things to make presentations more accessible for students.

- *Visuals for visually impaired learners.* A traditional approach for learners with visual impairments is converting text to Braille. Another approach is to increase the interaction between teacher and students during and immediately after the presentation. Increasing verbalization and descriptions of the text and images increase the probability of visually impaired students' comprehension and retention. This really applies to all students!
- *Visuals for struggling learners.* Students who are developing new mathematical concepts may find the addition of visuals to be very helpful. The ability to connect the components of a subject, such as mathematics, with visuals helps students make their own mental images and thus helps them understand the concepts being taught. For these students, such things as graphs, line drawings, or charts might be beneficial for them to recall essential information during an assessment.
- *Visuals for gifted learners.* Putting ideas into visual form is a great way to challenge students who are ready to move beyond more traditional formats in demonstrating their learning. Asking students to prepare visuals in the form of drawings, charts, or graphics may allow them the flexibility to express their knowledge in unique and interesting ways.

Figure 8.2 Photographs as Representational Visuals: Photographs, illustrations, graphics, and words represent a continuum of realism for different kinds of symbols.

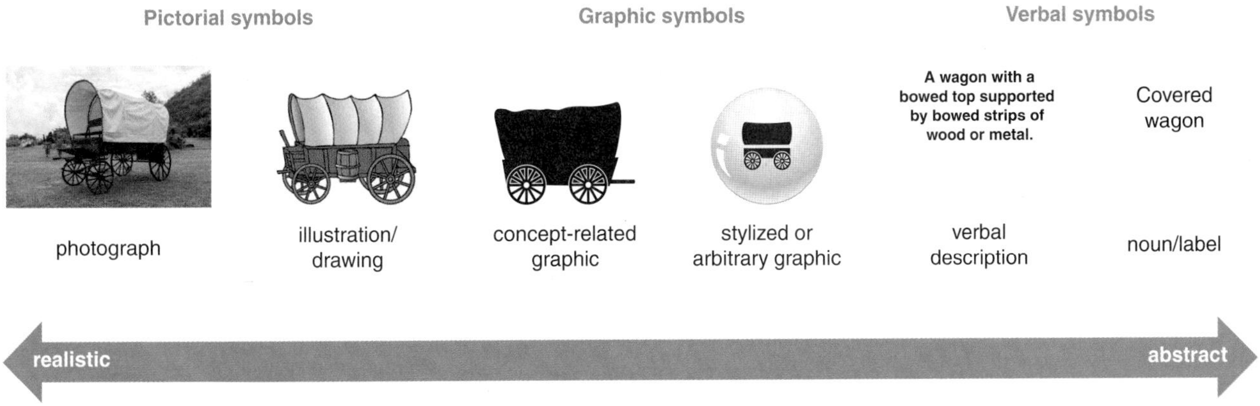

ORGANIZATIONAL. **Organizational visuals** show the qualitative relationships among various elements. Common examples include classification charts, timelines, flowcharts, and tabular charts (see Figure 8.3). These graphic organizers can show relationships among the main points or concepts in textual material. This type of visual helps communicate the organization of the content.

Figure 8.3 Organizational Visuals.

Organization charts show the structure or chain of command in an organization such as a company, corporation, civic group, or government department. Usually they deal with the interrelationships of personnel or departments.

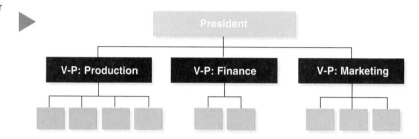

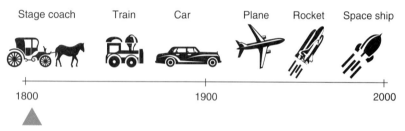

Stage coach · Train · Car · Plane · Rocket · Space ship

1800 · 1900 · 2000

Timelines illustrate chronological relationships between events. They are most often used to show historical events in sequence or the relationships of famous people and these events. Pictures or drawings can be added to the time line to illustrate important concepts. Timelines are very helpful for summarizing a series of events.

Animal Kingdom Classification

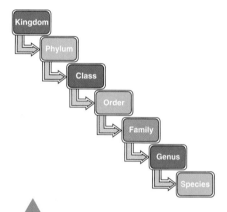

Classification charts are similar to organization charts but are used chiefly to classify or categorize objects, events, or species. A common type of classification chart is one showing the taxonomy of animals and plants according to natural characteristics.

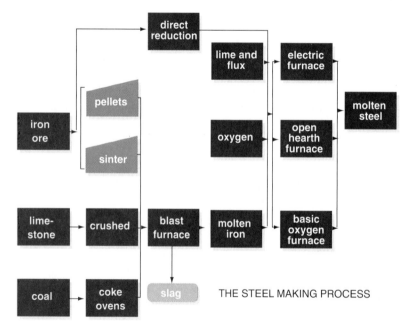

THE STEEL MAKING PROCESS

Flowcharts, or process charts, show a sequence, a procedure, or, as the name implies, the flow of a process. Flowcharts show how different activities, ingredients, or procedures are interrelated.

Import Percentages

	Wheat	Cotton	Steel	Oil
USA	0	0	20	35
England	65	95	35	10
France	15	95	30	90
Japan	85	15	0	95
Brazil	0	0	20	70

Tabular charts, or tables, contain numerical information, or data. They are also convenient for showing time information when the data are presented in columns, as in timetables for railroads and airlines.

RELATIONAL. **Relational visuals** communicate quantitative relationships. Examples include bar charts, pictorial graphs, pie charts, and line graphs (see Figure 8.4).

TRANSFORMATIONAL. **Transformational visuals** illustrate movement or change in time and space. Examples would be an animated diagram of how to perform a procedure such as tying a shoelace, a person running, or a moving object. Transformation is depicted with movement indicators as seen in the animation of the water cycle (Figure 8.5) and line drawings in Figure 8.6.

INTERPRETIVE. **Interpretive visuals** illustrate theoretical or abstract relationships, such as cause-effect. Examples include a schematic diagram of an electrical circuit, the food pyramid, or a school evacuation plan (Figure 8.7). Interpretive visuals help learners build mental models of events or processes that are invisible, abstract, or both.

Producing Visuals

Planning is an important component of creating visuals. Graphic organizers and presentation or storyboarding apps are excellent for using planning techniques such as concept mapping and storyboarding. It is also helpful to understand techniques for creating presentation visuals.

Figure 8.4 Relational Visuals.

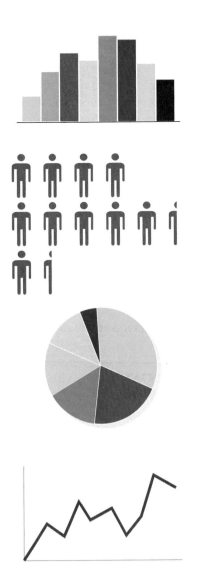

Bar graphs are easy to read and can be used with all students. The height of the bar is the measure of the quantity being represented. The width of all bars should be the same to avoid confusion. A single bar can be divided to show parts of a whole. It is best to limit the quantities being compared to eight or less; otherwise the graph becomes cluttered and confusing. The bar graph is particularly appropriate for comparing similar items at different times or different items at the same time; for example, the height of one plant over time or the heights of several students at any given time. The bar graph shows variation in only one dimension.

Pictorial graphs are an alternate form of the bar graph in which numerical units are represented by a simple drawing. Pictorial graphs are visually interesting and appeal to a wide audience, especially young students. However, they are slightly more difficult to read than bar graphs. Since pictorial symbols are used to represent a specific quantity, partial symbols are used to depict fractional quantities. To help avoid confusion in such cases, print values below or to the right of each line of figures.

Circle (or pie) graphs are relatively easy to interpret. In this type of graph, a circle or "pie" is divided into segments, each representing a part or percentage of the whole. One typical use of the circle graph is to depict tax-dollar allocations. The combined segments of a circle graph should, of course, equal 100 percent. Areas of special interest can be highlighted by illustrating a piece of pie separately from the whole.

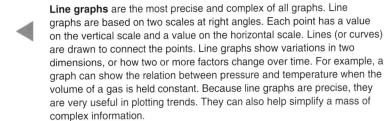

Line graphs are the most precise and complex of all graphs. Line graphs are based on two scales at right angles. Each point has a value on the vertical scale and a value on the horizontal scale. Lines (or curves) are drawn to connect the points. Line graphs show variations in two dimensions, or how two or more factors change over time. For example, a graph can show the relation between pressure and temperature when the volume of a gas is held constant. Because line graphs are precise, they are very useful in plotting trends. They can also help simplify a mass of complex information.

Figure 8.5 **Transformation Visual:** Arrows in the water cycle image depict movement.

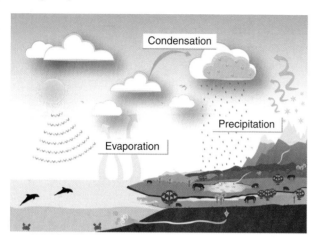

Figure 8.6 **Transformational Visuals:** An active posture, as in the line drawing on the left, communicates movement more reliably than arbitrary graphic conventions such as speed lines, as in the drawing on the right.

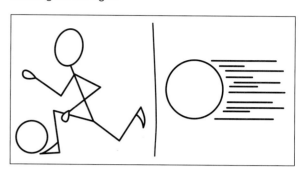

Figure 8.7 **Interpretive Visual:** An evacuation plan is an example of an interpretive visual.

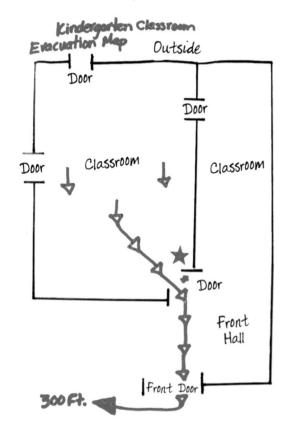

Source: Annie Pickert/Pearson, Pearson Education

PLANNING. If you or your students are designing a *series* of visuals—such as a series of digital screens, a set of presentation slides, or a video sequence—**storyboarding** is a handy strategy for planning. This technique, borrowed from film and video production, allows you to creatively arrange and rearrange a whole sequence of thumbnail sketches. You can use a digital or non-digital approach to create a storyboard. First, you create digital pages or paper index cards to record a simple representation of the visual and text you plan to use. If the series will include narration, this would also be included on the storyboard, along with production notes that link the visuals to the narration. For example, divide the individual storyboard pages/cards into areas to accommodate the text or narration and the production notes (Figure 8.8).

The exact format of the storyboard card should fit your needs and purposes. Design a card that facilitates your work if the existing or recommended format is not suitable. You can make a simple sketch, write a short description of the desired visual on the card, or use digital images. After developing a series of such pages or cards, organize them in the rough sequence of the planned order of presentation (Figure 8.9).

CREATING DIGITAL PRESENTATIONS. With presentation apps, such as Microsoft's PowerPoint, Apple's Keynote, and free apps such as Google Slides, and Prezi, even users without specialized training can create attractive and professional visual displays. Guidelines for preparing digital presentations include the following:

- *Carefully select font type, size, and color.* Arial is a *sans serif* font (a font that does not have the "hands and feet" at the ends of the letters) and is easy to read (see Figure 8.10).

Figure 8.8 Storyboards are useful for planning and presenting rough drafts of presentations.

Figure 8.9 The storyboard page or card contains places for the visual, production notes, and the narration.

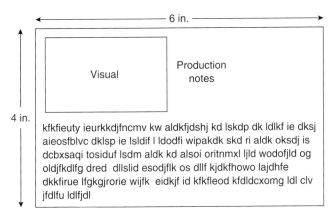

Figure 8.10 Font styles should be selected to suit their purpose.

A sans serif typeface, such as Helvetica, is well suited to projected visuals.

A serifed typeface, such as Palatino, is recommended for printed text.

serifs

A font size of 24 points or larger ensures readability when using a digital projector. The text color should provide adequate contrast with the background color. Use upper and lowercase letters where appropriate.

- *Use a plain, light-colored background.* Busy backgrounds can be distracting to your students. Dark text on a light background is typically easier to read than light text on a dark background.

- *Use center or left justification for titles.* To help your students follow the organization of your presentation, use a brief descriptive title or subtitle at the top of each slide.

- *Use concise communication.* Keep the number of words on a slide to an absolute minimum. The "6 × 6 rule" recommends no more than six words per line and no more than six lines per slide. If you need more words, use a second slide.

- *Use master slides to establish a consistent visual and text format.* Master slides allow you to place text of a specific font on each page, and visuals to be repeated in the same position on every slide. Most apps use master slides when creating presentation themes.

- *Use appropriate visuals.* Avoid images that are irrelevant to your content. Select or create visuals that effectively communicate your message, as noted in the Types of Visuals.

- *Use consistent transitions.* Transitions—the movement from one slide to the next—should be consistent throughout your presentation. Do not use random transitions and avoid "noise" or audio effects with transitions.

- *Use simple "builds."* Build effects are how bulleted text or images are introduced within a single slide. Avoid build effects, like "swirling" (where new text spins onto the slide), that can divert student attention. Watching the effect often takes longer than reading the new text.

- *Carefully use animation to support the instructional message rather than to add a dramatic element to your presentation.* For example, components of a model can be added as each is discussed, such as adding one layer at a time to the food pyramid or adding planets in order of their distance from the sun.

- *Minimize the use of sound.* Use sound only if it enhances your presentation. Screeching tires and cash register sounds quickly become distracting.

Capturing Digital Visuals

Most current digital devices include a camera and apps that allow users to capture, edit, display, and share photos and videos. The technology of digital cameras and scanners makes the process of capturing visuals easy for both teachers and students. Digital cameras allow you to see a photo before you take it and after it has been "captured." You can delete images and reshoot on the spot until you get exactly what is needed. When editing digital visuals, it is important to recognize the need for caution to avoid altering an image in a way that might distort reality and present a false message to the reader or that might violate a copyright holder's rights in regard to the original image. See Copyright Concerns: Visuals.

Whether you or your students are recording the things you see on a field trip, creating a photo essay, shooting an historical subject, or developing an instructional picture sequence, a few guidelines can make your photographs more effective.

- Include all elements that are helpful in communicating your ideas.
- Eliminate extraneous elements, such as distracting backgrounds.
- Include size indicators (e.g., a car, a person, a hand, a coin) in the picture if the size of the main object of interest is not apparent.
- Divide the picture area in thirds both vertically and horizontally. The center of interest should be near one of the intersections of the lines. This is called the "rule of thirds." Don't cramp the important part of the image near the edge of the picture.

Copyright Concerns
Visuals

The following guidelines address use of visuals by teachers and students.
You are permitted to use:

- One illustration per book, periodical, or newspaper
- One diagram, chart, or picture from a single source
- One visual per source for presentation visuals (*PowerPoint* slides, overhead transparencies, etc.)

You are *not* permitted to use:

- The reproduction of copyrighted cartoon characters

- When making how-to documents, take the picture from the viewpoint of the learner, not the observer.
- If a feeling of depth is important, use foreground objects (e.g., blossom-covered tree branches or moss-covered rocks) to frame the main subject.

Video Example 8.4: Visuals in Learning

Observe instructions and guidance provided to students when capturing visual images for their weather broadcast. How does Scott James assist students with managing images they locate? What copyright guidelines does Mr. James expect students to follow?

Innovations in Teaching

The Maker Movement

The Maker Movement is a global revolution that is impacting today's schools by engaging students in using new technologies to become makers of innovations. Students use new technologies such as robotics, 3-D printers, and open-source microprocessors combined with a variety of other resources; for example, parts from broken devices and recycled materials, along with computer programming to make new products.

Making engages students in "tinkering" or playing with technology to find out how it works, typically by taking it apart and then making something new by adding different components. Makers are creative, open to exploring and trying multiple configurations to make a product that outperforms the previous model or to create a brand new invention.

When students are engaged as makers, motivation increases and learning is enhanced. The maker projects fulfill today's curriculum standards and workplace requirements by engaging students in real-world applications that demonstrate the interdependence of science, technology, engineering, and mathematics. *MakerEd* and *MakerSpace* provide support resources and digital communities for schools interested in the Maker Movement.

 Check Your Understanding 8.5

Summary

This chapter discussed multimedia literacies and ways to enhance learning with audio, video, text, and visuals and placed key emphasis on the chapter's learning outcomes.

- *Compare and contrast multimedia literacies for audio, video, text, and visuals.* Audio literacy requires attentive listening and deciphering of messages to identify what is meaningful and important to learning and connecting it with prior knowledge. Video literacy requires meaningful viewing or production of video that results in increased knowledge and skills. Text literacy is the ability to gather, comprehend, and evaluate the message and to synthesize and to write about what you read or experience, whereas visual literacy is the learned ability to interpret visual messages accurately and to create such messages.

- *Explain how to use audio recordings to enhance learning for students.* Both teachers and students can use various types of audio recordings to enhance learning. Teachers can prepare their own recordings or use commercially available or free digital recordings to supplement instruction. Students can record oral histories, book reviews, field trip notes, personal recitations of poems or other works, small group performances, and other classroom activities that involve audio content.

- *Give examples of how the four types of educational videos support student learning.* Documentaries attempt to depict essentially true stories about real situations and people. Dramatization enables students to compare and contrast the differences between a book and video of the same story, as well as to build positive student attitudes concerning such areas as multiculturalism, disabilities, self-esteem, and working cooperatively. Video storytelling develops visual literacy skills, writing skills, and video production skills. Virtual field trips enhance and build upon knowledge gained from reading textbooks, Internet descriptions, or listening to lectures.

- *Describe strategies to increase student comprehension of text resources.* When developing lessons that integrate text resources, include activities that engage students in reading resources that are of high quality. Plan activities that require students to pay close attention to the content and critically examine key concepts. Apply research-based reading comprehension strategies, which engage students in working toward continual improvement of understanding when reading complex information or literary text.

- *Explain how use of each of the six types of visuals will enhance student learning.* The six types of visuals, and how they enhance learning, are as follows: (1) *representational* visuals show the actual object under study; (2) *mnemonic* visuals help learners recall factual information through the use of graphic cues; (3) *organizational* visuals show the qualitative relationships among various elements; (4) *relational* visuals communicate quantitative relationships; (5) *transformational* visuals illustrate movement or change in time and space; and (6) *interpretive* visuals illustrate theoretical or abstract relationships.

ASSURE Lesson Plan

The Classroom Case Study for this chapter is based on an interdisciplinary fifth-grade lesson created by Scott James. The video shows Scott James implementing the multimedia lesson in his fifth-grade classroom and providing his insights for achieving successful use of audio, video, text, and visuals.

This ASSURE Lesson Plan describes the instructional planning used by Scott James, a fifth-grade teacher, to create an interdisciplinary lesson that incorporates the use of audio, video, text, and visuals. Mr. James wants to increase student awareness of natural disasters while increasing their expository writing skills. To address this challenge, student pairs select a natural disaster of their choice and conduct online and library research for their selected topic of interest. Students use this information to write an audio narrative and develop storyboards for their digital video

news broadcasts. Below is Scott James' ASSURE lesson plan for the natural disaster news broadcast lesson.

Scott James
Fifth Grade
Topic: Natural Disasters
Analyze Learners

General Characteristics of Learners

The students in Scott James' fifth-grade class are of mixed ethnicities and from low- to middle-income homes. They are fairly equally distributed with regard to gender and are either 9 or 10 years old. Student reading ability ranges from below to above grade level. Student behavior problems increase when completing traditional seatwork.

Specific Entry Competencies

The students are, in general, able to do the following:

- Conduct online research
- Use iMovie software to edit digital video

Learning Differences and Needs

Scott's students learn best when engaged in activities that are relevant to the content and for which they can self-select topics. His students' interest and motivation increase when they use technology. The students vary greatly in their comfort level with creating audio narratives and acting for the digital video news broadcasts. Differences are also seen with regard to selection and use of visuals and sound; some students use a traditional approach, while others use a creative and fun method for the final products.

State Standards and Objectives

Curriculum Standards. *National Council of Teachers of English, Curriculum Standard 4:* Students adjust their use of spoken, written, and visual language (e.g., conventions, style, vocabulary) to communicate effectively with a variety of audiences and for different purposes; *National Science Education Standards for 5–8: Earth and Space Science:* Structure of the Earth System: Global patterns of atmospheric movement influence local weather. Oceans have a major effect on climate, because water in the oceans holds a large amount of heat; *Common Core State Standards, ELA Literacy, Grade 5.3:* Write narratives to develop real or imagined experiences or events using effective technique, descriptive details, and clear event sequences.
Technology Standards. *ISTE Standards for Students:* Creativity and Innovation
Learning Objectives. The learning objectives for this lesson are as follows:

1. Using content from Internet and library research on a student-selected natural disaster, the fifth-grade students will write an audio narrative for a news anchor and an on-the-scene reporter.
2. Using the student-written audio narratives, the students will create storyboards that include visuals and segments for a news anchor and an on-the-scene reporter and meet the lesson criteria for storyboards.
3. Using their student-created storyboards and audio narratives, each student records his or her audio narrative (news anchor or on-the-scene reporter) of the news broadcasts with digital video.
4. Using the digital video of their news broadcast, students will use iMovie to produce a final edit of their news broadcast that meets the lesson criteria.

Select Strategies

Scott James selects teacher- and student-centered strategies for the natural disaster lesson. The teacher-centered strategies involve providing a detailed text-based description of the lesson objectives and how the student pairs will conduct their research and create their news broadcasts. The student-centered strategies include conducting Internet and library research, writing audio narratives, developing storyboards, and planning, recording, and editing their news broadcast video.

Select Resources

This lesson involves student use of laptops, a digital camcorder, microphones, a green screen, and iMovie to edit their natural disaster videos. Scott uses the following guidelines to assess his technology and media selections:

- ***Align to standards, outcomes, and objectives.*** The library, Internet sites, and iMovie software provide the necessary tools for students to meet the learning objectives.
- ***Accurate and current information.*** Students use text-based and Internet resources to conduct their research on natural disasters.
- ***Age-appropriate language.*** Students use websites and books that are appropriate for fifth-grade students. Scott provides assistance and text-based job aids for student use of iMovie.
- ***Interest level and engagement.*** Students choose a natural disaster of interest to them and create a personalized news broadcast, which increases student interest and engagement.
- ***Technical quality.*** Both the Internet sites and iMovie have high technical quality.
- ***Ease of use.*** Student use of iMovie requires initial training and support, but is fairly easy for fifth-grade students to use after basic skills training.
- ***Bias free.*** Students use multiple references for their research to better ensure use of bias free content. iMovie software is bias free.
- ***User guide and directions.*** The online help features of iMovie are not very easy for fifth-grade students to use. Therefore, students most frequently ask each other or Scott for assistance with technical difficulties.

Utilize Resources

- ***Preview Resources.*** Scott selects and previews the "kid-friendly" Internet sites, library materials, and iMovie software to ensure they have the needed features.
- ***Prepare Resources.*** Scott prepares a text-based assignment sheet that describes the lesson requirements and criteria used to assess the final student products.
- ***Prepare the Environment.*** Scott tests the Internet connections on the laptops and ensures that iMovie is installed on each one. He also tests the digital video camera to ensure that it is working and downloads to the laptops.
- ***Prepare the Learners.*** The students have experience with Internet research and iMovie, thus the lesson begins with an overview of lesson criteria, technical skills, and an introduction to natural disasters.
- ***Provide the Learning Experience.*** Scott guides student learning during each lesson phase: research, audio narrative, video production, and presentation of final videos to the class.

Require Learner Participation

- *Student Practice Activities.* The students in Scott James' class use laptops, the Internet, library materials, and iMovie to complete their natural disaster news broadcasts. Student pairs select a natural disaster and then conduct Internet and library research to find information about the topic. The students use this information to write the news anchor and on-the-scene reporter audio narratives and storyboards. Digital video is then recorded during students' presentations of their news broadcasts, and students use iMovie to create final cuts of their videos for class presentation.
- *Feedback.* Scott James provides continuous feedback as students conduct their research, write their audio narratives, create storyboards, edit videos, and present their news broadcasts.

Evaluate and Revise

- *Assessment of Learner Achievement.* Scott assesses learner achievement in two ways. First is demonstration of content knowledge, as seen in student audio narratives, storyboards, and iMovie presentations. The second is demonstration of technology skills, which is assessed according to the assignment criteria as stated in the learning objectives.
- *Evaluation of Strategies and Resources.* Scott evaluates the lesson strategies through continuous communication with the students. He also examines student products to determine whether the strategies were effective. Evaluation of the technology and media involves noting technical problems that occur during the lesson. This involves examining the functionality of the various software apps, Internet and library resources, and the digital camcorder.
- *Revision.* After reviewing the evaluation results from the lesson implementation, Scott concludes that the lesson worked well, with one minor exception. He thought three weeks was too much time to devote to the designated standards and objectives. Therefore, he revised the lesson by borrowing digital video cameras from a regional media center to decrease the time needed to record all students.

Professional Development

Demonstrating Professional Skills

1. Create an audio recording your thoughts and ideas about what it means to integrate multimedia in your teaching. Listen to your narration after a few entries. What have you learned about your ideas? How does the use of audio impact your collection of reflections? What are the pros and cons of using audio as compared to a written journal? (ISTE Standards for Teachers 5.C)

2. Select and preview a video that would enhance a lesson you teach or plan to teach. Use the Selection Rubric: Video Resources to record your review. Analyze the rubric findings and write an argument presenting the pros and cons for classroom use of the video (ISTE Standards for Teachers 2.A, C).

3. Select three text resources you would use when teaching and appraise each one according the list of advantages and limitations of text. (ISTE Standards for Teachers 2.A, C).

4. Locate six visuals that you believe would be useful in your own teaching and evaluate them using the *Selection Rubric: Visual Resources*. Analyze the rubric findings and write an argument presenting the pros and cons for classroom use of each text resource (ISTE Standards for Teachers 2.A, C).

Building Your Professional Portfolio

- *Creating My Lesson.* Using the ASSURE model, design a lesson for a scenario from the Lesson Scenarios in the Appendix, from an example in the chapter, or use a scenario of your own design. Use instructional strategies that you believe to be appropriate for your lesson and information from this chapter related to integrating multimedia (audio, video, text, and/or visuals) into your instruction. Be sure to include information about the audience, the objectives, and all other elements of the ASSURE model (ISTE Standards for Teachers 2.A).

- *Reflecting on My Lesson.* Write a reflection describing decisions made during development of the lesson. Also describe the multimedia resources (audio, video, text, and/or visuals) included in the lesson and how each resource will enhance the learning experiences of your students. (ISTE Standards for Teachers 5.C).

- *Enhancing My Lesson.* Enhance the lesson you created by including specific strategies for meeting the diverse needs of learners. Specifically, describe additional strategies you would include for advanced students who already possess most of the knowledge and skills targeted in your lesson plan. Also, describe strategies and resources you could integrate to assist students entering the lesson who have not met the specific entry competencies. What adaptations would be needed for the selected multimedia resources if you had a student with limited hearing? (ISTE Standards for Teachers 2.B; 2.C; 3.D; 5.C)

Suggested Resources

Print Resources

Anderson, E.K., Robinson, R.S., Brynteson, K. (2015). Teaching visual literacy: Pedagogy, Design and implementation, tools, and techniques. In D. M. Baylen & A. D'Alba (Eds.), *Essentials of Teaching and Integrating Visual and Media Literacy: Visualizing Learning* (pp. 265-290). Switzerland: Springer International Publishing.

Berg, J. (2015). *Visual leap: A step-by-step guide to visual learning for teachers and students.* Brookline, MA: Lamprey & Lee.

Hayes-Jacobs, H. (2016). *Active literacy across the curriculum: Connecting print literacy with digital, media, and global competence, K-12,* (2nd Ed.). New York, NY: Routledge.

Martin, F. & Carr, M. L. (2015). An exploratory study on K-12 teachers use of technology and multimedia in the classroom. *Journal of Educational Technology, 12*(1), 7–14.

Newby, T. J., Stepich, D., Lehman, J., Russell, J. D., & Leftwich, A.T. (2011). *Education technology for teaching and learning* (4th ed.). Upper Saddle River, NJ: Merrill/Prentice Hall.

Orús, C., Barlés, M. J., Belanche, D., Casaló. L., Fraj, E. & Gurrea, R. (2016). The effects of learner-generated videos for YouTube on learning outcomes and satisfaction. *Computers & Education, 95*, 254-269.

Rasinski, T., & Padak, N. (2012). *Research to practice: Text considerations in literacy teaching and learning.* Ohio Literacy Research Center. Retrieved March 22, 2013, from http://literacy.kent.edu/Oasis/Pubs/0200-14.htm

Online Resources and Apps

Audio

NPR Podcast Directory

The National Public Radio (NPR) partners with over 50 radio stations and producers to provide podcasts on topics such as art and life, economy, opinion, politics, pop culture, the world, and many more. The organization of the podcasts is by topic, title, or provider.

Sound Learning

Sound Learning offers connections between Minnesota Public Radio programming and subject area resources for history and civics, world religions, economics and personal finance, language arts, and science and health. The site also offers a technical guide to help you access audio files, and suggestions for effective learning strategies.

StoryKit App

StoryKit is a free multimedia storytelling mobile app. It allows its users to create electronic storybooks and share them with others. StoryKit is a practical tool for teachers as they can use it to create their own storytelling books and share them with their students. StoryKit is compatible with iPod touch, iPhone touch, and iPad.

Video

PBS Video

PBS offers an outstanding collection of free online videos in the following categories: arts and music, culture, drama, food, history, home & how to, Indie films, news and public affairs, and science and nature. Many videos link to additional resources.

TED: Ideas Worth Spreading

TED is a nonprofit organization devoted to "Ideas Worth Spreading" regarding technology, entertainment, and design (TED). The award-winning site has a collection of hundreds of free talks from the world's most fascinating thinkers and doers, who are challenged to give the talk of their lives (in 18 minutes or less). All of the talks feature closed captions in English, and many feature subtitles in various languages. These videos are released under a Creative Commons license, so they can be freely shared and reposted.

iMotion HD App

iMotion HD is a video app that lets students create a time-lapse or stop-motion film by combining still photos. They can set this app to take photographs at timed intervals to show elapsed time (like a plant growing or a sunset) or for stop-motion film (using action figures or puppets). With the full version of the app, users can add music and get access to extra export features like uploading their movie straight to YouTube.

Text

Common Core Writing in Action

The Common Core Writing in Action website provides a variety of classroom resources focused on building the writing literacy skills of students. The resources are organized by (1) text types and purposes, (2) production and distribution of writing, (3) research to build and present knowledge, and (4) range of writing.

ReadWriteThink

The International Literacy Association (ILA) and the National Council of Teachers of English (NCTE) provide the ReadWriteThink site. The classroom resources on this site include lesson plans, student interactives, mobile apps, calendar activities, and printouts. Lesson plans and activities are aligned with NCTE Standards and the Common Core State Standards (CCSS), when applicable.

Google Docs App

Google Docs is a free online word processor that lets you create and format text documents and collaborate with other people in real time. Google Docs can be saved as Word, OpenOffice, RTF, PDF, HTML or zip files. The app also provides a document revision history, which enables access to any previous version, or translates a document to a different language.

Visuals

International Visual Literacy Association

The International Visual Literacy Association (IVLA) is a not-for-profit association of researchers, educators, and artists dedicated to the principles of visual literacy.

Visual Learning

This site provides tools and examples of how visual learning helps students understand and retain information when associations are created between ideas, words, and concepts. Specific information and subject area examples are included for graphic organizers, concept mapping, mind mapping, webbing, outlining, and plots and graphs.

Drawp App

Students use the Drawp app to create personalized visuals art with over 200 colors and textures (e.g., Cotton Candy and Mighty Metal), photo tools, and voice recording to share their thoughts and inspiration. Drawp was developed with an easy-to-use interface for children. Artwork can be easily shared with teachers or added to a student gallery.

Chapter 9
Preparing for Tomorrow's Challenges

 Learning Outcomes

This chapter addresses ISTE Standards for Teachers 2, 3, and 5.

9.1 Describe how the ASSURE model supports tomorrow's learning as described in the National Education Technology Plan.

9.2 Discuss the characteristics of tomorrow's thinking and learning as represented in models and learning environments.

9.3 Explain how tomorrow's teachers exemplify digital age thinking and learning practices.

9.4 Describe future ready professional learning with regard to professional engagement, organizations, and journals.

9.5 Give examples of funding technology for tomorrow and list the basic components of a grant proposal.

 Goal

Understanding factors influencing the advancement of tomorrow's teaching and learning.

Introduction

Today's schools and teachers must be prepared to continually advance learning as our society transitions to more sophisticated, dynamic, and innovative digital tools for work, communication, and entertainment. This advancement can be supported with forward thinking, use of the ASSURE model, and technology-focused professional learning to guide teacher implementation of advanced learning models and environments. Technology grants can assist schools in increasing student access to cutting-edge technology and media that build the knowledge and skills needed for tomorrow's careers.

The ASSURE Model for Tomorrow's Learning

Among the trends that are driving instructional technology and media for tomorrow's learning are redesigning learning spaces and rethinking the roles of teachers (NMC, 2016). For example, the learning spaces of tomorrow will need to have a robust infrastructure to better accommodate student use of multiple digital devices and a flexible configuration to support collaborative learning. Teachers will need to maximize the redesigned spaces by being digitally savvy and knowing how to meaningfully integrate a variety of technologies into formal and informal learning.

Overall, the ASSURE model is structured to help teachers achieve the innovative changes needed for tomorrow's learning. The comprehensive, yet flexible ASSURE model, provides teachers the support and guidance to develop, implement, evaluate, and revise lessons that integrate technology to increase student learning and prepare them for future careers. The ASSURE model directly supports the following Future Ready Learning, National Education Technology Plan Learning goal (US DOE-OET, 2016a):

> All learners will have engaging and empowering learning experiences in both formal and informal settings that prepare them to be active, creative, knowledgeable, and ethical participants in our globally connected society (p. 7).

The first step in the ASSURE model, *analyze learners*, asks teachers to identify the needs of all learners to better ensure that they have the resources and personalized support to participate in learning experiences that are engaging and empowering. The next four steps—*State standards and objectives, Select strategies and resources, Utilize strategies and resources,* and *Require learner participation*—help teachers to strategically plan and implement active and creative learning experiences that support deeper levels of learning. Students emerge with the preparation to be "knowledgeable and ethical participants in our global society" (US DOE-OET, 2016a, p.7). The final ASSURE model step, *Evaluate and revise,* involves assessment of both student progress and the

Video Example 9.1: Digital Conversion

Listen to Dr. Mark Edwards' description of his school's digital conversion to prepare students for the future. What are key student benefits of using personalized tools? What contributing factors are discussed with regard to students gaining a sense of connection from innovative use of digital tools?

instructional process to determine what worked well and what needs to be revised before implementing the lesson again. Tomorrow's teachers can implement the ASSURE model to continually engage students in future-ready learning activities that prepare them for successful careers.

 Check Your Understanding 9.1

Tomorrow's Thinking and Learning

In looking toward tomorrow's thinking and learning, new digitally inspired models and learning environments are emerging. Innovation is at the heart of these emerging trends as seen in ongoing systematic research and development to improve learning (Guston, 2016). Foundational to tomorrow's trends is cyberlearning, or the use of Web 2.0 computing and communication technologies to support learning. Even though cyberlearning involves the integration of new and ever-changing technologies and interacting with it others beyond the classroom, it does rely on research-based learning theories and practices requiring student to think critically and solve meaningful problems. Implications for tomorrow's thinking and learning are discussed regarding models and learning environments.

Tomorrow's Models

Among the promising models for tomorrow's thinking and learning are coding as literacy, and connected, personalized, and transdisciplinary learning. Brief descriptions of each follow.

CODING AS LITERACY.   There is an increasing emphasis for tomorrow's educators to emphasize coding as a new literacy. The prominent and transformational role of technology in our society has increased demands in the labor market for employees with computer science knowledge and skills. Specifically, the U.S. Bureau of Labor Statistics (2013) estimates that by 2022, there will be nearly a 20% increase in the number of available jobs in computer- and math-related occupations. The computer science position of tomorrow will go beyond basic coding skills in that they will require creative problem solving based on solutions from multiple dimensions.

As educators, it is imperative that we prepare PK–12 students for these future opportunities by ensuring they gain a diversified range of computer science knowledge and skills. These opportunities can occur through computer science classes in which students learn basic coding to collaboratively create educational games, apps, and websites to address real world challenges in their school, community, and beyond. It is recommended that the collaborative hands-on coding experiences involve three phases: 1) deliberative practice, or "tinkering" with immediate material feedback to make ongoing corrections, 2) rapid peer feedback to maintain progress, and 3) rapid cognitive feedback to develop transferrable skills (Berland, 2016, p. 204).

Students can greatly benefit from learning computer science basics, such as coding, as it not only promotes complex thinking, but also engages students in fun and creative problem-solving activities. Students can start learning basic computer science concepts at a young age. For example, elementary students can begin creating simple, paper-based algorithms by writing step-by-step instructions to solve a problem, e.g., write instructions to move eggs from different locations to a basket. These types of experiences support basic coding literacy and prepare them for progressing toward more sophisticated applications of computer science in middle and high school.

Even though most teachers and administrators agree with the importance of adding computer science as a required subject, because of challenges such as standardized testing, technology access, and identifying qualified teachers, very few school districts have transitioned computer science to a priority (Gallup, 2016).

CONNECTED LEARNING. Connected learning "revitalizes the educational process by forging links between students' academic studies, their personal passions, and opportunities to engage with peers who support and share their interests" (CLRN, 2016a, para. 2). Specifically, the connected learning model develops lifelong learners by building connections between academics, a learner's interests, and mentors and peers with similar thinking. The model integrates digital age technologies to engage learners in making, creating, and producing to achieve deeper learning and understanding. These hands-on experiences prepare students to be "entrepreneurial in their learning, recognizing that this is what is now needed to be successful in work and in life" (CLRN, 2016b, para. 6).

Connected learning is based on six learning and design principles and three core values. First are the three learning principles of peer-supported, academically oriented, and interest powered. Next are the three design principles of production-centered, openly networked, and shared purpose. The core values of connected learning are social connection, full participation, and equity (CLRN, 2016c). The model has proven to be effective, particularly when working with underrepresented youth from disadvantaged communities (Rheingold, 2016).

PERSONALIZED LEARNING. All students are unique and have specific learning needs as well as diversified interests, cultural backgrounds, and experiences. Therefore, personalized learning is the ultimate approach to prepare PK–12 students for success in tomorrow's workforce. This need for personalized learning isn't a new idea; however, the technology and methods to achieve this level of learning is a key focus for tomorrow's students as these approaches aren't readily available in today's schools.

Technological advances in online learning environments coupled with the ability to adapt and differentiate instruction based on the individual learning path of a student are showing promising strides (Penuel & Johnson, 2016). Continued research to expand the evolving implementation of adaptive personalized learning needs to not only explore how to effectively facilitate personalization, but also address barriers that inhibit widespread use. For example, "compounding the challenge is the notion that technology alone is not the whole solution — personalized learning efforts must incorporate effective pedagogy and include faculty in the development process" (NMC, 2016, p. 7).

TRANSDISCIPLINARY LEARNING. The transdisciplinary learning model is another promising trend that corresponds to the growing need to equip students with real world problem-solving knowledge and skills that go beyond discipline specific content for careers in a global economy. Although the transdisciplinary model is not new, it is experiencing emergent interest due to the infusion of real world inquiry with core subject content, as well as arts, poetry, economics, social life, and politics (Bazhanov & Scholz, 2015). The transdisciplinary learning model corresponds to the growing need to equip students with real world problem-solving knowledge and skills that go beyond discipline-specific content for careers in a global economy. Although the transdisciplinary model is not new, it is experiencing emergent interest due to the infusion of real world inquiry with core subject content, as well as arts, poetry, economics, social life, and politics (Bazhanov & Scholz, 2015).

Emergent use of transdisciplinary learning is seen in STEAM education that integrates science, technology, engineering, arts, and mathematics. This approach aligns with the Next Generation Science Standards' (NGSS) (2012) three dimensions of learning: practice; crosscutting concepts; and disciplinary core ideas. Specifically, when the transdisciplinary model is applied with STEAM education based on NGSS, it provides students with digital tools that "enrich opportunities for introspection, interaction, and disruptive innovation" (Keane & Keane, 2016, p. 64).

Implementation of transdisciplinary learning models requires rethinking about how schools work—or a shift in traditional classroom paradigms based on discipline-specific organization (NMC, 2016). These approaches require innovative designs that create seamless and flexible links between classes and content areas. Additionally, reliable, current, and readily accessible technology is needed to maintain creative use of technology to support authentic transdisciplinary learning.

Tomorrow's Learning Environments

The learning environments of tomorrow will more closely "resemble real world work and social environments that facilitate organic interactions and cross-disciplinary problem solving" (NMC, 2016, p.2). These environments will require access to a robust and comprehensive infrastructure that includes ubiquitous connectivity, powerful learning devices, and high quality digital learning content that is all undergirded with responsible use policies (US DOE-OET, 2016a). These environments will also support and enhance student use of emerging technologies such as artificial intelligence, augmented reality, robotics, and wearable devices.

ARTIFICIAL INTELLIGENCE.   Artificial intelligence (AI) enables computers to simulate human actions. These human-like actions are accomplished by combining knowledge engineering with the user's physiological data from oral responses, eye movements, and gestures (fig 9.1). AI uses programed neural networks to create a more Natural User Interface (NUI) that allows "humans to interact with machines similarly to how they interact with each other" (NMC, 2016, p. 10). Our everyday experiences include interactions with AI. For example, smartphone virtual assistants respond to our verbal questions; phone answering systems use customer responses to branch calls to address identified needs; and shopping sites recommend new items based on purchasing history.

The use of AI is seen in education. For some time, large integrated learning systems such as SuccessMaker (Pearson, 2016) and Carnegie Learning (2016) have used AI to personalize the educational experience of students. These systems help students to work at their own pace by using learner input to branch to new areas of content or provide remediation when needed. New and exciting applications of AI that will

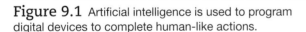

Figure 9.1 Artificial intelligence is used to program digital devices to complete human-like actions.

enhance tomorrow's learning are also emerging in PK–12 educational settings. Among these are intelligent tutors and virtual collaborative agents.

Intelligent Tutors.   Intelligent tutors go beyond integrated learning systems in that they provide a virtual tutor that simulates one-to-one tutoring sessions for core content areas such as mathematics, science, geography, and reading. The tutors engage students in dialogues that involve discussion, questioning, and opportunities for self-reflection on learning (Luckin, Holmes, Griffiths, & Forcier, 2016). The tutors provide a safe learning environment in which the learners receive nonjudgmental feedback for wrong answers in an encouraging manner.

Lifelike robots are also used for intelligent tutoring, as seen in fig 9.2. An example of an AI tutor is RALL-E or the Robot-Assisted Language Learning in Education (ALELO, 2016). "Such robots will allow students to engage in a social role-playing experience with a new language without the usual anxieties of speaking a new language. The RALL-E also encourages cultural awareness while encouraging good use of language skills and building student confidence through practice" (US DOE-OET, 2016a, p. 16).

Virtual Collaborative Agents.   Virtual collaborative agents use AI to assist teachers with online collaborative projects. The agents can "join" collaborative groups and participate as an expert or a virtual peer. When joining a collaborative group as an expert, the virtual agent contributes by offering new content and recommended resources to online conversations. They can also interject questions to help guide the online discussions.

Virtual collaborative agents can also serve as a virtual peer. In this role, the agent serves as a student in the course who is programed with a cognitive level similar to other classmates. However, the virtual agent "is capable of introducing novel ideas . . . deliberate misconceptions, or provide alternative points of view to stimulate productive argument or reflection" (Luckin, Holmes, Griffiths, & Forcier, 2016, p. 27). The virtual collaborative agents often provide a less intimidating contributor to an online collaborative activity than participation from the teacher.

AUGMENTED REALITY.   Tomorrow's learning environments will include increasing opportunities for students to engage in varying forms of augmented reality (AR). AR uses digital technologies to overlay real-time camera views with virtual components, such as 3D digital visualization, to create "augmented" or enhanced, real time interactive experiences. This "interaction between the virtual object and the real world brings to life abstract concepts and seeks to enhance understanding" (Hamilton, 2016, para. 2).

Often, the terms augmented reality (AR) and virtual reality (VR) are used interchangeably. However, distinct differences exist between the two "realities." Simply

Figure 9.2 Intelligent tutor robots simulate face-to-face conversation during tutoring sessions with students.

put, AR enhances, extends, and expands reality, whereas, VR is designed to simulate or replace reality with a computer generated environment. Augmented reality is most frequently experienced with mobile devices such as laptops, smart phones, and tablets.

Use of AR apps is experiencing continued growth in social networking, advertising, and entertainment. It is also seeing advances in PK–12 settings as AR apps become more popular, accessible, and easier to use. Additionally, there are multiple benefits when integrating AR into instruction because of the hands-on, interactive engagement with virtual objects immersed in a real world context. AR can be integrated with developed apps that support the PK–12 curriculum or with apps that enable students to create their own augmented reality environments. Through AR, "dynamic processes, extensive datasets, and objects too large or too small to be manipulated can be brought into a learner's personal space at a scale and in a form easy to understand and work with" (NMC, 2016a, para 1). For example, AR can enhance an astronomy lesson with the augmented reality app, *Star Walk*. This app uses a mobile device's sensors and GPS system to identify the user's location and correlate the data with the constellations from that viewpoint. *Star Walk* provides images and detailed information about the stars, constellations, and planets based on the current location. The users are also able to access the Time Machine feature to view the night from past times or future dates.

Other AR apps use printed "triggers" to interact with the AR software. For example, *Elements 4D* includes printable images to create blocks representing elements from the periodic chart. Students manipulate the block within the AR environment to safely experiment with chemical reactions by joining different elements. Another option is for students to create their own AR experiences with the use of AR creation apps, such as *Augment, Aurasma Studio, Blippar*, and *TaleBlazer*. The *TaleBlazer* AR app provides a variety of educational games and an editor feature that allows users to make their own games using a step-by-step process on a browser-based tool. The games are situated in real world settings that include different aspects of the landscape and other physical objects. Virtual characters, objects, and data are added to a rich and interactive experience.

As with other innovative trends, a major challenge to integrating augmented reality into instructional practices is equity of access for all students. Critical are access to robust Internet service as well as digital devices that support the required connectivity for AR integration.

ROBOTICS.   There is a long history of fascination with robotics, often due to the humanoid features of some robots. These man-made machines are designed to accomplish a wide range of tasks associated with such things as work, space exploration, safety, education, health, and entertainment. Futurists predict that by 2020, robotics will be a $100 billion industry (Tobe, 2016). Among the robots to be produced by this advancing industry are microbots, exoskeletons, body-machine interfaces to help amputees, telepresence robots controlled from a remote location, and alternatively powered robots, many of which will be programmed with artificial intelligence capabilities (Deloitte, 2016.)

The spreading robotics industry has implications for PK–12 education because of the growing need for qualified robotics engineers and technicians who design, build, and work with robots in numerous occupations. The foundational knowledge and skills required for these future careers underlie the Next Generation Science Standards (NGSS) as well as other curriculum areas. Robotics programs, competitions, and internships are emerging as an innovative approach to preparing PK–12 students for future opportunities in highly technical STEM careers. Although student excitement and engagement are easily observable benefits of student involvement with robotics, deeper benefits include student use of standards-based critical, analytical, and computational thinking; problem solving; and creativity and innovation; as well as development of collaboration and communication skills (Botball, 2016).

The National Aeronautics and Space Administration (NASA) is a leader in supporting robotics education for K–12 students through The Robotics Alliance Project (RAP) (NASA, 2016a). A key objective of the Robotics Alliance Project is to "Invest in the workforce pipeline by recruiting students via robotics competitions and engage them in NASA robotics missions leading them to pursue higher education and careers in the robotics Industry" (NASA, 2016b, para. 3). Of importance to K–12 teachers, is the Educational Robotics Matrix with current curriculum, competitions, and internships displayed by K–5, 6–8, and 9–12 grade levels. The curriculum includes standards-based lesson plans, activities, and resources, while the competitions and internships list grade appropriate opportunities.

There are multiple national robotics competitions for K–12 students. Among the most popular are the FIRST Robotics Competition, the Marine Advanced Technology Education (MATE) ROV Competition, and the Botball® Educational Robotics Program. Student excitement for robotics competitions is generated through the sports-like atmosphere of student teams competing against each other to solve challenging missions with student-created and field-tested robots (fig 9.3). Engagement in these competitions not only builds STEM knowledge and skills but often involves development of workplace skills such as writing reports and giving presentations to a panel of practicing professionals (competition judges). These benefits, combined with the future need for robotics professionals, are fueling the increased interest of integrating robotics into tomorrow's classrooms.

WEARABLE DEVICES. Wearable devices are becoming increasingly popular, especially in the form of smart glasses, virtual reality headsets, and wireless wristbands. These powerful devices "not only track where a person goes, what they do, and how much time they spend doing it, but now what their aspirations are and when those can

Figure 9.3 Engagement with robotics prepares students for future careers.

be accomplished" (NMC, 2016, p. 10). The two types of wearable technology predicted to have the greatest impact on PK–12 education are smart glasses and virtual reality headsets. Use of wireless wristbands will also increase; however this growth will primarily be seen within health and physical education due to their capability to track various aspects of physical activity.

Smart Glasses. As with most technology, each new version of smart glasses is more powerful, versatile, smaller, and more fashionable. Available functions include Wi-Fi and Bluetooth connectivity, HD camera, ambient light sensor, GPS receiver, gyroscope, accelerometer, magnetometer, altimeter, and thermometer. Some offer 3D display and stereo sound, while some include facial recognition capabilities to help remember the names of the people you meet.

Smart glasses are showing potential benefits for PK–12 education. For example, wearable smart glasses support student creation of first-person videos from a unique perspective that also records detailed time, location, and setting data (Ribeiro, 2016). Teachers can also benefit from the use of smart glasses by using the facial recognition feature to record student attendance.

Virtual Reality Headsets. Virtual reality headsets, or head mounted devices (HMDs) are used to experience a digital environment as if you were actually in the virtual setting. The headsets are similar to a pair of blackout goggles equipped with an HD screen and surround sound (fig 9.4). They must be connected to a digital device and often involve the use of hand-held controls.

Although the most common use of virtual reality headsets is with gaming, educational uses are beginning to appear in PK–12 schools as inexpensive cardboard models and fully functional, more expensive devices as seen in Figure 9.4. Both types of headsets can benefit student learning through virtual reality experiences presented in 3D and 360° visualization enhanced with point of interest details, narrative, and reflective questioning.

As the name implies, Google Cardboard is a virtual reality headset that students build from a template (fig 9.5). The headset is designed to hold a smartphone that connects with Google Expeditions to engage students in over 200 virtual experiences. Students can explore the coral reefs, Mars, the Egyptian pyramids, Antarctica, and multiple other places. Teachers are provided curriculum guides and tips for integrating the Google Expeditions into their instruction.

As wearable technology becomes more common in school settings, concerns are being raised with regard to privacy and safety when students use devices that track personal

Figure 9.5 Simple cardboard tools can be used to create engaging and responsive environments to extend learning experiences.

Figure 9.4 Virtual reality headsets provide students with immersive, 3D learning experiences.

information. Fredrick (2015) notes, "The ease of data use, however, needs to be balanced by a need for privacy and security of each individual. Just as current systems can be hacked, so too will wearables face challenges in security" (p. 26). It will be critical for districts employing this and other technologies to ensure they implement the infrastructure guidelines for Responsible Use Policies and Protection for Student Data and Privacy as recommended by the National Education Technology Plan (NETP) (US DOE-OET, 2016a).

 Check Your Understanding 9.2

Shared Writing Exercise 9.1

Tomorrow's Teachers

Teachers of tomorrow will need to exemplify digital age thinking and learning practices that ubiquitously integrate emerging technologies that not only leverage student digital age experiences, but also support global collaborations. This combined approach engages students in knowledge construction that benefits all learners.

Video Example 9.2: Capturing Learning with ePortfolios

Consider Katheryn Higgins' description of changes in teaching and learning in a digital environment. What changes in teaching are recommended? In what ways does a digital environment require student change and what are the potential benefits of these changes?

Exemplify Digital Age Thinking

The teachers of tomorrow must exemplify digital age thinking. They need to be digitally savvy and active social media participants. Teachers of tomorrow will also actively collaborate in global learning communities.

The teachers of tomorrow will need to remain digitally savvy by staying informed and current with regard to emerging technologies. The expectations of digitally savvy teachers are summarized in the NMC Horizon Report (2016):

> Educators are increasingly expected to be adept at a variety of technology-based and other approaches for content delivery, learner support, and assessment; to collaborate with other teachers both inside and outside their schools; to routinely use digital strategies in their work with students; to act as guides and mentors to promote student-centered learning; and to organize their own work and comply with administrative documentation and reporting requirements (p. 5).

Digital age thinking will also be reflected by teachers of tomorrow through active participation in social media to remain connected with students, parents, and community members, as well as to engage with global communities of educators. Locally, this will involve teacher use of social media tools such as Facebook, Twitter, Instagram, and other current tools to share information and feedback with students, keep parents informed, and discuss collaboration opportunities with community members.

The teachers of tomorrow will actively engage in global education communities comprised of teachers, researchers, and community members interested in PK–12 teaching and learning. Members of these global communities engage in conversations and share resources regarding innovative approaches to student learning and discuss how to address common concerns while meeting individual cultural needs of students.

Application Exercise 9.1

Ubiquitously Integrate Emerging Technologies

The digitally savvy teachers of tomorrow will know how and when to seamlessly integrate technology to enhance student learning. Students will learn how to use a variety of digital devices beginning in the primary grades to better ensure that class time is focused on content area knowledge and skills rather than learning computer basics. There will be greater use of digital devices to support problem solving, critical thinking, and exploration of information and data. These uses will better reflect work place applications of technology rather than using the devices for basic skill remediation.

Additionally, in an environment where tomorrow's teachers ubiquitously integrate technology, instruction doesn't "stop" so students can "do technology"—but rather, digital devices are interchangeably used before, during, and after class. Ubiquitous integration of technology leverages the digital expertise of students. Tomorrow's teachers should encourage input from students regarding innovative tools, new resources, and novel ways to approach and share learning.

Support Global Collaboration

Tomorrow's teachers are challenged to ensure students "learn with the world, not just about it," (iEARN, 2016). As such, they need to be global-ready and have expertise in applying inquiry-based, technology-supported approaches to integrate global content, contexts, and perspectives into their instruction (VIF, 2014). Engaging students in global collaborative learning will prepare them to better understand the dynamics of international relationships and to be active citizens who effectively work with others to address complex global issues.

One method for teachers to support global collaboration is through the non-profit organization of iEARN, which has more than 50,000 educators and 2 million youth from over 140 countries that represent over 30 languages involved in collaborative project work worldwide (iEARN, 2016). There are over 150 teacher-developed projects that involve students from multiple countries who work collaboratively to address issues noted in the United Nations Sustainable Development Goals, such as to end poverty and hunger and to improve health, education, and gender equity (UN-DESA, 2016). The projects not only align with curriculum standards, but also engage students in comparing local issues and solutions with those from other locations. Every iEARN project must be focused to "answer the question, 'How will this project improve the quality of life on the planet?' This vision and purpose is the glue that holds iEARN together, enabling participants to become global citizens who make a difference by collaborating with their peers around the world" (iEARN, 2016, para. 7).

 Check Your Understanding 9.3

Future Ready Professional Learning

There is a national call for PK–12 teachers to be "future ready" (US DOE-OET, 2016a). Considering the constantly changing technology innovations that impact everyday living, working, and education, it is imperative for teachers to stay informed and current through a long-term commitment to professional learning. Professional learning is supported through professional engagement, professional organizations, and professional journals.

Professional Engagement

The professional engagement of tomorrow's teachers will extend beyond school district inservice training to encompass global learning opportunities, interactions, and collaborations. To achieve this level of involvement, tomorrow's teachers need robust digital connectivity to remain professionally engaged with "people, data, content, resources, expertise, and learning experiences that can empower and inspire them to provide more effective teaching for all learners" (US DOE-OET, 2016a, p. 25). As these professional engagement trends expand, schools and districts need to rethink "the ways educators engage in their own continuing professional development, much of which involves social media and online tools and resources" (NMC, 2016, p. 5). Professional learning opportunities are readily available through real-time and archived webinars, video tutorials, online resources, and collaborative social media sites.

Teachers who are professionally engaged regularly continue professional growth through collaborations with online communities of practice, often referred to as **professional learning networks (PLNs)**. Teachers can join or create a PLN of those who teach the same grade level and content area and/or have similar interests, such as technology integration, special needs, collaborative projects, and more. Engagement with PLNs continues to expand due to the benefits of being online, anytime, anywhere communities with the possibilities for global involvement of educators (Trust, Krutka, & Carpenter, 2016). However, with these expanded engagement opportunities, it is important for tomorrow's teachers to understand that "improvements in student learning are related to improvements in educator practice and that strengthened practice is supported by research- and standards-based professional learning" (US DOE-OET, 2016b, para. 1).

Today is an exciting time for teachers as the professional engagement opportunities to expand teaching and learning are becoming more and more pervasive in formal and informal education each year. Associated with this growth are the increasing numbers of professional organizations and journals that support educators interested in application of technology and media to improve learning.

Video Example 9.3: Professional Development and Online Communities

Listen to how Chris Gammon describes professional learning opportunities for new digital environments. According to Mr. Gammon, in what ways does teacher collaboration enhance professional learning? How do professional online communities support teacher integration of technology lessons?

Professional Organizations

Professional organizations offer teachers multiple opportunities to remain engaged with educators within and beyond their disciplines to stay informed with current research and practice, build teaching skills, and create professional relationships. Meghan Everette (2016), a third grade teacher, summarizes the benefits of professional organizations in the following statement:

> I love my colleagues that I connect with virtually, but my closest connections were made in person and continued online . . . Being truly connected means not only paying the dues, but participating in meetings, going to conferences, writing and reading, and being an active community member. When you do those things, the connections become strong and meaningful (para. 4).

As a teacher, you will want to maintain active participation in at least one national organization as well as one or more regional, state, or focused organization, one focused on your area of teaching and interest, for example technology integration or online learning. Several of the national professional organizations also have regional, state, and/or local affiliates (AECT, ALA, ISTE, USDLA). By joining one or more of these, you will quickly make contact with nearby professionals who share your particular interests. Many organizations offer full-time students a reduced rate and often have special interest groups for students.

Brief descriptions of key professional organizations for educators interested in various aspects of technology integration are presented to guide your understanding. The descriptions provide a general overview of the organization, and include such topics as goals, members, opportunities, and major publications.

ASSOCIATION FOR EDUCATIONAL COMMUNICATIONS AND TECHNOLOGY (AECT). AECT is an international organization representing educational technology professionals working in schools, colleges, and universities, as well as the corporate, government, and military sectors. Its mission is to provide leadership in educational communications and technology by linking professionals holding a common interest in the use of educational technology and its application to the learning process. AECT has 9 divisions designed around areas of special interest represented within the membership as well as a graduate student assembly: culture, learning and technology; design and development; distance learning; emerging learning technologies; international; organizational training and performance; research and theory; school media and technology; and teacher education. The association maintains an active publications program, including the journals *Tech Trends*, and *Educational Technology Research and Development*, as well as a large number of books, portals, databases, and conference proceedings. AECT sponsors an annual conference that features over 300 educational sessions and workshops focusing on how teachers are using new technologies and teaching methods in the classroom. It also hosts a summer professional development conference and a biannual research symposium every other year.

ASSOCIATION FOR THE ADVANCEMENT OF COMPUTING IN EDUCATION (AACE).   AACE is an international educational and professional organization dedicated to the advancement of the knowledge, theory, and quality of learning and teaching at all levels with information technology. AACE disseminates research and applications through publications and conferences. Journals published by the AACE include *International Journal of E-Learning (IJEL)*, *Journal of Computers in Mathematics and Science Teaching (JCMST)*, *Journal of Interactive Learning Research (JILR)*, *Journal of Educational Multimedia and Hypermedia (JEMH)*, *Journal of Technology and Teacher Education (JTATE)*, *Journal of Online Learning Research (JOLR)*, *AACE Journal (AACEJ)*, and *Contemporary Issues in Technology & Teacher Education (CITE)*.

AMERICAN LIBRARY ASSOCIATION (ALA).   ALA is the largest library association in the world. Over 60,000 members represent all types of libraries—public, school, academic, state, and special libraries serving persons in government, commerce, the armed services, hospitals, prisons, and other institutions. The association has 11 divisions focusing on various types of libraries and services. The American Association of School Librarians (AASL), one of the divisions, holds national conferences focusing on the interests of school media specialists. AASL also publishes the *School Library Media Research*, which presents research that pertains to the uses of technology for instructional and informational purposes. Special issues have dealt with such themes as communications, technology, and facility design for learning environments that require a great deal of technology.

COMPUTER USING EDUCATORS (CUE).   CUE is a nonprofit educational corporation with an active membership of thousands of educational professionals representing all disciplines from preschool through college. CUE supports many regional affiliates and Learning Networks as well as an annual national educational technology conference in California, which brings together over 6,000 teachers from across the nation.

GLOBAL SCHOOLNET FOUNDATION (GSN).   GSN engages 120,000 educators and millions of students from 194 countries to explore community, cultural, and scientific issues that prepare them with multicultural understanding, civic responsibility, and communication skills needed for the workforce. Global SchoolNet's free membership program provides project-based learning support materials, resources, activities, lessons, and special offers from its partners.

INTERNATIONAL ASSOCIATION FOR K-12 ONLINE LEARNING (iNACOL).   iNACOL is comprised of a diverse and global membership of K–12 educators and receives support from three leading foundations: Bill and Melinda Gates, Nellie Mae, and The Walton Foundation. iNACOL conducts research to develop and share new learning models, publishes National Quality Standards, and provides the Network Hub for student-centered, personalized learners. The organization also provides multiple iNACOL symposiums focused on various current topics associated with blended and online learning.

INTERNATIONAL SOCIETY FOR TECHNOLOGY IN EDUCATION (ISTE). ISTE is a global nonprofit organization serving more than 100,000 educators. ISTE supports its membership through the annual ISTE Conference and Expo, the ISTE Standards for students, teachers, administrators, coaches, and computer science educators, and numerous professional learning webinars, online courses, books, and publications. ISTE publishes the *Journal for Computing Teachers, Journal of Research on Technology in Education, Journal of Digital Learning in Teacher Education*, and *entrsekt*. Of particular interest to PK–12 teachers is the *entrsekt* journal, which focuses on innovative aspects of connections between learning, technology, and the community.

INTERNATIONAL TECHNOLOGY AND ENGINEERING EDUCATORS ASSOCIA-TION (ITEEA). ITEEA is the professional organization of more than 35,000 secondary technology, innovation, design, and engineering educators in the United States alone. Its mission is to promote technological literacy by supporting the teaching of technology and engineering and promoting the professionalism of those engaged in these pursuits. ITEEA strengthens the profession through leadership, professional development, membership services, publications, and classroom activities.

ITEEA publishes two peer-reviewed scholarly journals, *Technology and Engineering Teacher* and the *Journal of Technology and Education*. Another journal offered is *Children's Technology and Engineering* (CET). CET is a useful, interesting tool for K–6 teachers interested in technological literacy in grades K–6. ITEEA also provides the *Science, Technology, Engineering, and Mathematics (STEM) Connections*, a free online newsletter to keep teachers current on cutting-edge STEM strategies and resources.

UNITED STATES DISTANCE LEARNING ASSOCIATION (USDLA). USDLA promotes the development and application of distance learning for education and training. The members and sponsors represent PK–12 education, home schooling, higher education, continuing education, corporate training, telemedicine, and military and government training. The association has become a leading source of information and recommendations for government agencies, the U.S. Congress, industry, and those involved in the development of distance learning programs. USDLA has chapters in all 50 states. It is a sponsor of annual USDLA National Conferences and provides a variety of online resources. In addition, USDLA holds regular meetings with global leaders of distance learning and sponsors an annual National Distance Learning Week.

Application Exercise 9.2

Professional Journals

A key contribution of professional organizations in instructional technology and media is to publish journals of interest to their members. Various other digital periodicals are targeted to educators interested in using educational technology and media. Online journals are quickly becoming the journals of choice because they provide teachers with current information that includes interactive links to additional information and they are a "green" solution. Examples of highly relevant online journals targeted toward PK–12 educators are listed here.

T.H.E. JOURNAL. *T.H.E. Journal* is dedicated to transforming education through technology. The free subscription includes a monthly journal available in print and digital versions. The journal content is archived in a searchable format with a browse-by-topic feature. Among the topics are Common core, K–12 news, grants, special needs, professional development, and STEM. The free subscription also includes the option to receive various online newsletters such as: *THE News Update, IT Trends, THE 21st Century School, K-12 Mobile Classroom,* and *THE STEAM.*

eSCHOOL NEWS. *eSchool News* is a free print and online publication that provides the latest news, resources, and reports on the applications of technology to improve learning. The newspaper has over 300,000 subscribers and the website has over 500,000 unique visitors each month. Topics of focus include: top trends, technology, thought leadership, digital curriculum, colleague corner, resources, and webinars. Among the top trends are: innovation centers, apps, blended learning, and mobile learning.

EDUCATION WEEK. *Education Week* offers free subscriptions to E-Newsletters in the following topics: Edweek Update; Teacher Update; Digital Directions; Curriculum Matters; Industry & Innovation, Career Coach; and Common Core Update. The Education Week Teacher site offers special reports, blogs, events, opinions, and career links.

TECH & LEARNING. *Tech & Learning* is a free online journal with practical PK–12 recommendations for resources and strategies to integrate digital technologies. The journal has over 250,000 subscribers and includes articles on current topics as well as regular features on the latest products, what's trending, and big ideas. The journal site includes searchable archived editions. The Tech & Learning website provides links to news, events, and the following resources: contests, eBooks, whitepapers, buyer's guide, app of the day, site of the week, PD tips, poll, live PD library, future-ready schools, video, K12 blueprint, and blogs.

Through regular reading of educational technology journals, teachers can expand their professional knowledge and growth by staying informed of new technology and media that have positive impacts on student learning. Teachers can use this knowledge and growth to develop and implement innovative learning practices and environments that better prepare students for tomorrow's careers. These online journals also include current resources and connections to PK–12 teachers with similar interests to engage in collaborative professional growth opportunities.

 Check Your Understanding 9.4

Funding Technology for Tomorrow

Even though PK–12 access to technology is continually increasing, many teachers prefer to have a class set of digital devices rather than limiting student use to one or two days per week in the technology lab or bringing in a cart with digital devices such as tablets or laptop computers. To solve this dilemma, districts, schools, and/ or teachers often apply for technology grants. These grants typically provide funding for devices, apps, and very frequently require professional development for teachers to ensure they understand how to meaningfully integrate the digital tools into their instruction. Technology can also be acquired with grants focused on core content, social behavior improvement, and career training, if the digital devices are integrated as a program component.

Types of Grants

There are two basic types of technology grants: government grants funded at the federal, state, district, or school level, and organization grants from businesses and corporations or nonprofit organizations such as foundations, groups, or associations.

GOVERNMENT GRANTS. Information regarding government grants can be explored on the comprehensive Grants.gov site. This location has a robust tool to search by keyword, opportunity status, funding type, eligibility, category, and the agency, which lists most government departments as well as the National Science Foundation and National Endowment for the Humanities. Teachers can search for posted or forecasted grant opportunities by terms relevant to the area of interest, such as "teacher," "K-12," "Technology," "Education," or specific subject areas. The search results present a link to a description of the grant as well as the application materials. The grants range from statewide funding for longitudinal data systems to program-specific initiatives such as funding to improve the provision of assistive technology for individuals with disabilities. Government grants can provide substantial funding, but frequently require the submission of a lengthy, detailed proposal and budget; multistate collaborative partnerships between districts and universities, as well as community organizations; and matching funds from the districts and partners. Thus, federal grants are normally awarded to districts or regions rather than to schools or teachers. However, the U.S. General Services Administration sponsors the Computers for Learning (CFL) program as a way to promote the reuse of government computers scheduled for replacement. The CFL program transfers excess computers and technology equipment to high-needs schools that complete the application and meet the program requirements.

Other opportunities for funding involve federal formula and competitive grant programs, such as the Elementary and Secondary Education Act (Titles I, II, III) and IDEA, which may allow portions of the funds to be used to support digital learning. For example, these funds might be used to support digital learning when integrated to improve and personalize teacher professional learning, collaboration, and communication and/or increase student access to high quality digital content and learning resources. These allowances have been approved as a way to better coordinate federal program support to maximize the impact of available resources. It is imperative to keep in mind that any use of technology for these purposes must comply with applicable privacy laws and the specific program requirements of each funding source (US DOE-OET, 2016a).

ORGANIZATION GRANTS. Grants from nongovernment organizations and foundations often involve a less extensive proposal process that is flexible enough to award funding to individual schools or teachers as well as to districts and local collaborative partnerships. In addition, most schools can typically meet the requirements of grants sponsored by well-known organizations such as AT&T's Aspire funding, the Kellogg Foundation's Educate Kids Grant, and Cisco Systems Education Investments. However, please note that some grants have a very targeted focus. For example, the Lockheed Martin Corporation Philanthropy only funds K–16 science, technology, engineering, and math initiatives in schools located in communities in which Lockheed Martin has employees, which includes locations across approximately 25 states.

Numerous websites provide lists of organizations that offer PK–12 technology grants. Examples include THE Journal's K-12 Grants; Teachers Count Grant Resources, Grants For Teachers, and Digital Wish. There are also fundraiser sites to assist teachers with obtaining funds for digital learning. Popular sites include Digital Wish, DonorsChoose, Adopt A Classroom, and Fund My Classroom. There are also generic sites such as GoFundMe that are used by teachers to obtain digital resources. For further examples, see Technology Grant Resources in the Suggested Resources at the end of the chapter.

Figure 9.6 Grant Proposal Components: Technology and other types of grants typically have seven key components.

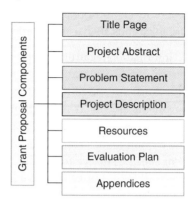

Writing a Grant Proposal

Writing a successful grant proposal begins with a clear and structured process to describe how the funds will be used to achieve the overall purpose of the grant. It is critical to follow the specific guidelines in the Request for Proposal (RFP) or Application, as most proposals have a strict page limit and require specific topics to be addressed and presented in a designated order. Many grants use an online application that follows an outline similar to the one presented in fig 9.6.

Brief descriptions of, and useful tips regarding, the seven grant proposal components are described in the following section.

TITLE PAGE.   Select a title that is concise and clearly states the intent of the project. Avoid the use of clever or cute titles that may not transmit the intended message. Include names and contact information of the key people who will implement the project, as well as the name of the grant and funder information.

PROJECT ABSTRACT.   This is typically a one-half to one-page description of the project that includes overall goal/purpose, description of the project and how it will be implemented, who will benefit from the project, key staff, evaluation plans, overall costs, and timeline. Avoid overuse of academic jargon.

PROBLEM STATEMENT.   The intent of this section is to convince the funder that your proposed project will benefit students. Your argument should be supported with data and research. It is important to include data about your current situation by providing information such as the student-to-computer ratio and a description of student and teacher needs. For example, will the project focus on students who are from low-income families, who are English language learners, or who have special learning needs, including providing advanced studies for gifted students?

PROJECT DESCRIPTION.   The project description includes the goals and outcomes, target population, methods, project staff, and timeline.

- *Goals and outcomes.* Begin this section with clearly stated goals and measurable outcomes that will be achieved at the end of the project.

- *Target population.* Describe who will benefit from the project. Include descriptions of the students by grade level and subject areas that will be emphasized, the teachers who will implement the project, and targeted parents or community members who may participate.

- *Methods.* Provide clear and concise descriptions of the methods that will be used to implement the project. Show how your project will use research-based approaches to guarantee successful outcomes. Address the following questions: How and what type of technology will be provided to the targeted population? How will teachers be prepared? How will the project change classroom practices and learning opportunities? How will parents and/or community members be involved?

- *Project staff.* Most grants designate the lead project staff as the principal investigator (PI) and secondary lead staff as co-PIs. Begin your list with the PI and co-PIs, then list other key staff: professional development facilitators, technology coaches, and technical assistants. It is not necessary to list those who provide accounting or secretarial support, as those services are typically considered "in-kind" contributions. Include names and a brief description of qualifications for the assigned roles of each staff member.

- *Timeline.* Use a timeline to depict when each major activity will take place and the staff responsible for the activity. A table works well to display the information by using the following columns: date, activity, and person(s) responsible. It is sometimes helpful to outline how the project will continue beyond the ending date of the grant to demonstrate how you plan to sustain the project beyond the grant-funded time period.

RESOURCES.   Describe the available, or "in-kind," resources that will be used to support the project (e.g., facilities, personnel, and digital equipment: devices, printers, projectors, interactive whiteboards). Then describe resources that will be purchased with project funds. Include a rationale for each purchase that shows how it will support achievement of the project goals and outcomes.

EVALUATION PLAN.   Provide a clear description of the methods, procedures, and timeline for evaluating the degree to which the project goals and outcomes are met. This may include collecting data during and after program implementation. Describe which participants will be included in the evaluation, the evaluation instruments to be used, how the results will be analyzed, and how the findings will be shared.

APPENDICES.   The RFP typically limits the appendices to specific types of content and number of pages. Common information in an appendix includes detailed descriptions of professional development models, example student work, data collection instruments, and staff curriculum vitae. Also, a detailed budget is often required in the appendix. If the grant is funded through your district, it is critical to work closely with your accounting and development officers to determine budgeting guidelines.

One way to improve technology grant proposals is to review past proposals submitted by your school or district, which often have descriptions of your student population and local setting that can be adapted for your proposal. It is also useful to review online example proposals submitted by other schools and districts.

Application Exercise 9.3

   Check Your Understanding 9.5

Summary

This chapter discussed factors influencing tomorrow's teaching and learning and placed key emphasis on the chapter's learning outcomes.

- *Describe how the ASSURE model supports tomorrow's learning as described in the National Education Technology Plan.* The ASSURE model is structured to help teachers achieve the innovative changes needed for tomorrow's learning. By following the step-by-step model, teachers receive the support and guidance to develop, implement, evaluate, and revise lessons that integrate technology to increase student learning and prepare them for future careers.

- *Discuss the characteristics of tomorrow's thinking and learning as represented in models and learning environments.* Among the promising digitally inspired models for tomorrow's thinking and learning are coding as literacy, and connected, personalized, and transdisciplinary learning, all of which are based on a foundation of cyberlearning. The learning environments of tomorrow will require access to a robust and comprehensive infrastructure that includes ubiquitous connectivity, powerful learning devices, and high quality digital learning content. These environments will also support and enhance student use of emerging technologies such as artificial intelligence, augmented reality, robotics, and wearable devices.

- *Explain how tomorrow's teachers exemplify digital age thinking and learning practices.* Teachers of tomorrow will exemplify digital age thinking and learning practices by ubiquitously integrating emerging technologies that not only leverage student digital age experiences, but also support global collaborations. This combined approach will engage students in knowledge construction that benefits all learners.

- *Describe future-ready professional learning with regard to professional engagement, organizations, and journals.* Considering the consistently changing technology innovations that impact everyday living, working, and education, it is imperative for teachers to stay informed and current through a long-term commitment to professional learning supported through professional engagement, professional organizations, and professional journals. The professional engagement of tomorrow's teachers will extend beyond school district inservice training to encompass global learning opportunities, interactions, and collaborations. Professional organizations offer teachers multiple opportunities to remain engaged with educators within and beyond their disciplines to stay informed with current research and practice, build teaching skills, and create professional relationships. Professional journals provide teachers with current research and practitioner information to inform classroom instruction.

- *Give examples of funding technology for tomorrow and briefly describe the basic components of a grant proposal.* There are two basic types of technology funding: government grants funded at the federal, state, district, or school level, and organization grants from businesses and corporations or nonprofit organizations such as foundations, groups, or associations. Writing a successful grant proposal begins with a clear and structured process to describe how the funds will be used to achieve the overall purpose of the grant. It is critical to follow the specific guidelines in the Request for Proposal (RFP), which typically requires information to include the following components: title page, project abstract, statement of the problem, project description, resources, evaluation plan, and appendices.

Professional Development

Demonstrating Professional Skills

1. Review ASSURE lesson plans that you have developed or other technology integration lessons and describe how each lesson aligns with the 2016 NETP Learning Goal and in what ways the lesson can be modified to address components of the goal not included in the lesson. (ISTE Standards for Teachers 2.A, 2.C)

2. Select one or more of the models for tomorrow's thinking and learning and describe how you could integrate the approach into the curriculum you teach or plan to teach. What specific content area would work best, and why? What digital devices would be needed and what, if any, technology support would be needed? In what ways would students benefit from engagement with the new model? (ISTE Standards for Teachers 2.A, 2.B)

3. Conduct a self-reflection to assess how your teaching aligns with expectations for tomorrow's teachers. Address the following questions in your self-assessment: What are your strengths and weaknesses with regard to your ability to exemplify digital age thinking? What strategies would you implement

to ensure that emerging technologies were ubiquitously integrated into your instruction? How would you engage your students in global collaboration? (ISTE Standards for Teachers 3.A, 3.B)

4. Interview two or more teachers who you consider to be "future ready" educators regarding their involvement in professional learning. Structure your interview to discuss specifics of professional engagement, participation in professional organizations, and use of professional journals. In a three- to five-page paper, compare and contrast the professional learning strategies of each teacher and how you plan to engage in professional learning. (ISTE Standards for Teachers 5.C)

5. Analyze the technology needs of the school in which you work or would like to work and locate a grant that would help the school address the identified needs. Use the grant proposal outline to write a brief description of how you would write each section of the proposal. (ISTE Standards for Teachers 5.C)

Building Your Professional Portfolio

Reflecting on My Learning. Reflect on the need to prepare for tomorrow's challenges, as described in this chapter, and write a description of how you think this need will impact your teaching. Explain what you think the most rewarding aspects of tomorrow's thinking and learning will be and why. Explain what you think will be the most challenging aspects and why. (ISTE Standards for Teachers 2.A, 5.C)

Enhancing My Portfolio. Select a technology integration lesson from the Web, or one that you have developed. After citing the source of the lesson, analyze it according to topics discussed in this chapter. Specifically, take note of how or if the lesson addresses tomorrow's thinking and learning by examining: (1) the role of cyberlearning in the lesson, (2) changes needed to implement "connected learning" in the lesson, and (3) how augmented reality could enhance student learning. (ISTE Standards for Teachers 2.A, 2.B)

Suggested Resources

Print Resources

Burns, M. (2016). *Deeper learning with QR codes and augmented reality: A scannable solution for your classroom.* Thousand Oaks, CA: Corwin/Sage.

Carr, C. E. (2015). *The nuts and bolts of grant writing.* Los Angeles: Sage.

Couros, G. (2015). *The innovator's mindset: Empower learning, unleash talent, and lead a culture of creativity.* San Diego, CA: Dave Burgess Consulting, Inc.

New Media Consortium (NMC). (2016). *NMC Horizon Report: 2016 K–12 Education Edition.* Austin, TX: The New Media Consortium.

Orey, M. (2015). Worldwide list of graduate programs in learning, design, technology, information, or libraries. In M. Orey & R. M. Branch (Eds.), *Educational Media and Technology Yearbook* (Vol. 39, pp. 217–316). New York: Springer.

Pawlicki, D. & James, C. (2014). *The insider's guide to winning educational grants.* San Francisco, CA: Jossey-Bass.

Reeves, D. L. (2016). *Find your future in technology.* North Mankato, MN: Cherry Lake Publishing.

Online Resources and Apps

Discovery Education

Discovery Education provides solutions for districts, free resources for teachers, parents, and students, and conversations and connections through their community blog. Free teacher resources are available by grade level and content area and include lesson plans, virtual field trips, Brain Boosters, learning adventures, science curriculum center, WebMath, Worksheets to Go, and much more.

Edutopia

Edutopia provides multiple resources regarding "what works in education." The site is supported by the George Lucas Educational Foundation (GLEF) and provides three opportunities to "Join the Movement for Change." These include: 1) *Get Inspired* through various strategies for learning, teacher development, and technology integration; 2) *Find Solutions* with blogs, videos, classroom guides, quizzes, and A to Z topics by grade level; and 3) *Join the Conversation* through Facebook, Twitter, YouTube, Google+, Pinterest, and signing up for RSS.

Common Sense Graphite

Graphite is a free platform from Common Sense Education that provides thousands of reviews of educational apps and tools. The reviews are written by and for teachers to help them discover the best educational technology tools while learning best practices for teaching and connecting with the growing community of educators. The overarching goal is to "Help us raise a generation of kids who think critically, act responsibly, and interact positively in the digital world."

Edtechteacher

The mission of Edtechteacher is "to support educators in their quest to enrich student learning experiences through emerging technologies." This site offers teacher-created free resources in the following areas: Frameworks and Models; Tutorials and Helpful Links; Innovative Projects and Lessons; Tech Tools by Subject and Skill; Free Live Webinars and Recordings; Google Apps for Education; App Recommendations; and Assessment and Rubrics.

National Center for Technology Innovation

The National Center for Technology Innovation (NCTI), funded by the U.S. Office of Special Education Programs (OSEP), advances learning opportunities for individuals with disabilities by fostering technology innovation. The website provides resources and information to promote partnerships for the development of tools and applications by developers, manufacturers, producers, publishers, and researchers.

iTunes U Education App

iTunes U [University] is an app for iPhones, iPads, or iPods that provides teachers with apps to learn from the world's largest collection of free education content as well as to plan lessons, grade assignments, and upload resources. iTunes U also engages learners through apps, books, videos, podcasts, and more and enables the teacher to answer questions in one-on-one chats or start debates with the entire class using group discussions.

Pinterest App

Pinterest is a social media app populated with "pins" added to "boards" created by its users. Pinterest has numerous boards for teachers, including: In the Classroom, Technology Integration, Professional Development, Learning, Lesson Plans, and much more. The boards include photos, images, diagrams, tips, notes, and other information that are grouped with other Pinterest boards with similar content. When the Pinterest app is downloaded, teachers can create personalized boards by "Pinning" new information they locate or boards of interest created by others.

Technology Grant Resources

Big List of Educational Grants and Resources

A current collection of educational grants, contests, awards, free toolkits, and classroom guides provided by Edutopia that are aimed at helping students, classrooms, schools, and communities. This site is updated on a weekly basis. The Grants and Contests and Awards categories include active links to the resources, plus the title, application deadline, and a brief description that designates the specific prize, for example, "Average awards range from $5,000 to $10,000."

SchoolGrants

This site contains a variety of information and resources on grant writing, grant opportunities, and sample grant proposals. Also provided are newsletters and an index of links, including one for technology resources.

Teacher Tap: Grants and Grant Writing

This website provides professional development resources for teachers and librarians focused on grant resources starting points, exploring grant possibilities, getting started, identifying the need and your solution, goal setting, and writing a grant proposal.

Appendix:
Lesson Scenarios

Scenario	Content	Students	Goal
Mr. Wilson wants his preschool children to have a better understanding of the weather cycles.	Weather/seasons	Preschool-aged children, 4–5 years old, with little instruction in weather patterns	At the end of the lesson, the children will have a general understanding of the seasons and the weather patterns associated with them.
Mrs. Harris plans to introduce the concept of simple addition to her K–1 class.	Mathematics	Students, 5–6 years old, with knowledge of number concepts	At the end of the lesson, the students will be able to complete simple addition problems with sums less than 10.
Mr. Martinez wants to reinforce his students' understanding of prepositions.	Language arts	Elementary students, 7–8 years old, who are building their vocabulary skills	At the end of the lesson, students will be able to place graphics in the location specified in given prepositions.
Ms. Eller's class expresses interest in the states surrounding their own.	U.S. geography	Students, 8–9 years old, with limited knowledge of the influence of geography on states' development	At the end of the lesson, the students will be able to identify the geographic factors that influence the states' economic, social, and political histories.
Mr. Cheon wants to introduce his students to art forms made from natural stone.	Art	Intermediate grade students, 9–10 years old, who have limited knowledge about using stone for artwork	At the end of the lesson, the students will be able to identify several types of artwork that are created with natural stone.
Ms. Chinn wants to introduce her students to the concept of life cycles by studying the life cycle of a frog.	Life science	Students, 11–12 years old, with strong physical science and limited biological science background	At the end of the lesson, the students will be able to identify the stages in the life cycle of the frog and be able to describe the relationships among the stages in the development of the frog.
Mr. Heller's class is interested in issues related to health, especially those identified in eating a balanced diet.	Nutrition	Middle school/junior high students, 13–14 years old, with knowledge of the Food Guide Pyramid	At the end of the lesson, the students will be able to select a balanced menu covering three meals per day for one week.
Ms. Galloway has decided to collaborate with the world history teacher's lesson on World War II by introducing her students to the literature of the period.	World literature	High school, college-bound students, 16–17 years old, who have an interest in reading and exploring period literature	At the end of the lesson, students will be able to discuss the relationship between international events during World War II and the literature produced in that period.
Mr. Wasileski's high school English class is ready to learn how to write a research paper.	English writing	High school students who have limited experience writing a research paper	At the end of the lesson, students will be able to write a paper that includes appropriate use of references, following the pattern of introduction, research questions, analysis, and conclusions.

Glossary

Acceptable use policy (AUP)   An agreement among students, parents/guardians, and school administrators regarding appropriate use of the Internet.

Affective domain   The domain of human learning that involves changes in interests, attitudes, and values and the development of appreciation.

Alt-tag   Alternative textual material to provide brief descriptions of graphics or images.

Analogical visuals   Visuals that convey a concept or topic by showing something else and implying a similarity.

Animation   A technique in which the artist gives motion to still images by creating and juxtaposing a series of pictures with small, incremental changes from one to the next.

Applications   Games, simulations, tutorials, problem-solving programs, productivity software, and graphic software programs.

Asynchronously   Not at the same time.

Asynchronous setting   A distance learning setup in which the teacher and students are not together at the same time.

Audio literacy   Understanding the role of hearing and listening in learning.

Audio teleconference   A teleconference involving transmission of voices only. The voices are amplified at each end by a speaker system.

Auditory fatigue   The process by which attention to a sound gradually decreases because of the monotony of the sound.

Augmented reality (AR)   Combining real-world data with virtual data.

Authentic assessment   Evaluation that is usually performance based and that requires students to demonstrate their learning in a natural context.

Behaviorism   A theory that equates learning with changes in observable behavior. With this theory, there is no speculating about mental events that may mediate learning.

Benchmarks   Standards against which students are tested.

Bit   An acronym for binary digit, the smallest unit of digital information. The bit can be thought of as a 1 or a 0 representing a circuit on or off, respectively.

Blended instruction   A combination of e-learning with live, face-to-face instruction.

Blended learning   The result of instruction that is a combination of e-learning and live, face-to-face instruction.

Blog   Web log serving as a publicly accessible personal journal for an individual.

Blu-ray disc (BD)   A medium that stores high-definition video, games, and other data. The disc is the same size as a standard DVD, but stores almost ten times more data than a DVD. The name comes from the blue laser used to read the disc.

Bookmarking

Byte   The number of bits required to store or represent one character of text (a letter or number); most commonly, but not always, it is made up of eight bits in various combinations of 0s and 1s.

Cable modem   A television cable connection that provides very high speed access to the Internet.

Cartoon   Line drawing that is a rough caricature of real or fictional people, animals, or events.

Central processing unit (CPU)   The core element of a computer that carries out all the calculations and controls the total system.

Chart   Visual representation of abstract relationships.

Classroom voice amplification system   Audio technology system that optimizes the listening environment for all students using a lightweight wireless teacher's microphone linked to a set of speakers strategically placed around the classroom.

Clip art   Prepared visual images (drawings and digital pictures) that can be inserted into digital documents and presentations.

Cloud computing   System in which applications are available through networked computers to distribute greater access to processing power and applications.

Cognitive domain   The domain of human learning involving intellectual skills, such as assimilation of information or knowledge.

Cognitivism   A theory according to which mental processes mediate learning and learning entails the construction or reshaping of mental schemata.

Collaborative   A sharing or cooperative nature of an experience.

Community of practice (CoP)   A group of educators from across the nation and around the world who have common goals and share ideas and resources.

Compressed video   Video images that have been processed to remove redundant information, thereby reducing the amount of bandwidth required to transmit them. Because only changes in the image are transmitted, movements appear jerky compared with full-motion video.

Computer-assisted instruction (CAI)   Instruction delivered directly to learners by allowing them to interact with lessons programmed into the computer system.

Computer conferencing   Connecting two or more computers together for textual and/or graphical information exchange.

Computer-managed instruction (CMI)   The use of a computer system to manage information about learner performance and learning resources and to then prescribe and control individual lessons.

Computer platform   Different types of computer operating systems, such as Mac OS, Unix, or Windows.

Configuration   A computer's specific combination of hardware components.

Constructivism   A theory that considers the engagement of students in meaningful experiences as the essence of learning.

Cooperative learning   An instructional configuration involving small groups of learners working together on learning tasks rather than competing as individuals.

Copyright   Regulations that describe the manner in which an original work can be used and copied. Copyright laws regulate the manner in which authors or artists can be reimbursed for their creative work.

Course management tool (CMT)   Software designed to make it easier for teachers to use resources in the distance learning system, such as the discussion board, test options, and grade book.

Cyberlearning   The use of Web 2.0 networked computing and communication technologies to support learning.

Decode   To comprehend information that is presented.

Digital fabricator   Three-dimensional printer or rapid prototyping machine, also known as a "fabber" (short for fabricator), that can build 3-D objects by carefully depositing materials drop by drop, layer by layer, using a geometric blueprint from a CAD program.

Digital subscriber line (DSL)   A telephone line that provides very high-speed access to the Internet.

Digital video editing   Taking apart and putting back together video segments using a computer and associated software.

Diorama   A static display employing a flat background and 3-D foreground to achieve a lifelike effect.

Discovery   A teaching strategy that proceeds as follows: immersion in a real or contrived problem situation, development of hypotheses, testing of hypotheses, and arrival at conclusion (the main point).

Discussion   A teaching strategy involving the exchange of ideas and opinions.

Display   An array of objects, visuals, and printed materials.

Distance learning   An instructional situation in which students learn via telecommunications.

Documentary   A video program that deals with fact, nonfiction, or fictionalized versions of fact.

Document camera   A video camera mounted on a copy stand to show documents, pictures, graphics, and real objects to groups.

Drawing   Graphic arrangement of lines to represent persons, places, things, and concepts.

Drill-and-practice   A teaching strategy in which learners are led through a series of exercises or problems and given feedback.

Educational gaming   A competitive environment in which learners follow prescribed rules as they strive to attain a challenging goal.

Electronic mail (email)   Transmission of private messages over a computer network. Users can send mail to a single recipient or broadcast it to multiple users on the system.

Electronic portfolio (e-portfolio)   A digital collection of student work that demonstrates progress in learning as shown in student self-reflections of the portfolio contents.

Emoticon   An email symbol generated from punctuation marks.

Encode   To visually express an idea to others.

Entry tests   Assessments, both formal and informal, to determine whether students possess desired identified prerequisites.

Exhibit   A display incorporating various media formats (e.g., realia, still pictures, models, graphics) into an integral whole intended for instructional purposes.

Fair use   Basic criteria an educator can use to determine whether it is appropriate to use copyrighted materials in a classroom setting.

Feedback (learner)   Information provided to the learner regarding correctness of performance and suggestions for improvement.

File server   In local area networks, a station dedicated to providing file and mass data storage services to the other stations on the network.

Firewall   Intranet software that prevents external users from accessing a proprietary network, while allowing internal users access to external networks.

Flash drive   USB minidrive, a form of removable storage device that allows the user to store files outside the computer; also called a jump drive.

Gateway   A computer that interconnects and makes translations between two different types of networks. Also called a portal.

GB   See Gigabyte.

Gigabyte (GB)   Approximately 1 million bytes, or 1,000 megabytes.

Graph   Visual representation of numerical data.

Hardware   The mechanical and electronic components that make up a computer; the physical equipment that makes up a computer system, and, by extension, the term that refers to any audiovisual equipment.

Hearing   A physiological process in which sound waves entering the outer ear are transmitted to the eardrum, converted into mechanical vibrations in the middle ear, and changed in the inner ear to nerve impulses that travel to the brain.

HTTP   See Hypertext transfer protocol.

Hybrid   A mixed learning environment that combines Internet resources (e.g., WebQuests) with traditional classroom curriculum.

Hybrid instruction   See Blended instruction.

Hypertext transfer protocol (HTTP)   The web protocol that ensures compatibility before transferring information.

Iconic   Any referent that resembles the thing it represents.

ILS   See Integrated learning system.

Informal learning   An instructional setting that provides students with opportunities to learn from experiences outside of the classroom.

Information   Knowledge, facts, news, comments, and content as presented in memos, lectures, textbooks, or websites.

Informational text   Nonfiction text materials including textbooks.

Information literacy   The ability to use a range of critical thinking and problem-solving skills to effectively participate in today's society.

Input device   Hardware that transmits information to the computer, for example, a keyboard and mouse.

Instruction   Deliberate arrangement of experience(s) to help learners achieve a desirable change in performance; the management of learning, which in education is primarily the function of the teacher.

Instructional material   Specific items used within a lesson that influence student learning.

Instructional technology   Hardware, software, and/or processes to facilitate learning.

Integrated learning system (ILS)   A set of interrelated computer-based lessons organized to match the curriculum standards.

Integrated services digital network (ISDN)   A network that provides high-speed access to the Internet using digital communication.

Internet   A global interconnection of a broad collection of millions of computer networks serving billions of people around the world.

Internet radio   A system used for broadcasting online programs over the Internet.

Internet service provider (ISP)   A company that provides account holders with access to the Internet for a fee.

Internet video   Internet broadcasts of events or activities on a website using compressed video or video streaming; some broadcasts are live and others are recorded.

Interpersonal domain   The domain of learning that involves interaction among people and the ability to relate effectively with others.

Interpretive visuals   Visuals that illustrate theoretical or abstract relationships.

Intranet   A proprietary or closed internal network that connects multiple sites across the state, within the country, or around the world; systems connected to an intranet are private and accessible only by individuals within a given school or organization.

KB See Kilobyte.

Kilobyte (KB or K) Approximately 1,000 bytes; more precisely, 1,024 bytes.

Learning center A self-contained environment designed to promote individual or small-group learning around a specific task.

Learning communities Student and teacher use of electronic connectedness to share ideas, engage in inquiry, and search for additional information.

Learning style A cluster of psychological traits that determine how a person perceives, interacts with, and responds emotionally to learning environments.

Listening A psychological process that begins with someone's awareness of and attention to sounds or speech patterns, proceeds through identification and recognition of specific auditory signals, and ends in comprehension.

Literary Fictional text materials including stories, dramas, poems, and myths.

Local area network (LAN) A simple network that connects individual computers to one another within a limited area—normally a classroom, building, or laboratory—to permit the exchange of files and other resources.

Log-on The process of entering a specific username and password to access online materials.

Manipulative Object that can be viewed and handled in a learning setting.

Mashups Websites that bring together content from a variety of resources, creating resources that are new and different from the original sources, for example, online news media sites.

MB See Megabyte.

Media See Medium.

Media centers School facilities that offer traditional library reading resources as well as a variety of information technology assets.

Media format The physical form in which a message is incorporated and displayed; examples include whiteboards, webpages, PowerPoint or Prezi slides, CDs, DVDs, and computer multimedia.

Media literacy The ability to interpret and produce a wide variety of media, including text, audio, visuals, and video, which are often combined to form multimedia.

Medium A means of communication. Derived from the Latin *medium* ("between"), the term refers to anything that carries information between a source and a receiver. Plural: media.

Megabyte (MB or M) Basic unit of measurement of mass storage.

Metacognition Knowledge of and thinking about one's own thinking process.

Mobile app Software application designed for mobile devices that enable many of these devices to take photos and short video, email, surf the Web, play games, provide location-based services (GPS), and use calendars and other personal management tools.

Mobile assessment tool Mobile computing resource that enables teachers to record student assessment data directly into a mobile device that transfers the data to a computer for report generation.

Mobile technology Portable technology such as smart phones, portable music players, tablet computers, e-readers, and other handheld technologies.

Mock-up Representation of a complex device or process.

Model A 3-D representation of a real object; it may be larger, smaller, or the same size as the thing represented.

Multiple intelligences Theory developed by Howard Gardner that suggests humans have multiple methods of learning: verbal/linguistic (language), logical/mathematical (scientific/quantitative), visual/spatial, musical/rhythmic, body/kinesthetic (dancing/athletics), interpersonal (understanding other people), intrapersonal (understanding oneself), naturalist, and existentialist.

Musical instrument digital interface (MIDI) Technology that allows students to create music by focusing on musical ideas rather than the mechanics of playing an instrument or learning musical notation.

National Education Technology Standards for Students (NETS-S) A document that specifically outlines expectations for student use of technology to guide their learning.

Netiquette Guidelines relating to email and other interactions on the Web.

Network A communication system linking two or more computers.

One-way video Video transmission in which visual and auditory information is delivered to learners with limited opportunities for immediate connections with the teacher or source of the information.

Online learning The result of instruction that is delivered electronically using computer-based media.

Open source Websites that offer free productivity suites (e.g., word processing, spreadsheets, presentation software).

Operating system Software that functions as the computer's interface with the user.

Oral history Historical documentation of a time, place, or event by means of recording the spoken recollections of participants in those events.

Organizational visuals Visuals that show the qualitative relationships among various elements.

Output device Hardware that displays the information from a computer to the user, for example, a monitor or digital projector.

Persistence of vision The psychophysiological phenomenon that occurs when an image falls on the retina of the eye and is conveyed to the brain via the optic nerve. The brain continues to "see" the image for a fraction of a second after the image is cut off.

Personal response system Handheld wireless devices (similar to TV remotes) used to collect and graphically display student answers to teacher questions.

Photos Two-dimensional representations of people, places, and things.

Pinboards Online websites that enable users to organize photos, videos, and other information onto digital boards by lesson, unit, grade level, or subject area.

Place shift Experiencing instruction at some place away from the live teacher.

Podcast Internet-distributed multimedia file formatted for direct download to mobile devices.

Podcasting Distribution of recorded audio files in MP3 format over the Internet.

Portable digital audio player Device that allows users to take digital audio files with them, such as an Apple iPod.

Portal See Gateway.

Poster A visual combination of images, lines, color, and words.

Practice Learner participation that increases the probability of learning.

Prerequisites Competencies that learners must possess to benefit from instruction.

Presentation An instructional strategy in which a source tells, dramatizes, or disseminates information to learners.

Presentation software Computer software used to create attractive graphic displays without specialized production skills and to display visuals with a digital projector.

Pretest   A test administered before teaching a lesson to identify students who need remediation prior to lesson implementation and also to identify those who have already mastered what you plan to teach.

Problem-based learning   A process in which students actively seek solutions to structured or ill-structured problems situated in the real world.

Problem-solving skills   Reaching a solution to a novel problem using higher-order thinking skills such as defining the problem, considering alternatives, and using logical reasoning.

Productivity tools   Web applications that allow users to create and edit documents online while collaborating in real time with other users. Examples include web apps for word processing, slideshows and presentations, spreadsheets, note taking, concept maps, and calendars.

RAM   See Random access memory.

Random access memory (RAM)   The flexible part of computer memory. The particular program or set of data being manipulated by the user is temporarily stored in RAM, then erased to make way for the next program.

Read-only memory (ROM)   Control instructions that have been "wired" permanently into the memory of a computer. Usually stores instructions that the computer will need constantly, such as the programming language(s) and internal monitoring functions.

Realistic visuals   Visuals that show the actual object under study.

Real object   Not a model or simulation but an example of an actual object used in instruction.

Relational visuals   Visuals that communicate quantitative relationships.

Removable storage device   High-capacity portable computer storage unit that allows the user to store information and move it from one computer to another.

Response to Intervention   A program of assessment and appropriate instructional assistance in schools.

ROM   See Read-only memory.

Scaffold   To build on prior knowledge as part of the learning process.

Scanner   A computer device that converts an image on a piece of paper into an electronic form that can be stored in a computer file.

School media center   An area of the school where a variety of media are organized and made available to students and teachers.

Search engine   A program that identifies Internet sites that contain user-identified keywords or phrases.

Semantic-aware application   Application that works with a user's computer to help it "understand" what the user wants to know and guides the search for an answer that addresses the question the user has posed.

Simulation   An abstraction or simplification of some real-life situation or process.

Slow motion   High-speed videography that slows down a motion so that we can observe the process.

Social bookmarking   Online service that enables users to organize, store, manage, and search for bookmarked resources online and provides users with links to online resources they want to remember and share.

Social media   Mobile and web-based applications that enable users to interact, collaborate, co-create, share, and publish information, ideas, and multimedia.

Social networking service   Website that facilitates online connections and interactions of users based on shared backgrounds, interests, and experiences. Users are able to share ideas, messages, information, and multimedia with people in their network.

Social psychology   The study of the effects of the social organization of the classroom on learning.

Standardized tests   State-wide tests that are administered in a consistent manner and using the same scoring procedures. These are used to identify student learning that is meeting or exceeding state standards and to determine where there is a need for improvement.

Storyboarding   An audiovisual production and planning technique in which sketches of the proposed visuals and verbal messages are put on individual cards or into a computer program; the items are then arranged into the desired sequence on a display surface.

Streaming   Transmission method by which an audio file itself stays on a network server, but the file is available to listeners on an audio device.

Streaming audio   Audio sent in packets to allow listening to portions of a file before all portions are downloaded.

Streaming video   A video file downloaded from the Internet that starts playing before it is completely downloaded.

Student-centered strategies   A type of learning experience in which the learners are involved in the direction of the experience.

Synchronously   Distance learning when all the participants are together at the same time.

Synchronous setting   A learning situation in which the teacher and the student are together at the same time, for example, a face-to-face classroom or real-time video conferencing.

Synthesizer software   Computer software used to create original music, radio programs, and other materials to demonstrate student learning; also called softsynth.

TB   See Terabyte.

Teacher-centered strategies   A type of learning experience in which the teacher directs the learners in the experience.

Technological competence   Knowing not only the basics of computer literacy, but also how and when to use technology to enhance student learning.

Technology   (1) A process of devising reliable and repeatable solutions to tasks. (2) The hardware and software (i.e., the products) that result from the application of technological processes. (3) A mix of process and product, used in instances where the context refers to the combination of technological processes and resultant products or where the process is inseparable from the product.

Technology lab   A room set apart from regular classrooms and furnished with multiple computers, usually established in schools that do not have computers in individual classrooms.

Technology literacy   Students' abilities to engage in the use of technology to support their learning and show competency in six key areas: creativity and innovation; communication and collaboration; research and information fluency; critical thinking, problem solving, and decision making; digital citizenship; and technology operations and concept.

Telecommunications   A means for communicating over a distance; specifically, any arrangement for transmitting voice and data in the form of coded signals through an electronic medium.

Terabyte (TB)   Approximately 1 million megabytes.

Text literacy   The ability to use text as a means to gather information or to communicate.

Time lapse   Videography that compresses the time it takes to observe an event.

Time shift   Experiencing instruction at some time after the live lesson.

Transformational visuals   Visuals that illustrate movement or change in time and space.

Tutorial   A teaching strategy in which content is presented, questions are posed, responses are given, and feedback is provided.

Two-way video   Video transmission in which visual and auditory information are exchanged across the system between learners and the teacher synchronously; also referred to as videoconferencing.

Understanding   The final step in the listening process that involves comprehension of auditory signals.

Uniform resource locator (URL)   The address for an Internet site or World Wide Web page containing the protocol type, the domain, the directory, and the name of the site or page.

URL   See Uniform resource locator.

USB (universal serial bus)   A hardware interface technology that allows the user to connect a device without having to restart the computer.

Video conferencing   Distance teaching using the computer and classroom cameras to both see and hear your students at a distance.

Videography   The creation of video.

Video literacy   The knowledge and skills needed to understand and evaluate video messages and to create video that appropriately achieves the intended outcomes.

Virtual field trip   A type of field trip in which the students do not leave the classroom setting; instead they use media to provide the experience of "being there."

Virtual public schools (VPS)   State-level initiatives that use the Internet for delivery of instruction and that offer courses or whole programs of study that students can access, including courses that might not be available to them at their local schools or advanced

placement classes from other high schools or from colleges and universities anywhere in the world.

Visual literacy   The learned ability to interpret visual messages accurately and to create such messages.

WAN   See Wide area network.

Web   See World Wide Web.

Web application   Browser technology used as a client to accomplish one or more tasks over a network, for example, webmail.

Webpages   Documents that make up the World Wide Web. See also Website.

WebQuest   A set of steps that provide guidance when seeking information about a simulated problem.

Website   A collection of webpages available on the Internet that provides information about products, services, events, materials, and so forth.

Web 2.0   Available online resources that provide students with many types of learning opportunities beyond simple information access.

Wide area network (WAN)   A communications network that covers a large geographic area, such as a state or country.

Wiki   A web-based document subject to edit by any of its users.

Wireless network   Computers connected by radio frequency, microwave, or infrared technology instead of wires.

Word cloud   A visual representation of text-based data used to convey concepts, key vocabulary, significant events, ideas from brainstorming, and much more; also called a tag cloud.

World Wide Web (the Web)   A graphical environment on computer networks that allows you to access, view, and maintain documents that can include text, data, sound, graphics, and video.

References

Chapter 1

Barnett, R. (2013, Feb.). Rise of Internet learning creates digital divide. *USA Today*. Retrieved from www .usatoday.com/story/news/nation/2013/02/16/ internet-learning-crates-digital-divide/1925189

Becker, G. H. (2003). *Copyright: A guide to information and resources* (3rd ed.). Lake Mary, FL: Gary H. Becker.

Bergmann, J. & Sams, A. (2012). *Flip your classroom: Reach every student in every class every day*. Washington, DC: International Society for Technology Education.

Calkins, L., Ehrenworth, M., & Lehman, C. (2012) *Pathways to the common core: Accelerating achievement*. Portsmouth, NH: Heinemann.

Center for Applied Special Technology [CAST] (2014). *Universal design for learning*. Retrieved from www.cast.org/ about/index.html

Common Core State Standards [CCSS] (2012). *Common Core State Standards*. Retrieved from www.corestandards.org

Gee R. (2012). Kickboard for teachers encourages data collection in the classroom. *Huffington Post*. Retrieved from www.huffingtonpost/yought-radio-youth-media- international/kickboard-for-teachers-en-b1506845.html

Hertz, M.B. (2012, July). The flipped classroom: Pro and con. *Edutopia*. Retrieved from www.edutopia.org/glog

International Society for Technology in Education [ISTE] (2012a). *National Educational Technology Standards for Students*. Retrieved from www.iste.org/students/index.html

International Society for Technology in Education [ISTE] (2012b). *National Educational Technology Standards for Teachers*. Retrieved from www.iste.org/Content/NavigationMenu/ NETS/ForTeachers/NETS_for_Teachers.htm

International Society for Technology in Education [ISTE] (2015). *ISTE Policy Brief*. Retrieved from www.iste.org

Lehman, B. A. (1998). *The conference on fair use: Final report to the commissioner on the conclusion of the conference on fair use*. Retrieved from www.uspto.gov/web/offices/dcom/olia/ confu/confurep.pdf

Lenart, A. (2015). Mobile access shifts social media use and other online activities. Pew Research Center. Retrieved from pewresearch.org

Moss, K. & Crowley, M. (2011). Effective learning in science: The use of personal response systems with wide range of audiences. *Computers in Education, 56*(1). P. 36–43.

Partnership for 21st Century Learning (2015). *Framework for 21st century learning*. Retrieved from www.21stcenturyskills. org/index.php?option=com_content&task=view&id=254&l temid=119

Prensky, M. (2006, December/January). Adopt and adapt: 21st century schools need 21st century technology. *Edutopia*, 43–45.

Rainie. L. & Cohn, D. (2014). Census: Computer ownership varies widely across U.S. Pew Research Center. Retrieved from pewresearch.orgé

Chapter 2

Bloom, B. & Krathwohl, M. D. (1984). *Taxonomy of educational objectives, Handbook 1: Cognitive domain*. New York: Addison-Wesley.

Churches, A. (2008). Bloom's taxonomy blooms digitally. *Tech & Learning*, 1. Retrieved from www .techlearning.com/studies-ined-tech/0020/ blooms-taxonomy-blooms-digitally/44988

Driscoll, M. P. (2013). *Psychology of learning for instruction* (4th ed.). Boston, MA: Allyn & Bacon.

Gagné, R. (1985). *The conditions of learning* (4th ed.). New York: Hold, Rinehart & Winston.

Gardner, H. (2011). *Multiple intelligences: New horizons*. New York: Basic Books.

International Society for Technology in Education [ISTE] (2012a). *National Educational Technology Standards for Students*. Retrieved from www.iste.org/students/index.html

Morrison, G. R. & Lowther, D. L. (2010) *Integrating computer technology into the classroom* (4th ed.). Upper Saddle River, NJ: Merrill/Prentice Hall.

Newby, Stephich, Lehman, & Russell (2010). *Educational technology for teaching and learning* (4th ed.). Columbus, OH: Pearson.

Partnership for 21st Century skills (n.d.). *Learning for the 21st century: Report and mile guide for 21s century skills*. Retrieved from www.21stcenturyskills.org

Piaget, J. (1977). *The development of thought: Equilibration of cognitive structures*. New York: Viking Press.

Slavin, R.E. (1990). Research on cooperative learning: Consensus and controversy. *Educational Leadership, 47*(4), 52–54.

U.S. Department of Education [USDOE] (2010) *National Education Technology Plan (NETP)*. Retrieved from www .ed.gov/technology/netp-2010

Waugh, C.K. & Gronlund, N.E. (2012). *Assessment of student achievement* (10th ed.). Columbus, OH: Pearson.

Chapter 3

American Association of School Librarians (ALA) (2007). *Standards for the 21st –Century Learner*. American Library Association. Retrieved from http://www.ala.org/aasl/ sites/ala.org.aasl/files/content/guidelinesandstandards/ learningstandards/AASL_Learning_Standards_2007.pdf

American Association of School Librarians (2007). *Standards for the 21st –Century Learner*. American Library Association. Retrieved from http://www.ala.org/aasl/sites/ala.org.aasl/

files/content/guidelinesandstandards/learningstandards/ AASL_Learning_Standards_2007.pdf

Bloom, B. S., Engelhart, M. D., Furst, E. J., Hill, W. H., & Krathwohl, D. R. (Eds.). (1956). *Taxonomy of educational objectives: The classification of educational goals. Handbook 1: Cognitive domain.* New York, NY: David McKay.

Brookhart, S. M. (2008). *How to Give Effective Feedback to Your Students.* Association for Supervision and Curriculum Development. Alexandria, VA. Retrieved from http://www .ascd.org/publications/books/108019/chapters/ Feedback@-An-Overview.aspx

Dick, W., Carey, L., & Carey, J. O. (2014). *The systematic design of instruction* (8th ed.). Boston, MA: Allyn & Bacon.

Gagné, R. M. (1985). *The conditions of learning* (4th ed.). New York, NY: Holt, Rinehart & Winston.

Gagné, R. M., Wager, W. W., Golas, K., & Keller, J.M. (2004). *Principles of instructional design* (5th ed.). Beverly, MA: Wadsworth Publishing.

Gardner, H. (2011). *Frames of the mind: The theory of multiple intelligences.* New York, NY: Basic Books.

Gronlund, N. E. (2009). *Writing instructional objectives for teaching and assessment* (8th ed.). Upper Saddle River, NJ: Merrill/Prentice Hall.

Hatami, S. (2012). Learning Styles. *English Language Teaching Journal, 67*(4), 488–490.

International Society for Technology in Education (ISTE). (2007). *National Educational Technology Standards for Students (NETS-S)* (2nd ed.). Eugene, OR: Author.

International Society for Technology in Education (ISTE). (2008). *National Educational Technology Standards for Teachers (NETS-T).* Eugene, OR: Author.

Keller, J. M. (2010). *Motivational design for learning and performance: The ARCS model approach.* New York, NY: Springer Science + Business Media.

Marzano, R. J., & Heflebower, T. (2012). *Teaching and assessing 21st century skills: The classroom strategies series.* Bloomington, IN: Marzano Research Laboratory.

Usher, A., & Kober, N. (2012). *Student motivation: An overlooked piece of school reform.* Retrieved December 2, 2012, from http://www.cep-dc.org/displayDocument .cfm?DocumentID=405

Chapter 4

Graesser, A. C. (2017). Reflections on serious games. In P. Wouters & H. Van Oostendorp (Eds.), *Instructional Techniques to Facilitate Learning and Motivation of Serious Games: Advances in game-based learning* (pp. 199–212). Switzerland: International Publishing.

Gupta, N. (2016, August 4). Tips to conduct successful classroom discussion. Retrieved from https://logicroots .com/MathBlog/14-teacher-tips-to-conduct-successful- classroom-discussion/

Heick, T. (2013, February 26). 4 teaching tips for more effective direct instruction. Retrieved from http://www .teachthought.com/pedagogy/instructional-strategies/4- teaching-tips-for-more-effective-direct-instruction/

Johnson, D. W., & Johnson, R. T. (1999). *Learning together and alone: Cooperative, competitive, and individualistic learning.* Boston, MA: Allyn & Bacon.

McLaughlin, C. (2016, May 16). Low-graduation-rate schools concentrated in charter, virtual school sectors. Retrieved from http://neatoday.org/2016/05/16/ low-graduation-rate-charter-virtual-schools/

National Center for Education Statistics (NCES) (2017, March). *The Condition of Education. English Language Learners in Public Schools.* Retrieved from https://nces.ed.gov/programs/coe/ indicator_cgf.asp

Slavin, R. E. (1989–1990). Research on cooperative learning: Consensus and controversy. *Educational Leadership, 47*(4), 52–54.

Smutny, J. F., & von Fremd, S. E. (2009). *Igniting creativity in gifted learners, K–6: Strategies for every teacher.* Thousand Oaks, CA: Corwin Press.

Chapter 5

Adams Becker, S., Freeman, A., Giesinger Hall, C., Cummins, M., and Yuhnke, B. (2016). *NMC/CoSN Horizon Report: 2016 K-12 Edition.* Austin, Texas: The New Media Consortium.

Gee, J. (2013), Games for learning, *Educational Horizons, 91*(4), 16–20.

International Society for Technology Education (ISTE) (2017). *National Educational Technology Standards for Students.* Eugene, OR: ISTE.

Jonassen, Howland, Moore, & Marra, (2003). *Learning to solve problems with technology: A constructivist perspective.* Upper Saddle River, NJ: Merrill/Prentice Hall.

Papert, S. (1993a). *The children's machine: Rethinking school in the age of the computer.* New York: Basic Books.

Papert, S. (1993b). *Mindstorms: Children, computers, and powerful ideas.* New York: Basic Books.

Shute, V., Rieber, L., & Van Eck, R. (2011). *Games . . . and . . . Learning.* Columbus, OH: Pearson.

Chapter 6

Greenhow, C., & Askari, E. (2017). Learning and teaching with social network sites: A decade of research in K-12 related education. *Education and Information Technologies, 22*(2), 623–645.

Pickett, P. (2017, May 09). Open-source software definition. *The Balance.* Retrieved from https://www.thebalance.com/ what-is-open-source-software-2071941

Tang, Y., & Foon Hew, K. (2017). Using Twitter for education: Beneficial or simply a waste of time? *Computers & Education, 106,* 97–118.

Chapter 7

Becker, G. H. (2003). *Copyright: A guide to information and resources* (3rd ed.). Lake Mary, FL: Gary H. Becker.

Dodge, B. (1999). *The WebQuest page.* Retrieved from www .webquest.org.

Keegan, D. (1980). *Foundations of distance education* (2nd ed.). Pyrmont, NSW: Law Book Co of Australasia.

Simonson, M., Smaldino, S., & Zvacek, S. (2014). *Teaching and learning at a distance: Foundations of distance education* (6th ed.). Charlotte, NC: Information Age Publishing.

Chapter 8

Clark, R. C. & Lyons, C. (2010). *Graphics for learning: Proven guidelines for planning, designing, and evaluating visuals in training materials* (2nd Ed.). San Francisco, CA: Pfeiffer.

De Moll, E. H., Routt, E., Heinecke, G., Tsu, C., & Levitt, J. (2015). The use of imagery mnemonic to teach porphyrin biochemical pathway. *Dermatology Online Journal, 21*(4), 1–6.

Gardner, H. (2011). *Frames of the mind: The theory of multiple intelligences.* New York, NY: Basic Books.

Handsfield, L. J., Dean, T. R., & Cielocha, K. M. (2009). Becoming critical consumers and producers of text: Web 1.0 and Web 2.0. *The Reading Teacher, 63*(1), 40–50.

Harris, C. (2014, January, 31). Tips for creating instructional videos. Instaructional Development Center Blog: Information Technology at Purdue. Retreived from https://www.purdue.edu/learning/blog/?p=6696

International Reading Association (2012). *Literacy Implementation Guidance for the ELA Common Core State Standards.* Retrieved from http://www.ldonline.org/article/56488/

Jolls, T. (2008). *Literacy for the 21st century: An overview and orientation guide to media literacy education.* Retrieved May 11, 2010, from http://www.medialit.org/reading_room/article540.html

Mayer, R. E. (2012). *Multimedia learning* (2nd ed.). New York, NY: Cambridge.

Mayer, R. E. (2014). Incorporating motivation into multimedia learning. *Learning and Instruction, 29*, 171–173.

Morgan, H. (2013). Technology in the classroom: Creating videos can lead students to many academic benefits. *Childhood Education, 89*(1), 51–53. http://www.tandfonline.com/doi/abs/10.1080/00094056.2013.757534

National Association for Media Literacy (2016). Resources, Media Literacy Defined. Retrieved from https://namle.net/publications/media-literacy-definitions

National Center for Education Statistics (NCES) (2015). *National Assessment of Educational Progress (NAEP), 2015 Reading Assessment.* Retrieved from https://nces.ed.gov/nationsreportcard/reading/distributequest.aspx

National Center for Missing & Exploited Children® (NCMEC) (2016). Netsnartz Workshop. Retrieved from www.netsmartz.org/RealLifeStories

National Assessment Governing Board. (2010). *Writing framework for the 2011 National Assessment of Educational Progress.* Washington, DC: U.S. Government Printing Office.

National Governors Association Center for Best Practices (NGA Center) & Council of Chief State School Officers (CCSSO). (2010). *Common Core State Standards, English Language Arts.* Retrieved March 26, 2013, from http://www.corestandards.org/assets/CCSSI_ELA%20Standards.pdf

Paivio, A. (1971). *Imagery and verbal processes.* New York, NY: Holt, Rinehart & Winston.

Putnam, A. L. (2015). Mnemonics in education: Current research and applications. *Translational Issues in Psychological Science, 1*(2), 130–139.

Rowe, S. S. (2012). A new kind of currency: Informational text literacy in elementary school. *National Association of School Psychologists. Communiqué.* Retrieved March 26, 2013, from http://www.readperiodicals.com/201201/2576109791.html#b

StoryCenter (2016). *About StoryCenter.* Retrieved from http://www.storycenter.org/about/

United States Access Board (2015). Section 508 of the Rehabilitation Act: Application and Scoping Requirements, E103.4 Defined Terms: Audio Description. Retrieved from https://www.access-board.gov/guidelines-and-standards/communications-and-it/about-the-ict-refresh/proposed-rule/text-of-the-proposed-rule

Chapter 9

ALELO (2016). RALL-E Project. Retrieved from https://www.alelo.com/rall-e-project/

Bazhanov, V., & Scholz, R. W. (2015). *Transdisciplinarity in philosophy and science: Approaches, problems, prospects.* Moscow: Navigator.

Berland, M. (2016). Making, tinkering, and computational literacy. In K. Peppler, E. R. Halverson, & Y. B. Kafai (Eds.), *Makeology: Makers as learners* (pp. 196–204). New York, NY: Routledge.

Botball (2016). Aligned standards and national impact. STEM alignment. Retrieved from http://www.botball.org/standards-impact

Carnegie Learning (2016). Cognitive tutor software: For students grades 9–12. Retrieved from https://www.carnegie-learning.com/learning-solutions/software/cognitive-tutor/

Computer Using Educators (Cue) (2016). About. Retrieved from http://www.cue.org/

Connected Learning Research Network (CLRN) (2016a). Relevant education for today's world. Retrieved from http://connectedlearning.tv/educators

Connected Learning Research Network (CLRN) (2016b). A learning approach designed for the demands and opportunities of the digital age: Powerful, relevant, engaging. Retrieved from http://connectedlearning.tv/what-is-connected-learning

Connected Learning Research Network (CLRN) (2016c). Connected learning principles. Retrieved from http://connectedlearning.tv/connected-learning-principles

Deloitte (2016). Robotics technology. Retrieved from http://government-2020.dupress.com/driver/robotics-technology

Discovery College (2016). Transdisciplinary teaching and learning. Curriculum: Primary Years Programme. Retrieved from http://www.discovery.edu.hk/curriculum/primary-years-programme/transdisciplinary-teaching-learning/

Everette, M. (2016). Join now: Why teachers need professional organizations. Scholastic Teachers. Retrieved from http://www.scholastic.com/teachers/top-teaching/2016/04/join-now-why-teachers-need-professional-organizations

Fredrick, K. (2015). Dressing for the future: Wearable technology. *School Library Monthly, 31*(4), 25–26.

Gallup (2016). Pioneering results in the blueprint of U.S. K-12 computer science education. Retrieved from http://csedu .gallup.com/home.aspx

GlobalSchoolNet (GSN). Our mission. Retrieved from http:// www.globalschoolnet.org/

Guston, D. (2016). Welcome to the new school of the future of innovation in society. Retrieved from https://sfis.asu.edu/ about/directors-welcome

Hamilton, K. E. (2016). Augmented reality in education. Retrieved from https://augmented-reality-in-education .wikispaces.com/

iEARN (2016). Learn with the world, not just about it. About. Retrieved from https://iearn.org/about

International Association for K-12 Online Learning (iNACOL) (2016). About. Retrieved from http://www.inacol.org/

International Society for Technology in Education (2016). Our mission. Retrieved from https://www.iste.org/about/ iste-story

Keane, L., & Keane, M. (2016). STEAM by design. *Design and Technology Education: An International Journal*, 21(1), 61–82.

Luckin, R., Holmes, W., Griffiths, M. & Forcier, L. B. (2016). Intelligence Unleashed. An argument for AI in Education. London: Pearson. https://www.pearson.com/content/ dam/corporate/global/pearson-dot-com/files/innovation/ Intelligence-Unleashed-Publication.pdf

Nagel, D. (2016). Google Expeditions in full rollout, iOS version to follow. Retrieved from https://thejournal.com/ articles/2016/06/27/google-expeditions-in-full-rollout-ios-version-to-follow.aspx

National Aeronautics and Space Administration (NASA) (2016). The robotics alliance project. Retrieved from https:// robotics.nasa.gov/

National Aeronautics and Space Administration (NASA) (2016a). Robotics alliance project objectives. Retrieved from https://robotics.nasa.gov/milestones.php

Next Generation Science Standards (NGSS) (2012). Three Dimensional Learning. Retrieved from http://www .nextgenscience.org/

NMC Horizon Project (2016). NMC Horizon Report Preview: 2016 K-12 Edition. Retrieved from http://cdn.nmc.org/ media/2016-nmc-horizon-report-k12-preview.pdf

Pearson (2016). Successmaker. Retrieved from http://www .pearsonschool.com/

Penuel, W. R., & Johnson, R. (2016). *Review of continued progress: Promising evidence on personalized learning.* Bolder, CO: National Education Policy Center.

Rheingold, H. (2016, June 20). Research shows connected learning works. Digital Media + Learning Central. Retrieved from http://dmlcentral.net/research-shows-connected-learning-works/?variation=b&utm_expid=42725708-5.oNX7Gn2HRIOm8WhS1GUvRg.1&utm_referrer=http%3A%2F%2Fdmlhub.net%2F

Ribeiro, J. (2016). *Wearable technology spending: A strategic approach to decision-making.* Hershey, PN: IGI Global.

Tobe, F. (2016). Fascinating projections: $100 billion robotics industry by 2020. *Robohub*. Retrieved from http://robohub .org/fascinating-projections-100-billion-robotics-industry-by-2020/

Trust, T., Krutka, D. G., & Carpenter, J. P. (2016). "Together we are better": Professional learning networks for teachers. *Computers & Education*, 102(November), 15–34.

United Nations Division for Sustainable Development (UN-DESA) (2016). Sustainable development knowledge platform. Retrieved from https://sustainabledevelopment .un.org/sdgs

US Department of Education Office of Educational Technology (DOE-OET) (2016). *Future ready schools: Reimagining the role of technology in education.* Retrieved from http://tech.ed.gov/ netp/

US Department of Education Office of Educational Technology (DOE-OET) (2016a). Future Ready Schools: Building Technology Infrastructure for Learning. Retrieved from http://tech.ed.gov/futureready/infrastructure/

U.S. Department of Labor Bureau of Labor Statistics (2013). *Employment projections – 2012–2022.* Retrieved from https:// www.bls.gov/news.release/archives/ecopro_12192013.pdf

VIF (2014). International education: Global-Ready Teacher Competency Framework. Retrieved from https://www .viflearn.com/featured-resources

Name Index

Adams Becker, S., 96
Ahu, T., 43, 51, 54, 56, 60
Alonso, D., 183
Amanpour, C., 128
Ambrose, S. A., 63
Anderson, E. K., 208
Anderson, R., 38
Anderson, W. G., 166
Armstrong, N., 126
Askari, E., 132

Baker, F. W., 63
Barlés, M. J., 208
Barnett, R., 3
Barrett, H., 36
Bassett, K., 94
Bates, A. W., 94
Baylen, D. M., 208
Bazhanov, V., 214
Becker, G. H., 18, 152
Belanche, D., 208
Berg, J., 208
Bergmann, J., 7
Bessesen, M., 183
Bird, K., 96–97, 101, 113, 115
Bloom, B., 26, 54
Bridges, M. W, 63
Brookhart, S. M., 56
Brooks-Young, S. J., 63
Brynteson, K., 208
Burns, M., 231

Calkins, L., 11
Carey, J. O., 42
Carey, L., 42
Carpenter, J. P., 222
Carr, C. E., 231
Carr, M. L., 208
Carr-Chellman, A. A., 63
Casaló, L., 208
Cennamo, K., 20
Chappuis, J., 63
Chun, J., 140, 141, 145, 146, 157, 164
Churches, A., 26
Cielocha, K. M., 170
Clark, R. C., 195
Cohn, D., 3
Conrad, R. M., 166
Cook, A., 38
Courbat, C., 79
Couros, G., 231
Crowley, M., 8
Cummins, M., 96

D'Alba, A., 208
Damodaran, S., 138

Davis, V., 118, 120, 122, 133, 135
Dean, T. R., 170
Dell, A., 117
De Moll, E. H., 198
Dick, W., 42
DiPietro, M., 63
Dodge, B., 153
Doering, A., 38, 117
Donaldson, J. A., 166
Dowd, H., 117
Driscoll, M. P., 22

Earhart, A, 126
Edwards, M., 212
Engelhart, M. D., 54
Ertmer, P., 20
Everette, M., 223

Foon Hew, K., 128
Forcier, L. B., 216
Fraj, E., 208
Franey, J. J., 94
Fredrick, K., 220
Freeman, A., 96
Furst, E. J., 54

Gagné, R. M., 26, 40, 52
Gammon, C., 10, 223
Gardner, H., 28, 42, 178
Gee, J., 101
Gee, R., 8
Giesinger Hall, C., 96
Golas, K., 52
Golding, W., 183
Graesser, A. C., 73
Greene, K., 138
Greenhow, C., 132
Gregory, G. H., 63
Griffiths, M., 216
Gronlund, N. E., 37, 46
Gupta, N., 66
Guretzky, J., 94
Gurrea, R., 208
Guston, D., 213
Gwee, S., 138

Hamilton, B., 117
Hamilton, K. E., 216
Handsfield, L. J., 170
Harris, C., 186
Hatami, S., 43
Hayes-Jacobs, H., 208
Heflebower, T., 48
Heick, T., 66
Heide, S., 138
Heinecke, G., 198

Hertz, M. B., 7
Higgins, K., 220
Hill, W. H., 54
Holmes, W., 216
Horsley, M. K, 94
Hourigan, T., 94
Howland, J., 38, 99
Hunter, J., 20

James, C., 231
James, S., 169, 179, 187, 193, 204, 205
Johnson, D. W., 71
Johnson, R., 214
Johnson, R. T., 71
Jolls, T., 181
Jonassen, D. H., 38, 99

Kaiser, L., 65–66, 66, 78, 85, 91
Karlin, M., 138
Keane, L., 215
Keane, M., 215
Keegan, D., 140
Keller, J. M., 51, 52
King, M. L., 174
Kober, N., 49
Kohmetscher, A., 94
Krakower, B., 20
Krathwohl, D., 26, 54
Krutka, D. G., 222
Kuzmich, L. M., 63

Laufenberg, D., 31
Lee, D., 94
Leftwich, A. T., 208
Lehman, B. A., 16
Lehman, C., 11
Lehman, J. D., 25, 208
Lehmann, C., 30
Lenart, A., 3
Levitt, J., 198
Lipinski, T. A., 166
Lovett, M. C., 63
Lowther, D. L., 25, 81, 131, 177, 185, 192, 197
Luckin, R., 216
Lyons, C., 195

Mager, R. F., 33, 38
Marcus, A. S., 94
Marcus-Quinn, A., 94, 138
Marra, R., 99
Marshall, J., 65–66, 66, 78, 85, 91
Martin, F., 208
Marzano, R. J., 48
Mayer, R. E., 170, 195
McCullough, D., 12

McJohn, S., 20
McKnight, K., 94
McLaughlin, C., 86
Miles, S., 138
Mims, C., 38, 81, 131, 177, 185, 192, 197
Moore, J., 38, 99
Moore, M. G., 166
Morgan, H., 180
Morrison, G. R., 25
Moss, K., 8
Murphy, P., 94

Namuth-Covert, D., 94
Newby, T. J., 25, 208
Newton, D., 117
Norman, M. K., 63
Nugent, G., 94
Nye, B., 128

O'Bannon, B., 117
O'Malley, K., 94
Orey, M., 231
Orús, C., 208
Ozogul, G., 138

Padak, N., 208
Paivio, A., 195
Palloff, R. M., 166
Papert, S., 99
Pawlicki, D., 231
Penuel, W. R., 214
Petroff, J., 117
Piaget, J., 22

Pickert, A., 201
Plante, S., 20
Polgar, J., 38
Powell G., 138
Pratt, K., 166
Prensky, M., 15
Puckett, K., 117
Putnam, A. L., 198

Rainie, L., 3, 11
Rasinski, T., 208
Reeves, D. L., 231
Rheingold, H., 214
Ribble, M., 63
Ribeiro, J., 217, 219
Rieber, L., 101
Robinson, R. S., 208
Roblyer, M., 38, 117
Rodriguez, A., 169
Rose, M., 173
Ross, J., 20
Routt, E., 198
Rowe, S. S., 170
Rowling, J. K., 128
Rushby, N., 94
Russell, J. D., 25, 208
Ruzic, R., 94

Sams, A., 7
Scholz, R. W., 214
Schrock, K., 50
Shank, P., 166
Shute, V., 101

Simonson, M., 140, 166
Skinner, B. F., 22
Slavin, R. E., 24, 71
Smaldino, S. E., 81, 131, 140, 166, 177, 185, 192, 197
Smutny, J. F., 72
Stepich, D., 25, 208
Stiggins, R. J., 63
Stoddard, J. D., 94
Strong, W., 20
Stroud, T., 183
Surry, D. W., 94

Tang, Y., 128
Tobe, F., 217
Traw, R., 154
Trust, T., 222
Tsu, C., 198

Usher, A., 49

Van Eck, R., 101
Veletsianos, G., 94
von Fremd, S. E., 73

Wager, W. W., 52
Waugh, C. K., 37
Woodward, W. W., 94
Wright, S., 155

Yuhnke, B., 97

Zvacek, S., 140, 166

Subject Index

AAC audio, 175
AACE (Association for the Advancement of Computing in Education), 224
ABCDs of learning objectives, 45–47
ABC News, 89
Abstract information, 181, 195
Acceptable use policies, 149
Accessibility of online resources, 157
Acoustica, 179
Adaptability, as technology benefit, 3, 4, 13
Adaptive learning environments, 214
Administrators, teacher evaluations by, 58, 59
Advanced Audio Coding (AAC), 175
Adventures of Cyberbee website, 166
Advertising in free materials, 88
AECT (Association for Educational Communications and Technology), 20, 223–224
Affective learning, 180
Algorithms, 213
Alphabet books, 68
American Association of School Librarians, 224
American Library Association (ALA), 20, 224
Amersfort School of Social Awareness, 77
Analyzing learners (ASSURE model), 41–43, 212
Animations, 203
Annenberg Foundation, 147
Appendices in grant proposals, 229
Apple, 87, 179, 186, 201
Applications (apps), defined, 105. See also Software
Application stage (Bloom's Taxonomy), 26
Arial font, 201
Artificial intelligence, 215–216
Askkids.com website, 160
Assessment
  in ASSURE model, 57, 212–213
  computer use for, 98–99
  in distance learning, 143
  entry competencies, 42
  linking to standards and objectives, 41
  major approaches, 32–37
  of prior knowledge, 24
  use of audio with, 175
Assessment Focus website, 36
Assessment tools, 8–9
Assistive technologies, 4, 13

Association for Educational Communications and Technology (AECT), 20, 223–224
Association for the Advancement of Computing in Education (AACE), 224
ASSURE model. See also Case studies
  analyzing learners step, 41–43, 212
  evaluation and revision step, 57–61, 212–213
  learner participation step, 54–56, 212
  overview, 1, 3, 40, 41
  provisions for innovation, 212–213
  resource use step, 52–54, 212
  standards and objectives step, 44–47, 212
  strategy and resource selection, 48–51, 212
Asynchronous settings, 86, 145
AT&T Aspire program, 227
Attention, directing with visuals, 195
Attitudes, video's effects, 180
Attitude scales, 33
Audacity app, 174
Audience for learning objectives, 45
Audio
  as communications medium, 5, 6
  copyright protections, 18, 178
  language instruction podcasts, 132
  in portfolios, 36
  in presentations, 203
  selecting resources, 49, 175, 176–177
  sharing, 125, 126
  strengths and limitations, 171–172
  suggested applications, 100, 173–175
  use in distance learning, 143, 144, 145–146
  when to use, 172–173
Audio description of video, 182
Audio literacy, 170
Audio Literature Odyssey, 126
Audio teleconferences, 145–146
Augment app, 217
Augmented reality, 216–217
Aurasma Studio app, 217
Authentic assessment, 32–34, 57
Awesome Library, 117

Backgrounds, in presentation slides, 202
Bar graphs, 200
Behaviorism, 22
Behaviors, learning objectives for, 45
Benchmarks, 23
Best Kids Apps website, 117
Bias, 88, 133
Biblionasium, 128

Big List of Educational Grants and Resources, 232
Bill and Melinda Gates Foundation, 224
Bits, 109
Blackboard, 141, 146, 160
Blended instruction, 86–87, 141
Blended learning, 15, 16
Blippar app, 217
Blogs, 12, 121, 156
Bloom's Taxonomy, 26–27
Bookmarking, social, 124–125
Book reviews, 173–174
Books, digital, 190
Botball® Educational Robotics Program, 218
BP Global, 89
Broadcast materials, 89, 167, 182–183
Build effects, 203
Business organizations, instructional materials from, 89
Bytes, 109

CAD programs, 114
Calculators, 100
Cameras, 203
Carnegie Learning, 215
Case studies
  distance learning, 139, 141, 145, 146, 148, 157, 164–165
  electronic portfolios for English instruction, 40, 43, 51, 53, 56, 60
  Lewis and Clark lessons, 65, 71, 78, 85, 91–93
  multimedia tools, 169, 179, 187, 193, 204, 205–207
  water cycle instruction, 96, 97, 101, 113, 115–116
  Web 2.0 tools, 118, 120, 122, 133, 135–137
Cell phones, 3. See also Mobile devices
Center for Education and Research in Information Assurance and Security, 148
Central processing units, 109
Charts, 199, 200
Checklists for assessment, 32–33
Children's Technology and Engineering journal, 225
Chunking, 68
Circle graphs, 200
Cisco Systems Education Investments, 227
Civil War miniseries, 183
Class blogs, 121
Classification charts, 199

Classroom environment. *See* Learning environments
Clickers, 8
Closed captioning, 174
Cloud computing, 119
CNN Interactive website, 167
Coding literacy, 213–214
Cognitive learning skills, 26–27
Cognitive mapping apps, 77
Cognitivism, 22–23
Collaboration
  in distance learning, 142, 144
  instructional technology for, 77, 78
  in learning activities, 54–55
  between teachers, 155–156, 221–222
  virtual agents, 216
  Web 2.0 tools, 119, 120
Color, in presentation visuals, 202
Common Core State Standards, 11, 44, 189. *See also* Standards
Common Core Writing in Action website, 209
Common Curriculum website, 63
Common Sense Education, 94, 231
Communication tools, 12–13
Community information, 156
Community of practice activities, 9
Competition
  cooperative learning versus, 24, 72
  to promote STEM careers, 217, 218
  with use of games, 72, 73
Comprehension stage (Bloom's Taxonomy), 26
Computer-assisted instruction, 101–102
Computer conferencing, 155
Computer-managed instruction, 102
Computers. *See also* Digital devices; Instructional technology
  artificial intelligence, 215–216
  distribution in classrooms, 110–113
  evolution of instructional role, 97–98, 99
  hardware, 108–110
  monitoring student use, 112, 148–150
  use in distance learning, 147
Computer science skills, 213–214
Computers for Learning program, 227
Computer Using Educators (CUE), 224
Conative skills, 48
Concept-mapping software, 77, 99
Concrete–abstract continuum, 194
Concrete referents, visuals as, 194–195
Conditions for assessment, 45–46, 47
Conference on Fair Use, 16
Configurations, computer, 108
Connected learning, 214
Constructivism, 23, 32
ContentBarrier software, 149
Contexts for learning, 83–87. *See also* Learning environments
Convenience of distance learning, 150
Cooperative Extension Services, 89

Cooperative learning
  instructional technology for, 78, 79
  research support for, 24, 25
  strengths and limitations, 71–72
  when to use, 82
Copyright
  audio and music, 18, 178
  distance learning and, 142, 150, 151, 152
  as factor in material selection, 50
  overview of legal concerns, 16–18
  pinboard images, 126–127
  software protections, 98, 102
  video, 18, 187
  visuals, 203
Copyright Act (1976), 17, 98
Costs for distance learning, 151
Course management tools, 146
Creative Commons, 94, 127, 166
Critical thinking, 55
Cross-cultural understandings, 27–28, 180
CUE (Computer Using Educators), 224
Cues, in video, 183–186
Culture, instructional effectiveness and, 27–28
Currency of online resources, 150
Curriculum standards, 10–11. *See also* Standards
Curriki website, 90
Cyberbullying, 133, 148, 149
Cyberbullying Research Center, 133

Decisions, Decisions software, 111
Decoding visuals, 170
Degree, in ABCDs of learning objectives, 46
Demonstrations, 67–68, 76, 82. *See also* Presentations
Department of Education (U.S.), 89
Department of Health and Human Services (U.S.), 89
Desks, interactive, 90
Desktop computers. *See* Computers
Desktop publishing, 100
Digital audio, 175–179. *See also* Audio
Digital books, 190
Digital cameras, 203
Digital citizenship, 149–150
Digital devices. *See also* Instructional technology; Mobile devices
  evolution of instructional role, 96–99
  funding for, 226–229
  general impact on instruction, 96, 99
  major types, 99–102, 108–110
  selection criteria, 105–108
  strengths and limitations, 102–103
  successful integration in classroom, 103–104
Digital divide, 3
Digital learners, 11–14
Digital manipulatives, 6

Digital Millennium Copyright Act of 1998, 178
Digital Performance Right in Sound Recordings Act of 1995, 178
Digital portfolios, 36. *See also* Electronic portfolios
Digital projectors, 109
Digital Resources for Lifelong Learners of All Ages website, 64
Digital Taxonomy, 26–27
Digital teachers, 7–11, 221
Diigo, 124
Dioramas, 85
Disabled students. *See* Individual differences
Discovery, 74–75, 82
Discovery Education website, 231
Discussions, 69–70, 77, 143
Displays, 85
Distance learning
  case study, 139, 141, 145, 146, 148, 157, 164–165
  critical issues, 148–150, 152
  elements of, 15, 16, 140–142
  evaluating resources for, 160–162
  instructional technology for, 142, 144–147
  integrating with classroom instruction, 152–157
  networks for, 158–160
  strategies, 143–144
  strengths and limitations, 150–151
  when to use, 85–86
Documentary video, 182–183
Document cameras, 76
Downloads, copyright protections, 152
Dramatizations, 180, 183
Drawp app, 209
Drill-and-practice, 68–69, 76, 101–102
Dynamic Indicators of Basic Early Literacy Skills (DIBELS), 9
Dyslexia, 190

Editing video, 186
Edmentum, 77
Edmodo, 127, 146
EDSITEment, 89
EdTechTeacher website, 64, 231–232
Educational games. *See* Games
Educational Robotics Matrix, 218
Education Week, 226
Education World website, 50, 64
EduClipper website, 126
Edutopia website, 20, 231, 232
Electronic pen pals, 153, 154
Electronic portfolios
  as assessment tools, 36
  case study, 40, 43, 51, 53, 56, 60
Elementary and Secondary Education Act, 227
Elements 4D app, 217
Ellis Island Experience, 104
Email, 149–150, 152, 153

Emoticons, 150
Encoding visuals, 170
English Language Arts standards, 189
English language learners
   benefits of audio for, 172, 174
   digital tools for, 4, 68, 132
   growing number, 22
Enrichment centers, 84
entrsekt journal, 225
Entry tests, 42
Environment. *See* Learning
   environments
eSchool News, 20, 38, 226
Evaluate and revise step (ASSURE
   model), 57–61, 212–213
Evaluation plans, in grant
   proposals, 229
Evaluation stage (Bloom's
   Taxonomy), 26
Exhibits, 85
Extreme Event simulation, 79

Fabbers, 114
Facebook, 119
Face-to-face learning, 15–16, 83–85
Facial recognition technology, 219
FactMonster.com website, 160
Fair use
   audio recordings and music, 178
   for distance learning settings, 142
   guidelines, 17
   pinboard images, 126–127
   software, 98
   video recordings, 187
Federal grants, 227
Federal publications, 89
Federal Reserve Education, 94
Federal Resources for Educational
   Excellence, 144
Feedback
   in distance learning, 143–144
   informative, 54, 56
   instructional effectiveness and, 25
   software features, 108
Fees for use of copyrighted
   material, 18
Fermilab, 94
Field trips, virtual, 156, 183
File servers, 158
Filtering software, 149
Fire departments, instructional
   materials from, 89
Firewalls, 159
FIRST Robotics Competition, 218
Five-point scales, 33
Five Ps process, 41, 52–54
Flashcards, 68
Flash drives, 110
Flipped classroom model, 7
Flowcharts, 199
Fonts, 201–202
Foreign governments, instructional
   materials from, 89

Format changes, 18
Forwarding copyrighted content, 152
Four-point scales, 33
Free and inexpensive materials,
   87–90, 119
FREE.ED, 89
Funding for technology, 226–229
Fundraiser websites, 227
Future Ready Learning goals, 212

Games
   augmented reality, 217
   for English language learners, 68
   for problem solving, 55
   selection criteria, 49, 80–81
   strengths and limitations,
      72–73, 101
   variety of instructional types, 78–79
GarageBand software, 179
Gardner's multiple intelligences,
   28–29, 42–43, 178
Gary Becker's Copyright Information
   Site, 20
Gateways, 159
General Services Administration
   (U.S.), 227
GeoBee Challenge, 147
Gifted and talented students
   technology adaptations for, 4
   use of audio, 174
   use of video, 182
   visual resources, 198
Gigabytes, 109
Gizmos website, 74
Global collaboration, 221–222
GlobalSchoolNet, 27
Global SchoolNet Foundation, 224
GLOBE program, 156
Glogster, 129
Goals in grant proposals, 228
GoFundMe website, 227
GoGooligans.com website, 160
Google Cardboard, 219
Google Docs, 36, 87, 123, 209
Google Expeditions, 219
Google Maps, 128, 129
Google SafeSearch technology, 160
GoogleScholastic.com website, 160
Google Slides, 201
Gooru website, 90
Government grants, 227
Governments, instructional materials
   from, 89
Grants, 226–229
Grants.gov website, 227
Graphics, 100–101. *See also* Visuals
Graphite platform, 231
Graphs, 200
Greatest Speeches of the 20th Century
   website, 126
Group activities in distance learning,
   144. *See also* Collaboration
Guggenheim Museum, 156

Hardware, computer, 108–110, 159
Hashtags, 128
Head mounted devices, 219–220
Hearing impairments, 4, 174
Helpful Hundred list, 45
High-speed Internet, 3
High-tech assistance, 4
History/social studies literacy, 189
Humor, in email and texts, 150
Hybrid learning environments, 154
Hyperlinks, 147, 152, 157
Hypertext transfer protocol, 159

Icons, visuals as, 194
IDEA, 227
iEARN, 222
Ill-structured problems, 70
Illustrative Mathematics website, 90
iMotion HD app, 208–209
iMovie app, 186
iNACOL (International Association
   for K-12 Online Learning),
   224–225
Inappropriate content
   in distance learning settings, 149,
      150, 151
   on social networks, 127, 133
   on video sites, 125, 133
Inclusion, technology's role, 13
Independent study, 87
Individual differences
   accommodating in
      presentations, 66
   accommodating in tutorials, 69
   advantages of digital devices, 102
   advantages of video, 181
   audio resources to address, 157
   distance learning resources for, 157
   identifying, 13–14, 42–43
   instructional effectiveness and,
      25, 29
   learning objectives for, 47
   software and apps to address, 105
   technology's benefits, 4
   text learning resources, 190
   visual resources, 198
   Web 2.0 tools to address, 132
Informal study, 87
Information, instruction versus,
   25–26
Informational text, 189
Information chunking, 68
Information literacy skills, 55
Information storage, as technology
   benefit, 3
Informative feedback, 54, 56
Innovation, 54, 212, 213
Input devices, 108–109
Inspiration software, 186
Instruction, effective, 24–29
Instructional environment, 26. *See also*
   Learning environments
Instructional formats, 15–16

Instructional materials
  accessibility standards, 13
  copyright protections, 16–18
  for distance learning, 142, 143, 144, 147, 150–151
  free and inexpensive, 87–90, 119
  overview, 6–7
  previewing and preparing, 52
  selecting and modifying, 49–50
Instructional strategies. *See also* Learning environments
  in ASSURE model, 41, 48–49, 212
  cooperative learning, 71–72, 78, 82
  demonstrations, 67–68, 76, 82
  describing in grant proposals, 228–229
  discovery, 74–75, 82
  discussions, 69–70, 77, 143
  drill-and-practice, 68–69, 76, 101–102
  emerging models, 213–215
  evaluation and revision, 57–61, 212–213
  gaming, 72–73, 78–79, 80–81
  linking to standards and objectives, 44
  presentations, 66–67, 75–76, 82
  problem-based learning, 70–71, 77, 82
  simulations, 73–74, 79–81
  tutorials, 69, 76–77
Instructional technology. *See also* Digital devices; Media; Software
  adoption process, 15–16
  benefits for students, 11–14
  benefits for teachers, 7–11, 220–222
  describing in learning objectives, 47
  for distance learning, 142, 144–147
  emerging applications, 213–215
  evaluating use, 57–61
  funding for, 226–229
  future tools, 215–220
  for presentations, 66
  previewing and preparing, 52
  principles for effective use, 29–30
  role in learning environments, 2–6, 96
  search engines for kids, 160
  selection criteria, 49, 104, 105–108
  support systems for, 14
  for various instructional strategies, 75–82
Integrated learning systems, 77
Intelligence, artificial, 215–216
Intelligences, multiple, 28–29, 42–43
Intelligent tutors, 216
Interactive multitouch desks, 90
Interactive tools, 12, 75
Interest centers, 83–84
International Association for K-12 Online Learning (iNACOL), 224–225
International Literacy Association, 209
International Reading Association, 189

International Society for Technology in Education (ISTE)
  activities of, 225
  learning objectives, 44
  standards development, 96–97
  standards for students, 13
  standards for teachers, 9–10
  website, 38
International Technology and Engineering Educators Association, 225
International Visual Literacy Association website, 209
Internet radio, 175
Internet Safety Game, 157
Internet service providers, 159
Internet use
  digital learning tools, 12–13
  disparities, 3
  media centers for, 16
  overview, 159
  supervision, 112, 148–150
Internships, 217, 218
Interpretive visuals, 200, 201
InTime, 117
Intranets, 157, 159
iTunes, 175
iTunes U app, 232
iWork software, 87

Journals, 224, 225–226
Justification, in presentation slides, 202
Just-in-time peer demonstrations, 67

Kathy Schrock's Guide to Everything, 50, 64, 117
Kellogg Foundation, 227
Keynote software, 201
Key pals, 153, 154
KidPix software, 54
KidRex.org website, 160
Kidsclick.org website, 160
Kids.com website, 157
Kidspiration software, 186
Kits, use in distance learning, 144
Knowledge stage (Bloom's Taxonomy), 26
Kurzweil, 190

Labs, technology, 112–113
Language instruction, 4, 132. *See also* English language learners
Learning, defined, 21
Learning abilities, analyzing, 41–43, 212
Learning Ally, 190
Learning centers, 83–84, 111, 174
Learning communities, 120
Learning environments. *See also* Instructional strategies
  effective, 24–29
  emerging models, 213–215
  future needs, 212
  future technologies, 215–220

  hybrid, 154
  preparing, 52
  social-psychological perspective, 24
  technology's role, 2–3, 15–16
  various contexts, 83–87
Learning management systems, 160
Learning objectives, 25, 41, 44–47
Learning Styles Inventory, 38
Learning theories, 22–24
Lesson Plans for Teachers website, 63
Lewis and Clark case study, 65, 71, 78, 85, 91–93
Libraries, 89, 144, 224
Library media centers, 16. *See also* Media centers
Library media specialists, 50, 142
Line graphs, 200
Literacies
  coding, 213–214
  Common Core standards, 189
  for learning, 14
  media use, 31, 170–171
  technology use, 30
Literacy in History/ Social Studies, Science, and Technical Subjects standards, 189
Literary text, 189
Living documents, 147
Local area networks (LANs), 158
Lockheed Martin Corporation Philanthropy, 227
Long-term memory, 23
Low-tech assistive devices, 4

MakerEd, 204
Maker Movement, 204
MakerSpace, 204
Manipulatives, 6, 84–85
Marine Advanced Technology Education ROV Competition, 218
Mashups, 120, 128–129
Master slides, 202
Matching games, 68
Math Blaster, 55, 102
Mathematics resources, 9
Math-Only-Math Blog, 121
mCLASS: Reading 3D software, 8–9
Media. *See also* Instructional technology
  copyright protections, 16–18
  free and inexpensive, 87–90, 119
  linking to standards and objectives, 41
  major formats, 3–6
  previewing and preparing, 52
  principles for effective use, 31
  selection criteria, 6, 49
  use in distance learning, 143, 144, 145–147
  with various instructional strategies, 75–82, 104
Media centers
  distance learning access, 142

libraries as, 16
    specialized staff, 50, 142
    tutorials in, 77
Media formats, 3–6
Media specialists, 50, 142
Medium-tech assistive devices, 4
Megabytes, 109
Memory (computer), 109
Memory, cognitivist perspective, 23
Mental disability, 4
Metacognition, 23, 25
Methods, describing in grant
    proposals, 228–229
Microphones, 186
Microsoft Office, 87, 123
Microsoft PowerPoint, 54, 75, 146,
    201–203
Microworlds, 99
MIDI, 178–179
Mini-drives, 110
Minnesota Public Radio, 208
Misinterpretation of videos, 181
Mixcraft software, 179
Mnemonic visuals, 198
Mobile apps, 96
Mobile devices. *See also* Smart
    phones
    as assessment tools, 8–9
    for augmented reality, 217
    on carts, 112
    as learning tools, 11–12, 96, 163
    recording audio on, 174
Mobile learning, 163
Mock-ups, 84–85
Models, 84
Modifying instructional
    materials, 50
Monarch Butterfly Journey
    North, 147
Monitoring distance learning
    students, 112, 148–149
Moodle, 146, 160
Motion, 180
Motivation, 48–49, 72, 195
Movie Maker app, 186
MP3 and MP4 audio, 175
Multi-device classrooms, 111–113
Multimedia product rubric, 35
Multimedia sharing, 125–127
Multimedia strategies, 104
Multimedia tools. *See also* Audio;
    Video
    case studies, 169, 179, 187, 193, 204,
        205–207
    developing student literacy with,
        170–171
Multiple intelligences, 28–29, 42–43
Multitouch desks, 90
Museums, 89, 156, 174
Musical instrument digital interface
    (MIDI), 178–179
Musical/rhythmic intelligence, 178
Music apps, 174–175, 178–179

National Aeronautics and Space
    Administration, 218
National Assessment of Educational
    Progress Reading Framework
    (2015), 189
National Center for Technology
    Innovation, 232
National Council of Teachers of
    English, 209
National Education Technology Plan,
    29, 212, 220
National Education Technology
    Standards for Students, 29–30
National Geographic Society, 147
National Instructional Materials
    Accessibility Standard, 13
National Park Service, 89
National Public Radio, 208
National Technical Information
    Services, 89
National Weather Service, 153
Natural History Museum, 156
Natural User Interface, 215
Nellie Mae Foundation, 224
NeoK12 website, 126
Net Nanny software, 149
NetSmartz, 183
Networks
    computer, 112–113, 149, 156–160
    neural, 215
    professional learning, 222
    social, 119, 127–128
Neural networks, 215
News articles, copying, 152
News broadcasters, 89
New Tech Network, 27, 28
Next Generation Science Standards,
    214, 217
NMC Horizon Report, 221
Non-profit organizations, 89
Nonstructured informal
    study, 87
Note-taking for presentations, 67
Nova (TV program), 183
NPR Podcast Directory, 208

Objectives, 25, 41, 44–47
Obscenity, 150
Office 365, 87
One-way video, 146–147
Online instruction, 141, 147. *See also*
    Distance learning
Online journals, 225–226
Online reviews, 50
Online virtual schools, 86
OpenEd website, 126
OpenOffice, 123
Open source products, 87, 119
Operating systems, 105
Oral histories, 173
Oregon Trail app, 79
Organizational visuals, 199
Organization charts, 199

Organization grants, 227
Output devices, 108–109

Pablo app, 138
Parents, online communications
    with, 155
Partnership for 21st Century
    Skills, 27, 38
PBS LearningMedia website, 89
PBS website, 167, 208
Peer demonstrations, 67
Peer evaluation, 58, 59
Peer tutoring, 144
Pen pals, 153
People, as communications media, 6
Performance checklists, 32–33
Permissions (copyright), 17–18
Personalized learning, 214
Personal response systems, 8
PhET Interactive Simulations, 94
Photography, 203–204. *See also* Visuals
Physical disability, 4. *See also*
    Individual differences
Picmonic app, 198
Pictorial graphs, 200
Pie graphs, 200
Pinboards, 125, 126–127
Pindex website, 138
Pinterest, 126, 232
Pivot 2.0 app, 9
Place shifting instruction, 140
Planning video productions, 186
Planning visual productions, 201
Platforms, computer, 159
Podcast Alley, 175
Podcasts
    defined, 12, 125
    instructional use, 126, 175
    for language instruction, 132
Poet laureate, 173
Police departments, instructional
    materials from, 89
Portals, 159
Portfolio assessment, 34–36
PowerMapper, 157
PowerPoint
    features, 75
    guidelines for using, 201–203
    suggested applications, 54
    use in distance learning, 146
Practice, 25, 54–56
Preproduction planning (video), 186
Prerequisites, 42
Presentation evaluation form, 59
Presentations. *See also* Visuals
    for distance learning, 143
    by groups, 78
    guidelines for producing, 201–203
    instructional technology for,
        75–76, 101
    strengths and limitations, 66–67
    when to use, 82, 101
Pretests, 42

Prezi
  collaborative use, 123, 124
  features, 75
  guidelines for using, 201–203
  use in distance learning, 146
Principal investigators, 229
Printers, three-dimensional, 114
Prior knowledge, assessing, 24
Privacy concerns, 148, 219–220
Problem-based learning, 70–71, 77, 82
Problem-solving skills, 72, 180
Problem statements, grant proposal, 228
Producing audio, 178
Producing video, 186
Product evaluation checklists, 33, 34
Productivity apps, 123–124
Professional growth for teachers,
  222–226
Professional journals, 224, 225–226
Professional learning networks, 222
Professional organizations, 223–225
Project abstracts, 228
Project descriptions, grant proposal,
  228–229
Projectors, 109
Promotions, in free materials, 88
Public broadcasting
  instructional materials from, 89, 167
  video from, 182–183, 208
Public Broadcasting Service, 167,
  182–183, 208

Question-and-answer activities, 143
Quick Response (QR) codes, 9, 181

RALL-E, 216
Random access memory, 109
Rapid prototyping machines, 114
Reading assessment tools, 8–9
Reading comprehension
  standards, 189
Read-only memory, 109
ReadWriteThink website, 209
"Real-Life Stories," 183
Real objects as manipulatives, 84
Real-world contexts, 25
Recording audio, 171, 172, 173–175,
  178–179
Recording video, 186
Reinforcement, 22
Relational visuals, 200
Remediation, distance learning for, 151
Removable storage devices, 110
Representational visuals, 198
Request for proposals, 228
Research skills, 155
Resources. *See also* Instructional
  technology
  in ASSURE model, 41, 49
  describing in grant proposals, 229
  evaluating use, 57–61
  linking to standards and
    objectives, 41

Response to Intervention, 13–14
Responsible use policies, 220
Reviews of educational resources, 50
Robot-Assisted Language Learning in
  Education, 216
Robotics, 216, 217–218
Robotics Alliance Project, 218
Role-playing, 73, 79
Royalty-free materials, 18
Rubistar website, 36
Rubrics
  audio resource selection, 176–177
  for authentic assessment, 33–34, 35
  creating for resource selection, 49
  game and simulation selection,
    80–81
  online resource selection, 161–162
  for selecting visuals, 196–197
  software selection, 106–107
  text resource selection, 191–192
  video resource selection, 184–185
  Web 2.0 tool selection, 130–131
Rule of thirds, 203

San Diego Zoo and Wild Animal Park
  website, 167
Sans serif fonts, 201
Sarcasm, in email and texts, 149
Scaffold approach, 74
SchoolGrants website, 232
School Library Media Research
  journal, 224
*Science, Technology, Engineering, and
  Mathematics (STEM) Connections*
  newsletter, 225
Science Bank, 94
Science Buddies Blog, 121
Science literacy, 189
Scientific method, 74
Search engines, 134, 159, 160
Second-language English speakers.
  See English language learners
Security in distance learning settings,
  148, 157
Security of wearable devices, 219–220
Seesaw app, 63–64
Selection rubrics. *See* Rubrics
Self-evaluation, 58, 59
Semantic-aware applications, 134
Servers, 158
Sesame Workshop website, 167
Share My Lesson website, 94
Short-term memory, 23
SimCity, 55
Simulations, 73–74, 79, 80–81
Simulators, 85
Single-device classrooms, 110–111
Six by six rule, 202
Smart glasses, 219
Smart phones, 3, 8–9. *See also* Mobile
  devices
Smithsonian National Zoological
  Park, 156

Smithsonian website, 89
Social bookmarking, 124–125
Social networking, 119, 127–128, 221
Social psychology perspective, 24
Social studies, 155
Software. *See also* Instructional
    technology
  audio, 174–175, 178–179
  concept mapping, 77, 99
  copyright protections, 98, 102
  firewall, 159
  Internet monitoring, 149
  major types used in instruction,
    99–102
  open source, 87, 119
  for problem solving, 55
  reading assessment, 8–9
  selection criteria, 104, 105–108
  video editing, 186
  vocabulary building, 54
  for writing activities, 29, 132
Sonny Bono Copyright Term
    Extension Act (1998), 18
Sophia website, 20
Sound Learning website, 208
Sounds in presentations, 203
Special effects, 108
Special needs. *See* Individual
    differences
Spreadsheets, 54, 55, 100
Staff, describing in grant
    proposals, 229
Standardized testing, 37
Standards
  applied to distance learning, 141
  in ASSURE model, 41, 44–45
  curriculum, 10–11
  for digital students, 13
  for digital teachers, 9–10
  National Education Technology
    Standards for Students, 29–30
  for reading comprehension, 189
Star Walk app, 217
STEAM education, 214–215
STEM skills, 217
STEM Teen Read program, 155
Stock Market Game, 79
Storyboards, 186, 201, 202
StoryCenter, 183
StoryKit app, 208
Storymaker software, 29
Storytelling, 174, 183
Strategies. *See* Instructional strategies
Streaming audio, 175
Stream odor case, 104
Structured independent study, 87
Structured problems, 70
Struggling learners, 190, 198. *See also*
    Individual differences
Student-centered learning, 48
Students
  analyzing learning abilities,
    41–43, 212

monitoring computer use, 112, 148–150
overview of technology benefits for, 11–14
participatory learning, 54–56
preparing for instruction, 52–53
scientific data collection by, 156
teacher evaluations by, 58
SuccessMaker, 77, 215
Supervising distance learning students, 112, 148–149
Supplementary instruction, distance learning for, 151
Swirling effects, 203
Synchronous settings, 86, 144–145
Synthesizer software, 179

Tabular charts, 199
TaleBlazer app, 217
Talking heads, 181
Target populations, 45, 228
Teacher-centered learning, 48
Teacher evaluations, 58, 59
TeacherFocus, 9
TeacherLingo blog, 121
Teachers
  designing distance learning, 140–142, 147
  as model users of technology, 98
  online collaborations, 155–156
  overview of technology benefits for, 7–11, 220–222
  professional growth, 222–226
TeachersFirst Edge blog, 121
Teacher Tap: Grants and Grant Writing, 232
TeacherTube, 125, 126
Teach-nology website, 36
Tech & Learning, 226
Technical subjects literacy, 189
Technical support for distance learning, 151
Technology, Education and Copyright Harmonization (TEACH) Act, 142
Technology carts, 112
Technology gap, 3
Technology guidelines for teachers, 9–10
Technology labs, 112–113
Technology literacy skills, 30
Technology resources. *See* Instructional technology
TED website, 208
Telecommunications, defined, 140
Teleconferences, 145–146, 155
Terabytes, 109
Testing, 36, 42, 143. *See also* Assessment
Text
  as communications medium, 5, 6
  integrating with instruction, 189
  producing, 190
  selecting resources, 190, 191–192

strengths and limitations, 188
types of resources, 189–190
use in distance learning, 144, 147, 153
Text literacy, 170
Text messaging
  classroom applications, 100
  digital citizenship issues, 149–150
  rates of use, 3
  use in distance learning, 153
T.H.E. Journal, 226
Three-dimensional imagery, 128
Three-dimensional printers, 114
Three-point scales, 33
Time limits, fair use, 142
Timelines, 199, 229
Time shifting instruction, 140
Title pages, grant proposal, 228
TMHS Climate Change Debate, 122–123
To the Ends of the Earth (video), 182–183
Traditional assessment, 36
Traditional portfolios, 35–36
Transdisciplinary learning, 214–215
Transformational visuals, 200, 201
Transitions in presentations, 203
Tutorials, 69, 76–77
Tutoring approaches, 76–77, 216
Twitter, 127, 128
Two-way video, 146–147

Uniform resource locators (URLs), 159–160
United Nations Sustainable Development Goals, 222
United States Access Board, 182
United States Distance Learning Association (USDLA), 225
United States Geological Survey mashup site, 129
Universal design for learning, 14
USB connections, 110
U.S. Copyright Office website, 20
U.S. Government Publishing Office, 89
Utility companies, 89

Verbs for learning objectives, 45
Verse app, 138
Video
  as communications medium, 6
  copyright protections, 18
  with demonstrations, 76
  for English language learners, 68
  language instruction podcasts, 132
  in portfolios, 36
  recording with smart glasses, 219
  selection criteria, 49, 183–186
  sharing, 125, 126
  strengths and limitations, 179–181
  suggested applications, 100, 181–182
  types, 182–183
  use in distance learning, 143, 144, 146

Videoconferencing, 77, 146–147, 155
Video literacy, 170
Virtual collaborative agents, 216
Virtual field trips, 156, 183
Virtual Math Teams project, 9
Virtual reality, 216–217
Virtual reality headsets, 219–220
Virtual schools, 86, 153
Virtual tutors, 216
Visual Learning website, 209
Visual literacy, 170–171
Visually impaired learners, 4, 182, 190, 198
Visuals. *See also* Presentations
  as communications media, 5, 6
  culturally sensitive, 4
  integrating with instruction, 194–195
  major types, 195–200
  producing, 200–204
  royalty-free, 18
  selection criteria, 195, 196–197
  strengths and limitations, 193–194
Vocabulary software, 54

Walton Foundation, 224
WatchKnowLearn website, 126
Water cycle case study, 96, 97, 101, 113, 115–116
Water testing case, 104
Wearable devices, 218–220
Weather Channel website, 89
Web 2.0: Cool Tools for Schools website, 138
Web 2.0 tools
  case study, 118, 120, 122, 133, 135–137
  future needs, 213
  main types, 120–129
  overview, 119–120
  selecting, 125, 129–131
  strengths and limitations, 132–133
Webpages, defined, 159
WebQuests, 77, 153–155
Websites, defined, 159
WebWatcher software, 149
Whiteboards, 75
Wide area networks (WANs), 158
Wikipedia, 12–13, 122
Wikis, 12, 121–123
Windows Media Player, 175
Wireless devices. *See* Mobile devices
Wireless networks, 158
Word processing, 99–100, 190
World Wide Web, 159–160
World Wide Web Consortium Accessibility Initiative, 157
Writing instruction
  online mentoring, 154
  primary goals, 190
  technology tools for, 29, 132

YouTube, 125, 126

Zoos, 156

Credits

Design Elements: Chapter openers and Technology for All Learners image: Julien Eichinger/Fotolia; ASSURE Classroom Case Study, A Model to Help ASSURE Learning, and ASSURE Lesson Plan image: Pojoslaw/Fotolia; Copyright Concerns image: Tovovan/Fotolia; Media Samples and Technology Resources image: Vladgrin/Fotolia; Taking a Look at Technology Integration image: Dimec/Shutterstock; When to Use image: Keo/Fotolia.

Chapter 1: p. 1: Paul/Fotolia; p. : Elypse/Fotolia; p. 5: (Audio) Kokhanchikov/Fotolia, (People, teenagers) Michael Flippo/Fotolia, (Video, camcorder) Himmelssturm/Fotolia, (Manipulatives, blocks) JackF/Fotolia, (Text, children) Karin & Uwe Annas/Fotolia, (Video, filmstrip) Mickyso/Fotolia, (Visuals, hand drawing) Peshkova/Fotolia, (Visuals, anatomy) Adimas/Fotolia, (Text, tablet with book) Punto Studio Foto Ag/Fotolia, (People, icons) Niroworld/Fotolia, (Manipulatives, puppy) Ewas/Fotolia, p. 6: Joseph Sweeney/Pearson Education; p. 7:

Chapter 2: p. 21: Samuel Borges/Fotolia; p. 27: Joseph Sweeney/Pearson Education.

Chapter 3: p. 39: Poulsons Photography/Fotolia.

Chapter 4: p. 94: Joseph Sweeney/Pearson Education; p. 96: Joseph Sweeney/Pearson Education.

Chapter 5: p. 95: antonella/Fotolia; p. 93: Joseph Sweeney/Pearson Education.

Chapter 6: p. 118: Samuel Borges/Fotolia; p. 129: Joseph Sweeney/Pearson Education.

Chapter 7: p. 139: Paul/Fotolia.

Chapter 9: p. 211: Antonella/Fotolia; p. 215: Ktsdesign/Fotolia; p. 216: Frank/Fotolia; p. 218: Science photo/Fotolia; p. 219: left: Vectorfusionart/Fotolia; right: Ramil Gibadullin/Fotolia.